BADASS WISDOM

Badass Wisdom

A KILLER DAILY MEDITATIONAL TO TAKE YOU TO THE UGLY PLACES AND KICK YOUR ASS!

Sven Erlandson

Eksjö Yard Publishing

Other Books by this Author

There's a Hole in My Love Cup: The Badass Counseling Method for Healing the Soul and Unleashing Greatness

Spiritual But Not Religious: A Call to Religious Revolution in America

Rescuing God from Christianity: A Closet Christian, Non-Christian, and Christmas Christian's Guide to Radically Re-thinking God Stuff

I Steal Wives: A Serial Adulterer Reveals the Real Reasons More and More 'Happily Married' Women are Cheating

The 7 Evangelical Myths: Untwisting the Theology Behind the Politics

Badass Jesus: The Serious Athlete and a Life of Noble Purpose

Dedication

To the suicidal, the stuck, the over-thinkers,
and the procrastinators
To the widow, the orphan, the widower, and the outcast
To the I-missed-the-red-flags, to the abuse survivors, the extreme
taker victims, and the sibling they hated
To the broken, the bruised, the alone, and the lost
To the I'm-not-good-enough, the I-suck, the everyone-hates-me,
and the what-did-I-do-wrong
To the one they never loved, the ones for whom they never even
tried, the forgotten, and the angry
To the kids whose dad is still of the belief it's-the-past-get-over-it,
the adults whose mom was cold as ice, the souls who had their
childhood stolen, and the dear, dear little saints who suffered in any
way at the hands of an adult, sibling, neighbor, family member, friend,
or what have you
To the cheated, the robbed, the completely misunderstood, and the
ones who've completely screwed up
To the unheard, the unseen, unwanted, and unwantable
To the ones who stopped trying, the ones who still are, the ones
who've given soul, and the ones whose soul was raped
To the longing, the throbbing, the aching, and the begging
To the religion victims, the failing to launch, the insecure parents,
and the adult-children of all manner of parental f**ckery
To the men hiding in hyper-masculinity, the terrified souls hiding
their gender or sexuality, the moms who never wanted kids but can
never say it aloud, and the teens who are convinced no one truly cares
To the poetic hearts, spilling minds, fractured souls, and the distant,
distant, and staying more distant
To the ones who swear they have no hate, to the ones who can't
stop, to the ones ever in motion, to the over-the-top
To the people who are trying to understand and bring love to them,
but are yet so dispirited and confused themselves
And to the clerics, the social workers, the prison volunteers, the
rehab specialists, the psychologists, the listening friends, the nurses

who take time, the committed therapists, the mental health intake workers, the doctors so overwhelmed, the police department mental health liaisons, and the infinite folk who go unnamed and unrecognized – tragically so – in this fight we're all in to give life back to those from whom it was stolen by society, by parents, by value systems, and by viruses

This book is my SKØL to you!

For you inspire me, every one of you, even down to the poorest in spirit. Your courage to live one more day and the hope you bear oddly buoys us all.

Mostly, I know – yes, I actually KNOW! – that each of you bears the Divine Spark in you; each carries, perhaps unwittingly, a message from the god/gods themselves, a gift, a purpose, a skill, an insight, a talent,

a something.....

a something that this world needs, that I need.

Dammit don't quit; I need you!

Acknowledgments

Thanks to Emma Scott. Special thanks to Christine Whittemore for your hard work on all things Badass Counseling.

Special thanks to Rev. LeRoy and Charlotte Erlandson, now deceased, who are the inspiration for all of my work. You taught me how to garden flowers and vegetables, and how to garden souls. I can never repay the debt. I love you so much.

Profound, humble thanks to Karen Camporeale, my playmate, who has made so many things possible. It's just so much fun to go through life next to you, grow pretty flowers for you, bring morning coffee to you, listen to Writer's Almanac with you, and steamroller in bed over you. Thank you for everything you've brought to my life. I love you.

Very special thanks to Robert H. Friedman for his production and mastering of the audiobook. Thank you also for arranging and performing the music in the audiobook, which is an old Swedish folk tune. I'm truly grateful, Rob.

Lastly, to Svea and Colbjorn, my two young Vikings, who also happen to be the editors of this book. Thank you for your critical thinking, your willingness to jump in on anything and everything, and your forbearance with me. There's no one on earth whom I trust more than you two. Everything I have is yours.

Introduction

Every single morning of my childhood, before walking to the bus stop, Mom would cook a hot breakfast for each of us six kids to eat in our kitchen nook – high school bus earliest, then junior high siblings, then me in elementary school. Every single morning, Dad, a Lutheran pastor, would read from a daily meditational pamphlet put out by either the Episcopalians or the Catholics. Similar to our home, the readings were never too religiousy, but nearly always had a good thought for me to ponder as I walked through the dewy grass (or deep snow, in winter) in the back yards to the bus stop on the other side of our block.

As an adult, for decades, part of my daily ritual has been listening to *The Writer's Almanac* on National Public Radio, now only in reruns. It, too, has made me think, made me smile or laugh, and taught me a bit more about life and myself, while enjoying Garrison Keillor's enchanting voice. I still enjoy a good daily thought or two.

Additionally, when I was about 13, my mother encouraged me to start journaling, not just capturing my thoughts but, far more importantly, releasing my feelings. She knew every person needs an avenue to flush out their pent-up feelings and ever-spinning thoughts. So, as you might guess, the daily meditationals and insights became fodder for my journaling and healing, my change and growth, and ultimately my direction and inspiration.

Badass Wisdom is written in this same spirit, intended to grow you into greater intimacy with your own soul – your authentic self. It's to be nothing more than a challenge to you, something to turn your thinking upside-down, and give you questions to jumpstart your journaling for the day.

It is a companion to my book, **There's a Hole in My Love Cup**: *The Badass Counseling Method for Healing the Soul and Unleashing Greatness.*

Don't rush through this. Just take it in small doses, day by day. It's a meditational that you chew slowly, not a big concept book that you eat in a few sittings. The purpose is to stimulate deep thinking, healing, and inspiration to change, a little bit each day. Take your time.

Peace and laughter to you on your journey,

Sven
Summer 2023

January

January 1

> *Every new beginning comes*
> *from some other beginning's end.*
> -Seneca, Roman statesman and dramatist

The Roman god, Janus, was the god of beginnings and endings, depicted as having two faces – one looking forward, one looking into the past. The month of January, named after Janus, is not solely a month of beginnings. It is just as much about looking backward. For how can one create something new without studying the old and that which did not work? Without adequately assessing the problems (in the past), any new creation is but a half-solution. Creation is dependent upon the destruction of that which doesn't work.

Becoming your most badass self isn't just about goals, motivation, toughness, accomplishment, motion, and winning. That's only a piece of the equation. Being a killer badass is much more complex and deep. It's about knowing the self, examining and feeling your pains, past and present. It's about mining your pain and experiences for gems of wisdom, cascading waterfalls of new insight, and luxurious times of rest in the calm of life. The true warriors, poets, visionaries, and transformers of human experience have all known this. Until you not only master self, but truly understand self, you know nothing and are functioning at 50% efficiency and strength, at best. The real power of living a badass life comes from within, and that demands going into the past to determine how it is still driving your present and future.

So, what is it from your past that simply does not work, and perhaps never did? What relationship, career, way of thinking, or passion in your life simply needs to be put to death? What is still attached to you, either externally or internally, that was never you, to begin with? Do you realize that by saying 'no' to it you are saying 'no' to all that is not you and 'yes' to a more authentic you? Isn't that the real goal? When do you finally have the courage to walk through the fears you associate with that destruction?

How much do you fear not having that which has provided you with so much (perceived) security? Or is your fear one of having to put something to death? Do you shy away from the unsavory task of destruction, necessary as it may be? Is it because you fear how you will be seen? Fear being misunderstood or unliked? When do you finally have the courage to choose the needs of the soul over the insecurities of the ego? What's it gonna take?

January 2

Fill your paper with the breathings of your heart.
-William Wordsworth, English poet

After the rush of excitement on New Year's Day comes the daily grind that begins, really, today. January 2nd represents the days that often aren't inspired or fresh, but still require the slog of hard work in the growth and replenishment of the soul. So today's questions are the daily questions – the ones you come back to, again and again, over the coming year. When you have the itch to journal more and go deeper, come to these old friends. You need to dog-ear this page. Highlight it. Come back to it!

When journaling, write the first question at the top of your page. Flush out – write out – your answer. Move to the next or ask 'why' after the first question. Flush. Next question. Flush.

- What do I really, really feel right now, or about this, if I were to be totally honest?
- Why? (This should be the most common question you ask in your life and in your journaling.)
- What's really eating at me about this situation? Why is that?
- Why am I so angry? So sad? So afraid?
- What's the single biggest and most powerful FEAR driving this whole equation?
- Is there one person I'm having strong feelings about, positive or negative? Who is it?
- What are those feelings – anger, love, happiness, frustration, disappointment?
- How is this hardship or pain I'm experiencing the single greatest blessing that could have ever happened to me? What is my own soul trying to teach me with this pain? What am I still not learning or still resisting that the ongoing pain keeps trying to get through to me?
- In what ways am I feeling called to be an instrument of stronger love and compassion in the world? How has the past pain – the past workouts in the spiritual gym with the badass coach of my soul – perfectly prepared me for the workout ahead?
- What is the super scary thing I'm just terrified to look at (and be forced to feeeeel) in my life, or more importantly, in my soul today and lately? Why is that so scary to me? What's at stake?

- Do I have the courage to do what needs to be done? If not, what's it gonna take for me to summon it?
- What are the hard, ugly, toilet-cleaning tasks (the crap most people don't want to do) I'm being called to execute?

January 3

The hardest thing when you think about focusing (your attention and life);
you think focusing is about saying 'Yes!'
No.
Focusing is about saying 'No!'
And when you say, 'No,' you piss off people.
-Steve Jobs, Apple founder and American innovator

Jobs' words are never more true than in the invention of a life, in the finding of your own soul, in living authentically. For, it all starts with the courage to say that hard 'No' to all the paths, purposes, and people you have spent your life saying 'Yes' to, though they never felt right, never fit, and caused you to forever chafe at their presence and pressure on your life.

It is this 'No' that separates the safe from the bold, the unoriginal from the intrepidly authentic, and slow death from *ALIVENESS!* It is this 'No' that is the most fear-inducing part of the hero's journey – the original life, because it is often the rejection of the messages and beliefs of those we love and even lean on. Thus, it is a movement from the leaning, to the standing on one's own truth.

That's scary ground. It requires a sort of getting one's own sea legs, as it were. It is to feel one's own footing and to trust it. That takes repetitions of saying 'No.' Some people prefer to start on the big stuff with their 'No' then move to the granular; some start small then move toward the really big stuff.

What do you most fear saying the 'No' of your soul to? What path, person, or purpose is no longer yours? Do you have the courage to finally start pissing people off with your unflinching commitment to becoming self?

It's time.

January 4

*The real man
smiles in trouble,
gathers strength from distress,
and grows brave by reflection.*
-Thomas Paine, American political activist

In this month of Janus – looking forward and backward – what would you have done differently? We all know hindsight can be 20/20 (though, not always), but it can also be fantastically frightening. Having the courage to look at what really happened....and what was really motivating you – really, really deep down – is nasty-ass, ugly work.

So, what is the one decision, above all else, you most regret making in your entire life? Why that one? What would be different, today, if you had gone the other path? What would you have avoided? What would you be able to do or say, now, if you had gone there?

Do you tell people when you have made a mistake or you are wrong? Or do you connect shame with mistakes? Do you connect weakness to apologizing? Do you see how it actually takes a far stronger, more sure person to concede mistakes, admit fault, and be contrite for harm done? It takes courage of character to draw attention to one's own failings, lapses of judgment, and times of harming. Are you possessed of that courage? Why?

Was this one decision (above) driven by ego? In what way? Or, perhaps, you wish you had made it based on ego? Was it driven by spite, even malice? Was it driven by the neeed to look big...or perhaps to be small?

This cuts to the heart of the issue – to what degree are you covering up your authentic self (your true inner badass), because of this fear?

'What is the fear in this case' should always be one of your go-to questions, right up there with 'why?'

January 5

... I consider myself a jazz poet.
I am satisfied with that.
What intelligentsia says makes little difference,
as I've always spent my time in skid row or in jazz joints
or with personal poet madmen
and never cared what 'intelligentsia' thinks.
My love of poetry is my love of joy.
-Jack Kerouac, American beat poet, Heaven and Other Poems

Do you love anything so much that you'd be willing to be poor to do it, to be it, or to have it? Do you love what brings you joy, regardless of the hurled insults and attempts to pull you from that joy? Whose voice matters more to you, theirs or the one which rises from the depths of your own being?

Do you possess the courage for the adventure of it, happy to come to the end of your days having done it yourself, your way?

January 6

**You become mature
when you become
the authority for your own life.**
-Joseph Campbell, American writer and pre-eminent myth scholar

The reason Campbell is not just making a value judgment, as if to say "These people are just better than those people, in my opinion," is because removing the voices and authority of others from your life and inside you demands a courage and a willingness to leave the fear and dependence of childhood/adolescence behind. To claim ownership and authorship of your life means removing the other authors from the place of power they've previously held in your life.

That requires a willingness to lose them, if it comes to that, and a desire to stand on your own ideas, willing to fail but wanting to succeed on the authority of your own inner voice. And, that is the voice of the soul moving into full maturity. When an individual is willing to rise and fall on the decisions of their own self, they have become their own author. Of course, there's always room for more growth, but major work has been done.

Have you stood up and seized full ownership and authority over your own life? If not, whom do you fear removing from the position of highest power in your life? What is the price of doing so? What do you fear them saying or doing, if you did? If that did come to pass, though you would likely grieve, would you, in the end, be okay? If you can answer that question in the affirmative, you're ready to reclaim your life, ready to move into full maturity.

January 7

Labels are for the things men make,
not for men.
The most primitive man is
too complex to be labeled.
-Rex Stout, American novelist

Some of the grand cliches of our time (and stretching back well into the past) revolve around definitions of toughness, manhood, strength, and, lately, badassery. Instantly, those words conjure up caricatures of someone always snorting, always coarse, full of bravado, angry, and bearing an over-inflated ego.

When looking at life with an emphasis on the soul, however, it's very important that we understand that the word 'badass' and associated terms like tough, strength, power, and even man and woman, are no longer defined anywhere near the same as they have been in the past. Being tough all the time, hard guy all the time, and never showing emotion (unless it's anger) are no longer viable ways to function, no longer adequate definitions of a happy or fulfilled life.

There is no way that such an idea of self-mastery can be so one-sided. It hasn't always been that way. It just got maligned, over time, by men and women too afraid of the pain in life and having never been taught the tools for releasing that pain. So, 'pack those feelings down,' 'just be tough,' and, 'bottle up your sadness, pain, and anger' became their mantras. Yet, those mantras never worked, not in war, not in life. The pain always catches up with you, dragging you down from the inside, demanding to be dealt with.

True 'badass' means the courage to be authentic, to be whomever you damn well feel like being, moment to moment. If there's pain, there are tears. If there's anger, you let it out (in safe ways that don't hurt others). If there's joy, you laugh. But living in one mode of 'always tough,' is nowhere near authentic. If anything, it's weak, because it is driven by an utterly arbitrary blanket statement for how you should act in any given moment. That's not badass; that's somebody whose values have been determined by someone else. That's a tool.

Circumstances may require the purging of pain to wait an hour, day, or week. But the authentic badass affirms and lives in the need to get pain, frustration, boredom, sadness *out* from inside. Because, until the pain is out of you, it's still in you and it's still actively hurting you.

Do you have the courage to live authentically, or are you still shrouded in BS old-school notions of 'never show feelings' that were completely arbitrary and over time seemed to create more pain than they ever solved? What's your fear in living authentically? Whose admonition do you fear? A dead parent? A living one? Why? What would it take for you to no longer live in fear of living authentically?

January 8

Courage is doing what you're afraid to do.
There can be no courage, unless you're scared.
-Eddie Rickenbacker,
U.S. WWI Fighter pilot/Ace & Medal of Honor recipient

It's always fear.

Everything is fear. Everything that keeps us unhappy, keeps us stuck, causes us to do the foolish and, at times, the brilliant, is fear. We are primal at the core.

So, what do you most want, most need, most know you must do? And what is the fear that comes along with it?

What would it take to find the courage inside to do it anyway, despite the fear? Particularly in the quest for authentic and empowered living, what do you most fear, yet most know you must do or want to do? What do you most fear happening if you were to go after your dreams?

Has the pain of not doing it finally gotten so bad that walking into the fear is not nearly as intimidating as it once was?

If it hasn't then don't worry, it will get worse. For, your soul is trying to push you out of your comfort zone to finally live the authentic, badass life you were meant to live.

January 9

> *Our pain can be our greatest teacher.*
> *It leads us to places we'd never go on our own.*
> -Debbie Ford, American self-help author

Have you ever felt like you need to dry out because you're drinking too much alcohol? Or maybe you've felt the need to lay off the weed, stop gambling, quit cheating, stop the incessant and excessive shopping, or put an end to the madness of your over-parenting, over-exercising, or over-working. Or, maybe you know you just need to slow the heck down and stop creating busyness and chaos. What is it that's slowly killing you or slowly pulling apart the fabric of your life and relationships, or threatening to?

Yet, you can't imagine stopping, much less even scaling it back, can you? Too hard, perhaps, or too much to sacrifice. Or, you know if you stop you'll have to face the stuff you're really running from that is just on the other side of that wall that the booze provides, that wall of busyness that keeps the screaming of your insides and your past at bay. You're running from the pain and truths of the past.

The loss of life energy from the way you're living (so as to avoid the inner pain and your own past) is growing greater by the day and the year, isn't it?

Tragically, one of the grand truths of life is that change will not occur until the pain gets bad enough. Until the pain of how you're living exceeds the pain of changing and the pain of finally dealing with the past, ain't nothin' gonna change.

So, the obvious question is, 'Has your pain gotten bad enough?' See, pain can come in many forms – protracted discomfort, discontent, continued loss (of any stripe), physical pain, exhaustion, and so many others. But, until it's too much, it's still not enough, not enough to keep you motivated through the very hard times of recovery, change, and growth. And there will be hard times that challenge your motivation.

Where are you feeling the squeeze? Where is the pain, slowly but surely, intensifying? You do realize that this crud of life doesn't magically heal itself, right? It's not going to just magically go away. So, when is the time? When do you finally do what you know you need to do – face and finally defeat the beast inside?

January 10

Every act of creation is first an act of destruction.
-Pablo Picasso, Spanish painter and sculptor

The creation and destruction of harmonic and 'statistical' tensions is essential to the maintenance of compositional drama.
Any composition (or improvisation) which remains consonant and 'regular' throughout is, for me, equivalent to watching a movie with only 'good guys' in it, or eating cottage cheese.
-Frank Zappa, American musician

Back in the 90s, when I was writing what would become my first book, I had a crappy old Apple-whatever computer – the kind that took little 3" non-floppy, floppy disks. Hard to imagine anyone being this way nowadays, but I had almost no experience with computers, apart from one computer programming class I had in college that I cheated my way through en route to a final grade of 'D.' So, it may come as no surprise that I had well over half of my book written when the entire computer breathed its last breath and shut down. And, as fate would have it, even though I had a disk, I hadn't actually used it. So, yes, the entire 250 pages were lost. And yes, I'm an idiot.

Now, the obvious moral of the story is: Don't be an idiot; save your work! But there's another moral, a bit of an ugly-beautiful one, that only showed its face six months later when I had finally remade the first half of the book. The new product was infinitely better than the original. The destruction of the old forced the genesis and execution of a tighter, clearer, stronger manuscript. I hated every damn minute of re-writing and re-working it, cursing the gods of computer machines the entire time, at least in the beginning, because I was still mourning the loss. And, for a writer, that is a huge loss. But, once it began to gather momentum and take shape, I knew I had something far better.

As my clients hear me say, all the time, *'Creation is invariably preceded by destruction.'* Things must die in order for things to live. Old forms must be stripped away to allow for new ideas. Decayed relationships and life pursuits lead to whole new births, when let go of. And part of that process is the grieving of the loss, as well as the openness to new ideas and new purposes.

Are you open? Are you still needing to grieve the loss? How big was the loss? What specifically was it about the loss that makes it so hard to move through? Be more specific. Drill down to the 'why' beneath the reason you've given. Is the hardest part about it all having to start over? Yes, it's a pain in the ass, but what if the new is infinitely better than the old? Are you willing to slog through, 'til the momentum begins to kick in? Or is this where you quit?

January 11

Pack up your troubles in your old kit bag
and smile, smile, smile.
-WWI British marching song

My parents grew up in the 1920s and 30s, during the Great Depression, then WWII. Thus, a positive mental attitude, despite the cataclysmic events happening in the world, was very much a part of their DNA. Catchy tunes with phrases like "Look on the sunny side of life," "Pack up your troubles in the old kit bag and smile, smile, smile," were sung and whistled.

But, unlike their generation, LeRoy and Charlotte very much believed in talking problems out to each other, flushing out all of their thoughts and feelings when going through hardship or sadness.

Their deliberate parenting ethos was to pair positivity with reflection, to keep the focus upbeat, when possible, but not be afraid to dive into the roots of problems to see where healing is necessary, even if that took awhile. So, it was neither head-in-the-sand blind positivity, but neither was it a stuckness in depression and sadness. There needed to always be work to solve the equations of our personal and interpersonal problems.

When one of their six children was having a bad day or, later in life, experiencing hard times, they listened without attempting to fix the issue. They let us rant and cry, encouraging the talking out of all angles of our problems, knowing that we would often be able to solve them on our own, if we could just release all of the emotion that charged the situation. Then, after listening and listening, Mom would simply end with, "Tomorrow is a new day," or "Let today's worries be enough for today." And things didn't always turn the next day (though sometimes they did), but what got implanted in us was the reflex of hope taught within a context of reflection.

There is always hope. There is always a way through the dark times. It is necessary to simultaneously acknowledge and release the dark, while aspiring toward the hopeful, believing in better days ahead. It is to walk joyfully amid the sorrows of the world. Often with the sorrows inside. But believing in tomorrow.

Do you believe in tomorrow? What is the absolute hardest part about today, what sorrows are you amid? Do you flush it out, particularly through journaling or talking it out with a friend, cleric, or counselor, rather than just keeping it stuck and tumbling inside your head? Where is the hope, too? Can you purge the pain while visioning the future?

January 12

When do you finally
pull the trigger?

When do you finally make that dream you've dreamed forever happen?

What is it about that dream that scares the bejesus out of you?

Can you name the fears? Can you name the person whose voice you most fear if you fail? Many people say it's their own criticism they fear most. But the problem with that is that no child comes out of the womb self-critical and self-hating. That means somewhere between the womb and right now you were *taught* to hate on yourself. That means that the inner voice that has always been so doggone critical of you was never yours to begin with. It's not your native voice, no matter how much you claim to own it. It started as someone else's. But then, you heard it so loudly or so frequently that it embedded itself inside you, to the point where it became indistinguishable from your own. And, now you defend it as if it's your own, and thereby allow it to limit you (which you're more than welcome to do, if you like). But the question is, 'Why would you want to?'

So face the damn thing. Journal out all the fears. Write a letter to the person you most fear judging you (but do not send it; otherwise you'll edit it as you write, which defeats the purpose of flushing out ALL the feelings and thoughts that still corrupt your life). Keep flushing it all out. Get it out! And,

FINALLY
ATTACK
YOUR
DREAM!

January 13

*I discovered that my insecurities and my flaws
were things that I actually need to embrace,
and I let them become my superpowers.*
-Skylar Grey, American singer/songwriter

Have you ever had someone ask you the question, "What's your superpower?" It's a silly question, on one hand, for obvious reasons. However, taken less literally, it's a great springboard for a quick thought on relationships.

I believe that everyone needs a particular relationship superpower (and yes, I'm aware of the fact that if everyone has it, then it's no longer a superpower; but play along). My reasoning is simply this: Once you have the ability, once you no longer fear to walk away from a relationship that either hurts or is no longer breathing life into you, you'll radically reduce your relationship unhappiness either in this one or in future relationships. You'll stop hanging onto lovers, friends, and family members who only bring pain or unhappiness in their wake.

The thing that keeps too many people stuck in unfulfilling and even unhappy or hurtful relationships is their fear of walking away, perhaps because of a fear of backlash, fear of being alone, fear of starting over, fear of facing all their own issues, or fear of what people might say. So you keep eating it and eating it from the other person. You stay, hoping it'll change, hoping you'll one day get the relationship you want and finally get your needs met. Maybe promises of change are made. But, over time, the changes never come or never stay. So leave!

But so many people respond, "But I believe in staying in relationships and working on them, no matter what!"

Okay, but what if the other person exhibits, time and again, that they're not working on anything and/or not even willing to work on anything? All jive, no action. Or worse, what if the other person in the relationship insists you are the problem instead of themselves, hence there's nothing for them to work on? Would you still stay? For what possible reason?

I see no good reason for staying in a relationship with a person who has a proven pattern of 1. Not meeting your needs and 2. Increasing your pain or greatly diminishing your life joy.

Once you no longer fear leaving, once that becomes your superpower, everything changes; first and foremost, the caliber of your relationships, because you're no longer tolerating low quality crap.

What do you fear most about leaving? Can you state your fear, in one sentence or less? What would it take for you to get through and past that? Or, if that one great fear came to happen, painful as it might be, would you survive? Would life go on? When do you begin to face the fears and make the changes, so that you're no longer enduring low caliber relationships?

January 14

> *Out of suffering have emerged the strongest souls;*
> *the most massive characters are seared with scars.*
> -Kahlil Gibran, Lebanese-American poet/writer

I'm a huge believer in the healing power of journaling, which this book is specifically designed to facilitate. In that, I can see the value of gratitude lists, which we're all familiar with – simply listing all that's good and worthy of gratitude in our lives. However, I've always seen gratitude lists as more palliative than actually productive when it comes to healing the root causes of life's problems.

Melody Beattie, in her book, *Make Miracles in Forty Days,* adds a new wrinkle to journaling that, in decades of my own journaling I had never been taught or even heard of. She recommends what I call 'shit lists.' At the top of the page, I write, "I'm grateful for and grateful that..." and then I go on to bullet-point or write paragraphs about everything that is going like shit in my life; everything I'm pissed about; everything I hate or every person I hate, in the moment. Every last 'negative' feeling, thought, or inclination I write out completely. For me, it's like scouring the heck out of the greasy, dried bottom of a pan that I just broiled steaks on in my oven. I scour out every last damn bit of rage, scorn, vile bitterness, anger, contempt, sorrow, grief, disappointment, and every other stinky feeling that most people spend their lives bottling up, denying they have, trying not to feel, or self-medicating from even though those feelings inevitably spill out when under pressure, offended, or drunk.

So many avoid those ugly feelings, because, "Hey man, I'm not a hater." To which, I always respond, Listen, until the hate (and every other 'negative' feeling) is out of you, it's still in you. So, technically, until you flush it all out, you're already a hater. You're carrying it around with you every day. You just packed it down real tightly and real deep, presumably to make room for more, or at least to pretend you don't have any hate at all.

Journaling 'sh*t lists' enable us to finally 'talk about' all the stuff without judgment, and to do so with the full force of all the energy that accompanies it. We can deep-dive into it, cry about it, rage about it, swear at the people and events and universe/God/happenstance, and more. But denying it exists or avoiding it at all costs, just packs that crud, that anger, that rage, and that sorrow down deeper!

What are the pain points inside you? What are you pissed about, grieving over, hating, or feeling betrayed by? What are all of your feelings? Can you tell the stories of your life and all the emotional charges that go with them, at least to yourself in your journaling, so that you may begin to flush, more and more? Are you ready to do some weekly sh*t lists? Have fun with it!

PS. And why shouldn't you or I be 'grateful' for all these supposedly negative feelings? Because, they're the scabs that have not healed and become old scars.

They're opportunities for more healing, growth, and expansion into fuller self. They're great indicators of where we're not happy in life and where there's massive potential for growth and change. Plus, we're just grateful for being aware that all this sh*t is in there; it means we're *ALIVE*, feeling all of life, all of it!

January 15

> *Jackie Robinson made my success possible.*
> *Without him, I would have never been able to do what I did.*
> -Martin Luther King Jr., American Civil Rights Leader

Like every other boy in America in the 1970s, my summers were spent mowing lawns, delivering my paper route, and playing T-ball and then baseball. Yet, for all the years I played, I never once hit a home run. I was a big kid who dreamed of, just once, getting the glory of hitting a dinger. Never happened.

Heck, sometimes, just making contact and getting a hit was hard enough. I grew to appreciate the satisfaction of getting on base, in no small part because I got nervous at the plate and would often swing at bad pitches—really bad pitches. I had never really been taught how to hit a ball beyond "Just swing the bat." Plus, I had the added pressure of listening to all the dads and moms behind the backstop smoking their cigarettes and shouting stuff like, "Hey Erlandson, you gonna get a hit this time?" It's funny, in retrospect, but felt quite angsty then.

Y'know what, though? I didn't outgrow that desire for decades. I outgrew the mocking and criticism. But the lust for home runs in life, career, and relationships took decades to abate. I longed to be the big man, the hero, just like every other 20- and 30-something. However, life teaches us that singles and doubles are excellent too, not to mention the walk. As the 'small ball' teams of baseball, like the Minnesota Twins and Oakland A's later modeled, there is something to be said for building success, moving the players around the bases bit by bit.

The goal, as I see it, isn't success in your 20s, no matter how throbbing the lust for it is at that age. The goal is to build career success, strong relationships, and a happy life, over time, bit by bit. Yes, we'd still like the doggone home run, now and then. And there's nothing wrong with wanting that. Occasionally, they come. But basing your life on needing that is not a mindset likely to yield, or sustain, happiness. You gotta celebrate the small victories and keep building.

Perhaps most importantly (if we extend the metaphor), there has to be a willingness to strike out. To play loose, to live in flow, to actually enjoy the game of life as you're building it means you gotta be willing to fail. Strikeouts are as integral to the game as anything else, an opportunity to learn, whether about your own stance, swing, and mental game, or about the pitcher's delivery. Fails are critical to success. To fear them means to play tight, not take chances, not try new ideas. And there ain't no joy, no success without those.

My real career home runs didn't happen until my late-40s/early-50s. I had to completely let them go long before that. Sure, some small part of me was always tickled by that possibility, and I suppose that's part of what kept me dreaming big and swinging for the fence, even while I kept knocking singles and sacrifice flies. I had to basically let it go and really consign myself to just enjoying the road.

Happiness was no longer allotted to the future when I would have success. It became a mandatory part of the journey. Then I could finally relax at the plate of life.

So, how much is your longing for massive success hamstringing your game? What do you need to change in your mental game to allow you to swing away, go after big ideas, appreciate small wins, and let your creativity flow? Mostly, do you have the ability to let go of wanting the big stuff, even while you simultaneously still want it? Can you live with an open hand, simultaneously holding onto and letting go of that which stirs your soul?

January 16

If you want to overcome the whole world, overcome yourself.
-Fyodor Dostoyevsky, Russian author

"Sven, I get soooo caught up in my head. I can't stop overthinking. I'm constantly gaming out possible scenarios and all the bad stuff that could possibly happen, not to mention all the mistakes I've made and embarrassment I feel over all that stuff. How do I get my mind to stop racing?" I hear this a LOT!

To stop the racing, start the flushing. See, the overthinking is driven, at its core, by fear, specifically of all the things that could happen... and hurt. It's a pain-reduction mechanism. The gaming out of possible eventualities is for risk analysis: Determine what the ultimate pains might be, then choose the route guaranteed to bring the least pain.

This is the thinking of someone who was likely raised in a highly critical or fear-filled environment or home where any misstep, poorly chosen word, failure, or anything out of the accepted norm was met with scorn, criticism, perhaps physical pain or some other pain delivery device, even if it was only a look of bitter disappointment from those in power. It hurt so much back then that as a matter of survival, the child's brain became an expert at assessing situations, scenarios, plans, and people that might be a possible conduit for pain. Massive fear drives the equation of this person's life.

So, the solution is to dig down to the fears driving the action. Dig down to the messages that were conveyed to you AND about you, whether overt or implied; name the messages, as succinctly as possible; name the origins/persons who delivered those messages; then begin flushing all of the attendant feelings that come with these new levels of awareness. Often the awareness itself takes a massive bite out of the fear and overthinking. However, for full scouring of the soul for the fears and messages you have to go into all the feelings and also the repercussions of these new revelations.

What are you overthinking? What are the fears driving you? What were the messages you received about you that caused you to fly below the radar and always live in fear of future pain? Who were you afraid of? What are the implications of realizing this person taught you to live in fear? Was there a second person who allowed this? How does it feel to know they did allow it?

January 17

Taking fun simply as fun,
and earnestness in earnest,
shows how thoroughly, thou,
none of the two discernest.
-David Miller, Author of Gods and Games

If you were to take a swing at it, knowing you could change your mind tomorrow if you like, what percentage of your life either is play or feels like play, and what percentage feels like drudgery or something other than the lightness of play? Is it 63% play and 37% heavy? Is it 12% and 88%, play to drag? What is it for you?

We've all heard it said, "Do what you love and you'll never work a day in your life." But the element of life as play goes even deeper than choosing a career, lover/mate, friends, and interests that are enjoyable. That's a huge part of life.

When you are on a task with something you love – be it career, working on your house, gardening, sorting out problems in a relationship, or working under the hood of your 1960s muscle car – you bring all of your 'work' powers to create something better, but it doesn't feel like work. It's just fun for you.

What's missing from your life? What would it take for life, for your work, and for your play to become play again for you; for it to become actually fun – a delightful engagement of all of your faculties towards an end that you want, choose and are happy to work at?

January 18

Bullying is the result of an unequal power dynamic –
the strong attacking the weak.
-Maria Konnikova, Russian-American author

One of the things I hear so frequently from people feeling stuck in their marriages or long-term relationships is, "My partner refuses to change. They say there's nothing wrong (or wrong with them) and they refuse to do anything for, or even acknowledge, my needs and wants." Thus begins our conversation on pain points.

Do you know why bullies bully? Sure, it's because they like the power, like the attention, or like to see others in pain or weakness (makes 'em feel big). Whatever the reason, all of it stems from a lack of love in childhood. However, there's another very simple explanation that accompanies those reasons: They bully because they can. Husbands and wives, boyfriends and girlfriends knock around their mates – whether physically or in words, neglect or public eye-rolling, and a million other ways – because their power is met unchecked. They create a power imbalance, usually early on in the relationship, that, when unchallenged, results in an escalation of their power. They forever escalate and expand their power so as to re-establish dominance. In short, they don't fear their partner. And, sadly, the only thing that keeps bullying personalities in check is the fear of a great, or greater, power source that can hurt them – i.e., the fear of pain. It's a horrible type of person to try to be in a loving relationship with and a horrible way to have to live when you find yourself with one. But there you are, and so you must respond with power or be ground to dust over the years.

There has to be a pain point. Otherwise, why would they change? They get everything, as it stands. There's no incentive to change. Why change if I don't have to?

So, you have to find your power, which you've likely been taught doesn't exist since childhood. You have to believe in yourself and your own birthright to be happy so much that you are willing to exercise your power and create pain or the potential for pain in your partner. Very often, for the person who does the self-work to re-find their power, the pain you create for the bully in your life is that you no longer *allow*. It's not specifically what you allow. It's that you generally stop allowing really anything at all from this person. That may seem like an unfathomable place of confidence to be in when you've been so beaten down, but it is very doable and doesn't have to take forever.

Sometimes, the greatest power you wield, if you've been bullied, is the power to simply walk away. For then a vacuum is created in the life of the bully. They no longer have someone they can beat up on. Hence, they no longer have a sense of self-worth. Remember, a bully's worth comes from pushing others down – feeling big by making others small. Remove the 'small' one and the bully shrinks into the head-full of messages planted in him/her/them as a kid, telling them of their worthlessness.

Stuck in a friendship, love relationship, work setting, family mess, or some other with a bully? Are you still hoping they'll change and actually start giving a crap about you? You're going to be waiting a very, very long time. Perhaps it's time to find your power by going inside and beginning to identify and remove all of the negative messaging you've had embedded deep inside since childhood. What were you taught about yourself? How were the messages of childhood the perfect, horrible setup for this relationship or work setting you find yourself in now? Are you ready to change it all?

January 19

> *Fight any instinct to be humorless.*
> *For, humorlessness is the worst of all absurdities.*
> -Jean Cocteau, French poet

One of the biggest insults I can hurl at someone, at least in my head (as I try not to hurt people with my words because I've done too much of that in my life), is to walk away from a conversation with them and think, "Humorless!" Few things bore me and cause me to not want to interact with someone more than the absence of the ability to kid around. It gets old quickly if all they can do is kid around and make everything a joke. But the person who cannot, at all, is painful for me to interact with.

See, the primary and most powerful male influence in my life was midwifed into existence on the family farm in the bitter cold tundra of one of the northernmost points of the contiguous United States on January 19, 1928. He had grown up in a family that loved music, the hard work of farming in the wretched cold, and a whole lot of laughter, which is rather ironic given the rather stoic nature of Swedish-Americans back then.

My dad was always a kidder, but never hurtfully so. He taught wisdom through irony, turning things upside-down, causing us to see things differently. But also, as a pastor, he modeled how to playfully interact with people, thus disarming them and instilling a sense of safety with him. I admired his ability to make crusty old men chuckle, not with a joke usually, but with an old fact or never-thought-of notion that made 'em raise their eyebrows, cock their heads, or say 'hmmm' and let out one laugh. Yet, oddly, he was a man who took life and his life's work very seriously. It was never seriousness at the expense of playfulness, nor vice-versa.

Who taught you playfulness? Or do you lack that tool in your toolbelt? Do you play life loose or play it tight? How does the whimsical factor into your life's work? Is it part of your creativity? In what ways?

January 20

> *We've let the blade of our innocence dull over time,*
> *and it's only in innocence*
> *that you find any kind of magic, any kind of courage.*
> -Sean Penn, American actor

Ever seen the workers on their knees, laying new sidewalks, smoothing it perfectly flat? Ever returned the next day to see that some little peckerhead kid put his handprint in that now-dry cement or some teen sweethearts wrote 'David loves Amy' with a stick in it?

No child comes out of the womb hating herself or criticizing herself, miserable about life. That means somewhere between the womb and right now, you were *taught* to beat yourself up and think little of yourself, slowly grinding down your life of dancing and twirling. The messages – often not explicit but implied in actions, a counter-message to the other positive messages you received, or in a look – we receive as a child get pressed into the wet cement of our child-soul. They harden into the core beliefs driving our lives, often becoming the virus infecting the operating system of our lives, hidden and silent, sucking the laughter and twirling from life.

When did you stop twirling in life? At what age do you remember life becoming ugly, heavy, unhappy, or laden with a distinct sense of being really self-conscious?

Why then? Why that age? What happened in the times leading up to that? What do you remember being said (or unsaid)?

Who perpetrated the action(s) or words that caused you to stop twirling? Have you ever in your life said one word to that person about it? Write a letter today or this week to that person. DO NOT SEND IT; just write it out. Flush out the most powerful feelings you have about those events and all that followed in the years afterward. Use the strongest, even most offensive language you possibly can. Express your anger, hurt, rage, tears, sorrow, and regret for not saying something sooner, perhaps. Say it all. Don't hold back. What is the single biggest thing you want to say or have never said to this person? What is it you most want to say to this person?

I'm not saying you should, but would you ever speak to or confront this person? Would it feel right or feel good to you? Why or why not? What is it you most fear in doing so – their defense, their denial, or their indifference? Why? Identifying those fears is the key to unlocking your authentic self. Again, you never have to confront that person in order to heal. What you do have to confront is what happens inside you when you consider doing so, and why.

January 21

You have been criticizing yourself for years,
and it hasn't worked.
Try approving of yourself and see what happens.
-Louise L. Hay, American motivational writer

Furthering yesterday's notion of core beliefs/messages driving your life, what is the biggest GOOD thing you can possibly imagine being written into the cement of your soul? What would feel the best? Is it something like...

"I am wonderful and totally kickass"

"My life matters; I MATTER"

 "I am good and good enough"

"I LOVE who I am and who I am becoming"

"I believe in you"

"I am wanted"

"I like me; heck, I love me"

Or is it something completely different? Why that phrase? How does that one speak to your soul?

What is the single most negative thing you can think of that was pressed into the former cement of your soul? Are you ready to smash that belief and let it go forever, replacing it with new beliefs? What would be the hardest thing, person, or pattern to let go of if you changed your core belief system?

What are five sentences that explain what that would feel like? Who would be most excited for you to become who you really are? Who are the people who would be your biggest supporters? What is the one sentence each of those people would say in support of you? (Make it different for each person.)

January 22

Author's note: I looked far and wide to find a quote
on the mistake that forgiveness can be.
I didn't find a single damn one. In fact, the greatest minds and most
deeply moral all sell forgiveness as a near panacea – from Gandhi to Jesus,
Pope to popes, MLK Jr to Fred Rogers (I mean, Mr. Rogers, for Pete's
sake), and from Maya Angelou to Bruce Lee.
And, truth be told, I see value in forgiveness. I do.
I just think one of the single most insidious mistakes made in relationships
is forgiving too soon,
forgiving before you've healed your own soul.
Forgiveness is a result of healing,
not the precursor to or cause of healing.
Putting forgiveness before healing
only stuffs the original pain down deeper.
And, burying deep pain even deeper never led to anything good,
only more pain later,
which serves nothing more than to be an ugly headstone
for a squirming body buried alive.
-Sven

Are you in a friendship, love relationship, work situation, family mess, or some other situation where someone is pushing you to forgive them? Does it feel uncomfortable or somehow not right?

99 times out of 100, if someone is pushing you to forgive them it's because *they* benefit by you doing so. If you're feeling pressured or really struggling with the rush of it, or the forgiveness at all, it's because somewhere inside you you're struggling to see how *you* benefit by doing so. More pointedly, the push to forgive is causing a squelching of your own feelings of hurt, unfairness, feeling unheard, or some other negative feeling that usually weaves into situations where forgiveness is being orchestrated.

The underlying message someone conveys when they push you to forgive them is that the healing of your pain is superseded by the desire of the other person to be exonerated and relieved of the burden of guilt, shame, or being exposed in the relationship, or simply their desire to get back to receiving the perks of a relationship with you. In other words, their wants are more important than your needs. They are more important than you.

Or, if someone is selling the importance of reconciliation in the relationship as more important than your healing by getting all of your pain out, they're saying the relationship is more important than you. And since the reconciliation of the relationship is what they're pushing hardest for, but you're not, then once again their wants are more important than your needs. And, if you agree to that, you're confirming your own lack of worth to yourself, to them, and to life itself. You are saying to that little eight-year-old you once were, "Yes, they're right. Your feelings and needs don't matter." And the worst part is that it's now YOU saying it to yourself. You are re-victimizing that child.

And the consummation of the damage is that in 'forgiving,' before you get all the pain out, you de-prioritize your own pain and, in fact, drive it deeper. You effectively shove that pain deep into that vault inside so that you don't have to feel it. Of course, the unfortunate downside of this is that pain in the vault grows and festers, bleeding problems into every aspect of your life, not the least of which is hidden resentment toward the one who pushed you to forgive in the first place, thus undermining the very relationship you're supposedly mending.

The most important priority in your life has to be your taking time and giving the energy to heal your own self. Do not be pushed to forgive. Where are the areas of life that you have healing work you need to do before you're ready for reconciliation or any movement, at all?

January 23

> *I'm guilty of giving people more chances than they deserve.*
> *But when I'm done, I'm done.*
> -Turcois Ominek, Author

I had been working with a young woman for six months while she considered a big career move across the country with her partner. She had been laboring, successfully, for a major record label, waiting, hoping for a promotion. Denied or beat-out each time a new opening arose, she lost more and more faith in the organization's appreciation of her, despite her love for it. She was never mistreated, just not cultivated. So, she and her partner made the huge decision to go start anew, elsewhere.

Within only a week after making the decision, while closing out her final three weeks with them, the label reached out to her and said, "We've got a promotion for you!"

She thought about it but laughed. "Nah, to hell with them," she told me. "I'm so done with them. I love 'em, but this is just the most beautiful example of them jacking me around, yet again. They didn't listen or take me seriously for five years, while happy to accept all the overtime and added value I brought. Now, there's really nothing they have that I want anymore. I'm so done."

In a bold stroke, with no job waiting, she and her partner moved to the West Coast, where her partner was hoping to go to a top law school. Within months of arriving, she had secured a higher-up position with one of the most storied agencies in Hollywood. Two years later, she had been moved to upper management, bought a house, and was loving a life of learning to surf and mountain getaways.

I'm done. I'm just done.

Those are powerful words, especially when accompanied with the realization that there's really not a damn thing you want from that position, place, or person anymore. You've done everything you can to make it work. Yet, you've been jerked around, pillar to post, so much that you're sapped of any positive affect for the person, place, or position. You're so over it.

That sort of clarity is invariably followed by bold action. Whereas, if there's still some nagging want that you have for that person or position, you'll keep one foot still back in it. But when it's toast, it's toast. When you know, you sooo know!

What's just done in your life? Do you still want it or something about it, or are you actually, truly done? If there is something you still want, what specifically is it, in one sentence or less? Could you honestly live, move on, and thrive without it? Are you finally ready to make the bold stroke?

January 24

Chains of habit are too light to be felt,
until they are too heavy to be broken.
-Warren Buffet, Investor, former richest man in the world

What's the difference between taking on massive debt at 22 and that same debt, unpaid, with accrued interest 20 years later, when 42? Depends on the interest rate, right? But even a small interest rate is going to cause that debt to grow massively. Left unpaid, that debt and new, growing interest now create their own worse problems: plummeting credit score, inability to make new investments and go new directions with life, massive mental anxiety, and depression, to name a few. It's the ugly stepsister of the law of compound interest.

Do you want to know how many people come to me in their 40s or 50s; we work together; they heal and finally start coming alive; then, very often say, "Man! I wish I would've known all this and done all of this 20 years ago! I feel like I wasted so much time!" Too many people to count.

I think the real problem isn't that people in their 20s aren't aware of their pains, fears, and the crud they were taught about themselves as a kid. Many are. I think they're not aware of how debilitating those things become when they're not dealt with. So, the 20-something dabbles in therapy or self-help but still thinks they can power through, or that the problem is not that bad.

But the 40-something is infinitely more motivated because they've been carrying that exact same life pain around for 20 years. They've tried, unsuccessfully, to shake it, bottle it, and medicate it. As a result, they become much more desperate, open to bold strokes, and uber-hungry for change, sometimes even open to going all-in on therapy. When life grinds you down harder you become more supple and willing to be moved and transformed.

Have you been ground down enough that you're willing to open up, trust, and begin to do the real work of healing? It doesn't have to take years. You can heal, but are you truly ready and hungry? Or do you just want to keep running from the tidal wave of pain that you've been running from (through self-medication, busyness, gambling, cheating, over-working, over-parenting, over-exercising, surrounding yourself with chaos, or some other way) your entire life?

If you truly are ready to deep dive, start by journaling about the ways you've been running. List on paper all the means you use to avoid feeling all the stuff you don't want to feel. Journal about how much life you're wasting by running; about what memories and feelings you're most afraid of; about the fear of feeling pain; about your fear of feeling overwhelmed by it all; about the implications of becoming fully aware of what was done to you or left undone. Just keep flushing it all out, bit by bit, day by day.

January 25

> *As you go the way of life,*
> *you will see a great chasm.*
> *Leap!*
> *It's not as wide as you think.*
> -Joseph Campbell, American scholar and writer

Since I was young, dating way back to early elementary school, I was quite good at mathematics. I was rarely at the top of my math classes, but I was always near the top. When young, we were told, "Make a career at what you're good at." So, from junior high all the way into college, I was encouraged to pursue a career in mathematics. I was actually majoring in mathematics at an engineering university when I realized, "Yes, I'm good at this stuff, but A) I'm not great at it; and B) I just don't enjoy it."

Could I have somehow made a career out of math? Sure. Are there many great careers in that field? Yep. Nonetheless, I didn't enjoy it enough to work at it, to become better, to learn more, to master it. I just didn't care.

And that's when I realized they were wrong – the well-meaning people in my youth who had encouraged us to pursue what we're good at. I did that and it taught me that that's not enough. I realized I want to enjoy, actually get lit off of that which I do with the bulk of my time, energy, and life. So, I started pursuing paths I loved 'til I no longer enjoyed that path anymore, just as I had done with math. Every challenge became a new open door that I plunged deeper into because it electrified me. I recognized that every path has hard times and stifling hardships. Yet, what powered me through the hard times was striving not just for success but enjoyment of the path. This ensured that I wouldn't be constrained to only enjoying life when I reached success, but that I would enjoy the journey towards it, as well. It was when the hard times, or even the good times, ceased to feel like my path that I knew it was time to let go of the security and move on. Shoot, eventually you find what you enjoy, are great at, and have no desire to quit. That's when life really starts to coalesce and flow.

What are you good at but hate or are just plain bored by? What do you love but are terrified to go after? What's the biggest fear: staying in misery or leaping? If you're going to have to weather the storms of life, would you rather do it doing what you love or what you are good at but really don't get lit up by? When do you have the courage to change paths? What would it take for you to finally make the switch?

January 26

"It's only life, afterall."
-Indigo Girls, American rock group

One of the most necessary elements in the process of not only healing from past pain but removing the insidious beliefs about ourselves that get pressed into us, from a young age, is finding and ascribing words to the experiences we've had. Words are so important for understanding and overcoming that which pulls us down from the inside.

Journaling can be so helpful in that process, as can writing poetry, counseling, talking with a trusted friend, writing letters (that you don't send) to those who've caused pain and hardship. But there is another thing that can be immensely powerful in speaking to the soul – the lyrics of music. Many clients have said to me, over the years, how this or that song or group spoke to their soul in dark times. It's really the same function as poetry and great literature – bringing words to our experiences, so that we may "...know we are not alone," in the words of CS Lewis.

What music groups and songs have spoken to you over the years and now? Write out the lyrics that really sing to your soul. Who are the authors and poets that have taught you about yourself and your experiences? What specifically were the words they wrote that stuck? What is the struggle you're still trying to find the words to? Ask the universe and your own soul to send you the music or words that will perfectly crystallize your experience and provide insight into this struggle.

January 27

> *I have always tried to live by the 'awe principle.'*
> *That is, can I find awe, wonder, and enchantment in*
> *the most mundane things conceivable?*
> -Craig Hatkoff, American investor

In my late-40s, I was in a men's touch football league that was pretty rough and tumble. Despite being the oldest guy on the field, I was trim and could keep up quite well. As an offensive lineman, whose job is to protect the quarterback (and occasionally release into a pass pattern), I took pride in giving good protection. But I rediscovered something I had learned back in my D-1 football days: There were a couple of guys in the league who played defensive line, who were, without exaggeration, 100 pounds overweight, yet who moved fast as lightning in a flat-out rush and could easily peel back into pass coverage. It didn't make any sense. It was remarkable, really. F = M x A. These animals could generate massive force because they could move these giant bodies so astoundingly fast. And it was jacked to play against 'em, for that exact reason.

Turns out, stuff ain't always as it appears, is it? Ever looked at something and thought, "How the heck can that be?" It just makes no sense, at all. And, in some ways, all you can do is sit back and marvel at it.

What's standing in front of you that just blows you the heck away? Person, place, or thing? What do you marvel at? Why? What specifically about it causes you to experience what the writer, Rudolf Otto, called *mysterium tremendum* – something massive that just blows you away? Do you allow yourself to be overwhelmed, to experience the sheer awe in your life?

Or, perhaps you're missing it. You're missing life. And, you know it.

January 28

"Those whom the gods would destroy,
they first make proud."
-Tom Clancy, derivative of Euripides quote

I'm a huge believer that pride is both good and necessary for a happy life. In fact, one of the personality attributes most missing in the lives of the clients I've worked with over the years, is genuine pride, genuine self-love. It has too often been supplanted by self-loathing or, at the very least, a lack of self-worth. Raised in homes of criticism, ridicule, or even absence of words and actions of love, too many enter adulthood and the making of adult decisions – marriage and career, in particular – skewed heavily toward, or over-compensating for, deep-rooted self-contempt. Pride, even if it is only in one's work, can be lifesaving and life-enhancing.

That said, in larger doses it can also be a recipe for disaster. See, every life encounters crashes, big ones. And the more one thinks of oneself and the less one also carries humility, the more precipitous the fall and harder the impact when the inevitable crash hits. Life is very fair, insofar as no one escapes life without pain and crashes. *No one.*

Painful as they can be, crashes are good for the soul. They make us human, bringing us back down to earth, infusing us, hopefully with a greater sense of compassion. Or, at the very least, they remind us of our finite abilities, our smallness, our inability to control the changes that life brings. They remind us, simply put, that the gods delight in kicking our heinies when we get too big for our britches.

So, where do you fall in this equation – utterly lacking pride in the beauty and joy of your own existence, or so overly full of yourself that one can almost hear the gods snickering in the distant ethers? Who taught you that you suck, such that you've either fully bought into it, or that you're declaring your greatness from the rooftops, so that no one will think what you already think about yourself deep inside?

January 29

What mystical force is at play when a place speaks to our soul?
We talk about soulmates.
But no one mentions how connected we can feel upon first meeting a
place,
how the magnetism pulls us out of ourselves
and longs for this location we just met.
-Mandie Hines, American author

Who are your people? More than just your relatives and family, who are the people with whom you identify? What about the geographical places that, for whatever reason, sing to your soul?

For me, there are several. I will one day be buried in a tiny, church cemetery in northern Minnesota, not because I know anyone there, anymore, or even feel a kinship with the people there, but because I grew up in that church yard, after service and Sunday School, playing among the headstones of Swedlunds, Esbjornsons, Hedmans, Olsons, Svensons, and Bernstroms. The Swedes took to that lush topsoil of Minnesota farm country when they immigrated to America and my people – the clergy – served them. Those kind people of the cold country are my people.

Yet, during seminary and many subsequent years, my heart sang and drew inspiration from the highly creative ethos of Berkeley/Oakland, CA. I have written many books and articles while living there. Being around the wild thinkers on the fringes, who have the raw courage to think and live way outside the boxes of a ticky-tack society, fire my creativity and desire to express.

Living in the NYC/Lower New England area has shown me a preponderance of people similar to the few I knew like them when I was growing up – the on-fire, focused, and unapologetically driven people. Oh, I love these people. We get each other. There's a resonation between kindred spirits.

And then, finally, there are that small handful of writers, all of them dead, whom I only ever found in the geography of their work and the geography of a library or bookstore. It was they who furthered the work started in me by my deep-questioning mother. These deep thinkers are my elders who've guided me through this life to become whom the gods wanted me to be. Joseph Campbell, James Hillman, Martin Luther, Richard Bach, Shakti Gawain, Lester Levenson. It would be a bit pretentious to call these titans my people, but at the least they are the elders in a tribe I like to dance with.

Who are your people as you define them? Why? What is the geography they share in common? What do you get from them? What do you bring to the table?

January 30

It is the soul's duty to be loyal to its own desires.
It must abandon itself to its master passion.
-Rebecca West, British author

The heart tugs. I believe that. It's always speaking to us, whispering new paths, new openings for heartfelt expression. But we get so caught up in and spun around by the necessities and vicissitudes of life, which very often outweigh or overshadow the calling of the heart to extend new kindness in new directions, to be an instrument of love in the world.

But the real infusion of new joy and genuine fulfillment in our lives comes not just from the giving of loving kindness to others, but allowing the heart to find creative expressions in the forms and directions it seeks to do so. And for many, there is a particular richness to the giving of the heart's love when it is directed toward those who can benefit oneself in no possible way. Perhaps it is directed toward those with less power, strength, agency, or money. There is not only an innate beauty to the act, but a different sense of deep satisfaction when it is completely other-focused.

Where is your heart calling you today, or lately, to give of yourself? What are the things inside you that keep you from going in those directions? Is there a reprioritization necessary in your life, even if only temporarily? What do you fear losing if you redirect your energies? What do you fear happening if you engage in these new avenues of creative expression of the heart? Do you have the courage to do it, anyway?

January 31

Really, when you take a step back and you really know yourself,
you're able to make better decisions.
-Omarion, American singer

Part of what creates so many problems in our careers, relationships, friendships, finances, and health, is that we're not clear about who we really are and what we really want. Specifically, far too many people make far too many compromises on their non-negotiables, because they don't know what their non-negotiables are.

One of the exercises in my book, *There's a Hole in My Love Cup*, involves drawing three horizontal lines across a page of paper, making three equal sections; then labeling the top section 'Non-negotiables,' the middle section 'Want, but negotiable (and %),' and bottom section 'Don't give a crap.' You can do a different page for each aspect of your life. One for finances. One for romantic relationships. One for career. One for friendships. And so on.

So, let's say you're doing one on relationships. The top section of your real dealbreakers generally contains about 4-8 things. Any more than that and you're probably listing things that you're somewhat negotiable on that should be saved for the middle section. The top section is for those things that no one should ever be able to coerce you into compromising on. When people say, "Relationships require compromise," this top list is exempt from compromise, by definition.

But, where the real action happens is in this middle section. Here you list every last thing you want in a relationship. *And then*, in parentheses after each item, you state the percent you want this and the percent you could live without it. As an example, let's say that in the center section you've listed, 'Someone who can cook well.' Let's say that you think about it and decide that this is not an absolute necessity and you could have a happy relationship with someone who didn't cook well. You might end up realizing that your wanting of that is 70% want and 30% room to live without it. So you'd write (70%-30%).

Perhaps a part of you would enjoy someone who is athletically active, but it's not a huge priority for you, so your percentage is 25% want and 75% don't care. Hence, (25%-75%). As you continue to fill in the percentages on all of them, your room for negotiation with the universe becomes clearer. You begin to see areas where the universe could really delight you with someone who meets your dealbreakers but is this odd amalgam of different percentages of that center section. Further, once you're in the relationship, you now have built-in room to be flexible and make something work, without ever feeling as though you're compromising your dealbreakers.

Oh, and the last section is simply the stuff that perhaps you think you should care about but don't; or things that others might care about, but you don't. This section is important to always keep in mind. Far too often in relationships our pride or fears get us caught up in arguments over things that, when it boils right down to it, we don't even care about.

What would your pages look like for each section of your life? Dive in and do the exercise, especially in the sectors of life where you're struggling the most.

February

February 1

*My fear now is of being cliché, of complacency,
of not being able to feel authenticity in myself and those around me.*
-John Hawkes, American actor

We've all heard the cliché quote that, "life begins outside your comfort zone." While it may well be true, the problem with stepping outside one's comfort zone is that it's damn scary out there! Few things will induce more fear than endeavoring something new, going after something you really want, something big. Yet, that is where this quote is clearly leading us.

Interestingly, the discomfort is not usually in the action that you're endeavoring. Instead, the discomfort is happening *inside* you. Therefore, the comfort zone that has to be stepped out of is the one inside you. It's as if you have to step outside of yourself, or outside of your old self. But, even that is still happening inside of you. Thus, mastering the future – i.e., turning it into what you would like it to be – requires mastering your own damn self, first. Inner game, then outer game.

When we're young, we can often do this by sheer willpower: "Just push through your fears!" But that's a game trumpeted by young men to even younger men. What is learned by men and women who age into their 40s and 50s, is that the soul is more powerful than the will. The pains and emptiness, negative messaging and external millstones that get implanted into the soul from a young age eventually grind even the most fearless and powerful of wills to an inexorable and insurmountable halt.

Eventually, mastery of the inner game requires something other than force. Moving forward, particularly in bold, new directions requires going into the pain and beginning the process of releasing both it and the fear of it, the latter of which is what causes inhibition and inaction. Fear of the pain keeps people locked in comfort zones like nothing else in the human experience can.

To tap into a power you've never known, to truly begin to step outside of your comfort zone, demands naming the inner pain sources and beginning the process of facing and releasing them. Thus, conquering the challenges ahead in your life demands conquering the challenges inside you. Few things in life demand more courage than that.

What is it about the pain inside that scares you most? Which particular stories, memories, people, or thoughts inside scare you at the mere mention of them? Isn't it fascinating how a mere thought that you can have, while sitting in your favorite chair with your pet or sipping your favorite coffee in your favorite slippers, can scare the absolute holy hell out of you? You can be completely safe with good locks on the doors and all of your favorite and warm life possessions and people around you, but still be terrified... of something *inside* you!!!

Still think this stuff isn't powerful? Still think this stuff doesn't have the power to short circuit, undermine, hamstring, and outright ruin a career, relationships, and a life, as a whole? Can you still justify minimizing the essential nature of doing this work to finally become free, happy, and *ALIVE?*

February 2

> *It takes a big man to admit he's wrong.*
> *I am not a big man.*
> -Fletch, Fletch Lives

That is easily one of my Top 5 all-time favorite movie quotes. Apart from being funny as hell, it also points to a greater truth among men. All people, I suppose, but particularly a whole lot of men, just ain't big enough to admit being wrong, ever.

This type of person is extraordinarily difficult to have a relationship with because the relationship is predicated upon protecting the ego of the frail male, who cannot own up to anything that makes him look 'less than,' in any way. He sees being wrong as a sign of weakness. He sees striking out as failure, rather than part of the process of hitting and getting on base. Every at-bat has to be a hit or be forever wiped from the memory banks of the scorer's table.

This type of person is even worse to have as a parent (again, this trait can be found in both mothers and fathers). This type of parent will use his own children to gratify his ego's need for power and control. When he inevitably hurts his child, he will not apologize because that, in his eyes, makes him look bad, makes him look weak. Which, to be clear, he is deep inside, but he just can't bear to have anyone else see it.

This man is both a fool and a scourge to humanity. His belief in his own toughness and rightness not only drives others away, leaving him eventually alone and bitter, but harms them in the process. This is all because he was taught, at a very young age, that he was worth nothing. And so, he attempts to feel worth by undermining the worth of others. It's a child's game executed by a grown man with power. And it's ugly.

Are you this man or woman? To what degree is your frail ego harming your relationships and others? At what point do you have the courage to see the damage you're doing and change, thereby becoming a member of the human race, rather than falsely seeing yourself as some sort of god who hovers above the lesser mortals? Further, when do you finally go inside to explore the initial wounds that you've been covering up for decades with this false bravado?

Or, do you have one of these people in your life? To what degree are you allowing someone(s) in your life to act this way with you? I'm not saying you're causing it, as if to blame the victim. I'm asking if you're allowing it, which is a very different question. If so, what are you truly afraid of? Do you see the price of your own character weakness, how it causes pain to yourself and possibly others who need you to stand up against this, and how it undermines your relationships and overall happiness?

February 3

***Find a group of people who challenge and inspire you;
spend a lot of time with them, and it will change your life.***
-Amy Poehler, American comedian

I was in my early to mid-thirties when I moved to Los Angeles to follow a woman whose career was there. Now, I had lived in Colorado on my own for a few years of college and had spent a few years in Northern California for seminary but moving to L.A. was something different. We were starting a life together there.

She knew some people there already, as she had lived there a few years. But, it was completely new to me. So, we were forced to build relationships through our jobs, our neighborhood, and by other random encounters. What grew out of this was a cluster of friendships that became the foundation of people with whom we spent Thanksgivings, 4ths of July, as well as birthdays and Christmas parties. These friends became our new family, at times even closer than family.

Have you had that experience before? Have you encountered situations in life that bred relationships that became 'closer than family?' It's a powerful experience because it opens one's eyes to what has been missing in some family relationships. It also breathes new meanings into holidays and events formerly spent with your family of origin. There is a new thankfulness when surrounded by people you depend on for joy and connection, who also depend on you. There's a sense of 'we're in this together' that is sometimes absent or skewed with families of origin.

Who are the friends in your life who have become family? What longing in you gave birth to these new family members? What do you get from these relationships? What do you bring to them that they value? How have these relationships changed your perception of your family of origin?

February 4

We were free of self-judgment when we were babies,
and yet at some point, we developed a sensitivity that taught us to react
with self-consciousness and negative self-talk.
-Elaine Marie, American author

One of the most consistent messages I heard about myself from teachers growing up was, "Sven, you're different. You need to be more normal." While some teachers gave a message of "Different is great," this particular phrase became a bit of a repetitive mantra coming from those in power. Clearly, the underlying, unspoken message was, "I don't like who you are. You need to change to be more of what I like." At times, it was so adamant as to take on the flavor of, "Who you really are doesn't matter. Be what we want you to be."

Those underlying messages are damn powerful. My WWII generation mother used to call them "the messages behind the message." Add them to other messages coming from other sources and the strength of the notion starts to build up inside a young person. For example, I can recall getting turned down by many a girl in junior high and high school. Naturally, a young guy starts interpreting that repetitive scenario as "I'm unwantable."

Here's the thing, though: Those messages then embed into the wet cement of the soul. The child, or young person, begins to believe, to a large degree, that those messages are true. Far worse, sometimes the young person isn't even aware that those are the messages that he has received and that they're being pressed so deeply into the foundation of his being. Those unknown messages can take decades to identify and extract while, in the meantime, they wreak havoc on that person's career, love life, and family.

What were the most powerful messages you received growing up, either consistently or a few times, that embedded deeply? And, as you consider those messages you received, begin to poke around and consider what the real underlying messages were. Remember, a child's mind often converts all messages, even the most benign, into some judgment of his or her existence. So, what were the underlying messages? Usually, the underlying message was some derivative of 1) You're not wanted; 2) You're no good, or not good enough; and/or 3) You don't matter, or the real you doesn't matter.

What does it feel like to see those conveyed to you in your past? How have these core messages undermined your life? Do you have the desire to remove those messages from your life and replace them with new, life-giving ones? What would those new messages be?

February 5

There is no success in any venture in life without the capacity to focus your mind.
-My mantra I would hammer my athletes with
when I was an NCAA strength coach

Sometimes, when I'm in the middle of a workout, one I know I want to be in and enjoy, I find my mind straying or my intensity level a little off. Very often in those cases, I will say aloud to myself, "Just do the work."

Sometimes, in my writing and counseling, or even in the creation of my videos over the years, I've found myself holding back, not going full throttle, not completely putting my truths out there. I feel very much called in my soul to be aggressive in my work, 'leaving it all on the mat,' as we used to say in wrestling – i.e., holding nothing back, saying all that I need to say and in ways I need to say them. But when I see myself pulling punches, I simply tell myself, "Just do the work."

When I find myself getting distracted by life or minutiae, I remind myself, "I've got work to do," life work. That serves as a scolding and an internal "Quit screwing around!" to the petty stuff I'm letting myself get caught up in. I've got only a short spin on this earth, and I have lots that I can and must do.

What do you need to work harder at? What do you need to focus harder on? What is it you know you want or are called to, but also know you have another level or two of ability, focus, and drive that you are not tapping into yet? What too easily distracts you? Who too easily distracts you? What's the work you've been put on this earth to do? Are you squandering your time and life energy? Also, apart from the work you know you're called to do with your life, are you staying on top of the spiritual work that you know you need to do to operate at peak efficiency, especially the work of continually flushing out all the pain, fears, and BS beliefs you've been taught about yourself?

Come on, now. Just do the work!

February 6

Creation is invariably preceded by destruction.
If the seed does not die, there is no plant.
Bread results from the death of wheat.
-Joseph Campbell, American scholar
(whose work was a large inspiration for the Star Wars movies)

One of the grand, ugly truths of life is that life feeds on death, not just in the physical world of nature, though that is an obvious example and a great teacher. But, it is also true in the personal and interpersonal world. Relationships must die to give birth to new relationships. Old forms of self must be shed for new growth, for new iterations of self, much as the snake sloughs its skin.

What new forms are not coming because you're resisting the sloughing? What security do you cling to because it is what you've always known? What deaths are you refusing to acknowledge and see for the glorious beauty of new life that they are? Is it time to begin the grieving process, so that the pain can be released and the ritual of new birth may begin? For what deaths, and in which forms, are you failing to give thanks to the gods of nature and life itself? And what is next?

February 7

Sven, there are a lot of things in life we don't want to do, but we just gotta do.
-My Mom

In my childhood home there were eight of us, total. And as early as when I was four or five, I had weekly chores, which included dinner dishes, one night per week. This being long before our home ever had a dishwasher, it was no small feat (and I'm sure I screwed it up gloriously). Quite distinctly, I recall complaining to my mother, likely on many occasions, that I didn't want to do the dishes. To which she gave the response above.

I believed it strongly for a good 20+ years. Then, more and more, I let go of my belief in that little theory. While it is still true – there are toilets that have to be cleaned, dirt that has to be shoveled, oil that has to be changed – and I still take some odd pride from doing the undesirable work of life, I now see it as a bed of quicksand too easily sucked into if chosen as a dominant life principle. Yes, there are times we just gotta grind, either in pursuit of our bliss or because we're playing on a team/relationship and that means we don't always get our own way. However, I simply made the decision for my life that I would, more and more, do only those things that breathe life into my soul. And, that has made all of the difference.

In fact, I'm of the belief that the simplest answer to living a life of joy and aliveness is, at its most basic, just saying 'no' to that which sucks the life and energy out of you – people, places, plans, pursuits, purposes, preparations....and inner principles you believe about yourself. If you do just that one thing, over and over again, everything changes. You don't even have to 'pursue' your interests after doing that, for it will become inevitable, unavoidable, and nearly effortless. The grand answer to life and its absence of joy is nothing more than the courage to say 'no' to that which bleeds you.

That's it.

So, what bleeds you? Have you lived too long doing those things you don't want to do? Is it, perhaps, time to tweak the equation of your life? What are the top 10 things you're giving life energy to that need to be gone, because they are net-losses for you? Or, even if they cannot yet be cut out entirely, what are the people, plans, pursuits and principles that you need to scale back from an 80% presence in your life to 20%, or so? What do you most fear losing if you do, indeed, scale back? But is it finally necessary, nonetheless, for your own sanity?

February 8

Every morning, when you wake up, while you're laying there in that moment,
before your day begins with your short walk to the bathroom,
life is whispering two questions in your ear:
'Who the hell are you, really?' And,
'Do you have the courage to be who the hell you really are?'
-Sven

My mom, long before dying at 93, used to tell me, "Sven, I don't want to 'should on you.'" I don't know if she had learned something while working her way through raising my five older sibs, but she was adamant that she was not going to oppose my internal GPS, or in any way impose her will on me or allow anyone else to.

Wherever she had picked it up, she had deeply understood the value of the child being able to hear his own inner voice. She knew that adults spend lifetimes trying to extricate themselves from the internalized 'shoulds' of long-deceased parents, oftentimes experiencing inauthentic and unhappy lives in the meantime. She committed to allowing the teen room for originality, while still existing within the communal aspects of family and community and handling the expectations that go with that (chores, being a team player, kindness, respect). The permission and room to become original is gold. She knew it. Do you?

Who are you, really? What is the longest and most complete identification and definition you can give of yourself? What are the gaping holes inside where you don't yet know fully who you are? List the categories. List the specifics within those categories. Answer the question 'why' you still don't know, or what's missing, in order to know those specifics – i.e., what the precise question is that you're still trying to answer in figuring out those specifics. List the biggest fears that keep you from finding, answering, or feeling that new specific answer.

Do you have the courage to finally be who you really are? Lastly, what or who is the biggest obstacle to you being, saying, and becoming that which you most fully are? What precisely – in one sentence or less – do you most fear happening or fear being said if you start becoming your original self? If that fear actually does happen, will you be okay? Yes, it will hurt and you'll grieve, but will you be okay? Is it possible that your grand fear isn't the giant dragon you have always feared it to be? If so, now what?

February 9

A coward is incapable of exhibiting love;
it is the prerogative of the brave.
-Mahatma Gandhi, Indian revolutionary

"Oh, it was mutual, Sven," she responded about her divorce.

I smiled. "I doubt that very much. I am certain one of you consented. I agreed to go to a 'hot yoga' class once, knowing damn well I loathe doing *anything* in the heat, especially working out, sex, or anything physical. Shoot me now! I consented, and, true to form, hated it. So, who wanted your divorce and who didn't?"

"You're right. He didn't want it, but agreed, in the end."

Exactly.

Is it possible you force your reality onto others? Talk them into it; talk them into believing they want it, too? Do you need someone else's consent to simply spend your life your way, including walking away from that which no longer makes your soul sing?

Is that really love to force someone to accept your wants, needs, or reality?

It was in no way manipulative or bad for her to walk away from her marriage. That was completely her right. The manipulation started when she used her leverage to get him to think he wanted it, too, and then sold that as the company line. She wanted the cover that would provide, so that she wouldn't have to look like the bad guy.

How much of your life is consumed by fear of dislike, blowback, or criticism? Do you force someone else to see life your way so that you won't feel bad? Is that love? Do you see the cowardice in that? Do you see the manipulation and the fear driving your actions? Can you start sitting in and flushing out your fears in any given situation? Can you start living plainly, just being you without needing others as cover? Where is your cowardice showing?

February 10

When we miss someone,
often what we miss is
the part of us that this someone awakens.
-Luigina Sgarro, Psychotherapist

I have four brothers and one sister. I wouldn't say we were all tight growing up, as the span from youngest to oldest was 11 years. But, after thousands of family dinners, vacations, the dying and care of both parents (mostly attended to by 4 of the 6 kids, bless their hearts), and more, we are a somewhat close family, even to this day. I respect the hell out of every one of them and their spouses. Yet, as in any big family, you're naturally closer to some than others.

I had a major falling out with the one brother I was closest to and, some might say, most similar to, both in personality and temperament. It happened in our forties and lasted well into our fifties. We could still be cordial at family events, but it was nowhere near the same. And I missed him greatly. I missed the one person on God's green earth who I felt was most like me.

It ended, formally, after my father's memorial service. I apologized for all I had done to hurt him. He apologized for all he had done. It was really nice. Both of us humbled by the man we both respected, if for different reasons – him admiring dad's honesty, me his contrarian playfulness.

Now, a few years later, we're still not as close as we once were, and we may never be. I still miss him. I have no doubt he'd have cocktails with me, if I were in his city. I'd certainly welcome him into our home, if he came to the NYC area.

But, I miss him; the kindred-spirit-ness, the fellow wild soul in the universe, his charm, and his intensity. I don't miss his politics or that he was smarter than me in so many ways. But I do miss him.

Who do you miss? It doesn't have to be family. Who from your past brings a bit of emptiness or sadness into your soul as you ponder their memory? Maybe they're alive; maybe they're dead. What do you miss most? What do you miss least?

There's no need to push to reconcile. If it comes, if it feels right, you'll do what comes next. If not, that's okay, too. There's no push in life, no need for force. Nonetheless, it is good to allow that wistfulness for people from our past to blow through us, to feel them again; to smile, to laugh, to cry.

Who is your person?

February 11

If you're going to try, go all the way. Otherwise, don't even start.
This could mean losing girlfriends, wives, relatives
and maybe even your mind.
It could mean not eating for three or four days.
It could mean freezing on a park bench.
It could mean jail. It could mean derision.
It could mean mockery – isolation. Isolation is the gift.
All the others are a test of your endurance,
of how much you really want to do it.
And, you'll do it, despite rejection and the worst odds.
And it will be better than anything else you can imagine.
If you're going to try, go all the way. There is no other feeling like that.
You will be alone with the gods, and the nights will flame with fire.
You will ride life straight to perfect laughter. It's the only good fight there
is.

-Charles Bukowski, American poet

I am incapable of agreeing with this more. This statement by Bukowski both sings to my soul and speaks the truth I have lived since leaving the Air Force Academy 37 years ago. It was then that I began the slow, fast, arduous, free journey of living and expressing myself, of doing what I love and what feels right TO ME. I lost everything. I gave up everything. I lived on the street, lived in my car, lost family, lost my kids, was accused of losing my mind, and on and on. But g**damn, I was *ALIVE*, dancing with the gods. The exhortations of Joseph Campbell and others like him to, "follow your bliss," burrowed deep into my soul. And I lived it, still do, except that now it is all masked in the worldly success that came decades later. But, happiness and peace had come long before any hint of success.

Bukowski's words aren't for the timid; or maybe they are. Maybe it's precisely the timid who need it most. I think we all need it most, lest we slip into Thoreau's "lives of quiet desperation." Really, I think Bukowski's words reverberate in the souls of every person. There is something native to the human spirit that longs to live unleashed and on fire. But, too often, safety is chosen over passion.

To what degree are you robbing yourself of life because you fear the mocking, the losses, the isolation, and the terror of failure? Even if you cannot go all the way, as Bukowski cajoles us to, can you go further in that direction, even a bit – maybe a meter, maybe a mile? To what degree does your soul need to be set free? To what degree are you tired of living what you know to be your 'lower life,' killing you a bit more, each day? What's the grand fear? When do you tire of that fear stealing your life?

February 12

We must be willing to let go of the life we planned,
so as to have the life that is waiting for us.
-Joseph Campbell, Revolutionary mythologist

If you do follow your bliss, you put yourself on a kind of track
that has been there all the while, waiting for you,
and the life that you ought to be living is the one you are living.
Follow your bliss and don't be afraid,
and doors will open where you didn't know they were going to be.
-Joseph Campbell

The courage to express yourself and live on the outside who you really are on the inside, deep down, at the soul level of your being, is life's greatest challenge. The more you have the courage to be, say, do, and become your true self on the outside, not just the inside, three things begin to happen:

One, *you start to lose people.* Many of the people in your life, especially those who hold the most sway over you, are married to the idea of who you *used* to be. Begin to express your authentic self, even in small doses, and people will fight you to stay as you always were. Their own fears will run their mouths and actions. And, eventually, if you persist, some will walk away from you and you'll walk away from others, including some you thought would be with you forever. The thought of this is scary for anyone, so much so that it can keep people from opening up, even a little; keep them from putting their original self out there. Nonetheless, you should persist through this difficult part of life.

Two, *you start to effortlessly attract people.* We've all met people who just have clean energy, who are *ALIVE*, who just attract others. That's what you slowly start to become. People say, "Hey, I love who you're becoming," and, "If you went back to being who you say you used to be, I wouldn't be the least bit interested," or, "I love that you don't even know fully who you're becoming, but you have the courage to become." A whole new life starts to rise up around you.

Three, *stuff starts to fall out of the sky.* Good stuff! I know this sounds completely whackadoodle to a lot of folks, but I've seen it happen far too many times to question it, even in my own life. For example, in the last 8 years, I've been approached nine different times by production companies wanting to make a TV show out of me and/or my work, or use me in an existing show. Not once did I do anything to precipitate or pursue that happening.

One client did the work and, on my coaching, did only that which breathed life and energy into her, such as getting back into painting and singing in a garage band, neither of which she had done in nearly 15 years. A while later, I got an email saying that she and her son had held a yard sale and up walked a man, whom she started chatting with. Quite unexpectedly, new love had begun to blossom in her long-quiet dating life.

Another client, after walking out of my office at the end of our second very intense session, called me from the ground floor lobby to tell me that while on the elevator, she had gotten a call from someone she didn't know who had found her company and wanted to bring her in to consult his very successful company, which was in a field she had not even considered expanding to.

Who are the people you are most likely to get blowback from if you were to, more and more, believe in and become who you really are? In this list, circle the people you are most afraid to lose. Write out the three main reasons for each person of why you are afraid to lose them. What would it feel like to no longer have them in your life? Could you live with it and move on? Does it change your perspective on more fully becoming your truest self to know that, in the end, you can accept, live with, and move on from the loss of any of those people? How?

Who on your list do you not fear losing? Do you not fear losing them because A) they would not leave you if you were to more and more become yourself; or because B) you simply are not afraid of living without them (or without their diminished presence in your life)?

Does it change your perspective on living your truth to know you'll begin to attract new people, who are better suited to who you're becoming? What types of people would you most love to attract? What would make your heart sing?

February 13

People almost invariably arrive at their beliefs
not on the basis of proof
but on the basis of what they find attractive.
-Blaise Pascal, French mathematician and philosopher

As a former pastor, who still does the occasional wedding or funeral, I regularly get people asking me if I'm religious or some God-guy. I tell 'em I'm quite fluent and comfortable in the language of God, but I'm not religious and largely believe that God is simply all the things science hasn't explained yet. I'm an intellectual atheist, but experientially am very much of the belief that there's a whole lot of stuff science can't touch, hasn't touched, and at times, is terrified to touch – the trippy, inexplicable stuff.

Allowing myself to believe in that basic principle, especially as a pastor coming from a robust lineage of clergy, completely changed the trajectory of my life and career. It was the true beginning of my living authentically. My parents wouldn't have disowned me if I had expressed this earlier, but they might have worried about my eternal soul, or something. I was afraid to just be real, until I wasn't.

For me, the issue was god stuff – the beliefs of others that didn't fit with me. However, for many people, the inauthentic living they're stuck in has nothing to do with god stuff. There are a million beliefs that determine our lives, beliefs about the world, self, humanity, nature, the cosmos, the purpose of life, marriage/relationships, work, play, health, and more. To go deep and name your honest beliefs on paper is to know yourself as you are, not as you think you should be. It is to see self evolving into greater truth.

So, what do you believe? And has it occurred to you that the lurching and stalling of your life and career are directly related to the fact that you don't know who you really are, at the deepest level, or perhaps don't want to know? Can you see that there might be value in specifically, courageously articulating, even if just for yourself, what the heck you really believe? Even if you never choose to act on it, can you at least write it down? Can you, at the very least in life, be honest with yourself?

When do you begin to live authentically? When do you stop allowing your fears of what others will think to keep you from just being who you really are?

Can you trust that all these different, random pieces of your authentic self will begin to weave together into a brilliant tapestry if you have the courage to live them? They will. They always do. But the precursor is the courage to be aware of what the disparate threads are, to at least look at them.

February 14

The more you love,
the more you suffer.
-Vincent van Gogh, Dutch painter

Do you like sex? Yeah, me too.

Do you like love; like passionate, intense, can't-stop-thinking-about-'em love? Yeah, me too.

Do you like snuggling, laughing with a lover, and playfulness? Yeah, me too.

Often in deep, self-helpy work there is a downplaying of passion and the fires of love. And I appreciate the need for understanding and expanding concepts of love. Totally get that.

But, that doesn't deny the fact that love is awesome, feels great, and is just one of life's great delights. And, on this Valentine's Day, why the hell not celebrate the divine embrace of passionate love when the god Cupid pierces us with that madness-inducing concoction that is love, itself? Skol to that!

That said, I wouldn't be me if I didn't say, 'Isn't it damn interesting how the most intense of life's experiences also wields massive power to sear the heart, or even utterly torch it? Isn't it fascinating how love can be so much more powerful than our own willpower?'

To experience passionate love, as most everyone has, or will, is to know pain...absolute pain that comes with the destructive force of all the gods and fires. To know the love and pain is to be provided with the opportunity to grow, deepen, and wisen. To simply run from passion's inevitable pain is to miss the real gift it holds in its terrible clutches. That scorch bears insight into self, into others, and into the very soul of life. To be truly alive is to embrace them both – passion and pain. Both are blessings from the gods, if you have the eyes to see and the courage to look.

What are you missing because you fear the pain, pain that you can purge but clearly haven't yet? Are you running from passion because you fear the inevitable disappointments, frustrations, and deaths? Or have you experienced intense love, lost that love, and now you're running from the pain in its wake?

Depth begins when we embrace both the 'positive' and the 'negative,' when we realize all is a gift. What new challenge do you need to embrace, so as to live outside your limited sense of security? Can you learn from all this experience is teaching you? What rock is sitting there, waiting to be looked under?

February 15

> *I cannot always control what goes on outside.*
> *But I can always control what goes on inside.*
> -Wayne Dyer, American author

Oftentimes, the root problem when it comes to authentic living is that the voices of others occupy real estate in your head, heart, soul, veins, and cells. And whether you're 22 and struggling to launch or 48 and wildly successful, you're miserable inside because your authentic self, rising up from the deepest depths of your soul, is battling with the voices that have been rammed down your throat, likely since a very young age. There's a proxy fight for control of the company going on inside of you.

The emptiness you feel, the motivation you cannot find, the sadness over time lost, and all the negativity in your life finds its root in the fact that you are still driven by 'shoulds' inside that never are and never were your native self. Someone else's voice owns your life. Likely, more than one person or entity owns you, but there's always one who owns and controls you most, whether you're aware of it or not — someone you've been programmed to gain approval from or someone you live in fear of disappointing or getting criticism from.

What is the one sentence that you most fear someone saying to you or thinking about you? Or, what's the one sentence that would be the most painful to hear, or know someone is thinking? Or, what's the one sentence you've *most* spent your life running from?

Now, having answered that, who is the one person, above all else, that it would be most painful to hear that from, or know they're thinking that about you? Or, who is the one person most likely to say it? Or, who has always been the one quick to say such things? This is the person, more than any other, you are terrified of standing up to, terrified of reclaiming your life from. This is the person who owns you most. This is the real estate developer in a never-ending land-grab inside you. Do you have the courage to begin to explore, more and more, this person's extreme, multi-faceted influence in your life and the fear that accompanies it? Do you have the even greater courage to begin to extract this person from your depths? Regardless of how you treat the same, actual person outside you, what do you choose to do with this owner inside you? Do you see how your own true happiness is utterly dependent upon your willingness to reclaim all of your inner real estate?

February 16

Awareness is all about restoring your freedom to choose what you want instead of what your past imposes on you.
-Deepak Chopra, Indian-American New Age author

Question: What do Buddhism and my (deceased) mother have in common?

Answer: Not much, except this one thing, stated differently by each: In Buddhism, it's believed that everything in life changes when we become aware of both what's going on around us, and what's going on inside us. My mother, the deepest person I've ever known—who made a life out of healing wounded souls—repeatedly told me, "Naming the beast is half the problem."

There's no beast more insidiously powerful in our lives, chewing us up from the inside, than the beliefs we've been taught to believe about ourselves. These core beliefs about self come from pain and create fears, fog, and lethargy. It's those fears, pain, and BS beliefs we've been taught about ourselves that have to be named in order to be defanged. Awareness brings peace, strength, and clarity.

What is the beast in your life that is still unnamed? What are the earmarks, or symptoms, of the beast afflicting your soul? How is the affliction manifesting itself? Do you have sorrow, fatigue, disinterest, apathy, anger? How is that crud deep down causing storms on the surface?

It's sometimes hard to see it on our own, to go deep enough, but what can you see? If you were to be totally honest and dig as deep as you possibly can, what is the grand fear afflicting your life? Why?

What is your preferred means of running from your afflictions? Is it an eating disorder, the bottle, pills, gambling, over-working, cheating, surrounding yourself with chaos, swiping and scrolling, gaming, pot, or what? What would your life look like if you were to stop running, name the beasts, and free yourself from the terror they cause in your life?

February 17

Children shout loudest when feeling heard least.
Adults, too.
-Sven

Ever encountered a really annoying kid who is constantly loud, shouting, or in constant agitation? Or, maybe you were that person?

But, have you ever had the thought, 'What if there's nothing actually wrong with that kid, except that their needs aren't being met? What if the little one isn't some undisciplined snot, but a gentle soul running short on love, trying so desperately in the only way he knows how to be seen, touched kindly, heard, valued, and enjoyed?'

Are you that person, even now as an adult? Are you trying to be heard, your soul silently shouting in desperation and pain?

What is your soul longing to shout or longing to say? Do you even know?

Whose voice are you trying to be heard over? Who has most stifled your voice? In one sentence or less, what is the message most spoken to you that negates what you've been trying to say, or what your soul has been longing to say?

Do you live with a clean heart – your truths spoken, your authentic self seamlessly expressing on the outside who you are on the inside?

What would it take for you to finally have the courage to speak your truths, so that your heart might finally be clean and light? Do you have the courage to do so, even knowing the price might be high?

February 18

Argue for your limitations and, sure enough, they're yours.
-Richard Bach, American author and Navy aviator

Nikki handed me a book and said, "You need to read this! It'll blow your mind." I was a junior in college. She was pretty. Who was I to refuse?

That one book changed everything. It began my lifelong, deliberate spiritual journey. Even though I had grown up the son of a pastor dad and a mom who was a religious leader in the field of education, this was the real start. The book? *Illusions: The Adventures of a Reluctant Messiah*, by Richard Bach. Nikki was right; it was mind-blowing for me, at that age. It still challenges me when I pick it up every few years to flip through. One bite from the book that has always stuck in my head is the one above.

I got hit on my bicycle one summer rush hour on Lake Street in South Minneapolis. Side-swiped, I got sent ass over tea kettle, splayed out and bleeding under my bent-up bike. Police. Unnecessary ambulance. Walked home.

The next morning, I was frying some eggs and went to flip 'em when the doggone things flipped right onto the floor. Alone in my attic apartment of an old Victorian, I started laughing aloud, thinking of the bike yesterday and the eggs now, and stated matter-of-factly as I bent over to clean it up, "Man! I just cannot win!" I had been stating that sorta throwaway self-deprecating line for years. But in that moment, I had a complete 'AHA,' the second it came outta my mouth.

Somewhere in me, I believed it. No wonder my career had gone to crap and I had two failed marriages. Somewhere in me, after a decade and a half of struggle, I was repeatedly stating this crappy, seemingly funny and harmless line, thus limiting myself and sealing my fate. My language was contributing to my reality; and the language itself was a reflection of the beliefs driving it. From that moment on, those words never again passed over my lips.

What beliefs about yourself or your life do you adamantly defend that may not, in fact, be true, but you're making them true? Are you arguing for your limitations?

February 19

It is better to conquer yourself than to win a thousand battles.
Then the victory is yours.
It cannot be taken from you, not by angels or by demons, heaven or hell.
-Buddha, Ascetic spiritual teacher

I was in class at the Roman Catholic seminary I had been attending for two years. One of my favorite nuns was the instructor and somehow the class had gone off on a tangent about the purpose and meaning of the liturgy. A Lutheran among Catholic priests-to-be, I knew they had way more philosophy than me and their Latin was better than mine, but I also knew I was the only one in that room with significant study in both classical and koine Greek. So, I played the etymology card and the conversation got hot between my fellow students and me on the notion of liturgy as being "of the people," "by the people," and "for the people." It was a rare time where I had the upper hand with these incredibly intelligent men, and I took it because their argument was one that could so easily devolve into clergy arrogance. As the only son of a pastor in the room (and a humble pastor, at that), I knew the curse that it could be to employ effective ministry. Plus, I enjoyed screwing with 'em when it was clear they were in the wrong. I spanked 'em hard, secretly delighting in the whole damn affair.

Afterwards, walking out of class amid scowls and shaking heads of classmates, the nun pulled me aside. She seized my arm, looked me in the eye, and said, "Thank you, Sven. You can say things I can't."

Ho ho ho ho!! If my head wasn't big before that, it sure was for the rest of that day. I didn't tell anyone what she had said. I didn't need to. She validated me and my saying what needed to be said.

What was the takeaway from the experience? I love being me. I really enjoy being me. I haven't always, as the 8-inch blade scars up my forearms attest. But now, at middle age, it's pretty much all the time. I love the work I've put into creating the healthy body I have. I love having total control of my time, and am grateful for the years of work it took to get here. I love being able to help people with my thoughts and words. I love just being the odd duck that I am. I love that one of my best friends says he sometimes lives vicariously through me.

It ain't that I'm perfect. Furthest thing from it. But, I am the perfect me, the perfect Sven Erlandson. Since becoming fully authentic, come what may, I love my damn life. Most importantly, I love who I am even in those times when I stray away from my original self.

Do you love being you? I mean, do you really, really, really make yourself laugh with delight in being who you are? Does your life's work still excite and move you? Do your character and personality tickle you? And, if not, for God's sake why?

February 20

In the worlds of civil conversation and education,
the words, "I don't know" are the necessary precursor to all things good.
In the world of self-care,
"I don't know" is the giant X on the pirate's treasure map!
Right below it is the buried treasure chest
that will unlock all the gold you've been seeking.
Get digging!
-Sven

One of my favorite junctures to come to in a counseling session is when a client tells me something along the lines of, "I have no idea why I do/did that."

Playfully, yet seriously, I immediately shoot back, "Why'd you do it?"

"I don't know," they invariably respond, sometimes catching the subtle humor with a laugh.

"No. Take a shot at it. Now. Just take a wild guess at what might be in the ballpark of an answer, knowing you can change your mind tomorrow or next week," I push.

Sometimes, this push and "I don't know" will go back and forth several times before they realize that I'm not letting 'em off the hook. Then, they really focus, and out burps an answer. And – BOOM! – the lightbulb goes on, a powerful new insight is often birthed.

This was one of the most powerful tools I figured out in my own journaling over the decades. I just kept pushing myself to go deeper, to unveil the hidden. "I don't know's" are always packed with new revelations and wisdom. Always.

In your journaling, when you get stuck and can't think of the answer to the question, *guess* at what it might be, knowing you can always change your mind later that week, or in a month. And sometimes you will change it fully or just tweak it. That's great. It shows your brain is still working on the equation. But, start by getting into the ballpark; start by taking a swing at it. You can get into the infield and onto home plate as you whittle it down further.

But don't stop there. After you unveil the answer, attack it. Ask, now, 'Why?' Or, 'Where did that come from?' Or, 'How does that make me feel to finally see it?' Or, 'What fears are involved in this equation?' And, 'What might I have feared that caused me to keep it hidden from myself?' Or, 'What are the implications of now getting that?' In other words, keep digging. Keep pushing yourself.

So, what's the big "I don't know" in your inner life, at the moment? What are you most wrestling with? What questions about yourself or your life have you never found answers to?

February 21

Everything is a metaphor.
-Haruki Murakami, Japanese writer

There is never anything without something else.
-Brenda Hillman, America poet

- ☐ *All the world's a stage.*
- ☐ *She wears her heart on her sleeve.*
- ☐ *You gotta peel back the layers of the onion.*
- ☐ *Time is money.*
- ☐ *Don't be a couch potato.*
- ☐ *He's an open book.*

All of these are metaphors. It's basically a figure of speech where, to put it simply, one thing symbolizes something else. Two seemingly disconnected things are woven together to lend deeper insight into one of them.

But here's the thing: Pretty much everything is metaphor. Everything. Everything relates to something else, some deeper truth. My girlfriend of many years built a massively successful fashion design and manufacturing company in Manhattan. In her business, it's an unquestioned maxim that clothes tell so much about a person. Everything, even the micro, bears a deeper insight and connection to meta topics.

As you go through life becoming more aware of what's going on around you, are you seeing what's really going on with people?

What do that person's word choices indicate about what's really going on inside them? What's the message behind the message of that pregnant pause or that exhale of breath?

More importantly, as you become more aware of what's going on inside you, have you considered reverse-engineering your efforts to know yourself? That is, rather than asking yourself who you are and then plotting out your decisions and dreams from that, what if you were to look at all of your past decisions, successes and failures, behaviors and patterns, and then ask yourself (as sort of an objective observer might), what do those things tell you about the person doing them and experiencing them? What do they seem to indicate? And, are you okay with what your decisions tell the observer/you about yourself?

What is life teaching you in all you encounter? What are the deeper meanings and underlying messages? Why?

February 22

It is only by saying NO
that you can concentrate on the things that are really important to you.
-Steve Jobs, American tycoon

You can be a good person with a kind heart
and still say NO.
-Unknown

When we're children, the single scariest word in the English language is hearing the word 'no,' or some derivative of it. "No, you can't have the candy bar," in the checkout lane at the grocery store. "No, you can't have a go-kart." "No, you can't go to band camp." It's disheartening to not get what we want. In some small way, it can feel like a minimization of self, like who we are and what we want doesn't matter. It can make us feel like we're not loved. (Yet, one of the best things for a young human is to receive the simultaneous messages of "You are loved," and, "We don't always get everything we want.")

But, when we're adults, the single scariest word is not hearing the word 'no,' but *saying* the word 'no,' because we fear that it might:

- Feel unloving to the other person.
- Cause someone to dislike us or reject us.
- Shut off possibilities for the future

'No' is as much an expression of self as any 'yes' or as any behavior or action. 'No' is a statement of who I am not, what I won't allow, what I won't do, give, say, or entertain. It is a revealing of self. And that is scary, particularly if you've spent your life dialed into the lives of others, people-pleasing, or trying to win the approval (or avoid the criticism and rejection) of others.

Anyone struggling to find their 'no' and create and demand the boundaries 'no' implies, is someone who has likely forever struggled with a far deeper and scarier word. For, inside the word 'no' is the word 'I.' "No, *I* don't want to do that;" "that's not fair to *me*;" "you can't treat *me* that way." Finding and living your 'no,' demands finding and finally living your 'I.' And, that is a monumental shift in your life, if you've been raised to believe there is no room for your 'I.'

In many homes, children are not allowed to express certain feelings. In some homes it's happiness, others sadness, and in others it's anger. Inside of anger is the 'no'; inside the 'no' is the 'I.' The child was not allowed to have an 'I.' Thus, that child will spend the rest of his/her life trying to matter to someone, trying to get someone to see, want, and love their 'I.'

It's a massive shift to acknowledge your own 'I' and thereafter love yourself, rather than seeking that sense of mattering to someone else. It's huge to start loving yourself by taking the risk of saying 'no'/'I' if you've forever been trying to get love from others, because once you put your 'no' out there (or your 'I'), it means you will lose some people, especially those who are forever married to the person you used to be, the person who made it all about them. With 'I' and 'no' come blowback and loss...until they begin to yield the fruit of real relationships built upon mutual giving, respect, and love for each other's authenticity. For, believe it or not, there are people out there, many of whom you've not met yet, who only want your 'I,' your real self, and who will revel in it.

Are you still living in fear of the word 'no'? How bad does life have to get before you no longer fear blowback or losing people? When do you finally begin to honor the wonder of who you are? What will it take for you to finally find your 'I' and let it breathe in the sunshine instead of being buried? Perhaps today is the day.

February 23

Have you done everything you can to fix it?

It can be painstakingly difficult to extricate ourselves from a relationship, friendship, work situation, or family thing that we really wanted to work out but has been sour for a long time. "I don't know what to do! I don't know what to do!" is the thought that constantly wracks the brain as the situation degenerates.

Yet, after we know we have done everything we can, when we know there's nothing more we can do, the path becomes vividly clear and the longing for strength evaporates. The sense of knowing it's done makes the leaving nearly effortless. That's why holding on tighter and longer, rather than rushing to let go, is often the best path for the clarity and ease of movement it finally brings.

So, is it time to walk away? Are you done? Have you done everything you can do? If not, do you desire to still stay in it and keep trying? Do you keep stepping out then going back in? It's totally okay if you're doing this. There's no rush. But if you're doing these things, you gotta ask, "Why?" What persistent hope keeps you in it?

If you are still in it, if you're still in that state of inner wrangling and uncertainty, always responding, "I don't know what to do," when asked if you're walking away yet, then let me ask you this for your journaling: What is it you haven't done yet? What is it that you still have not said, or perhaps never said? What is the single biggest truth you're most afraid to say? What is it you still feel called to keep doing because you still don't have clarity? At least be totally honest with yourself: even if you hate doing it, what is it that you want to keep doing, at least for a little while longer? Because, if you don't have clarity in walking away, it means you still want to keep holding on, keep trying, keep hoping against hope. You're simply not done yet. There's nothing wrong with that.

But at least be honest with yourself about it.

Now, whatever you wrote as your answers to those questions, go do those things, scary as they may be. Truth is, that's the stuff that really frightens you most to do or say. That is the stuff that is keeping you from the clarity you need. But you're afraid to do it, because a part of you doesn't want to know the final truth, does it? These questions and actions are the very key to the prison you're keeping yourself in. The key is in your pocket. And until you say/do those things, you're not ready to go and you're just treading water, hoping something magically changes. It's because your prison cell is safe, isn't it? It's all you've known. You simultaneously want to be free of it and are terrified at that thought, aren't you?

What are you most afraid of – being alone, the voices and "I told you so's" that mock you in your head when you are alone, what people will say, or the thought that maybe no one will love you now, at your age, for who you really are? Or is it the simple logistics of making it on your own? (Btw, you CAN make it on your own, especially as you get stronger from living your truth.)

Is it possible that new love, or new friendships, or a new work situation, or a new family can happen? What are you feeling right now as you consider all of this? Is your heart beating faster? Stomach upset? Sweating? Agitated? Those are pretty good indicators that you want freedom but are scared. If you didn't want it, it wouldn't stir you up. It would be a big nothing burger with no physical effect. The physical/emotional response makes it clear that these thoughts and questions are stirring something very real inside you.

February 24

Relationships end for the same reason they began:
the feel. Not reasons; feel.
-Sven

Ask any person why their last relationship ended in a breakup and you will get any number of reasons, from "he was a jerk," to "the distance killed us," from "she was sooo selfish," to "his family never accepted me and just became too much," and on and on.

Similarly, ask someone why they're in their present relationship and you're likely to hear answers like "he's so kind," "she's so beautiful and smart," "he makes me laugh," "I respect her strength and the success she's built," and so forth.

But what's missing from nearly all answers to why you chose this person and why you broke up is the part that follows after the listing of reasons; because such and such things were present or absent, "I felt..." We get into a relationship because of how this person and this relationship make us feel. We get out of relationships because of how it makes us feel, or no longer makes us feel.

I have met many beautiful, kind, tough, playful women in my day that I didn't fall in love with, even though those characteristics would be at the top of the list of traits belonging to the women I did fall in love with. In other words, it's not the traits themselves; it's how I feel with this woman that draws me closer. And, it's the diminishment, or departure, of that feeling that causes me to leave (or her to leave me), even though those same reasons/traits still exist in her. It's always 'the feeeeel.'

This is why, when counseling couples or individuals considering a breakup, I encourage them to do as little reason naming as possible. Those reasons, almost invariably, create new neuroses in the other person. Now, of course, our insatiable desire to know 'why' often prevents those reasons from remaining hidden and the damage that often comes in their wake.

As an aside, some argue that getting out of a relationship where 'the feel' is gone is irresponsible, especially if a commitment was made to stay together forever, no matter what. And that is a choice only you can make. But, I'm a believer in happiness and peace in the soul. Thus, if a relationship persists in a state of pain, unhappiness, problems, and discontent for *a long period of time, such that it has now become a clear and irrevocable pattern,* that is the soul calling us to let it go and move on. Especially if one person is working on it and the other isn't, or if neither person has the will to work on it any longer. This is your intuition talking. Intuition does not only speak of what is coming, but of what is happening or needs to happen.

Are you honoring 'the feel' that beckons you in? Are you honoring 'the feel,' or lack of feel, calling you out? Why not? What's the fear? Why?

February 25

It's not what you say.
It's how you say it.
-Charlotte E. Erlandson, my mom

Dumb question: Have you ever had the experience of making a point, or telling someone something, and having them receive it very differently from how it was intended? The answer is obviously 'yes,' as that is a universal experience.

There are generally one of two reasons for this breakdown in communication: there is a miscommunication, or misunderstanding, of the actual content, either by receiver or sender; or the tone, style, or energy of the message delivery caused a disconnect for the receiver, perhaps even stirring up strong negative feelings about the message or even the sender.

How you deliver a message can be infinitely more impactful, whether favorably or adversely, than what you actually say. It can completely change your intent. This is particularly true when interacting with children. Their receptivity to energy and tone is unfiltered by age and experience. They're completely unaware of it (as are the adults communicating with them), and unaware of how to modulate it. Thus, it is incumbent upon the parents to continually engage in their own soul work to remove the strong emotions that could creep in, or unexpectedly shoot into, a situation where kindness and calm will have a far greater impact and do far less damage.

How much of how you are perceived, how you perceive yourself, and how you receive information from others is skewed because your 'how' (the way a message is delivered) outweighs your 'what' (the content of the message), and not in a way you want it to? What would it take for you to begin to better monitor your 'how you say it?' Why do you still allow this to happen?

Are you able to get past people's sometimes fumbling 'hows,' in order to experience and fully hear their 'what?' And, what is the 'how' in a sender's delivery that is most likely to cause you to turn off, tune out, reject, or dislike the 'what?' Can you go further into that answer and mine it for the 'whys' and 'wherefores,' so that you are no longer triggered by the inevitable 'hows' of human communication?

February 26

*Truly being present and listening to another
is like giving a bouquet of flowers.*
-Rev. LeRoy A. Erlandson, Dad

One of the things I've most frequently seen corrupt relationships between lovers, friends, family members, and work interactions is when one, or both, person's motor only has one speed. So many people are forever stuck in high gear in life. They are going, going, going. Forever in motion. Their brain is always in overdrive. So, they take pills or booze to calm down, stay forever busy, or sleep with the TV on because they can't bear a silent room and a loud mind.

Thus, when it comes time to have meaningful give-and-take with another person, they're often unable to sit still, or to have their brain sit still long enough to not just hear all the other person is saying, but to feel with them, to be truly present with them. There are few things more important to any relationship than the ability and willingness to be fully present to another human being.

Because the motor is forever racing, people will interrupt, finish sentences, and seek to fix (rather than hear). Maybe they only listen until they think of what they want to say next. Maybe talking over someone was normalized in their home of origin, maybe they get easily distracted. Whatever the case, the ability to be quiet and present, and not just hear but listen to another is absolutely golden. There are few greater gifts one can give another person.

Are you able to be present, able to silence your mind and your mouth? Do people feel your presence, or do they feel that you're forever distracted? Do you talk over others or interrupt? When do you begin to realize the long term negative effect it is having on your relationships? Do you have the courage to go inside and remove the pain and anxiety driving the motion?

Further, do you have the guts to insist that those closer to you slow down, let you finish, and truly listen to what you're saying? What does it say about you that you're allowing people to be close to you who do not honor your words, thoughts, and presence?

February 27

*Never have I dealt with anything more difficult
than my own soul.*
-Imam al-Ghazali, Sunni Muslim Persian polymath

*What people never understand
is that depression isn't about the outside;
it's about the inside.*
-Jasmine Warga, American author

One of the most critical elements to understand in the spiritual life – i.e. your relationship with your own spirit, or soul – is that spiritual unrest and unfulfillment nearly always manifest as depression and/or anxiety. Pretty much all unwelcome soul stuff results in some derivative of those two things. And, depression and anxiety are caused by a disconnection from one's own soul, which is the result of someone(s) ramming their expectations, wants, needs, feelings, and 'thou shalts' down your throat, or subtly sliding those things, if not outright ramming them. It starts very young. The child, eager to please and receive love, isn't even conscious that this is going on. Heck, many adults still allow it in their lives, quite unaware. Many adults fondly remember childhood with none of the forced messaging; but the messaging was there, nonetheless.

The more that gets stuck down that child's/adult-child's throat, the more it blocks out, beats down, and cuts off the native voice rising up from that young person's soul. And so, a grating begins deep inside the person, a grating between the message being forced in and the native message rising up from the bedrock. Like tectonic plates below the earth's surface, when they shift and grind on each other, it creates earthquakes on the surface and in the vicinity. Down below the surface, the suffocation of your own authentic voice by the voice(s) coming in from outside creates internal sorrow, pain, and agitation – i.e. depression and anxiety.

With time, it becomes both more difficult and more scary for that young person to express their authentic self, in no small part because doing so comes with a mighty price. The price is the further denunciation of those persons and voices that have been jammed in there, which serve as a confirmation of the deeper message the child has been receiving all along. That is, who you really are and your voice and feelings don't matter. Thus, for the individual to put their real self out there is terrifyingly risky. It counters all of the powers outside and all of the embedded messages inside.

With time, that person often begins to believe that the voices that were rammed down their throat are actually their own native voice. Thus, they believe that the criticism they most fear is their own, when those critical, condemning voices were never their own to begin with. This is where it gets really nasty. It's destruction from an outside source masking as self-destruction.

Have you been mistaking someone else's voice for your own? Whose? And what's the message? What are the messages you received, or were forced to choke down, as a kid from your parents? Even if they said nice, supportive things to you at times, were you ingesting negative, insidious, subtle, or hidden messages as well?

How does your inner life most manifest in your outer life? As depression or anxiety, or perhaps both? Which is greater?

February 28

*Is it possible that below the pains of what happened
is something worse –
the aching truth of what never will?*
-Sven

Until we've begun the process of deep healing, until our pain has gotten so damn bad and we've hit the point of needing to change and actually going into our inner crud, we run.

Running. Nonstop.

You're running, engaging in all manner of disengagement or hyper-engagement. We run using drugs, booze, busyness, incessant scrolling and swiping, over-parenting, addiction to chaos, cheating, shopping, gaming, pills, sleeping, and a million other ways. Running from the voices inside your head, the pain from your past, the messages that come rising up in that rare painful moment when you are still, undrugged, and undistracted. Worse, you're running from having to look at what you've perhaps always known (or just sensed), somewhere deep inside, to be earth-shakingly true. Seeing that would be too overwhelming, too achingly sorrowful, a fate worse than death.

So, what is your preferred means of running? Are you an addict? Do you like the ponies? Jack Daniels? Maybe your poison is something socially acceptable and seemingly highly functional, such as good ol' American over-working or over-exercising? Smoke a ton of grass? Paste your butt to the couch and binge incessantly on this Golden Age of Television they say we're in? Or maybe it's just constant movement – kid stuff, work stuff, endless hobbies and activities, driving hither and yon, dogs/cats, house crap, commotion, noise, and ever-present agitation? Maybe you absorb yourself in other people's problems? Or is it the real whopper – Whoppers, Oreos, bread, pizza, ice cream – FOOD?

How are YOU running?

But the meatier question is this: WHEN did you start running? I know you're going to say, 'I don't know,' or 'It came gradually.' And maybe both of those answers are true, but I want you to push harder. Give me an answer. Find it. When? When do you recall the balance being tipped? When did you really start running?

And, what triggered it? I mean, you didn't start running a year or five earlier. You could've started five years later, but you didn't. Why did you start running from your feelings at that particular time in life? What happened? Inside that answer is a whole lot of truth you've not wanted to face.

From what are you running? What is the one message you can't bear to hear or look at?

Can you imagine not running? What are the five biggest ways your life would be most different if you were no longer running, if the fear of whatever is chasing you were no longer there? What's the single biggest thing keeping you from stopping the running? What is the grand fear? Fear of being overwhelmed and dying? Fear of loss of control? Fear of that one voice, that one message that burrowed into your head decades ago, now being unleashed and attacking you from within? What's the voice? What's the message? Who taught it to you?

February 29

Side by side with the human race there runs another race of beings, the inhuman ones, the race of artists who, goaded by unknown impulses, take the lifeless mass of humanity and by the fever and ferment with which they imbue it turn this soggy dough into bread and the bread into wine and the wine into song.

Out of the dead compost and the inert slag they breed a song that contaminates. I see this other race of individuals ransacking the universe, turning everything upside down, their feet always moving in blood and tears, their hands always empty, always clutching and grasping for the beyond, for the god out of reach, slaying everything within reach in order to quiet the monster that gnaws at their vitals.

I see that when they tear their hair with the effort to comprehend, to seize this forever unattainable, I see that when they bellow like crazed beasts and rip and gore, I see that this is right, that there is no other path to pursue. A man who belongs to this race must stand up on the high place with gibberish in his mouth and rip out his entrails. It is right and just, because he must! And anything that falls short of this frightening spectacle, anything less shuddering, less terrifying, less mad, less intoxicated, less contaminating, is not art. The rest is counterfeit. The rest is human. The rest belongs to life and lifelessness.

-Henry Miller, American novelist, Tropic of Cancer

This is not a quote that someone normally puts in a daily meditation book. But, this is Badass Wisdom. My goal is to get you to live fiercely, intensely expressing your realest self, which I do not believe to be the domain solely of the artists. I truly believe that in every person is some calling that stokes an inconceivable force that must be unleashed, expressed, harnessed, or (at least) ridden.

What mad pursuit exists in your soul, yearning for expression, never dying even when it's not being expressed? What is the calling of your truest, most badass self?

March

March 1

Courage is the power to let go of the familiar.
-Raymond Lindquist, 20th Century clergyman

Camels are known for traveling long distances across deserts with little water or food, because they store fat in their hump that they use for nourishment.

A Relationship Camel can go a long time on a little bit of love – an extreme giver, who asks almost nothing in return. A Relationship Camel is someone in a relationship who says, "I'll do this for you and that, too. I'll take care of that. Let me get that for you. I'll do everything for you. Just give me a little bit of love in return, because that's all I need to go a long time." This person is beyond simply being a people-pleaser. The Camel gives everything, too terrified to insist on anything in return.

The Relationship Camel is afraid that if they make their wants and needs known, if they have any at all, they won't receive love; they'll be rejected; they'll be abandoned. The Relationship Camel was taught in childhood not to believe in themself, that they weren't lovable or were no good, or that they just didn't matter. So, in adulthood, they naturally and unwittingly choose people who are familiar, who reflect those same beliefs and are happy to take and take.

This ain't healthy. It leads to bitterness, unfulfilling relationships, and misery. It leads to holding onto relationships and people that hurt, take advantage, put us down or steal respect, time, money, and love. Often only extreme pain and loss lead the Relationship Camel to change into finally honoring their own needs/wants.

In which relationships in your life are you investing way more than you're getting? More importantly, are you beginning to understand the correlation between your core beliefs and the shape of the world around you, the world you've created?

Which relationships have you been sucked back into by shiny baubles and grand promises? How long did it take for these 'changes' to peter out? What do you think caused them to do so?

From whom did you learn how to be a Relationship Camel – the person who taught you to focus only on making a taker happy? Who taught you to walk on eggshells – the taker you likely still fear critique from and long for praise from?

How bad does the pain have to get before you're finally ready to let go, become unwound from the emotions of others, and finally live not just freer but lighter? When do you finally realize the futility of giving so much and getting so little in return? When do you finally do the work inside you and in your past, so that you no longer fear them leaving and fear them not liking you? You can do it!

March 2

Never regret anything that makes you smile.
-Audrey Hepburn, American actor

One of the biggest regrets of my life would probably be a seemingly small thing to an outsider. My first wife and I married when I was 23. Her father graciously offered us "either a small wedding and big honeymoon or a big wedding and small honeymoon." We went with the former, which meant a trip to Europe. However, the price of that was only being able to invite my immediate family and one friend (and spouse) to my wedding and reception. Problem was, I had two best friends growing up – Huge and Jon. In a rather impossible choice, I picked Huge, not Jon. I really don't even know why.

I saw Jon years later at a card game for the guys from the old neighborhood. Jon was both happy to see me and utterly dismissive of any notion of being offended by not being invited to my wedding, despite my immense remorse over it. He wouldn't have it. He loved me and thought nothing of the non-invite. Yet, my distaste for the situation and decision took a couple of decades to pass.

So, do I regret taking the small wedding? No, I regret not inviting my second best friend, anyway. My wife's father had enough money to afford a house on Chrissy Field in San Francisco, office space in Union Square, and a Maybach in the garage. He could afford it. As fate would have it, he ended up screwing his one faithful daughter (my ex) in his death, leaving her nothing, even though he was worth nine figures. Goes to character. But yeah, I regret not having more courage despite knowing that I was just a snot-nosed 23 year-old and he was an intimidating guy.

What do you regret? Whom have you hurt that you wish you hadn't? Or, whom do you feel you wronged, even if they don't see it that way, as with my dear old boy, Jon? Are you bolder now?

Have you changed? What triggered the change? Was it some form of pain?

List your regrets. All of 'em. Bullet points on a paper. Next to them, list the feelings, besides regret, that it most makes you feel. Next to that, list what it is you feel you most missed out on by doing/not doing the thing you regret. Can you forgive yourself and trust that your life has still worked out precisely as it needed to? How many of your regrets are because of ego reasons? What ego need would've been satisfied with each of those things, had you done them differently? And, is that ego need a piece of your highest self or not so much?

March 3

Whenever you have to make a decision, flip a coin;
not because it decides for you,
but for that moment it's in the air,
you realize what you're hoping for.
Always go with that choice, no matter what the coin says.
For that is your heart's true desire.
-Unknown

One of the fundamental differences between a high energy life of exuberance, power, inner calm, fulfillment, and clarity vs. a life of drag, heaviness, uncertainty, inner unrest, and the inability to sustain effort, is the difference between internal vs. external power sources.

See, the people who are most anxiety-ridden, depressed, and unclear are those who have spent their lives answering to external power sources. Usually, that external power source starts as mom and/or dad, or whoever raised the child, then morphs into whoever gets passed the baton, often a boyfriend/girlfriend/spouse. Yes, other influences become external power sources when growing up and in adulthood – friends, teachers, bosses – but rarely do any rival in power or influence the enormity of those initial external power sources, mom and/or dad.

That external power source gets internalized very often at a young age. Thus, often a parent no longer has to say a word, or that parent could die, and the child would still know quite clearly and live by those messages, expectations, and fears instilled by the silent parent. That's how powerful external power sources can be. And, until you clean house and rid yourself of those voices inside, they are what is driving your life. It is not enough to try to ram your own voice up and through those voices inside. No, the non-native voices inside must be put to death or excised. Otherwise, you'll forever be fighting those now-internalized voices, forever wasting energy on keeping them subdued inside. Those messages inside must be slayed. Only then can one's own soul voice rise up, unimpeded.

True energy, pure energy, comes from the voice of one's own soul. The lethargy you presently feel in your life is because you have conflicting voices inside, theirs and yours; the former blocking the latter, infusing the latter with doubt, heaviness, and murk. The deadness, indecision, and self-doubt you feel every day, are from living a life that you chose in reaction to those external power sources, not as a result of your own soul speaking.

So... Whose voices still infect your chest, your racing brain, and your soul? Apart from how you interact with those people in real life, whose voices inside you need to be put to death? Can you name the external power sources? What are their messages? Is it possible that those messages were never true, despite the fervor with which you have believed them and with which they have been sold to you? And if they are not true, then what is true? Is it possible you're actually good, wonderful, worthy of love, wanted, and the real you is glorious, lucid, powerful, and truly matters?

P.S. I realize that the quote at the top has nothing to do with the meditation and question. It was just a damn genius quote. If you can be aware, in the moment of the tumbling coin, which you're hoping it turns out to be, you've just answered your own query. Brilliant!

March 4

Grit is not about never quitting.
That's perseverance.
Grit is about the willingness, even hunger,
to do the ugly,
and do it for one reason only:
because the work's gotta get done.
That's grit.
-Sven

To what degree do you have the grit factor? In what areas of life are you willing, even eager, to do the dirty work that no one else wants to do or touch? Are you that way in your relationships, too?

I think of it sort of as the willingness to clean the bathrooms and toilets, when it comes to housecleaning time. But, far more importantly, getting gritty can apply to resolving conflict and your willingness to get granular in talking stuff out AND OWNING.....FULLY OWNING...THE STUFF YOU'VE DONE WRONG, THE PAIN YOU'VE CAUSED, AND THE TIMES YOU'RE JUST PLAIN WRONG!

Truth is, grit is never more important than in human interactions, conflict resolution, and apologies.

Quick question: if you were being fully honest, are your apologies packed with defenses, denials, deflections, and ramming the other person's wrongness down their throat, or making them feel like their crimes were far worse than yours? In other words, are you a relationship infant who cannot own the stuff they've done, who fears the grit because it implicates you? Do you run over your partner and make them feel small so that you can feel big and important?

Part of being a responsible human being is owning not just your successes, but your failures, especially your times of failing others, hurting them, taking advantage of their goodness, or just using your power to not have to fully account for what you've done. That is a person of true responsibility, not just someone posing as an adult.

Do you have life to give? Do you have the strength to walk with grit? What do you fear in doing so? Can you release that fear by allowing it up and out? Can you become a more socially responsible person in this gritty way?

March 5

Compassion is to look beyond your own pain,
to see the pain of others.
-Yasmin Mogahed, American educator

One of the most compassionate, genuinely kind men I've ever known in my life was a man named Grif who had his PhD from Harvard, a fondness for sushi and swimming laps at the community pool, and the largest classical music album collection I've seen outside of a music library, including a fondness for Mahler and Debussy.

Grif and I were both writers and roommates in a tiny, one-bedroom apartment in a bit of a sketchy Los Angeles neighborhood, him occupying the bedroom and me the living room.

What struck me as most interesting was that Grif could understand people's pain. He could think about a situation, even if it were one he had never had–such as losing your kids in a divorce–and then completely understand and genuinely sympathize. It was such a startling generosity of spirit that came from a place of intellectual understanding, as well as his own pain in other areas of life.

Similarly, a good friend of mine who has been going through massive family trauma the last few years, remarked, "I have always been able to identify and be compassionate toward people. But since this most recent death and the psychosis diagnosis of my son, and the excruciating pain I've been in, I just feel other people's pain and get it sooo much more powerfully. My compassion is completely different from anything it ever was before."

One of the most beautiful aspects of pain, whether experienced or intellectually understood, is that it has the power to open a door for us, the door to truly seeing and intimately understanding the pain of others. Pain can breed compassion, or it can breed a shutdown to one's own feelings and the pain of others. The former is the way of life, new connection to humanity, and compassion. The latter is a slow, bitter death.

Has your pain shut you down or opened you up? Are you bitter and dying, or grieving but healing and opening? Have you become more compassionate to the pain of others as you've aged? What broke you open? What was it about your own pain that changed you and expanded you? What type of pain do you feel more clearly and strongly now?

March 6

If it ain't fun, why do it?
-Sven

I've had seven books published and written several more beyond that. It takes a significant amount of focus, not to mention work, spread over months or even years to complete a book that punches people in the face.

Yet, what's strange in my experience is that, unlike many other writers, I've never experienced writer's block. Hell, I don't even believe in it, at least not for me. That's not to say that I haven't sat in front of a blank page and had nothing to say. So, I don't force it or try to conjure something. I just go do the next thing life is calling me to.

Thus, I've never seen that as blockage, or some negative thing. To me, it's just part of flow. Some days I have something to say; some days I don't, and thus, I let it go for that day or week. Blockage implies that something is supposed to be flowing today and it's not. Whereas, I see my creativity as subject to the callings and vicissitudes of my own soul. There are simply times for words from the soul and times for silence. And I don't force it. Quite frankly, I don't even care. If the project comes, it comes; if it doesn't, it doesn't.

It's frustrating, at times, because I want to control the process, control the output, control the results. But, I do my releasing work and fall back into the hands of the gods, or my own soul, and let go of needing to control anything.

As a result, when I am writing, it's highly motivated and driven because it's inspired. It's powerful, forceful, but not forced. I believe in hard work, and I do so when I'm inspired. Work is the engine; inspiration/fun is the GPS and the gasoline.

By my late 30s, my workouts had become the same as writing. As a former competitive lifter, I was highly disciplined and knew how to drag myself through workouts, even when I had zero frickin' desire to be anywhere near a gym. But, in my 30s, I stopped forcing life, workouts, career, writing, dating, and everything else. Now, at 56, my body is in better shape for far less work than it has ever been.

Motivation comes when it comes. Whether writing, working out, or what have you, the ability to let go of control, to be able to do without, to not force life, all happens inside me. Mastery of the outside happens inside. Mastery of joy and peace comes, oddly, from letting go of the need to control the outcomes. The motivation comes from enjoying the work itself, apart from the outcomes. Thus, in every endeavor I am simultaneously holding on to what I want, while letting go of ever having it or having it in the way I've envisioned it, all while enjoying the journey.

What are you controlling and, hence, forcing? What do you soooo not want to let go of? How are you choking life by attempting to control results? How are you holding on but simultaneously letting go? What do you fear happening if you do not hold on tighter, work harder, and force outcomes? Is it possible you're wrong?

March 7

The finish line is for the ego.
The journey is for the soul.
-Unknown

Do you have a dream of what you would most love to accomplish in life? Massive success? Lots of money? Big title? Fame? Big house(s)? What drives you? And what is the intensity level of that drive?

Are you convinced that once you accomplish that dream, then – THEN! – you can be finally, truly happy? Is it possible that the enormity of the dream and the intensity with which you pursue it are themselves an indicator of something else? Is it possible that the size of the dream perfectly matches the size of the hole inside you which it is supposed to fill?

How great is your lack of self-worth? How big is your self-loathing? How persistent is your longing to finally be loved by him, her, or them? Is it possible that your grand dream is desired to finally wipe away all the bad inside and acquire all the good from others, and therefore finally feel good inside?

Let me say it again, the mere fact that you need something so huge in order to finally feel fully *ALIVE* may well indicate how dead you really are inside; or else, why would you need such a colossus in order to finally feel that way? There is some dragon inside you that you believe will only be slain with the largest of swords swung in the largest of strokes.

I am all for big dreams. I have had and do still have them. I have spent my life in pursuit of them and slowly making them come to fruition. However, I have simultaneously dissected them many times to discern why exactly I'm pursuing that particular dream. Many times, in doing so, I have rerouted my course or deconstructed that dream only to construct a completely new one.

Because, as I looked at it much more deeply I realized I was pursuing that dream to satisfy some vindication, to achieve someone's attention and approval, or to feel big (or bigger). At times, my dreams were driven by "I'll show you;" sometimes by "Screw you;" and sometimes "Then you'll like me." In realizing that, I was able to let go of that dream, because I saw that I was essentially needing that accomplishment in order to get something from someone, thereby supposedly gaining my own happiness. But, that was giving someone else enormous power over my life. Further, it was putting my happiness out there in the future, contingent upon some turn of events that was not guaranteed.

What if I were to make today, tomorrow, and the next day, happy? What if I were to not wait? What if I were to make today about doing that which I love, or choose work and a life that are, in and of themselves, enjoyable? And/or, what if the giant desire for that massive acquisition sat inside a life where there was great joy already? Then the longing for that acquisition could still be present but not degenerate to the level of an absolute *sine qua non* for happiness and *ALIVENESS*. It's such a cliché but *ALIVENESS*, happiness, and peace are built in the mundane, the everyday, the small, bit by bit, until over time a life of happiness is created. That is not the same as a rejection of still swinging for the fence, so to speak. It is, instead, a falling in love with the small, while simultaneously working toward the large pursuits that move the soul.

What are the real reasons you want what you want and strive for that which drives you? Are you okay with those reasons? Or, are you still wanting something from someone else in order to finally be happy? Have you deconstructed your dreams to know precisely why you're doing what you're doing?

March 8

Every time you don't follow your inner guidance,
you feel a loss of energy, loss of power, a sense of spiritual sadness.
-Shakti Gawain, American author

How good are you at reading your own energy?

Our intuition, our soul, speaks to us not through our head but through our own energy. What is it that energizes you or brings you peace and relaxation? Are you following those things? For, those are the longing of the soul. Those are intuition speaking.

On the other hand, anxiety, force, pushing, agitation, and unrest are wants (ego drives) negatively controlling and infecting your life. Acting from anxiety produces anxiety, despite the hope that doing so will bring peace and happiness.

To live a life of intuition is to first and forever remove fear, then live from a place of feelings and energy. Your most authentic self speaks through intuition, producing either calm or exuberance.

When will you have the courage to live from a state of trust in feelings and energy, and let go of the fear-driven need to control life and force outcomes? What do you fear losing and fear letting go of? Are you ready to, more and more, trust intuition, energy, and feel?

March 9

When faced with a decision, choose the path that feeds your soul.
-Dorothy Mendoza-Row, American artist and blogger

By the time my mother was 51, she had six kids over 10 years old, including one in the Air Force, two in college, two in high school, and me, a rather difficult child still under her roof. She had done the work of a bachelor's and master's degree, counseled many people, and been a suicide prevention/intervention specialist.

This was a woman born in 1928, who was the highest-paid of her classmates coming out of teaching college, who taught in and ran the education programs of several churches in Minnesota, North Dakota, and Texas, and who had done all of that by her 50s. Over the next 20 years, she would publish numerous peer-reviewed articles in multiple journals and magazines in the field of early childhood education; serve as an adjunct graduate-level faculty member in the same field; counsel leaders and clergy; and serve on the highest-level transition team of the merger of two of the largest religious denominations in the United States, at the time.

At the age of 90, she fervently stated to her daughter-in-law that she was excited to be reading a new book on goal-setting and that she wanted to start a podcast and compile her writings into a book. This deep, quiet soul who had grown up on a farm with no running water or electricity behind a horse-drawn plow, who, as a girl, worked as hard as any man (to the point where her father had to downsize the farm after she left home at 16 to go to college), and by her 80s was carrying a cell phone, but still writing longhand, was nowhere near finished with her life's work.

And do you know what I remember most from childhood mom memories?

Mornings. Mom loved mornings, early mornings. As a boy, before sunrise, I would come downstairs for a hot breakfast only to find mom outside, on her knees, alone in the quiet, weeding her giant flower and produce gardens. "I taught you to cook well, Sven. Go do what you know," she'd say. Her gardening was sacred time, the only peace she got all day. There, she communed with her maker, loving nothing more than her hands in the soil, although she also often said that she enjoyed doing dishes with her hands in the warm water. In brutal Minnesota winters, her early mornings found her under soft light amid her sea of plants in her office or living room, reading and writing/journaling, surrounded by stillness. Writing was her way to flush out everything inside her, she'd say.

Mom's mornings fed her soul, as did the soil, pretty flowers, colorful vegetables, fresh raspberries, warm water, silence, and always a new deep question to wrestle with.

What feeds your soul? Are you doing it? Has it occurred to you that the reason you're feeling so depleted is because you're not simultaneously feeding your soul and flushing your soul of all that encumbers you inside. Do the damn work. Feed and flush the soul. What are you feeling today and why? Start your flushing there.

March 10

> ### *It's not hard to make decisions*
> ### *when you know what your values are.*
> -Roy Disney, Co-founder, The Walt Disney Company

One of the more difficult issues I see young people struggle with is giving themselves permission to not be like their parents or not be who their parents want them to be. They keep letting the years roll by, fearful of embarking on their own authentic paths because they keep waiting for the parent to grant them permission to be who they want to be, continuing to check the boxes their parents want them to. Still needing/wanting the parent's support and/or fearful of the parent's wrath, disapproval, or disappointment, this unwillingness to live authentically can even persist into one's 40s or 60s, the adult still waiting for permission from a parent, one who may even be dead. Worse, often the adult-child is not even aware that they are innately different from the parent, let alone allowed to be.

Thus, one of the rather jolting questions I ask of adult children is:

Is it possible that your parents' values
are different from your values?

What seems like a ludicrously obvious question and answer can have the effect of punching someone square in the nose, complete with blurred vision and disorientation. Confronted with this question, the rather obvious answer (because of course no two people have identical values and every child is different from every parent in many ways), enables them to see how silly it is that they continue to be trapped in inauthenticity and waiting for permission to live, particularly when followed with the question: Are you okay with the fact that you're continuing to live their values rather than your own? Oh, and one more: What does it say about your parents' love for you, and your parents as people, that they only approve of you, or support you, when you are living with their values?

Here's a little exercise: On a piece of paper draw a vertical line from top to bottom, halfway across the page. Now, atop the left column, write the words 'Parent Values' and in the left column make a bullet point list of all of your parents' values that you know of or perhaps are expected to live by. All of them. Next, above the right column write 'My Values.' In the right column, directly across from each of your parents' values, write either 'yes' or 'no' for whether you share this particular value or not. Then, most tellingly, if the answer is 'yes' to a particular value, write in parentheses next to the 'yes' the percentage that you hold this value. In other words, do you 100% subscribe to this value, or is it 67% or a mere 13%? What is that percentage?

By doing this exercise you begin to get a clearer definition of who you are, not to mention who you're not, or not fully: mom and dad. The more you are honest with yourself in your answers, despite the potential price or fallout, the more you will begin to see your own uniqueness. Very often, the mere awareness of the differences, on paper (rather than just nebulously tumbling around in your head), has a certain liberating power to it. It can be a real 'WOW!' moment. And, when followed by the other two questions, above, the sense of compulsion to be that someone you're not – i.e. to live their values – greatly diminishes and is often followed by a new sense of courage.

March 11

What would you do
if you knew you couldn't fail?

A great many motivational speakers and writers have volleyed that question to struggling or ambitious folks for a long time. It's a great question with enormous power to unlock potentialities, dreams, and new ideas. I recommend you write that at the top of a page, then just brainstorm – PLAY with it – ideas, thoughts, and possibilities. No matter how cockamamie an idea may seem, include it on the list. Don't edit!

I very much believe in that question as a helpful one. However, I ask a very different question when I'm speaking or counseling:

What would you do
even if you knew
there was a high likelihood you would fail?

This is a very powerful one. See, in the first question there is a strong possibility that you are considering that path for ego reasons, for fame/adulation, or perhaps for the long-sought approval of a parent or mentor. It is the desire to feel a sense of worth. In other words, that path is considered and perhaps engaged in to fill a hole inside, to provide something that's lacking; or, perhaps to provide immunity from a lifetime of disapproval and criticism. The latter question, however, while still possibly engaged in for ego needs, is much more driven by the sheer love of the work itself, not pain, fear, or emptiness. There's a slim chance one would traverse a path of likely failure if there weren't joy or immense fulfillment in the path itself, regardless of the destination.

Write that second question at the top of a page and kick around ideas and possibilities of work you love so much (or might love), that you'd endeavor them, even if the possibility of crashing and burning is high and the possibility of success is slim.

What are you feeling as you consider these two questions and the answers you've found? Do you need a destination so much that you'd sacrifice years of joy and fulfillment to achieve it? What then?

This leads to one final question:

Considering that first question at the top,
if you were to reach the mountaintop,
whatever you would do NEXT
is likely what you most want to do with your life.
If you want to continue that same work, then it is likely your life's passion.

If the zenith experience would yield a turn in a new direction, and you can name that direction,
then that new direction is your deeper life passion.

So, what would you do next, after making the millions, receiving the Grammy Awards, buying the mansion, or what have you? What's your next dream? Is it possible that's what your real passion is?

March 12

Turning and turning in the widening gyre,
the falcon cannot hear the falconer.
-W.B.Yeats, Irish poet, The Second Coming

With every new circle through the calendar we are pulled by the gravitational forces of other bodies and entities away from the falconer that is the original self – your own authentic voice. Falcon and falconer are one, but they lose the signal and intimate connection over time.

Unless they don't.

Do you lose – indeed, have you lost – intimacy with the falconer that is your soul? Have you been so pulled with each yearly gyre away from self, pulled out of your own orbits and orientations?

Who is the planet whose gravitational pull is so strong in your life that it pulls you from your center? Can you name it, yet? Or do you still struggle with awareness of what and who the problem really is? Are you done with living their definition of your life yet, whoever they are? Do you have the courage to no longer be pulled from rotation around your own original self? Do you have the courage to reject the pull of those formerly greater bodies? Are you ready?

Who are the other planets in your orbit that want and encourage you only to be your truest self, who desire only for you to find your own orbit, rather than heed their wants? Do you see the value in having people like this around you, encouraging you?

March 13

Not all storms come to disrupt your life. Some come to clear your path.
-Paulo Coelho, Brazilian lyricist and novelist

How do you exit relationships? Or, how is someone exiting one with you?

One of the tactics that has become far too common when it comes to leaving intimate relationships is, what I call, slow-walking. It happens when one person knows, or mostly knows, they're wanting to leave a relationship but they lack the courage to look the other person in the face and simply end it cleanly. Instead, they start to pull away slowly, ask for a partial break, or some derivative.

And so, the other person holds on, hoping – ever hoping. They cling, because they're uncertain of where they stand. They follow along like a little puppy, believing it's going to come back to life, even though the person issuing the pull-away mandate, deep-down, has no interest in returning.

If the door is not closed fully, if there is a "maybe in the future" left on the table or an "I'm not sure," then the other person will keep holding on, even if that was never the real intent of the one saying those words. It creates the illusion of hope where there really is none. That hope wastes time in the other's life and protracts their grieving, or keeps it from ever starting. It's a using of them and minimizing their feelings, so as to protect you from your fear of looking like the bad guy.

This is often the reason behind the "Let's be friends" notion that comes at the end of some relationships. While I am definitely in favor of friendships, I've seldom seen a breakup where the immediate shift into a friendship is possible, unless it had already been there without the in-love aspect for years. Normally, it takes a cooling-off period, a transition time of a year or two before that is possible. Thus, the "Let's be friends" thing is often the suggestion of the one doing the breaking up, so that they don't have to put a hard stop to the relationship. But, because a relationship seldom makes that hard shift quickly, this tack invariably leads to pain shortly down the road, as it leaves the other person longing, hoping, hanging on and hoping for a reunion, when that was never on the table; and the one leaving feeling frustrated.

Or, there are times when the one being broken up with suggests friendship. Invariably, this is a ploy to stay close and keep selling, so to speak, hoping to convince the one departing to stay or take them back. In either case, immediate friendship usually ends with acrimony, because the one doing the breaking up finally has to be tough and say it's over, precisely as they should have done months prior.

Fear of what the other person will say or think – fear of being the bad guy – is too often an excuse for acting irresponsibly toward others, particularly in breakups.

Do you break up in a respectful way? Are you giving your soon-to-be ex the benefit of a clean death for the relationship, even if it's hard for you to do so? Or, are you taking the easy way out, still protecting your feelings over theirs, still feeding your fears, rather than honoring their sadness and loss?

March 14

*It doesn't matter if thousands of people believe in you,
unless you believe in you.*
-Maddie Malhotra, American photojournalist

Plenty of generations, leaders, motivational speakers, clergypersons, and parents have espoused 'positive mental attitude,' throughout their lifetimes. And, for many, that can be a wonderful way to approach life, enabling them to support, compliment, encourage, and comfort others with kind, uplifting words.

However, the great problem for a whole lot of people is not that they lack the ability to find and focus on the good in others, but in themselves. There has been such a deluge of conditioning to the opposite that they forever see themselves as inadequate, terribly flawed, unlovable, and unimportant. This early life conditioning is so foreign to others that it can be difficult to fully understand and easy to judge. This inner belief that one doesn't matter is excruciatingly corrosive to relationships, careers, and any notions of peace. Many, if not most, who carry this infection from their past spend decades resorting to ill-fated attempts to power through and/or disprove it, unaware of the root of the problem dragging them down. They are forever fighting themselves, one foot on the accelerator, one foot on the break. The power of their core beliefs pulls them down from the inside.

The solution is to go into the pain, fears, and BS beliefs they've been taught about themselves, which they cannot see they have been running from their whole lives.

What is the pain you continue to avoid? What is the part of you that you most loathe? Do you have the courage to finally sit in it and allow it to wash over and pass out of you, again and again, until it is gone? Do you have the courage to change the language about that aspect (and others) of yourself?

What is the single most difficult, positive thing you could possibly say about yourself to yourself, even though every last word of it might feel embarrassingly untrue as you say it? What is the one affirmation you could almost never believe? Why? Has it occurred to you that the one affirmation that would make you most uncomfortable is pointing the biggest arrow at your largest insecurity and the associated negative childhood conditioning? What external power source implanted that belief into you? I challenge you to make that very affirmation the one at the top of your list, the one you tell yourself most repeatedly.

March 15

What's the difference between coaching female athletes and male athletes?

This was the question a dear friend of mine, himself an NCAA women's soccer coach who had previously coached both women's and men's collegiate soccer programs, was attempting to answer in his PhD work in Sports Psychology at one of the top 10 largest universities in the United States.

Over five years of deep research into all material on even remotely related subjects, in addition to interviewing every NCAA coach in charge of both a women's and a men's team, his research was approved, earning him his PhD. His conclusion, while definitely not an absolute, is quite fascinating to consider. And while he was not the first to assert it, he was the first to give it complex and thorough research. What was it?

Female athletes need to feel accepted before they perform. Male athletes need to perform before they feel accepted.
-Mike Navarre, PhD

It's interesting, isn't it? When I've deployed that thought, not just to teams and coaches I've worked with over the years, but to male-female couples in their relationships and parents in the rearing of their children, it has often yielded new insights and directions.

While it's no grand piece of fresh knowledge to say this, **what motivates me may not, in fact, motivate you.** What motivates you in the bedroom may not be compelling to your spouse. What one group of employees needs to be productive may have the opposite effect on another.

So, do you need to be more deliberate about building a sense of team, community, and family as you lead? Or, is the task in front of you to bring praise to solid performance? Perhaps you are giving praise too freely to your sons, when it has not been earned, causing you to actually lose credibility in the mind of the very person you're attempting to motivate. Perhaps your toughness, or harshness, is undermining the sense of family you're needing to create for success.

What was missing in your home growing up? Praise? Sense of warmth, connection, and love? The opportunity to prove yourself? The freedom to perform without criticism?

What stirs you to action?

March 16

If the path is bad, an obstruction is good.
-Neil Forsythe, Literary critic

I've grown to absolutely believe that when it comes to life, the real trick to living in flow is to allow for the possibility that closed doors are greater blessings than open ones. The universe is always talking. Your soul is providing little signs indicating not just what to go after, but showing you what to let go of. But, we get so caught up in brute forcing our way through life, breaking down every door (or trying to), and forcing our will on life, rather than allowing ourselves to flow with the universe.

What if the universe is in intimate communication with your soul and its longings? What if the closed door is simply a different version of a directional arrow? Or, at the very least, what if incessant closed doors are a repeated, unrelenting neon sign proclaiming "DETOUR"?

Similarly, what if the pain you continually run from actually holds gems of wisdom intended for your reaching new heights? In other words, what if what you see as bad in your life is actually veiling great good, but you have to peer behind the scary veil? Is it possible that curses are, in fact, blessings?

The path to discovering who you are
requires discovering who you are not.
-Sven

All of the negatives and pain sources in your life hold new insights for growth, but also indicate for you that which is not in your future. We have to go down paths and explore different purposes to discover those which don't feel right anymore, and why that is so.

1. List the top five things, events, situations, or people that you have considered the biggest curses of your life that would be almost impossible to find good in.

2. Now, under each one, write the questions: How was/is this event or person the single greatest blessing of my life? What was this thing sent to teach me about myself? About life? In what way is this learning I received precisely what I need for life moving forward?

3. What have been your 5 biggest disappointments or frustrations in life?

4. How was each one perfect? What would you have likely missed out on if you had gotten what you wanted?

5. Even if you never say it aloud or forgive the person who did it, what if the most wretched, horrible thing of your life was sent for your benefit – a gift from the universe? What if you simply can't see and don't want to admit the gems of wisdom it holds in its hand?

March 17

We are [each] the center of the universe;
we are [each] nothing, at all.
-Rabbi Nina Beth Cardin, American Rabbi

If you were to assign a percentage to it, what percentage of time in your life do you put yourself at the center of the universe and what percentage do you see yourself as nothing, or as very small?

I am of the belief that the fear that causes each of us to continually put ourselves at the center of the universe is the deep, underlying belief that if we are not at the center then we are nothing.

And, what often keeps us believing we are nothing, is the fear of sticking our necks out and subsequently having others say we are nothing; and/or the fear of being the center of the universe is the fear of being something and having all the attention, negative and positive, that can go with it.

How much of your life is driven by the fear of being nothing or being told you are nothing? Do you have the courage to be you, anyway, and expand your soul to its fullest potential?

March 18

Du vet.
-Walborg Erlandson, My grandma

My dad was about 25 in the early 1950s. He had gone back up to the large family farm in Hallock, in the northwest corner of Minnesota. Sitting at the kitchen table while his mother prepared the meal, he asked her a question that had been on his heart for some time: "Mom, how do you know when the girl is the one?"

Grandma put down her paring knife, turned to him, wiped her hands on her apron, and, looking him squarely in the eye, firmly stated the words he reminded me of nearly six decades later, months from his own passing: "Du vet." Her Swedish had kicked in. Dad knew it was serious. She then turned around and returned to her work.

Dad married the girl he had been thinking about a short time later. They spent the next 65+ years together. Grandma was right.

Translation? **"You'll know."**

1. If you were to be totally honest with yourself right now in your journaling, write out the honest answer to this question: What do you truly know? Not what are you willing to admit, but what is your truth? Can you feel it, yet? Let me put it this way: What is the truth that has been there, perhaps all along, that you have been avoiding, constantly second-guessing, or simply not seeing, hiding in plain sight?

2. What is the great unanswered question of your life or your future? What is it that you do not have an answer to?

3. Is it possible that you know exactly what your truth is already? Is it possible that you already know the answer to what you claim is the great unanswered question of your life? Is it possible that your problem is not that you don't know what your truth is, but that you do and you're terrified to admit it, because that would mean acting on it?

4. Living a truth or a new dream demands being judicious in whom you reveal it to, much as a tiny shoot coming out of the ground needs to be protected from too much sun or rain, or not enough of both, and the constant threat of rabbits or a human shoe. In what ways do you need to be judicious in what you share about what you're being, saying, doing, having, wanting, believing, and becoming? Who might do your dream/shoot harm?

5. What's going on inside you as you consider what you really know about your life and path? What do you feel as you consider those who might undermine your new paths and purposes?

March 19

*Energy cannot be created or destroyed;
it only changes form.*
-Law of Conservation of Energy (physics)

The grandaddy, immutable truth of them all, the one we are all simultaneously running from and being sucked further into, is that, with the lone exception of the Turritopsis dohrnii (the only immortal species known to humanity), all things die. Life feeds on life. Old forms, relationships, lives, paths, and purposes die and morph into something new. The tulip in spring is fodder for the rabbit, which is caught and eaten by the fox or coyote, which gives way to the wolf, bobcat, or maggots when it falls, each of which, in their turn, replenishes the soil on which it falls. And soil gives birth to tulips and shoots of all manner.

So too, the child grows to become a young woman, shedding many of her child ways, engaging in relationships that, over time, change from immature, selfish, or fear-driven ones to riper, deeper, more complex ones, which themselves give birth to the period of life where she has, perhaps, outlived suitors and her relationships are with memories, friends, children, or the deep relationship with the living silence that is the grand comforter, or terrifier, of all.

But, because we fear letting go of the old (read 'secure') and fear what's ahead, we hesitate at the headwaters of that which is to come. We have not yet fully embraced life's pleasures and pains. All of it is life. None of it bad, just a new experience. We keep trying to swim back upstream, having not yet mastered lifting our oars, living with an open hand, embracing all that life opens up to.

We must grieve the loss of the familiar and safe 'til the pain has been flushed, even as we flow forward, bumping up against a rock or two along the way. To live in this world is to forever be grieving that which was, while night-before-Christmas excited about that which is to come. We are forever living in the dance between grieving and opening.

What is life calling you, in this moment, to let go of and open up to? What do you most fear letting go? And in the opening? What is dying? What is being born?

What area of your life are you most inclined to fight to go back upstream? Why? What do you most fear losing, or never having, such that you conjure such monumental effort? In what area do you find it easiest to let go of old forms and open to new?

March 20

> *Pick a theme and work it to exhaustion...*
> *the subject must be something you truly love or truly hate.*
> -Dorothea Lange,
> American photographer best known for her iconic Depression-era photos

Dating well back to the days of the great sea captain and warrior, Lord Nelson, the Royal British Navy has woven into every center of every rope, from the thickest to the thinnest, a scarlet thread. This red thread was a simple way to identify whether a ship had been unlawfully stolen from the Crown. Call it a through line, that which runs through everything, identifying the owner.

What is the red thread of your life? What is it in all you say, do, become, possess, are, let go of, undertake, and fight for that identifies it as uniquely you, clearly an entity of its owner? How are you identifiable in that which you give life to? Is there anything original about who you are? Would there be if you had less fear, more courage, and a willingness to embrace the unknown of whatever is next?

March 21

Where there's force, there's ego.
-Lester Levenson, founder of the Sedona Method

Have you ever had those times where you knew you were forcing life? Perhaps you're a salesperson who really wants the sale, so you push and push, or you keep talking when you should be silent. Perhaps you're the rebuffed lover, who keeps sending unanswered letters, keeps pushing to meet and talk it out, keeps clinging, unable to bear the pain of not having this person. Or, perhaps you're the parent in the painfully quiet nest of your house that once teemed with chaos and frustrations, now begging or guilting your young adult to come home for a visit. Perhaps you're the neurotic exerciser, unable to stay away from the gym, convinced you can get better or look better if you just train harder.

You're forcing it. And it's ego; not just the kind of ego that needs to have itself inflated by adoration or by possession. Instead, it's the other ways ego infects and ruins life: ego's fears, ego's wants and emptiness, ego's need to control. It's the insisting that my own self be at the center of the universe, unable to let it all go, unable to trust that life flows beautifully, masterfully, quite apart from any fear-driven controlling or manipulation.

What are you forcing? Or, in what area of life do you most tend to force things? Do you see how that forcing of life is the exercise of ego over fear? Rather than facing, allowing, and releasing fear, you're spending life energy fighting it, constantly fighting it?

Have you ever experienced, in any sector of life, the sweet release of letting go of forcing it, only to discover life falling into place in ways you couldn't have devised or directed? If so, then doesn't it make sense that the mentality of letting go can be exercised across all platforms to much greater success? Or is fear so great in one or two areas that you just can't bring yourself to trust that flow, to let go of force? What do you see inside your fear? Do you think you will work through and get past your fears as you age?

March 22

Don't seek approval.
This may be the toughest suggestion for you to follow –
and the most important.
Whether you're a teenager seeking approval from your peers,
a middle-aged parent seeking the approval of your kids,
or a man or woman seeking the approval of your partner,
it all amounts to the same thing.
You're giving your personal power away
every time you seek validation from someone else for who you are.
-T.J. MacGregor, American novelist

Let me ask you a simple question: Of all the people in your life who have power over you or influence in your life, who has it because you actually had your own power, and you gave them a slice of it, and which ones took it, uninvited, and never gave it back? Which are voluntary and which are involuntary, forced?

See, there's nothing wrong with giving someone power over you or influence in your life. It's your life; you can spend it however you damn well please. However, you gotta ask yourself, 'Who has my power and why?' See, power/influence that is given is rooted in trust. Power/influence that is taken is rooted in the selfishness of the other person. And generally, that is a person you likely should not be trusting.

Who has power in your life that was taken from you when you were younger or weaker, and they've never given it back? When do you take your own power back? Or, maybe you're okay with them having power/influence over you? Are you really? Is it possible that the unhappiness in your life is linked directly to who has power over you? What would it take for you to finally reclaim the real estate inside you, to take back your power? Would you lose someone? And, what does it say about that person that they will only love you or only stay in your life if you give them power over you? Sound healthy to you? Or perhaps a bit pissy and selfish on their part?

March 23

Passion is energy.
Feel the power that comes from focusing on what excites you.
-Oprah Winfrey, American tycoon

My career never fully began to take off until my 40's – my 40s! I waited so damn long that eventually I let go of the need I used to have for success. I still wanted it, sure. But it had lost its ability to consume me. I found this weird joy and power in not-having. That's what enabled me to live in my car, way back when. That's what enabled me to give up all of my life possessions, drain my bank account, and go work among the homeless of Oakland, CA, living on the street among them, sleeping on concrete every night for 2 ½ years. My need to have success was toast, and had been for awhile.

But alas, after I let it go, success started to come to me. Mid-40s and things started to turn, slowly. Late 40s, I got a growing practice in Manhattan. Early-50s, I'd made it in New York City, the hardest place to do so! The most powerful, elite, and rich were coming to me to sort out their screwed-up lives and whisper advice into their ears. Yet, I still maintained a strong connection to the people of the street, middle class folk, and working horses in the trades. My books, which had seldom sold more than a few hundred copies per year, were now selling tens of thousands per year. I was being flown in private jets to remote locations to provide counseling.

Now, in my mid-50s, that lust for more roars like a lion inside me. Not just more money, which was an animal that never really consumed me, but more influence, more challenges, more lives to change, and, to be honest, more big experiences to sate my drive for adventure. And yes, the occasional big stuff to satisfy my big ego. I won't lie.

Even still, life continues to challenge me with new inner crud to overcome. The need for spiritual discipline never ends. The ability of the ego to destroy inner peace never ends. We're never 'there.' Life, at each and every stage, is a journey; always this dance with our own insecurities, wants, hungers, and ego.

That drumbeat of more, more, MORE, MORE is in me, as surely as there are other drum beats in other people. I am called by my soul, which was hammered by decades of nothingness and spartan living to collapse into those easily consuming aspirations. I don't try to reject them. For, the longing for more is as much a tool for greater work as it is a potential corruption of peace and energy. But, I do allow it to come, unresisted, and pass. By allowing it, it will not run the machine and drive my life. It becomes just one more tool in the belt.

What's the drumbeat inside you? Does it run you, or does it inform you? What would it take to simply allow it without allowing it to overwhelm you? Could life be just as joyful and just as meaningful if that drumbeat never came?

March 24

> *Nothing in life is to be feared.*
> *It is to be understood.*
> -Marie Curie, Polish-French physicist

I'm of the strong belief that when people say they fear failing, fear being penniless, fear the unknown, or fear changing, what they're really afraid of, deep down, is what people will say or think about them. Obviously, it's not all people, but damn near most of them. The power we give away to other people to guide, or at least inhibit, our life and choices is sadly a nearly omnipresent reality. This is why change, personal growth, and healing require so much courage. In fact, nothing is more important to becoming authentic than courage, because the forces array – in the words, looks, questions, and sneers of others – to keep you neatly boxed, stuck precisely as you are and have always been.

Do you have the courage to not just be different, but to be authentic, even knowing the price you will pay in terms of disapproval, mocking, and being thought of as foolish? And whose criticism do you most fear? In one sentence or less, what is the single most painful thing that person could say or think about you?

Let's say you heard that sentence from that person, what then? Would you die? Would life go on? I mean, sure, you'd grieve and be devastated. But after you flushed all the pain out, would you be okay? If so, if that's your great fear, and if you know you'd recover and be okay if it happened, then what precisely is it that's holding you back from becoming your original, true self?

March 25

With age comes wisdom,
but sometimes age comes alone.
-Oscar Wilde, Irish poet

Today is the birthday of the woman who was the wisest person I've ever known, my mother, Charlotte E. Erlandson. She was months short of 40 when she birthed me. From a young age, I knew my parents were older than those of my friends. Add to that, their life's work as a cleric and spiritual counselor meant they (with me or any of my siblings in tow) spent a lot of time at nursing homes, hospitals, and in the homes of old people, further adding to the sense of my own parents being old. I very much liked that and, over time, benefited from it.

Due to her nature and age (though she was very hard-working in raising six children and later taking her career full-time as an educator, professor, and writer), mom moved slower, was more contemplative, and asked deeper questions of me at a young age. Everything seemed to be either a question, a koan, or a metaphor. Plus, she had slow ears. The youthful hurry and impatience of many parents was long burned off by the time I came around, if it was ever there to begin with. She could quietly listen as my brain, mouth, and energy went on and on 'til they slowed, too. I had a mother who listened. As a result, I felt heard, calmed, and became a listener, myself, over time.

So, who are the old people who've taught and influenced you, whether blood or completely unrelated? What were the greatest lessons you learned, specifically from the old people in your past? What was different for you about sitting in the company of an old person that made you receptive to hearing them and being shaped by them? Are you the old person for someone else? If so, do they feel like you see and hear them? What are they learning from you? More importantly, what's the underlying message they're receiving from you?

March 26

People naturally follow leaders stronger than themselves.
-John Maxwell, American author/speaker

Maxwell calls this, "The Law of Respect." The inverse of that is that people won't follow or will only begrudgingly follow someone they don't respect, and then only because that person has some external power over them. If they don't see you as better than them, in some way, they won't follow.

I can recall reading a newspaper interview with the great conductor of the NY Philharmonic, Lorin Maazel, who said, to paraphrase, "There's nothing worse as a musician than playing in an orchestra when you don't respect the conductor."

Even if you've never played in an orchestra, you've likely experienced it in your work setting: a boss you don't respect because they are either dumber than you, weaker than you, worse at decision-making, or some other infirmity that makes your tenure under him/her unbearable.

Well, the same is true for love relationships and families. If there is an inequitable distribution of power, then the person in power better be respected and *trusted* by the other(s), or there's nothing but rocky shoals ahead.

And, one of the pivotal moments in the life of any relationship is when the one not in power becomes aware that if they were leading, there would be greater benevolence, clearer direction, less chaos, and a more equitable and charitable distribution of power and decision-making. At that point, a major decision has to be made inside this person: to stand up and make the needed and hard-won change, to continue to endure while knowing the root problem and the toll it will take, or to walk away.

The real eye-opener in life is when we realize *we* have to lead, because no one else is doing it or doing it effectively. It's a scary moment; it means that you must step out from the shadows and take risks.

Do you respect those you are allowing to lead you? Do you trust them? Is it time for you to stand up and lead? Are you afraid? What do you fear most? Do you have the courage to do it, anyway? For, that's what leadership is – doing what needs to be done, even when scared.

March 27

Cool means being able to hang with yourself.
All you have to ask yourself is,
"Is there anybody I'm afraid of?
Is there anybody who, if I walked into a room and saw,
I'd get nervous?"
If not, then you're cool.
-Prince, Iconic entertainer/Minnesotan

I was living in Los Angeles in the early 2000s. My girlfriend and I had broken up. I had gone for a long bike ride and found myself at a Barnes and Noble in Santa Monica browsing books. Then, completely out of the blue, someone said, "Whatcha reading," or some such thing. I looked up and here was this knockout, cute blonde woman with a tiny puppy in her arms. Instantly, I knew exactly who it was. I had seen her in movies by that time, as she was one of the top young actresses in the world. And in a colossal failure, I said something profound like, "Uh, this and that," and went about browsing.

"Stupid! Stupid! Stupid! Complete dipsh*t!" are the self-flagellating words that have rung in my head ever since! Seldom have I blown an opportunity greater than that one, at age 34. I mean, come on, a movie star!

I was so not cool, especially around women. Hell, I had grown up in a family of pretty much all males and male energy. Women terrified me, not to mention movie stars. I was the opposite of what the King of Cool, Prince, mentions in the quote.

Who intimidates you by their mere presence? Who still makes you nervous – an old lover, your boss, a hero, a silent crush? What are the fears, insecurities, and self-doubts that still infect your beliefs in yourself. I think we all have work to do in this area. Are you doing the work?

March 28

I would advise young artists to paint as they can,
as long as they can, without being afraid of painting badly.
-Claude Monet, French painter

Message to young artists:
Your opinion is the only one that matters...
...so don't worry about what anyone else thinks about your art!
-Alicia Tormey, American painter

One of the many struggles I went through, back in my late 20s and into my 30s when starting my twisty, turny career, was the idea of referring to myself as a writer and, more dauntingly, an artist. By 35, I had already had two books published, others I had written, as well as reviews and articles that had been published in scholarly journals, theological publications, and a national newspaper or two.

Yet, from the day I started writing my seminal book, *Spiritual but not Religious* in 1995, I've found the term 'writer' to be a bit pretentious for me, not because I considered writers pretentious, but because it felt self-inflating; as I hadn't really proven myself in the world's eyes – i.e. I hadn't sold enough. To consider myself the even loftier appellation 'artist,' was just way too much, as I was utterly inept with a paint brush or sheet of music, and I wasn't the nobler of the writing professions, as I saw them: poet, novelist, playwright. Those were the real artists, not a non-fiction writer who struggled to even call himself a writer.

But, the indisputable fact, in retrospect, was that I was both. I was a writer and an artist, developing and honing my craft. Is an acorn any less of an oak than the 80-footer it will become? The oak DNA is in there, and while it's not fully expressed, it's still perfectly expressed for this stage of the oak's journey. I see this so vividly in the young chefs, late-blooming poets/rappers, nascent painters, and beginning ceramicists I've been introduced to over the years. I also witness this struggle with creative, artistic identity in the professional dancer who has reached her 40s, the arthritis-ridden sculptor in his 60s, the formerly brilliant physicist who crafted theories that shocked an industry but now at 70 can only read the work of others, and the 90-year-old woman whose gardens she can walk through but no longer tend. The question these people are left with is often, "Am I still an artist, when I no longer bear fruit?"

Are you an artist? Are you a struggling artist? Or, perhaps, are you at such an early stage of your art that you even wrestle with the mere idea of calling yourself an artist? Are you an artist whose limbs no longer give ripe fruit in season, but whose work still provides cool shade, pretty leaves, and gnarled wood that whispers of winters past for those who bask under them?

BADASS WISDOM

Hear me say this: you are an artist, and I need you. I need the acorns bearing fresh ideas to inspire and excite me. I need the composer, the creative deep thinker, the insightful photographer, the wordsmith, and the craftsman. You tickle my brain and light fires in my heart. I need the old-limbed artists and even those long dead, I come back to you for wisdom and to feed my soul! My life's work depends on yours. Please do the world a favor and see yourself as the artist, or artisan, that you are. The world needs you! I need you!

March 29

No man is truly free,
until he can live as though his father is dead.
-Oscar Wilde, Irish poet

Due to the enormous power that parents have over children and the imprinting of their messages into the soul of the child, the parental voice owns massive real estate inside that child. As that child grows and ages into adulthood, the now adult-child may think of herself as a completely autonomous entity Yet, she ain't. Yes, sure, she has differentiated herself from the parent(s) to some degree. However, it's usually far less than she thinks, particularly if there was damage done by the parents or soul needs that went unmet.

Be that as it may, the innate and deliberate identity of that child/adult-child is still down there underneath all the crud done, or left undone, by the parent. Until that young person, or grown-ass adult, does the deliberate work of excising the presence of the parent inside, she is not self-authoring her life. She is still responding to deeply hidden messages about self, life, expectations, and criticisms.

Whether the parent is living or dead is irrelevant. The adult-child must do the work of slaying the parent inside. That requires going inside and identifying all that is parent (or unwanted parts of the parent), and all that is self, then removing the former. Only then do freedom and peace come. Parenthetically, all of this can be done without any input from (or need for) the actual parent.

List the top 10 things you love and adore your parents for, if you can. What does it feel like to think about each of those things?

Now the toughie: What are the 3-4 things for which you have the strongest negative feelings toward your parents (or the one parent you venerate most)? Describe those things, events, or memories in complete detail.

And, slightly tougher still: Let it all flow; describe in the strongest language the truest, realest, and most powerful feelings you have toward your parents for each of the memories in the last paragraph. If you were to be completely honest, what is it you really feel?

If you have no strong negative feelings toward a parent(s), is it possible you're lying to yourself, or keeping it bottled up way down inside? Is it possible you're denying your truth? Is it possible that your instinct to protect your parent, or the memory of your parent (and the sense of guilt from doing the opposite), is so great that you'd rather deny and avoid than face it? Is it possible you're still protecting the feelings of your parent(s) over your own, precisely as you were always trained to do?

March 30

Don't be pretending
that your love is real.
-Eric Clapton, British singer, "Pretending"

One of the hardest things to do in a relationship is to end it, especially if we're actually fond of, or love, the person we're in the relationship with. It's hard to even think of hurting this other person's feelings; hard to think of them being mad. And so, we pretend. Pretend to understand. Pretend to fully care. Pretend to love completely. Pretend to still be in love.

Yet, crazy as it seems, to end it is to be merciful. Painful as it's going to be for them and for you, it's the right thing. It's to give their life back to them, because everyday you keep them in the illusion that you're fully there, you're unfairly stealing life from them. Additionally, you're creating the illusion of hope inside of them – hope it can still work out, hope for it to get better, hope to be fully loved, once again.

Thus, to pretend is to steal. It's a selfish act, done because you don't want to touch the inevitable pain. But if you go into the pain and do the hard thing, that pain will end. It will pass. And at some point, you have to have the courage to not only live your life fully and completely without fear, but also to give full control of their life back to them. You owe them honesty. And that takes courage.

What do you fear most in this situation? What are you stealing from them because of your cowardice? Is that the kind thing to do? Further, when do you honor self and the longing of your own soul for greater happiness? When do you finally have the courage to pull the trigger and make it happen, scary as it may be? Today's the day.

March 31

The heart has its reasons
that reason cannot know.

-Blaise Pascal, French mathematician and spiritual writer

If you were to be totally honest, what percentage of your life have you spent following your heart, even at the expense of reason? And, just as importantly, whatever that percentage is, are you okay with that? Do you wish you had done it differently? Additionally, do you wish your future was different from your past, in terms of heart and reason?

To be clear, heart and reason are not always at odds. In fact, there are many times in life when they are in lockstep. But it doesn't take long in talking with someone to unearth what their real passions are, what they would most love to do with their career, relationships, love, time, health, and so forth. Too often in life, the fear of being thought foolish, unreasonable, irrational, the bad guy, selfish, or just plain dumb interrupts or outright blocks a life of passion and joy.

What are the passions you keep hidden? In what bold new directions is your heart calling you? What new plans, purposes, people, paths, and potentialities beckon your soul?

Got the courage to finally begin to boldly act on the calling of your heart *and not back down* amid the slander and critiques of your path and of you? When does your life finally become fully your own? When?!

April

April 1

Laughter is poison to fear.
-George R.R. Martin, American author

When I was nine, one of my best friends, Dave, put syrup in the family shampoo bottle and shampoo in the syrup bottle on April Fools' Day. I don't recall if his siblings or parents fell for it, but he thought it was pretty funny, nonetheless, and so did I. Dumb, pre-teen humor.

It has been said that the very first thing to disappear when entering a foreign country, is one's sense of humor. The mind becomes overwhelmed with the new environment, new stimuli, and new languages. There is a focusing, a tightening of the brain and body.

Laughter both requires and creates looseness. It can be an escape from seriousness or from life. It can be a means of avoidance or the subtlest way to deliver hard truth.

What's the silly, stupid stuff you do in life to get a rise out of people or simply make them laugh, or at least make yourself laugh? Where do you play? Who loosens you up? Where does your fun, lighthearted side show up? Are there people who enjoy the brightness, slyness, or sunshine you bring to life? Do you, at least at times, make yourself laugh? Can you laugh at yourself?

Or, has the tightness and heaviness of life tightened you to the point where laughter and looseness are lost?

One of the grandest benefits of doing deep soul work is that as we dig deeper and deeper, emptying the soul of the crud that has been dumped there, and one day, quite unexpectedly, we find ourselves laughing again. We notice the sun is shining brighter and warmer. This isn't contrived BS; it's just fact. As we empty the soul of all that overwhelms and tightens us from the inside, the loosening begins and, more and more, cleans our body and brain. What is the next level of stuff that you have maybe been avoiding and running from that needs to be cleaned out, so that looseness and laughter may start to calm your body and soul?

April 2

Blessed are the poor in spirit.
-Jesus

During my 20s and into my 30s, I spent an increasing amount of time thinking about suicide. I even bought razor blades more than once. But it wasn't until I was 33 that I actually went through with it. I was living in Los Angeles. I drove to Berkeley, where I had gone to grad school. I parked at the foot of the pier there and opened my veins. I bled for nearly an hour, but I didn't die. I actually started to laugh at the oddity of not dying.

It was then that I realized how much I really wanted to live. But, the real grand epiphany in that moment was no epiphany, at all. It was the very simple, even banal realization that if I were going to choose to live, I would have to make different decisions. That was it; my grand near-death insight.

I stepped out of my blood-soaked car and asked a passerby to call 911. I was whisked away in an ambulance and confined for 36 hours (less than the state standard).

But I did die that day. The old me died. It really did. It took time for the new me to come to full flourish, but come he did. I was still committed to my journaling and self-growth, and it simply wasn't true that all my decisions changed immediately. But, change they did. Six years later, during my years of ministering to and living among the homeless, I was having the irregular morning mocha and journaling, when completely out of the blue, I started laughing. It suddenly hit me. I was, both in that moment and in the new chapter of my life, happier than I had ever been in my entire life. I had done it. I was thriving! Nary a penny to my name, but I had never been happier, never freer, never more *ALIVE!*

A million decisions came in between the suicide and thriving. Career success, at least by worldly standards, wouldn't come for several more years. But I was happy. More pointedly, I was experiencing a lightness of life that I had not known since childhood.

What burdens your soul? Are you actively getting it out? Are you making different decisions, most notably in your commitment to healing and self-growth? Are you naming and releasing the pains and old beliefs that have bogged you down for decades? If not, are you ready to start? Has the pain gotten bad enough yet?

April 3

Shame is a soul-eating emotion.
-Carl G. Jung, Swiss psychiatrist

My mother was 93 when she passed away. Yet, long before that, in her 70s, she would share with me how she felt so much guilt over her parenting. I don't know if dad felt guilt, but mom did. Despite the fact that by pretty much all accounts, she was an amazing mother. Nonetheless, she felt it – opportunities she wished she had made possible for her kids, things she could've done better, poorly chosen words or responses.

She also shared with me that she reached the point in life where she had to flush out all of her feelings and then forgive herself. She had already apologized to her kids years prior, but it wasn't until her 70s that she could forgive herself, at times lamenting that she had not done so sooner. She knew she needed to do so for her own peace and joy.

What memories do you have from your past that carry with them great shame, guilt, or embarrassment? What keeps you from forgiving yourself? Is it possible you even carry shame over not what you did, but what was done to you? Can you see the unfairness you commit against yourself by continuing to carry that?

Can you take the time and endure the discomfort to allow all of your feelings surrounding those memories to rise up? Can you then begin to flush out the feelings through counseling or journaling or writing letters you don't send, and keep flushing until the memory no longer carries discomfort?

This is soul work. It's not just about releasing the week-to-week anxieties and pains. To fully clear the soul and finally burn clean energy means to dive into the past, allow up all the feelings that have been stuffed down for so long, and actively purge them.

That is what brings in the soul.

April 4

Don't spend time beating on a wall,
hoping to transform it into a door.
-Coco Chanel, French fashion designer

There's a common motivational conviction that insists you must keep attacking when doors are closed. And, at times, it is true that persistence will open the door. However, far too often we waste life energy trying to beat down obstacles rather than treat them as a part of the flow, as a sign to simply make a course correction, to allow life to shape you just as much as you're trying to shape it.

The question, of course, becomes: How do I know when to keep attacking and when to let it go and move on in an adjusted direction?

'How do I know...' questions always start with fear. The question that always has to be asked when determining whether to attempt to create a door where there's a wall is: Is this somehow, deep down, driven by fear? Or, does it feeeel right?

Now, that's sorta hokey language for a lot of people who are trying to build success and dreams. But a fear-driven career seldom ends in happiness. Whereas, if one has done the work of flushing out the pain, fears, and BS beliefs they were taught about him-/herself, there is a feel, and one can trust it. I have worked with many people in finance and the top echelons of business who flat out state that they can feel their decisions; and when they're exhausted, beaten down, or overwhelmed by life, they lose connection to that feel, lose trust in their own judgments, and make mistakes they never made before.

In the end, "How do I know..." questions are always answered by removing the fears, not the least of which is: Will I be okay if it all goes south? I may grieve, but will I survive and move on to live, attack, and dream another day? And, is it possible that this closed door is a blessing? Can I let it go, trusting that new doors will flow effortlessly into my path ahead? What fears are driving your insistent, incessant attacks on walls?

April 5

We don't get the father we most want.
We get the father we most need.
-Unknown

Today is my father's death day. He died a while back, in his 90s. I always loved my dad, and respected him for many reasons: he was physically strong, a down-to-earth farm kid who became a Lutheran pastor, a really witty guy who enjoyed kidding around with people and committed his life to serving them. Tough not to admire. A truly good man by any reckoning.

But for so many years, deep into my 20s, I wanted a father who was great, not good. I wanted a father who was known far and wide, famous, who had done life-changing things – a Darwin, Einstein, Churchill, or Carnegie. I wanted a father who didn't, at times, talk too much. I wanted a father who better understood my extreme different-ness.

Instead, I got a father who was in the trenches every day for 65 years, listening to people's problems, giving a kind word, holding the hand of hurting men and women, protecting teens who had gotten pregnant and ostracized by families, and more. He was a pastor committed to serving his God and to serving people. During my poor years, even though he would never remotely understand my life path, he often slipped a $20 bill into my pocket or bought a bag of groceries for me. He held his tongue when he probably wanted to criticize or question. He supported a son he didn't understand. If that's not love, what is?

Now, well into my own 50s, his goodness and commitment to kindness is the lodestar for the work I do – striving to stand for the weak, bring a healing ear and words to the hurting, walk through life with laughter and gentle goodness, even as my own success has soared. He was and is, particularly in the long run of life, precisely the father that this very different, odd duck of a son needed most.

When do you let go of what you think you want – whether regarding a parent, a mentor, a life path, or way of thinking – and see the upside-down gift the universe is blessing you with? In what ways has life given you the very thing or person you never knew you always wanted?

April 6

1. ***Summer Breeze,*** Seals & Crofts
2. ***Just You and Me****,* Chicago
3. ***Cool Change,*** Little River Band
4. ***Hollywood Nights,*** Bob Seger
5. ***Calypso****,* John Denver

After a whole lot of Mozart, those are my five favorite songs of all time. I could hear them a thousand more times and still never tire of them, still find them stirring my soul. But here's the thing: pretty much every person on God's green earth would disagree with me on all five of those songs, or on at least one or three of them. And yet, they're still just perfect for me!

This is one of the grand points of life, isn't it?

I often get people asking me, "Sven, if you could change one thing in this world, what would it be?"

"That's easy," I respond. "I would add the two words 'for me' to every person's declarations of best, most perfect, and greatest, no matter what they're referring to – religion, political viewpoint/affiliation, parenting, life path, geography, dreams, sports teams, values, etc." We so easily absolutize our own beliefs in life. That's all ego; the attempt to fill empty love cups by demonizing the cups of others. That is what creates the walls, the fights, the condescension, the separation, and the hate.

It's so easy in life to say that my way of doing things is the best or only way. My beliefs are the one, true belief system. My opinion is the most right. My path is the only real path.

Yet, what does it take to simply add "...for me" to each of those declarations, to allow room for others to live their own truths, beliefs, paths, and ways of doing and living? Can you see how that would bring so much more peace and better community between different people and groups?

In what area(s) of your life do you most absolutize your beliefs and values? Why? What do you fear if you were to be open to the possibility that other values, choices, or beliefs are just as valid for someone else as yours are for you? And, what would you gain in terms of living peacefully in a community? Do you have the ability to pull yourself out of the center of the universe? What would it take to do so?

April 7

> *Every hardship has a reason and every deprivation a purpose,*
> *if you look through eyes of insight.*
> -Diamante Lavendar, Artist/author

So, here's a strange sequence of questions for you in your daily journaling. But first, take a piece of paper and draw a vertical line in the center, top to bottom. Draw a horizontal line an inch from the top, above which you can write the title for each column. Over the first column write the word 'Self;' over the second, write 'Life.'

You're going to answer a series of questions as you go down the page. You may write the questions to the far left. Then, you're going to answer each question as it pertains to self and to life. The first question is, "What was the first decade of your life sent to teach you about you and about life?" You're not answering the question for all people, but just for you. What were *your* first ten years sent to teach you about *yourself* and life?

If you don't remember much, or anything, from the decade, what does what you actually do remember exist to tell you about yourself? Or, what does the mere fact that you don't remember anything teach you about self and life?

The next question is the same question but now for the second decade of your life. Write your answer in each column. What about the third decade? Fourth? Etc.

How deep can you go as you explore these answers? Do you see the value in each of these decades, even though some may have been searingly painful? Have you grown, expanded, become more compassionate, more focused, more relaxed, or what? How have these lessons about self and life changed you? How has learning these things changed, or evolved, over time? Do you like who you've become? Is it too late to change? What would it take to do so?

April 8

What the caterpillar calls the end of the world, the master calls a butterfly.
-Richard Bach, US Navy pilot and author

In our home, back in the 70s, there was a large bulletin board hanging inside the kitchen. The phone hung in the middle of it. The board was often covered with pictures, news clippings, the weekly chore list, and so on.

Somewhere in my preteen years, I recall a tiny, one-paragraph news clipping being pinned there. It stated, in short, that some religious group was predicting that the world would end on such-and-such a date that year, just a month away. Upon reading it, I have a very distinct memory of feeling very afraid. I didn't discuss it with anyone but I was truly scared, increasingly so as the day of Armageddon inched closer.

Somehow, though I don't recall how, I remember learning that it was my father who had placed it there. What makes that tidbit interesting is that my dad was a Lutheran pastor, and this was explicitly not a Lutheran group making this claim; it was unthinkable that a Lutheran would ever do such a thing. I can only conjecture why dad put it up, but there is a part of dad that got a giggle out of tweaking people's thinking and being a contrarian. Thus, he likely found humor in it.

Be that as it may, the day came with great anxiety for me. And, as we all know, it passed without the world ending. It is, of course, funny as an adult. But at the time, I was terrified. Afterward, however, something shifted in me. Granted the obvious, I now saw with skepticism any group that claimed end-of-world knowledge. Much more significantly, I had, in some odd way, survived the end of the world, or at the very least survived my immense fears and anxieties surrounding it. Thus, it made me feel oddly stronger. It changed my outlook on fear. First, I witnessed that even the biggest fears often do not come to pass. More significantly, I realized there's always the day after, even when you think the world is going to end. There's always the next day. And life goes on.

So, what are the world-ending fears you have? What are you convinced you could never survive? What would it do for your thinking and sense of strength if you actually were to survive? What have you learned about fear, survival, and new life afterward, as you've aged? What new life would you create and live if you survived that very thing you are convinced would be the very end of the world? So, why not just start living that life now?

April 9

Sit with the pain until it passes, and you will be calmer for the next one.
-Naval Ravikant, Indian-American entrepreneur

Revisiting this notion of living as a badass – fully self-mastered, fully authentic – it's extremely important that you realize you'll never *fully* master the self, if you think of mastery as imperviousness to sadness, anxiety, fear, and hardship. That's not what being a badass is about, not what authenticity and self-mastery are. Further, pretending to be impervious to pain and feelings, as far too many men continue to do, is definitely not badass. That's just playing pretend.

Becoming and being a spiritual badass aren't about imperviousness, as if life can't touch you. If you're engaged in life, you're going to be full of fear when your child, or adult-child, has to go in for major surgery. You're going to know sadness when the dog you've loved and maybe hunted with for a decade or more is at death's door. You're going to feel anxiety, pain, exhaustion, fear, and so much more when the very normal events of life hit. Old BS notions that those things won't affect you are ludicrous. Of course you're going to be knocked down, laid low by life's difficulties.

And, lest we jump right into dumb cliches, being a spiritual badass definitely is not about jumping right back up after we've been laid low. In fact, it's often that very act of pretending to be fine and attempting to bounce back too fast that keeps life's pains stored inside, eating away at a person.

The spiritual badass – the person who lives from their own center – still gets knocked down and often deliberately allows him-/her-/themself to stay down and allow the pain to be felt, purged, learned from, and healed. The spiritual badass has the tools for allowing and purging the pain. The novice just ignores or runs from the pains. The spiritual badass understands and lives in the value of taking the time and expending the energy necessary to look at, address, and sit in the pain, till the pain has seared the soul (as it does), the lessons have expanded the wisdom (as they do), and the soul has come back to even keel, new strength, and greater clarity (as it does).

To what degree do you still live in old forms of pain-avoidance, rather than allowing it to come and to pass? What do you fear in allowing the pain to be felt? What anxieties, fears, sorrows, and hopes have you not allowed to see the light of day? Do you still live in outdated notions of toughness and weakness? Is it possible that all the misery you feel inside is precisely linked to this very tired notion of strength that was never true to begin with? What disciplines still need to be worked on so that your default is to shift into purging and healing mode, rather than just powering through?

April 10

There is nothing heavier than compassion.
Not even one's own pain weighs so heavy
as the pain one feels
with someone, for someone,
a pain intensified by the imagination
and prolonged by a hundred echoes.
-Milan Kundera, Czech author of The Unbearable Lightness of Being

There's so much loss and pain in this world. And the simple truth is, sometimes we have to turn off our emotional pain receptors. Sometimes, just to function, do our work, feed our kids, and enjoy a bit of life, we have to let go of feeling that pain in the world and in others.

But, that comes when held with a commitment to feeling the pain of the world, allowing it to work on us, allowing the calling of the souls of others to reach our own soul. To live as a badass in the world is to be neither impervious nor indifferent to the pain of others, all around us. In fact, it is to live in communion with it, allowing it to touch and to move us. Each of us is touched by different pains of this world. Each of us is moved by different heartaches in other beings. Each of us is called to reach out to soothe or heal the different wounds of others and of the earth itself. To live as responsible stewards of the life we've been given is to invest in others, particularly those who cannot give back. The strong do have a responsibility for the weak, if for no other reason than every single one of us has areas of life where we are weak and need counsel and strength from others in order to exist.

Who is your soul calling you to reach out to? What is the pain in this world that touches your soul, causing you to hurt for their hurt? Can you get past your own ego needs and drivers? Can you step out of the center of the universe for this moment in time? What do you need to let go of? Can you identify what you're afraid of if you were to reach out and help someone or some cause that stirs your soul?

April 11

If it weren't for greed, intolerance, hate, passion and murder,
you would have no works of art, no great buildings, no medical science,
no Mozart, no Van Gogh, no Muppets and no Louis Armstrong.
-Jasper Fforde, English novelist

If you were to be totally honest, do you have traces of hate in your heart, whether toward a person, a memory, or an experience? I'm not saying you're a hater or a bad person. I'm just saying that some life experiences are so extraordinary that to experience them conjures one of the most extraordinary of human feelings.

It is so easy to demonize hate as the third rail of human happiness, the one with the grand power to ruin it all. And yet, it's not; fear holds that grand claim, especially fear of feeling hate. Hate is almost the exact opposite. Hate, quite often, is the very doorway to the happiness and peace for which you've longed. For, hate is a perfectly natural response to extraordinary circumstances. Like disappointment, elation, melancholy, and lust, it is nothing more than a feeling; and like every other feeling, it passes, if it is welcomed.

It passes, if it is welcomed. Read that again.

Where hate becomes problematic is not in the feeling of it, but in what you do with it, if anything. Unleashing that hate upon another person is not the answer. And it is this unleashing that gives hate a bad rap.

However, packing the hate down inside as if it doesn't exist, or shouldn't exist, is not the answer either. In fact, that is the real problem. That is the biggest blockage to the inner peace we all so strive for. Too often, this packing down or bottling up is done in the name of "I'm not a hater." But by denying, or even minimizing the very authentic feeling, we stick it down deeper where it wreaks its damage on our life, like a snake in the long grass.

It is, in fact, the fear of that hate – what it can do, what it feels like, what you think it might say about you, and the taboo of it – that drives the packing down, the grand avoidance of it. Hate is, ultimately, not the problem; fear of one's own hate is.

The goal and task is to flush it out, just like every other emotion. To welcome it, welcome it, welcome it. To allow it to flow out of you and flow out of you in safe ways and, best of all, in ways that give it words, words, words. For, until it is out of you, it's still in you. Until you allow yourself to speak the hate you feel (whether to a therapist, to your journal, in a poem, but always with words; mere physical expression is not enough), you're living in fear of the hate. You're packing it down. And that hate packed deep inside will turn on you and start eating away at your innards, both literally and metaphorically. Only when it is flushed out is there true healing. For then, and only then, it no longer consumes you.

A dear friend took my advice and allowed herself to express her hate for her mother. She said it lasted two years, even though her mother was deceased. Two years of giving herself permission to see that her mother had burdened her with responsibilities of caring for a sibling through life, and that she had been subsequently taken advantage of by that sibling, all at mom's behest. My friend allowed the truth of it all and the pain and hate to come up and out. And, after a while, the hate for mom abated and eventually passed. The wound had healed, after finally being allowed.

So, again, hate. Deep inside nearly all past trauma or hurt is some measure of hate. For whom or what do you store hate that you have never allowed yourself to even acknowledge? When do you begin to flush it out? When do you de-charge the memories that have strong charges of hate affixed to them? Wanna know healing in ways you never have? Admit, voice, and flush all the powerful feelings, such as hate, you've been running from or packing down your whole life.

April 12

Which is easier for you:
To say 'yes' to things you hate doing
or
To say 'no' to things you love doing?
-Sven

I often posed that question to my athletes back when I was an NCAA Strength Coach. I would tell them that you need to understand your own answer to that question to know what drives you in life. But, more importantly, you need to know the answer that others give to that, whether they come to you for personal training or if you're a coach yourself, someday. Knowing what drives people impacts how you sell to them, how you get them motivated, how you lead them.

For example, in the world of personal fitness, some people find it very difficult to say 'no' to food, which they love. But, that same person may find it quite a bit easier to say 'yes' to working out, even though they really dislike, or even hate, doing it. Knowing this enables the coach to help them get progress, particularly initially, by emphasizing the workout side of getting in shape without pushing too hard on controlling food intake.

Another example is lifestyle. Some people find it much easier to say 'no' to having all the things they want to have and do than saying 'yes' to a job they greatly dislike but pays well.

Where do you fall on this question? Is it, perhaps, different in different areas of your life? Which ones? Why is the 'yes' or 'no' so hard or so easy in each of those areas? What is it about the experience that makes the 'yes' so difficult or the 'no' so much easier?

April 13

Trauma is personal.
It does not disappear if it's not validated.
When it is ignored or invalidated the silent screams continue internally,
heard only by the one held captive.
When someone enters the pain and hears the screams,
healing can begin.
-Danielle Bernock, American Author

One of the phenomena I run into a lot, when working with adults who are still burdened heavily with childhood trauma that hamstrings their adult life and impacts so much of their decision-making is a reluctance to concede the enormity of what was done to them. And, one of the reasons for this that I hear most frequently is, "So many people had it worse. I really can't complain. I didn't have it as bad as them."

To this, I tell them that when race cars go through a quick pit stop in the middle of a race, their pistons firing incessantly at high speeds, their engine oil can reach temperatures as high as 300 degrees Fahrenheit! Now, imagine pouring that engine oil at that temperature into a child's Styrofoam or plastic drinking cup. It won't take more than a very small amount before there is a gaping hole in the bottom of the cup, if the cup doesn't flat-out melt. After that, it is quite irrelevant how much more scalding oil you pour into that cup. The damage is done.

The pain inflicted on a child is quite similar. Massive damage is done to them even in small amounts. Thus, minimizing that you only had a pint of piping hot oil poured into your soul as a child does nothing to mend, or even alleviate, the incredible pain caused. Yes, children can be quite resilient after damage is done to them, even in great amounts. But, resiliency does not mean the gaping hole inside and all the concomitant pain are not still there and wreaking damage on all relationships, life paths, and decisions.

It is not just the amount of damage done to a child that matters, but the mere existence of scorching pain in their past, at all. And, THAT is what must be gone into, felt, and flushed.

At what point do you stop minimizing your pain out of a sense of guilt or comparison? Is it possible that what is actually under your minimizing of your own pain is the fear of even going near what you experienced, because for as small as you make it out to be, it's extremely painful to even consider – ie it really was excruciatingly hot oil poured into your little soul, back then? What was the nature of the oil – what form did it take? Journal it out.

April 14

Most people want to be circled by safety, not by the unexpected.
The unexpected can take you out.
But the unexpected can also take you over and change your life.
-Ron Hall, American author/speaker

It was winter in Dayton, OH. Cold, gray, always an inch of snow on the ground, seldom more. I would retreat occasionally to a tanning booth for a little color, so the mirror wouldn't find me too depressingly pale. There I got to know the owner; young fellow, late 20s. He told me he had left his fledgling engineering career, feeling called by God to start this small business. A year and a half in, he divulged, he and his wife were barely scraping by, hemorrhaging money. Considering quitting the business and returning to engineering, he queried, "How can this be? I was certain, after lots of prayer, that God called me to do this. I was just certain. My wife, too."

"God only calls us to success?" I (rather annoyingly) asked him. "Is it possible," I continued, "that immediate profit isn't the calling here? I know that's what you want. But is it possible that this is part of your soul's growth – an experience to be mined, both personally and professionally, for long term experience and wisdom?"

"Sure, but that's not what I want. Not what I thought I was getting," he said.

"Our plans aren't always what *life* plans. Perhaps you're aiming way too low. Perhaps the long term extraction from this experience well exceeds anything you could have done with this. Perhaps this small seeming-failure is one piece in a much larger puzzle that you simply cannot yet see."

What have been the 3 primary paths – career, relationship, or otherwise – you've felt called, or certain, to go down that you later discovered were not you or no longer you? (And you can certainly do this exercise well beyond the top 3. In fact, you'd be wise to do so.)

Okay, now the telling part. What were each of the three paths sent to teach you, both about life and about you? What would you not know about you, or what would you not presently be, if you had never gone those directions?

There are no mistakes. No wasted relationships. No pointless endeavors. No wasted time, not if you're forever mining it, even the inaction, the boredom, the downtime.

April 15

I dread no more the first white in my hair, or even age itself – the easy shoe,
the cane, the wrinkled hands, the special chair:
Time, doing this to me, may alter too, my anguish, into something I can bear.

-Edna St. Vincent Millay, American poet

I can recall standing in the pew, singing, at the old Highland Grove Lutheran Church out in the country, likely as a 4 or 5-year-old. I can see the hand of the old woman in front of me shaking heavily. I still remember it.

I remember Duane, the slow-moving banker in our small town, whose head would swivel side-to-side as he walked. There was Lloyd, the old organist who had all sorts of quirks.

I remember the times dad would take me along, after morning worship, out to Sunnyside Nursing Home to deliver Communion to the shut-in members there; lots of old, decrepit people talking too loudly, wheeling around, sitting and staring out a window. Later, going with the Cherub Choir of our suburban church to Lynwood Manor Nursing Home, I remember seeing an old man in a chair drooling uncontrollably.

It would be an overstatement to say that, at a young age, I became accustomed to the ravaging effects of old age. However, I was most assuredly exposed to it, maybe even acclimated to it. It was part of being the pastor's kid, tagging along.

As a result, I don't mind the thought of dying alone in a nursing home. The pastor, himself, did, decades later in his 90s. He died from Alzheimer's, which slowed him greatly but didn't render him completely incoherent. He was still a quick wit – playfully, innocently needling.

I recall mom feeling lightened when dad was moved to Walker Homes, because she no longer had to care for him the entire day. She could now rejoin her church group and have a bit of a social life at 91. Then Covid hit and those two years took what remaining zest she had been saving for writing a book and starting her own podcast, as she told me her goals were. And she passed, surrounded by my beautiful siblings and their spouses, her grandkids, and me. The WWII Generation was gone. All of it.

Do you fear old age? Do you fear how you will look in the mirror, both the mirror in the bathroom and the mirror of life? Do you fear age pulling at you, tearing away your control of your body and mind? Do you hate the idea of nursing homes or being alone at home? Which scares you more, dying or death? Why?

Odd as it may sound, is there anything you actually look forward to about aging and/or dying? What is it? Why? And, why can't you have it and live it now?

What were you taught about the old and the dying, either explicitly or tacitly? How do these messages inform or somehow drive your life, today?

April 16

> *In order to live freely and happily,*
> *you must sacrifice boredom.*
> *It is not always an easy sacrifice.*
> -Richard Bach,
> Illusions: The Adventures of a Reluctant Messiah

For those who, over time, have cultivated lives of quiet and peacefulness, it can be a rather common experience to teeter between calm (preferred) and boredom (generally unwanted). That place of extended stillness, right before boredom touches it, is one of life's sweet spots.

And yet, it does cross over. Too often, when that boredom shows its pouty face, we engage in activity and distraction because it bears with it such discomfort and, oddly, anxiety. It is ennui born of longing, specifically the desire to be engaged, focused, swept up in something. Yet, rather than sitting in it and allowing it to pass just like every other feeling does, we tend to skirt it with frightened nonsense and activity.

Relaxation becomes boredom becomes agitation becomes needless distraction guised as (pretend) productivity, when all it is is fear-driven action. It's fear of that restlessness, like the squirming in your seat on a road trip gone on too long.

But, there's another boredom far more insidious and life-sucking, and it doesn't pass like that. It's the boredom born of living the life of not-you. It's the precise inverse of an authentic life that breeds aliveness and vigor. It's the life of voluntary constraint in the world of someone else's expectations, shoulds, thou shalts, and "you betters..." It is a life chosen because the idea of living authentically is too scary, the criticism too great, the fear of looking foolish too overwhelming. It is a life that does not rise up from the soul, but denies the soul and its yearnings. It is to simultaneously know you're living a fake life, and to choose it anyway, for fear of the cost of living otherwise.

Yet, amid that boredom, pain grows. Pain, like fire, always grows when left unattended. With it grows the amount of energy necessary to suppress it, suppress the boredom, and suppress the calling of the soul to be free, happy, and *ALIVE!* That energy suck pulls from our body's ability to fight infection. That bleed of energy to suppress the pain creates physical maladies, bad thoughts, and increased hopelessness. And, we are repeatedly faced with the awareness of this stuck place, the incessant boredom, and the longing for life.

Thus, the choice:

A) To continue to live in boredom, because the scorn, criticism, certain foolishness, and uncertainty seem too much to bear, or

B) To choose the ALIVENESS of self-authored living and to put to death the boredom of inauthenticity, while enduring and becoming mostly

126

impervious to the slings and arrows of those who would keep us in our place, where they have us neatly boxed up, voluntary residents of a box.

So, what do you choose, each day: boredom or ALIVENESS? And, do you see how the latter requires sacrifice and courage? When do you tire of being a volunteer resident of the box?

April 17

Until the culture recognizes the legitimacy
of 'growing down,' each person in the culture struggles blindly
to make sense of the darkness
that the soul requires
to deepen into life.
-James Hillman, American psychologist

Depression is not the enemy.

For those with courage to weather the storms and chase the tornadoes of the soul that call us down and down into ourselves, which is what depression is, there is a deepening of the self and the wide, rich opportunity to learn. It is the opportunity to burn off that which is not you and never really was. It is the opportunity to be taught by the gods of the soul who you've always been meant to be. This is what it means to 'grow down.'

But it is that courage that is also required to stand in the pain and ask the questions of the soul gods – that is to say, ask of one's own deepest self – what this pain was sent to teach you about you and about the very nature of life, beyond the crap of making money, endless chores and jobs, and the hurrying. God, the endless hurrying.

Deep inside lie the answers of the soul, the very GPS for your life. But they are down below all the pain, fears, and garbage beliefs you were taught about yourself. To get to the answers, one has to burrow through and eject the BS. The depression is required – that slow drag of the soul is necessary to overcome the power of your will that desires, passionately, to run from the pull of the soul – to finally get you down into the sludge that needs to be removed, so that shoots of new life may poke up through the soil and begin to see the sun.

Why do you keep running from and medicating your depression? What if the very thing you avoid is, in fact, the calling of your own soul to re-tool and re-purpose? What if the dragon you fear is not just a dragon, but the very dragon who guards the treasure you've sought all along? How badly do you want the treasure? How badly does life suck without that treasure? Got the guts to take on the dragon of depression to discover what it holds in its gnarled claw?

April 18

You miss 100% of the shots
you don't take.
-Wayne Gretzky, NHL G.O.A.T.

There are times in life when little else is required but your own abilities mixed with an aggressive mind. You have to be willing to take the shot. It's that willingness – hell, eagerness! – to wait for just the right moment, but not wait too long, to go 100mph with your hair on fire.

Life requires – both for our greatest happiness and the execution of our greatness – the capacity to shift into attack mode. That's it. To keep that tool out of your tool belt, because you don't like how it sounds or how you'll be perceived, is to cut off part of your authentic self, because you *fear* others. That means they still have power over you, so much so that you'd cut off part of your life's abilities and character. You'd choose acceptable inauthenticity over criticized authenticity. And that's your choice to make, but it won't lead to happiness, because you can't be happy or have peace in the soul when on someone else's agenda, someone whose criticism you fear or approval you seek.

Mastery of life is not to always live in some Zen, kumbaya state of constant peace. Mastery of life is mastery of self, which means that there is not just one tool in the belt that is used. It is recognition that the hammer is just as important as the clamp, the lathe of equal value to the hex nut. Mastery of self and life is the ability to employ whatever tool the moment calls for, and it ain't always Namaste. Sometimes there is work to be done, battles to be fought aggressively, passionately, on fire.

What would it take for you to integrate your attack mode into your personality, not as your governing principle, but as just one more tool in the belt to be employed when inspired to do so? What's the biggest fear keeping you from occasionally using your attack mode? What's your biggest fear in expressing the fullness of your character and soul, rather than just the acceptable, nice parts? What's the criticism that nags you inside?

April 19

Somewhere we know
that without silence words lose their meaning,
that without listening speaking no longer heals,
that without distance closeness cannot cure.
-Henri Nouwen, Dutch Catholic writer and theologian

Few things have greater power in causing another person to feel self-worth than feeling heard.

Too often we use listening as a jumping off point. We listen only until we think of what we want to say next rather than listening for understanding. Sometimes, we listen to hide, so that we don't have to show anyone our real self. Sometimes, we just don't listen at all. Sometimes, we can't bear to listen; it's just too much, today. Sometimes, we listen only for the opening into which we will drive our agenda, our fix, our need.

But, listening has the power to express compassion not through words but through no words and simply being present, engaged. It has the power to connect, to deepen relationships. It has the power to reveal power. It has the power to heal, for it conveys *mattering*.

What has been driving your listening recently? Do you have the power to, more and more, extract yourself and your agendas from the center of the universe? Do you have the ego strength to let go of mattering for just a little while, so you can give that mattering to someone else? Do you listen only in the big, but seldom in the small; or vice versa; or tragically neither? Do you wonder why your connections lack, well, connection? Is it possible you fear not being the center of the universe, not driving your agenda, not feeding your bottomless need for attention, and as a result you eventually drive everyone away, or at least everyone you're not using to get your fix?

To extract oneself from the center of the universe or not is not just a big question, but potentially a daily one. Are you even asking it of yourself?

April 20

I hire people brighter than me and then I get out of their way.
-Lee Iacocca, Developer of the iconic American sports car, the Ford Mustang, and later CEO of Chrysler

Ego.

Few things in life have greater power to derail greatness, derail relationships, derail careers, derail parenting, derail friendships and derail societies than ego – i.e. someone's fear of pain, in whatever form that pain may come. Fear of the pain of:

- not getting approval
- not mattering
- being criticized
- being small
- destitution
- meaninglessness
- what people will think (of me).

So, people construct stories, lies, and artifices around them to insulate against the smallness they feel inside. They act like the know-it-all, pose like the smartest guy in the room (at least in their own heads), render opinion as fact, and constantly undercut others. Ego is what keeps others down, undermining them, unwilling to let them get bigger (than me). That's the mark of a small man, a small person, a person who fears others getting past him/her, who fears not being in control and always looking put-together and better-than.

But greatness, or at least wisdom, is the unleashing and building up of others. Their excellence finding origin, or influence, in our own. True greatness is the eagerness to unleash others to become their greatest selves. Oh, and it's a glorious thing to watch someone absolutely come alive, who did not know it, believe it, or have the opportunity to unleash it before. Be it a child, a creative, an employee, a thinker, a go-getter, a hustler, an animal, or some other, it's a beautiful unfolding to watch someone bloom into full flourish.

Of course, the natural byproduct of giving room and power to others is that one day, even as you deliberately recede, you are seen for the generous benefactor you have become and for all that you have given life to. By giving up your power and ego, you have attained all the ego that you previously sought and pretended to be.

So, what fear is keeping you down, and thus holding back those you're called to lead? Where is your ego hamstringing your own happiness and greatness? What is the specific pain you fear most that keeps you holding others back, perhaps even your own children? When do you finally have the courage to sit in that fear and allow yourself to begin flushing it out, so that it no longer destroys all you can be for others?

April 21

The creation of something new is not accomplished by the intellect but by the play instinct acting from inner necessity.
The creative mind plays with the object it loves.
-C.G. Jung, Swiss founder of analytical psychology

What's your jam?

What is it that when you're engaged with it you lose all sense of time, forget about hunger, feel electricity in your brain and fire in your belly? What is it? Maybe it's more than one thing; I'd be shocked if it weren't.

To live in that state, to work in that sense of play, well, that's something special. That's *ALIVENESS!* That's the sweet spot, the Holy Grail. THAT is when you're just murdering the ball, sawing the strings off that cello, killing it in your stand-up, absolutely focused on the workings of that clock you're fixing or the garden you're weeding, destroying the darkness with the intensity of the midday sun.

It's play. It's sheer delight in the very work itself. That's when creativity is electrified, flowing effortlessly.

Where does your creativity flow? Are you spending enough time there? What's sucking your time and life energy, pulling you away from your jam? Why do you run from that sweet spot in which your greatness surely is embedded? Who convinced you that that which is blissful for you is a big nothingburger? Who denigrated that very thing that most gives you life?

When do you begin to construct a life around the most lively places in your life, the places where intensity, creativity, play, and grit all flow together in harmony? WHEN DO YOU GIVE YOURSELF PERMISSION?

April 22

If you're always trying to be normal,
you'll never know how amazing you can be.
-Maya Angelou, American poet and civil rights activist

The desire to fit in, fly below the radar, and be normal is always driven by fear. Most of the time, it's fear of success and sticking out that drives the desire to be normal, or at least be perceived as normal. Somewhere along the line, you got the message that sticking out was bad and/or painful. So, fitting in the box became a useful, necessary survival mechanism.

But then, long down the road, you realize that you chafe against the walls of that same box. It doesn't fit. It no longer provides safety, but discomfort and discontent, unrest of the soul.

Plus, somewhere deep inside the soul is the longing to see, to feel, to be seen for your real self, no masks, no boxes. It's the desire to be amazing.

And, there's the rub: the grating of the former safety of the box labeled 'normal' against the longing of the soul to be amazing, to be your glorious, radiant, original self. That's where you are, aren't you? Heck, maybe you've even half-escaped that box in your life, but still know you hide in the box of normalcy in other parts of your life, fearful of repercussions and that age-old fear of looking stupid or being called so. The pride (and the fear it masks) obstructs the amazingness.

So, you stumble through life, perhaps even successful in the box of normal you've chosen. Yet, the unfulfillment grows, doesn't it? The soul calls. How long can you blow it off, ignore it, or silence it with incessant distraction? When do you tire of the waste of it all?

April 23

There is a vitality, a life force, a quickening
that is translated through you into action.
And because there is only one of you in all time,
this expression is unique.
And if you block it,
it will never exist through any other medium and be lost.
The world will not have it. It is not your business to determine
how good it is, nor how valuable it is,
nor how it compares with other expressions.
It is your business to keep it yours clearly and directly,
to keep the channel open.
You do not even have to believe in yourself or your work.
You have to keep open and aware directly to the urges that motivate YOU.
Keep the channel open...
No artist is pleased...
There is no satisfaction whatever at anytime
There is only a queer, divine dissatisfaction,
a blessed unrest that keeps us marching
and makes us MORE alive than the others.
-Martha Graham,
considered the most important dancer of the 20th Century,
she revolutionized the world of dance; (here in a letter to Agnes DeMille)

To each one of us is given a gift – a gift that because of your individual attributes, aspirations, abilities, and ailments, is unique precisely to you. It is that for which you have been put here by the gods, or the universe, or chance, or fate. As Graham says, it will never exist again.

What is your gift? What is it? Do you see how that very thing you bring to life could be exactly what someone else needs? Do you see how that gift is a gift to you, as well, and that having the courage to live it will bring a sense of joy and purpose like nothing else you can give yourself to?

Let it come. Wrestle with it. Let it wound you. Let it heal you. Let it set you free and finally come alive!

April 24

Promises are like pie crusts –
easily made, easily broken.
-Mary Poppins, fictional protagonist in the eponymous Disney movie

One of the biggest mistakes I see people make when they've been wronged in a relationship – whether it be from cheating, neglect, outright hurtfulness, or even abuse – is that they forgive too soon. That is, they forgive before the evidence is in. They may have a remorseful partner or parent claiming repentance and that they'll never do it again. And, it can be very easy to forgive when there are crocodile tears and big promises. But that's the problem: promises.

Whether it be promises of never doing it again or "I've really changed," the promises are always of things that will (or won't) happen *in the future*. Believing the penitent person requires trusting that things in the future actually will be different. And, in those intense times in a relationship it's very easy to get swept up in the heightened emotion and passion, and all the beautiful promises. That passion for you that they show can feel so good when it's been gone for so long. Finally, you're getting what you want, or at least you're getting the promise of it happening in the future.

Yet, the odd question in all of this is simply, "Why now?"

Why are the big tears, big promises, and big changes happening now? Well, what's strange is that often the promises that are made and the things they've immediately now started doing are the things you've been telling them for years, which implies they were listening the whole time but just didn't want to change. If they could change today and promise to continue it into the future, they could've changed five years ago, or ten. However, now they feel obligated to change because they've lost power. So, they'll promise the world, at least 'til they get their power back over you. But, far more importantly, they're leveraging what they know you've always wanted and what they've secretly always had the ability to give you. They're using it to get you back NOT so that they can finally start pouring love into your love cup, but so that you will go back to pouring love into theirs.

But that's not the point. The main point is that we believe promises made for tomorrow and forever. We do it because we want that passionate intensity for us that they're now showing. But here's the thing: promises are based fundamentally on trust, which is the very thing they just shattered, whether it be by cheating, betrayal, decades of neglect or self-centeredness, gaslighting, and/or other crud. They're asking you to give them something based on nothing from themselves...except impassioned words. It's a big ask. All parties feel the enormity of the ask.

As if the years you've been doing it already aren't enough, you're once again being asked to give up real estate in the relationship and inside you, when they are really giving up nothing. They are delivering little, if anything, at the time they're pushing you to let them back in. So, despite having all the leverage, you give it up for nothing except high emotion and promises with no guarantees.

Put that way, it seems like a bit of a foolish investment. But, we've all been there and made that investment. We've all let them back or gone back to them because we think we have to keep trying, which is really just a cover for how good the love feels in this rare moment when they actually want us back. And, more often than not, it goes sour because we just handed the power right back to them, which means they have the power to put on a show for a few weeks or months, then slide right back into the comfort of how it used to be.

The only guarantee you have is to watch them, over a good long time, to see if the change is real and increasing. To forgive before that is to act based on some fear inside you of not getting some need/want met. To forgive before that is to not do what's best for you, which is to wait and watch for changed action over time.

Whom have you been forgiving too soon? Whom do you just need to go slowly with? And, more importantly, what's the fear inside you that would cause you to forgive too soon, while caught up in the passion and promises?

Lastly, the real question is: Have YOU changed enough that you can call them out each and every time they might slide back into old patterns, old treatments, and ways that don't feel good? Because ultimately, it doesn't matter if they've changed when you yourself haven't changed enough to hold them accountable for how you want to be treated.

April 25

Part One:
***You are never given a wish without also being given the power to make it
true.
You may have to work for it, however.***
-Richard Bach, American author

When there has been pain in life, particularly in the distant past, so much of life gets spent running. So much of life becomes forcing things to happen, doing anything to keep moving forward, trying to create distance between the tomorrow and the seemingly unshakable pain of what happened in all the yesterdays. When a person is running from the past pain, the will serves as a very powerful engine.

But, the engine ain't the problem. The problem is the GPS. See, in this scenario what's determining the direction of the life of the pained person is the pain. The goal is to create as much separation from it as possible; or to create a life so fast and furious that it numbs the past pain, at least momentarily, again and again; or to create something that will be so big that it makes the pain go away (in theory), or at least seem minuscule. Life is forever spent as a *reaction* to the pain. Thus, the pain is in fact, the GPS, determining the direction of your life, even if only by causing you to run from it.

That's not an authentic – self-authored – life. That's not you running life. It's you being run by a past so scary you just can't stop, no matter how tired you are.

A great many people have the 'work' part of Bach's quote figured out. They know how to work for what they think they want. Where they fail is on the 'wish' part. They think they're working toward their own wishes when they're actually working to stay ahead of the pain. Their own inner GPS got shut down years ago. That's why they may be accomplishing big things, yet feel empty inside. Those particular achievements were never something their truest self ever really wanted. They were chosen by the broken self as a way to fight against the pain of the past, as a way to give them a sense of self-worth.

To find those authentic wishes means to stop running and allow that pain and the BS beliefs you were taught about yourself that are hidden deep inside you to wash over you, to overwhelm you, and to finally begin to flush out of you. The more you flush, the more your own authentic voice begins to rise up from within. Your wishes will begin to surface, as if they've been there the whole time, which of course they have.

Now, it becomes a matter of employing that great willpower in the direction of your native GPS. Now, you've got a wicked combination. Now, you've got the recipe for peace, happiness, and a real sense of fulfilling purpose.

What pains are you still running from? What percentage of the path you're on isn't you, and you know it isn't you, but just a compensation for (or escape from) all the pain? How exhausted are you from a lifetime of running?

April 26

Part Two:

> ### You are never given a wish
> ### without also being given the power to make it true.
> ### You may have to work for it, however.
> -Richard Bach

Ever felt like you had big dreams but lacked the willpower to make them happen?

Unlike the person in Part One (April 25), for you, the struggle in Bach's quote is not the 'wish' part, but the 'work' part. Maybe you know what you wish for, and the first few times you attempt it you start with great gusto, but you peter out 'til eventually you realize you just don't have the power to see it through. Or, you're just so tired from life that you can't scrape yourself off the bed or couch to actually begin anything.

It's not that you don't want to work for it, you just can't find the energy. You're so dead, so unable to get motivated. The inner GPS seems to be working fine, but for some reason, the engine keeps sputtering. Or, you have the 'power' mentioned in the quote. That's the engine, but the gas to fuel the power is non-existent.

If motivation is the problem, either the wish you claim to most want ain't your deepest self talking (but is a reaction voice, as mentioned in Part One), or you've got a 500-pound bag of rocks on your back from all the pain, fears, and BS beliefs you've been taught about yourself in your past. As a result of that bag of rocks, you can't move. Life is just too heavy.

In either case, the problem is the obstruction – the pain, fears, and BS beliefs. These have tightened you, worn you down, bled you dry. Thus, the more of them you get out of you, the physically lighter you become. You actually begin to have more spontaneous energy that requires no conjuring and no willpower to sustain.

No wish can be worked for – no GPS dream can be powered forward by an engine – until the problems causing the shutdown are addressed.

In what areas of your life can you just not seem to get motivated, despite grand wishes and dreams from the GPS of the soul? When do you start doing the ugly work of getting those rocks out of the bag on your back? Or, when do you start doing that in more areas of your life? What is the biggest thing inside that you most fear facing and tangling with in your efforts to finally be free of it? Why do you fear that one most?

April 27

**Opportunities to find deeper powers within ourselves
come when life seems most challenging.**
-Joseph Campbell, American Badass Thinker

So much of life is spent running from the pain, the dark forest, and the hardest, ugliest of times. We self-medicate. We distract ourselves. We stay incessantly busy; all as this grand diversion from being consumed by the call of the soul. And it's all fear.

We get pulled down. Each and every one of us, whether early or late, gets pulled down into the dark forest of the soul to either quit or find the gems of wisdom, cascading waterfalls of insight, and hidden fires of new strength. It's the darkness and ugliness inside us that hold those new powers.

Are you still running and diverting? Has life tripped you or have you been beckoned by your soul, to finally go into the forest? Are you ready to find the new power? Are you ready to face the trials, face the pain, face the mysteries and memories you've kept hidden? Are you ready?

April 28

Only the weak are cruel.
Gentleness can only be expected
from the strong.
-Leo "Dr. Love" Buscaglia,
American author & professor at the University of Southern California

Because of the programming so many of us received in childhood (whether from parents, siblings, bullies, or society), we've gotten lost in the misbegotten belief that gentleness is a mark of weakness, that softness is for the timid, and that toughness is the only way to go through life. To do otherwise, we've been told, is to be vulnerable to attack and to show the world you're not much of anything.

But there's no truth to that. As Buscaglia writes, a person unafraid of how they are perceived will be whomever they damn well feel like being, moment to moment. If they are feeling softness and want to express that, they will, because they fear no repercussions and feel no vulnerability. If they are angry, they will express that, too. To be a badass is to be fully authentic, moment to moment, which includes being soft, kind, gentle, and to express your sadness and share another's pain.

It is the weak one who fears how they will be perceived, fears how they might be taken advantage of, fears, fears, fears. To live forever in those fears and to contort your life to allay or entertain those fears – rather than to live from a sense of centeredness, just being who you are – is to live in a state of perpetual weakness disguised as hardness and toughness.

And, the wise see through the false shell of hardness and cruelty. The wise see the hurting soul inside, even if the hurting person cannot see it themselves.

What is the area of your life where you most fear walking with gentleness? What is it you most fear that keeps you in a false shell, in weakness? What would happen if that thing you fear actually happened? Would you survive and be okay, after you grieved? Worse, what if it never happened, but you spent your life in fear that it would? Do you desire to walk through life with gentleness and generosity of spirit? Do you have the courage to do it, trusting that if something happens you can adjust, learn, and move on?

April 29

> **If people knew how hard I had to work to gain my mastery,**
> **it would not seem so wonderful, at all.**
> -Michelangelo, Italian sculptor & painter

By age 45, I had:

- Two divorces
- Written five books (four published) that few people read
- Two estranged children (to differing degrees)
- Been thrown out of Lutheran ministry as a pastor three times for my books and theology, my stance on gay rights, and a personality they felt was too "intensely passionate"
- Worked a million jobs that I made the best of but weren't my calling
- Lived in my car, while writing and ministering to the unseen and others in need
- Given up my life possessions and drained what little money I had to minister to the homeless on the streets of Oakland and Berkeley, CA, while sleeping on concrete every night for 2 ½ years, and
- Streaked buck naked across the Oakland Coliseum in the top of the 9th (A's vs Red Sox), September 1999 (just four months after graduating from seminary), for which I made $500.

Now, the last entry really has nothing to do with the larger point I'm about to make, but it's one of the few things I'm actually proud of in my life just because, even now, it's so damn funny.

45 and no real success. 45 and so much pride had been stripped from me as I watched pretty much every person I knew from back in the day celebrate many successes. I still had a sliver of longing for success, but I had also let go of it, an oddly joyful thing to do. I'd finally grown content in the path I had chosen back in my 20s when I got off the wheel of others' expectations. Back then, I knew what I wanted to do: speak, write, and counsel. Those were the three things that made me happiest. Those were the only things that took away the ridiculousness of listening to others and gave me inner peace and the thrill of *ALIVENESS*. So I just started doing them, damn the cost.

That meant letting go of my pride, as well as what others thought of me – old classmates, siblings, parents, my own kids and exes, society. That's no small task. But, hell, I have come this far, so let's see where it leads.

It took 20 years of toiling in obscurity, in the grit and joy of doing precisely what I loved, even if I had no idea where it was going; even if it came with no money, no fame, no recognition, just my own peace and the respect of the few people who really got what I was about.

Then it began. Over the next ten years, a great relationship with a wonderful woman blossomed. Renewed life and laughter with my children began. There stirred a brick by brick, slow growth of small successes, then medium, and then hints and hints of the approach of a critical mass. Then explosions came (the good kind), by age 55. It came 30+ years after the humiliation and stripping of pride, and came only as a result of grit and my belief in my own authenticity and need to just be me.

30 doggone years! And, no one helped my career, not to any sizable degree. I did it myself when no one believed in, or much understood, what I was doing and what I was about (at times, even I didn't). The successes now are funny, pleasant, huge, and unnecessary, but delightful.

So, how long can you wait and work – without success – for what you believe in? How hungry are you to just be freaking you? Can you endure being misunderstood and being thought foolish?

April 30

If you're ever trying to figure out why someone (or yourself)
is doing something that doesn't make sense,
always ask yourself the question,
"What's the primary fear driving the behavior?"
Then speculate the possible answers,
and go with the biggest, hairiest, scariest one.
-Sven

Everything is fear. Every aspiration and motivation is fear.

It may be love, too. It may be inspiration. But always, at the primal root of human existence and decisions, is visceral fear. Dig down to and name that fear and you begin to achieve your true power; you can move people, move yourself, move the proverbial mountains, and do so rather quickly. Anything else that omits the fear in the equation is a half-solution, based on a half-baked misunderstanding of the true problem.

Far more often than not, the real fear driving the equation of people's actions (or inactions), is the fear of getting emotionally hurt, fear of hurting someone else, or fear of how they will be perceived. Never, ever underestimate the power of that last one. In fact, few things have greater power to short-circuit an authentic life and grand aspirations than fear of what others will think. Name that greatest 'other' and what that one person could say that you most fear, and you've just short-circuited, in the mere naming, a thousand pounds of pressure bearing down on your soul.

Someone has power over you, to some greater or lesser degree. You fear that person – their words, their silence, their scorn, their disappointment. And so you either stand inert or move to their tune.

Done yet? Seeing whose song is your soundtrack, are you okay with that? What would it take for you to finally walk away to live your own life without fearing them?

Who is the person? What is the one sentence you most fear them saying to you or thinking about you? Name it!

May

May 1

Do not ask your children to strive for extraordinary lives.
Such striving may seem admirable, but it is the way of foolishness.
Help them instead to find the wonder and the marvel of an ordinary life.
Show them the joy of tasting tomatoes, apples, and pears.
Show them how to cry when pets and people die.
Show them the infinite pleasure in the touch of a hand.
And make the ordinary come alive for them.
The extraordinary will take care of itself.
-William Martin, American author of *The Parent's Tao Te Ching*

Very often in life, those who push themselves to the detriment of their own health, their relationships, and their sanity, are those who are least able to enjoy the ordinary, to truly savor it for the beauty and joy it holds. So, they stir and run, agitate and accelerate. They can't bear to slow down. They can't bear death or aloneness, can't bear the simplicities of life, can't bear stillness.

Yet, it is precisely when we can be still and alone, when we can look at our fears and at death and no longer run, when we can drink in the majesty of a glorious, simple day that we are no longer building a life based on running and fear, but built on the joy of the journey. And it is on that path that the greatest successes and moments emerge.

What percent do you have the true ability to savor the simple, and what percent do you fear it or can't slow down enough for it? 30%, 70%? 85%, 15%?

What percent do you fear being alone, and what percent do you enjoy it?

What percent is stillness your default, and what percent is busyness?

What are you teaching your children?

May 2

Naming the beast is half the problem.
-Charlotte E. Erlandson, American writer, graduate professor, mother of six

Are you able to name what you feel? At any given moment, do you have the ability to step out of your head and into your body, and simply choose a word for how you feel: cold, sad, angry, excited, disappointed, suffocated, peaceful?

To be able to go deeper and deeper inside yourself and be able to pull out that which no longer serves you and no longer feels good (if it ever did), means having the ability to simply start by naming how you feel, right now. "I feel..." Do it in your journaling. Practice it quietly in your head when you're at the grocer or at work or on your way home. What do I honestly feel, right this moment? If you come up with an answer like good, fine, weird, or some word that really doesn't say much, challenge yourself to go deeper; for example, "Well, what does 'good' mean, in this case?" Then choose different feeling words. Or, "When I say weird, in this case, what would be another feeling word or two to describe it?" Then write it out.

The second step is to explore options in your journaling for *why* you feel that way. "I feel this way because..." And often, we don't know right away. We have to write out many possibilities before we can then sort of feeeel which one seems like the biggest right now, in our gut, or on our skin, or in our energy. What's the origin of the feeling? What triggered it? When did this feeling start? Then, journal about the *why*. Dive deeper into the origin and events that gave birth to this feeling, now.

The more adept you become at naming your feelings with a good measure of specificity, the better able you are to explore further into your past. You'll be able to name feelings you remember, events from your past and how they made you feel, time periods that stick out in your memory for reasons you've never been able to put your finger on, but now you can detect what the feeling is that goes with it and can likely isolate the event that birthed it.

Now you're into the work of mining your past for hurt and memories that you can heal, often just by naming and then allowing the authentic feelings to come out.

Fast forward to the present, instead of waiting for someone else to validate my feelings, I can validate them for myself by merely naming them, in each moment, especially when something doesn't feel right or good. That is a statement of mattering, an act of self-worth. But also, by being more conscious of and able to name my feelings specifically, I become more present to myself in relationships. I am more equipped to make relationships that meet my deeper needs, which means I am creating happier relationships, because I can name when/why I'm not.

Which feelings are you good at naming specifically? Which family of feelings are more of a struggle for you? Challenge yourself to get as specific as you can about your feelings in each moment. Validate yourself by validating the feeling; do this by giving it a name, an exact one.

May 3

We must let go of the life we have planned,
so as to accept the one that is waiting for us.
-Joseph Campbell, brilliant scholar
and author of the *Power of Myth* book/PBS interviews

That really is the inflection point, isn't it, the letting go of the life we have planned? We each long for the grand life waiting for us, but to let go of the life we have planned is a completely different animal. It's a big ask, not to mention the rather disconcerting fact that the life that is waiting for us might be quite different from the one we have planned.

Yet, if there's one thing I've learned over 30 years of counseling others, as well as my own journey to let go of that which I wanted most, the universe always – as in, invariably – has a bigger imagination than I do. Or, call it your own soul. That deepest depth, that source energy inside you sees a life that your supposedly high-functioning brain simply cannot see, in no small part because the soul interweaves all the unforeseen logic that foresight cannot yet weave.

The smartest path to colossal *ALIVENESS* and greatest authenticity is to allow room for the breathing, in and out, of the breath of the gods into your plans, sometimes destroying them completely, only to rebuild them in ways you'd never imagine, ways infinitely more enjoyable and fulfilling in the long run.

So, it is not just about letting go of the life you've had planned, but also trusting that what is to come will exceed even your wildest, maddest dreams.

Do you have the ability to trust in that which you cannot see or predict? Ah, now there's where the great separate themselves from the peloton. (Oh and by the way, that choosing to trust is not a once-and-for-all. It's a daily re-trusting, re-orienting and letting go along with the spirit of the universe itself, as well as to the movements and orchestrations of your own soul.)

May 4

When work becomes play,
and play becomes your work,
your life unfolds.
-Robert Frost, American poet

One of the most frustrating parts of having the father I did was that he was an incorrigible contrarian. He would incessantly take the opposite position, not just to frustrate us but to help us see there was wisdom in the opposite path or argument. It drove me nuts. But, he was pretty much always right that there was truth in the other way. And it just tickled the heck out of him to bend my thinking.

Thing is, now I do the same thing. I love needling people. I love turning people's thinking upside-down, not in an argumentative way but by posing questions that completely change how they look at the entire equation of what we might be discussing. I've made a healthy living doing precisely that, and changing lives by doing so. My books, counseling, social media presence, the podcast success – all of it is play for me. I'm just having fun being me. There isn't a day where it's work for me, none of it, except the occasional paperwork. I work my heinie off at it, but it's total play.

Is your life play? Is it becoming more and more so, at least? Or, have you resigned yourself to drudgery? Why? What would need to happen to finally give yourself permission to reclaim your life? Or, are you waiting for some other person to give you permission to run your life more your way, so that it might become play for you? Or, what could you change to make it simply *more* play, even if it's not completely so? What needs to be deleted or added?

May 5

*There are two great days in a person's life -
the day we are born and
the day we discover why.*
-William Barclay, Scottish writer

In that wonderful classic American baseball movie, *The Natural,* the character played by Glenn Close says to Robert Redford's ball-playing character, "I believe we have two lives – the life we learn with and the life we live with after that."

The march toward self-discovery – or finding your 'why' – is not inevitable. It is less something that happens and more something we choose. It's born out of a sense of absence, or discomfort, in the me I've always been. It grows out of unshakable unrest. It is a process of continually sloughing off the old skins in different sectors of one's life until there is a skin that you do not need to let go of.

This is the finding of the sense of self. This is the knowledge of the truths inside one's own depths. This is where the 'why' is found. Rare is the person who knows, definitively, their 'why' at a young age. Or, perhaps, a great many know it at a very young age, but the 'shoulds' and 'thou shalts' and misbegotten beliefs that get pressed into them by largely well-meaning adults silence that sense of purpose. Perhaps, we all know the general 'why' at a young age (even if not the specific nature of it), but lack the agency, the fortitude, the knowledge, and the strength to bring it to fruition. And so, we must learn first, which requires unlearning, or the long process of shedding the not-me.

What is your 'why'? Or, what is the 'why' you've been living; and what is your real, deeper one? What is not your 'why'? What never was *your* 'why'? Who put a 'why' on you that never fit, despite your best efforts? What would it take for you to finally shed those constricting former beliefs?

May 6

Praise in public,
punish in private.

How much of your leadership, whether in business, sports, parenting, or side pursuits, is not what it could be, simply because you're missing the nuances of leading people?

When and where to punish and praise are just a few of those nuances. One of the real ways to lead people, to get the most out of people, to help people unleash their greatness, is to see yourself in them. Specifically, it is to be so well-attuned to what feels good to you and what doesn't that you can tap into that knowledge and overlay it onto your interactions with others. For example, it is to truly understand the humiliation of being scolded publicly versus being taught privately how what I'm doing isn't working, isn't allowed, and can be changed into this over here, instead.

To lead others is to understand others, which requires knowing and understanding yourself, at least to some degree.

Secondly, it requires a shift from all answers to far more questions from you. It means to engage by listening and being present to the responder and their responses. By listening more we become more human, more calm. We attack less, blame less. We largely remove fear from the equation of leadership. To motivate and lead means, first and foremost, to understand. How can you do that if you're not listening? This does not mean that you always act on their input, but sometimes you will because you realize the brilliance of it and the need for it.

So, then, the question becomes: How well do you know yourself and what motivates and demotivates you? How tuned-in are you to who this other person really is and the nuances of their needs? Could you be asking more questions and engaging your subordinates? Or, is it possible that the ability to read people (and what they want), that was baked into you as a young people-pleaser is, in fact, a great gift when it comes to leading, at least as long as it's accompanied by the willingness to make the hard decisions and have people not like you, at times, for those decisions?

What's the next step you can take in upping your leadership game, in terms of better understanding people? And, do you operate from a place of compassion and desiring to understand, or from a place of doing without feeling? Is that working?

May 7

Music can name the unnameable and communicate the unknowable.
-Leonard Bernstein, 20th Century American Conductor

There are few things in life that more powerfully speak to our soul and name the unnameable than music. There is a universality to the medium.

What was the music that got you through a hard time, that gave words you never had to the experience you were then having? Or, perhaps it is now that you need those words, that harmony, that lovely tune, the trill, the descant, the ostinato, the bridge, the riff, that opening, those insanely powerful lyrics? Whatever it may be, can you identify the music that has spoken, or is presently speaking, to the longings and pains of your soul? If so, what are the threads in that music? What are the truths and words that music is naming?

Conversely, what are the experiences you still haven't found a word or tune for? What is it you still seek understanding of? And, is it possible that you're looking in the wrong place? Is it possible you need to be feeling and truly hearing the music that speaks to your soul to find your answers?

Do you now begin to understand the importance of the musician, the singer, and the poet?

May 8

Judge a man by his questions
rather than his answers.
-Voltaire, French writer

It's a pretty universal human desire to be liked. In that vein, one of the most common themes within that truth is that nobody likes someone who talks too much, who has an opinion on everything, or who comes off as a know-it-all. If you want to drive people away and be friendless, do that.

Do you speak more in statements or in questions? Do you talk more or listen more? Do you realize that the truly knowledgeable and wise people often say the least? Do you cede the floor to others, or are you ever in a grab to get the microphone, the spotlight, and the attention? Has it occurred to you that you're driving people away from you because you're so desperate to fill your love cup by stealing attention? Has it occurred to you that your area of greatest growth is to fill your love cup on your time, so that you're not trying to use others to get it filled, thereby always driving them away from you, creating the very loneliness you can't bear the thought of?

Or, on the flip side, are you the person who is hiding by letting others talk all the time? Has it occurred to you that, perhaps, the reason you want others to talk is because you're ashamed of who you are and don't want to be seen? Sure, some may see you as enigmatic and intriguing, but deep down they may speculate that your silence is a lack of pride or self-confidence, rooted in the belief you've been taught that you're stinky, no good, ugly, dumb, fat, skinny, worthless, hopeless?

Has it occurred to you that your unwillingness to open up is the point of your greatest growth, if you have the courage to do the work of identifying the origins of that self-loathing?

May 9

There comes a time in your life when you have to choose
to turn the page, write another book, or simply close it.
-Shannon L. Alder, Inspirational writer

Then I discovered that being related is no guarantee of love!
-Stieg Larsson, Swedish author, *The Girl with the Dragon Tattoo*

What's the myth in your family, either the one you came from or the one you created – and what does it say about whose feelings are most important? How much of your life have you spent and continue to spend making someone else's agenda, needs, wants, feelings, and story infinitely more important than your own, thereby implicitly stating "I don't matter"? Is the family myth that you've been living capable of standing up to critical analysis – if you were to see your story from an outsider's perspective, would you continue to believe so wholeheartedly in the story?

Is it possible that at the root of all of your frustration, pain, anxiety, depression, madness, lack of motivation, absence of career success, and inability to move forward in life is the desire to not shatter the myth and, thus, not hurt a certain person, not incur their wrath, not admit who they really are, or not turn away from trying to win their affirmation?

For Pete's sake, how bad does life have to get before you begin to admit that the origin story of your life doesn't work, and never really did? Does it strike you as odd that you were conditioned to see some people as more important than you? It is precisely that belief that keeps you locked in a myth. Do you see the inherent selfishness in that act? Why is it that you still continue to protect your family at the expense of yourself? And, has it occurred to you that now that you're aware you're doing it, you're the one actually perpetuating the myth, you're the one shouting to the heavens, "I DON'T MATTER"?

You okay with that???

May 10

> *Don't let the noise of others' opinions*
> *drown out your own inner voice.*
> -Steve Jobs, American innovator

In any creative or bold endeavor the element most likely to hold back or derail plans is the doubt ringing inside the mind of the doer. Yet, doubt is invariably caused by the influence of external voices, past and/or present. This is what causes us to distrust, or not fully embrace and execute, our own inner voice. We listen to the voices of others rather than our own. Almost without exception, it's because we've been conditioned by external forces, often parents, to powerfully believe that our own voice either doesn't matter or isn't nearly as important as those closest to us.

So, we pull back at often the most critical moments. We hedge our bets. We seldom dive in with both feet. We don't trust ourselves, generally because we fear their retribution, scorn, "Dummy!" or "I told you so," if things go south.

So, what about you? When do you most pull back from trusting your own instincts, intuition, or passion? What is the big fear that causes you to not put yourself fully out there, as you most want to? Are you tired of holding back yet? Lastly, whose voice is it that you most fear that causes you to pull back from flying at full wingspan? What would it look like to fly at full wingspan? What does your dream look like? When do you finally just say, "Screw it," and go for it?!

May 11

"Y'KNOW WHAT YOUR PROBLEM IS??!"
-Them

We've all had those words shouted at or spoken to us, either at one point or twenty, in our lives. We've all felt the attack of those words, regardless of the inevitable further explanation that followed it. For, they're stating clearly that there *is* something wrong with *you*, not them....*you*. That is the problem.

Your problem is that you actually believe you have a problem. You've been taught in your life to believe that you *are*, in fact, the problem. But, the problem with that belief is that there was never anything wrong with you to begin with. No child comes out of the womb flawed; each is beautiful and good in its own way. You didn't come out of the womb hating yourself, criticizing yourself, fearful of the world, convinced you were the problem. Nah, you were taught a lie; that something is wrong with you, that you are wrong in your essence. Your core beliefs have always been that you're the problem, which has been quite convenient for the person(s) teaching you this, as it enabled them to keep the focus off themselves and their own failings.

Everything is core beliefs. Change that core stuff and everything changes in the behaviors that inevitably flow out of core beliefs.

So now, in your journaling, list each person in your past and present who has established, contributed to, or reinforced your belief that you have a problem or are the problem. Next to each person's name, list the specific phrases or messages they spoke to you that conveyed this message.

Or, maybe it wasn't conveyed with words, but with a look, an attitude, a guffaw, questions, opportunities withheld, no's, withholding of love, distance, absence, or some other way.

Now, list next to each of those names and statements how each one made you feel. Next, write down each of the feelings you are feeling right now, large or small, as you think about each of these people, events, and accompanying feelings.

If you want to go further into flushing these out, write a letter or email (THAT YOU DO NOT SEND!) to each of these people, expressing in the strongest terms possible precisely how you feel. Don't be afraid to curse in the letters. If it's a mix of love and hate, let it all out. This is good!

Which of these people are still in your life? Is it time to start cutting them out of your life, or at least start radically cutting back their influence and impact on your life – stop answering calls (or answering so quickly), stop engaging in text fights, stop going to family events? Are you ready? Do you have the courage to do so? Can you see the need for doing so? Do you see that honoring self requires distancing yourself from those who do not honor you, and that this is where it starts?

May 12

> ### *This life. This night. Your story. Your pain. Your hope.*
> ### *It matters. All of it matters.*
> - Jamie Tworkowski, American author

An old college friend reached out to me, indicating he was in my area on business and wanted to stop by one evening to say 'hello.' I happened to be having a fire in the outdoor pit that autumn night. So we talked over wine and flames. It was lovely.

He shared with me a story I've heard far too often. Recently, he had checked into the emergency room in his southern city, more than once, actually, because he was suicidal. No one knew. The pressures of a mentally sick daughter living at home for the last two years had become too much. He was never able to sleep and felt constantly antagonized by his daughter. The guilt and self-loathing, the fear and hopelessness as he considered that his daughter refused medication but could not function on her own out in the world without it. All of it had become too much.

We talked well into the night, him alternating between tears, rage, fatigue, a bit of laughter, and a whole lot of pain.

Whether under these circumstances or some totally different, have you ever been so overwhelmed by life for so long that it just became way too much, taking you to the point of suicide, or at least to the point of seriously considering it?

I was. For 12 years. I'll tell you what I know. I finally realized that I wanted to live. And, the path from that realization and the psych ward for a two-day stay afterward to the point of finally becoming truly happy and feeling a real sense of purpose and aliveness required two things above all else.

One, it demanded continually flushing out all of the pain, fears, and BS beliefs I had been taught about myself. It took years, day in and day out, and I had no counseling that could really help me. So I did it alone through incessant journaling, constantly going into the pain, constantly flushing it out. And reading lots of books for new insights.

Two, a massively changed life required different decisions, rejecting that which was not me, actively choosing those paths, plans, purposes, and people that gave me energy. And, in the process I lost a lot of people, a lot of respect, and a lot of support. But I kept on my path because I knew it was slowly working and I knew it was *my* path, which I had no choice but to embark upon if I truly wanted not only to live, but to know true ALIVENESS!

It worked. And, because I had to go it alone, I am now able to help others navigate those areas of the dark forest of life. My old friend stayed in touch with me after that night by the fire. He lived one more day, then woke up the next day and decided to live one more day, committing to journaling and counseling, then one more day, and onward, 'til over time he became lighter and more able to make hard decisions he couldn't have before. He changed his living situation and his life. Joy began to return to his life – a sweeter, deeper joy.

So, what's the point? Get the pain out! Don't do it alone. You can, but it's much harder and takes much longer. There is new life on the other side of flushing out all of the pain, fears, and BS beliefs you've been taught about yourself. Get counseling. Find a suicide support group, too. Keep flushing.

Are you ready to begin the journey to healing and new life?

May 13

Do what you feel in your heart to be right – for you'll be criticized anyway.
-Eleanor Roosevelt, Former 1st Lady of the U.S.

One thing that people don't understand about bold leaders, great thinkers, and free spirits is that for as original, fearless, and uniquely authentic they are, even they bump against the occasional boundary or rule, whereupon they ask themselves, "Oh man, should I do this? There's gonna be serious blowback if I do."

But, if you've been doing this whole thing of living boldly and authentically long enough, you've come to see, again and again, that there's always going to be someone to hammer you, no matter what path you choose. And, often the one hammering us the most if we don't do it, is our own damn self that forever wishes we had. So, powering forward demands a sort of "Screw it!" mentality. Sometimes, it can even be a bit ticklish to know you're going to be tweaking some folks by your real stuff.

What's your heart calling you to? Come on, go for it! Stop living small.

May 14

In every generation, people resist new ideas.
What are you resisting today?
-Sukant Ratnakar, Author and management consultant

As I sit here writing outside of my favorite coffee shop, I see kids coming and going, some of them in their pajamas, even teens. I've never been a fan of that. Similarly, I was not a fan when fashion (in the form of my young son decades ago), told me I needed to start untucking my shirts; not easy to do for a moderately well-behaved, clean cut kid from the 70s. Nor did I understand it when we all decided to start wearing black socks with tennies, precisely as the old, out-of-touch men who raised us in the 70s would do.

Yes, change can suck or just plain make no sense at all. It's easy, at times, to turn into a crusty old guy, just like all those old dudes when we were kids. It's easy to stomp our feet and complain. It's easy to become just like previous generations. Different battles, same war.

Or, we can stop being crusty and, even if we don't embrace those changes ourselves, roll with it. We can be not only more tolerant, but accepting. Yes, I hate the over-informality of pajamas. But, heck, score one for free spirits! Yes, at times, I even wear dark socks with white shoes. (Maybe those unfashionable old guys in the 70s were not out-of-touch, but decades ahead of their time!)

So, what are you crusty about? Are there opportunities to start letting go of some of the orneriness? Do you realize that your angry diatribes or even your subtle dislikes are robbing you of happiness just as much as they're increasing the clouds of unhappiness that swirl over all of our collective lives together? You're choosing to rob yourself of happiness. You good with that? What discontent do you need to most let go of, or at least try to find some good in?

May 15

No person is your friend who demands your silence,
or denies your right to grow.
-Alice Walker, American novelist

Have you ever given deliberate thought to what you want and need in a friend? I think it's reasonable to assert that not only have all of us done this, but that this very thing starts early in childhood and continues right up through all adulthood.

The somewhat thornier question is, after giving thought to your needs and wants in friends, do you then require, even insist, that those needs be met? Do you speak your needs and persist in friendships, even despite disappointment, backlash, or the threat of losing that friend? Or do you back down and squelch your wants and needs?

This then yields the subsequent question, if you back down from expressing your feelings, wants, and needs, do you simultaneously back down in more high-intensity times when you *really* need them and they fail to come through. Or do you not feel justified expressing your hurt and disappointment in those situations? Didn't you set up that big disappointment by not insisting your needs be met in smaller, seemingly less-consequential situations?

Or, are you the opposite – you feel justified to stand up for your wants and needs only when they're huge, but not when they're small or medium?

Truth is, unless you're willing to lose a friend over standing up for your wants, you're likely already backing down from and minimizing them. You're already choosing someone else's value over your own, just as you've likely been conditioned to do your entire life. And, you'll likely keep doing so until the pain gets bad enough.

How much unhappiness and discontent do you have to endure in your life before you finally start speaking up for what you want, need, and feel, especially in friendships? Or, when do you start creating new friendships with people who are delighted to bring the forms of goodness you seek in a friend, and vice versa?

May 16

Pain serves a purpose.
Without it you are in danger.
What you cannot feel
you cannot take care of.
-Rebecca Solnit, American writer

One of the more interesting phenomena I have seen over 30 years of counseling, has been talking with a client who has been treated poorly by someone they either love or greatly look up to. The particularly fascinating part is that those instances of greatly disappointing or hurtful actions by the other person are often followed by more and greater actions of hurt towards my client. It's as if everything is being brought to a head, heightened in intensity, being made to happen as such by fate.

Invariably, the question I ask of clients who experience this doubling down, or quadrupling down by the other (sometimes to levels my client might never have expected or foreseen), is, "Is it possible it had to finally get this extremely bad for you to see it clearly?"

"See what clearly, Sven," they ask.

"See how little they regard you, how little they give a crap! You had to feeeel so severely the pain of their indifference before you would ever believe it real. Is it possible that the extraordinary pain they've caused you is precisely what you needed in order for you to finally set yourself free of the very thing you thought you wanted most – a relationship with them, be it personal or professional? Is it possible that you removing them from your life is precisely what your deepest soul is most longing for and calling you to do, because your attachment to them will only hold you back from your greatness and highest happiness in the future?"

Is it possible your pain getting greater is precisely the yank you needed from your old life and old ways of believing about yourself? Just like the body reveals what needs healing by creating pain there, is it possible that you needed to get hurt so badly in order to finally feel again, really feel what hurts you and needs healing, and in so doing make your healing a priority? In your journaling are you asking your pain all that it is trying to reveal to you, teach you, lead you to, and set you free from? What is the path or who is the person your pain is trying to break your grip on? Is it possible the breaking of your grip is the greatest thing that could ever happen to you, despite how painful it feels now?

May 17

> *The gifted man bears his gifts into the world,*
> *not for his own benefit,*
> *but for the people among whom he is placed;*
> *for the gifts are not his.*
> *He himself is a gift to the community.*
> -Henry Ford, American innovator/carmaker

It's really a kick in the butt – that quote – isn't it? It turns on its head what the American spirit has devolved into over the decades. Back then, generosity of spirit still governed even the most successful of the most successful. I believe we're slowly regaining that. As generational mistakes roll by and we learn and grow from them, we rediscover the value in giving, rather than just solely taking; the nobility of it; the responsibility of it; the joy of it.

Who are you called to give your gifts to? Who are the people among whom you've been placed, or perhaps called by your soul to bring your gifts to next? What are the gifts you bring to humanity? Do you have the ability to hold both the pursuits of your own joy and passion, as well as the uplifting of those among whom you've been placed by life itself? Do you have the courage to bear and deliver them boldly, so that others might live and thrive in their pursuits and in their souls?

May 18

Build me a son, O Lord,
who will be strong enough to know when he is weak,
and brave enough to face himself when he is afraid,
one who will be proud and unbending in honest defeat,
and humble and gentle in victory.
-General Douglas MacArthur, American commander in WWII

How many men do you know who embody that WWII-vintage ethos of one of America's most iconic leaders?

This was no brute, no cocky 'just-be-tough-all-the-time' caricature of a man. This was a man embodying both the necessary ugliness of war and the graces of a gentleman. He bore the courage (and prayed for a son of similar bearing), to be soft and kind, not just tough and hardass all the time (though he could be that, too). And, it is precisely that embodiment of all of it that makes a badass! That is real manhood.

If you're a man, do you have the willingness to admit weakness, to concede defeat, to be silent when you know you don't know, to cede ground to the real leader in the situation where you know you aren't? Is gentleness a tool in your belt that you've mastered? If you're a young man, are you following the wrong men for inspiration? Have you been tricked into believing that never admitting one's faults is the only way to victory? Are you man enough to be humble, generous in spirit, gracious and soft? Or are you just a dick?

If you're a woman, how much of your perception of men or interest in men, whether as friends, colleagues, family members, or lovers is colored by notions of manhood that you did not write, that were pressed upon you? How uncomfortable are you with a man who lives outside of the boundaries of manhood definitions that you've bought into for a long time? Do you have a need for men in your life to be/not be these previous definitions? Why?

May 19

> *If your actions create a legacy that inspires others*
> *to dream more, learn more, do more, and become more,*
> *then you are an excellent leader!*
> -Dolly Parton, Iconic American entertainer

What's most fascinating about this quote from Dolly is the repetition of the word 'more.' Implicit in that word is that what is, right now, is not enough. It implies that native to the human soul is a longing for expansion, for growth, for movement outside of the self as it sits right now.

Thus, really what she's saying is that great leadership is about pulling people out of themselves, or where they're at. It's creating safety outside of themselves, out into which they feel safe to embark. This implies that for many people the world outside of themselves is frightening. They've been scared into reclusion in their own little turtle shell life. The excellent leader coaxes them out of that shell, pushing back the naysaying voices that drove them into it, giving them belief in the power within and expansion of their wings.

So, great leadership is not just about exciting people for what can be, but "inspiring" them – i.e. lighting the fires of the inner spirit and stoking those fires to the point where they burn brighter than the forces that drove them into the shell. It is about creating safety by pushing back the other voices, creating room and oxygen for those inner fires.

Who has lit your fires in life? Are you living outside of your shell? Whose fires do you light? Are you creating safety outside their shells, so that they can feel comfortable stepping out and opening their wings after far too long, perhaps even flying away from you? Be that gift to humanity. Be that excellent leader!

May 20

You have enemies?
Good.
That means you've stood up for something, sometime in your life.
-Winston Churchill, British Prime Minister during WWII

That really says it all, doesn't it? It explains why, so often in life, we actually *don't* stand up, *don't* speak out, *don't* look the bully in the eye, *don't* express our truths, *don't* get caught up in a new dream or vision, *don't* pursue a new passion. We're terrified of what others will think, terrified of criticism, terrified of making enemies, terrified of not being liked.

So, we stay in the safety of our own little bubble.

Thus, life then boils down to the simple question of which you value more: a life of safety or a life of inspired action, rooted in strong belief, willing to live honorably and willing to be unliked or thought foolish? That latter is a big ask, to which a great many in history and today answer a resounding 'No!'

This is why we still venerate people who have the courage to be unliked, make enemies, or be thought foolish. It's because they show themselves as better than the rest of us, willing to be criticized, at times, for the greater good, willing to stand up and not sit down.

So, for what reason are you willing to make enemies? What idea inspires you, what passion, what purpose, what pain of others, what impossible path draws you down it?

Are you willing to go?

Moreover, are you finally eager to go, after a lifetime of living safely inside your shell, bored as heck?

Why, or why not?

May 21

*I think everybody should get rich and famous
and do everything they ever dreamed of,
so they can see that it's not the answer.*
-Jim Carrey, American actor

Here's an odd question for you: What percentage of your belief system is filled with the belief that if you get a lot of money, *then* you'll be happy? Is it 80%? Or, if you prefer, what percentage of your beliefs are rooted in the notion that the rich and/or famous don't have serious problems? 43%? How powerful is that belief, or a similar belief, in how you look at life?

Well, I hate to be the bearer of bad news for your belief system, but when it comes to the deepest problems of life, money offers no exemption. Money can buy you swankier clothes and supposedly better food, and certainly a bigger house, or more of them. But, it solves exactly zero when it comes to the pain of the soul. In fact, it has the capacity to actually heighten that pain because it can mask it, numb it, or create guilt over even having the pain in the first place (because "Hey, you got money. You don't have problems!"). Thus, it never gets solved.

Having counseled extremely wealthy people, including billionaires and extremely powerful and famous people, I know this to be fact. Having lived among and counseled countless homeless individuals, I know this to be fact. Having listened to the tears and pain of the middle class, I know this to be fact.

The greatest pain, suffering, disappointments, hardships, and sorrows are those that are inside us. Anyone can go in and heal, rich or poor. Every one of us must do this, when we are ready. There is no life, no lasting joy, and definitely no peace until we go inside and begin to flush it all out. When you're ready, you'll know. There's no need to force it. When it is time, the courage will come.

May 22

*The desire for safety
stands against every great and noble enterprise.*
-Marcus Claudius Tacitus, Roman Emperor

We so desperately cling in life to that which is secure, to that which is familiar. We subconsciously base new relationships upon what is familiar about love in our childhood. We stay in careers that have a guaranteed paycheck even when our heart died for it long ago and that same heart longs to go a completely different direction. We allow family members to continue to be mean or indifferent towards us because we cannot imagine the idea of living outside of the mental comfort of believing we have a family that loves and supports us, even if it's just an illusion. We stay in relationships that have long exceeded their "Sell-by date," because it's secure, safe, and familiar, even if it's utterly life-sucking.

It's like we're on a sinking ship. We cling to the mast of the ship even though there's a hole in the hull; it's sinking; and it's hauling manure and reeks to high heaven. We do so because we are terrified of jumping in and learning to tread water and even to swim.

But eventually, the pain of clinging to security breaks our grip on the secure. Eventually, our own soul makes things so bad that we finally have the courage, born of exasperation, exhaustion, and even rage, to walk away. That is when life begins.

That is when we finally begin our journey toward building great and noble lives, or at least happy ones in which we finally have some inner peace and a true sense of fulfillment.

What are the securities, even if they're false or illusive, that you cling to? What is the fear driving the clinging? What are the "great and noble enterprises" that your heart longs to endeavor, either personally, professionally, or both? Why those?

May 23

Some people feel the rain.
Others just get wet.
-Bob Dylan, American songwriter and Nobel Laureate

Let's be honest, a whole lot of time for a whole lot of people rain sucks. You gotta drive in it, walk in it, get soaked and cold. Then you gotta take off your wet clothes and take a hot shower to warm back up. If you just got your hair done or just washed your car and it rains, you're screwed. Even farmers and ranchers who often love rain can loathe it when it comes at the wrong times or there's too much of it. It can kill crops and impede harvesting and planting. Rain can really suck.

And yet, it's no great revelation to say that we need rain. *Need*. As in, life cannot exist without it. The crops need it. Gardens need it. Trees and grass, animals, reservoirs, and more all need it.

And then, there are those times too rare when we neither need it or loathe it, we just feel it. We allow it to be what it is – another part of human existence, to be felt, to be experienced, just as Dylan is saying in the quote. Ever been inside a tent in the woods in the morning with no agenda for the day and the rain patters on the canopy of your tent? When my siblings and I were kids and would have summer vacation at our Uncle Bob's cabin, we'd go outside in our swim trunks when it was raining and splash around in the mud before jumping in the lake.

Nearly everything in life is both needed and loathed, depending on circumstances...and it's there to just be experienced, to be felt. But we get so caught up in judgments of good and evil, happy and depressing, that we forget to feel it, pain and pleasure alike. Even feelings themselves; we don't feel them, we deny or suppress them rather than allowing them to come, flow through us, and flow out of us.

What is it that you're quickly categorizing, putting either in Column Good or Column Bad, forgetting or ignoring the third column of simply experiencing that which is? What is it you're missing the chance to simply accept, for this moment? There is something pleasant and healing to accepting and experiencing. Can you slow down for a moment and withhold judgment? Can you just feeeeel for a moment? Can you let it flow through you and out of you, rather than either resisting it or trying to hold on to it and not let it pass? Can you allow life to come and go as it will?

May 24

> *Sven, I'm now far more vulnerable*
> *in my close relationships and with my employees.*
> *But, I feel far less vulnerable.*
> -Jesse, client, 2022

How can that be? First off, how can someone willingly choose to be *more* vulnerable with others? It's too scary to consider, isn't it? That alone is a triumph. It implies a fearlessness inside. It implies a comfort, a confidence, an 'I'll-be-okay' mentality. But to, secondly, feel *less* vulnerable is mind-boggling. How can that even be?

This is the result of doing the inner work you keep hearing me push you about. When you have cleared out more of the fears, pain, and BS beliefs you've been taught about yourself, when you've spelunked the caves of your inner self to find the reasons for your misery, when you've faced the truths of your past and passed through the pain that came with them (the very pain you've been running from your whole life), when you've jackhammered away all the cement that got poured over the bedrock of your soul and got written into with deafeningly destructive messages, you find what is really down there........you touch the ocean bed of your soul.

THAT!

JUST THAT!

THAT is the essence of all life, where your own authenticity becomes indistinguishable from the voice of the gods, God, the universe, a Higher Power.

That is the experience you've never had. That is the source. That is the origin of power you've never tasted. That is where the soul's calmness resides, a calmness you never knew existed. That ocean bed, that bedrock.

And, the difference between living from that touchstone versus forever living clueless of its existence, is courage. Courage is the fulcrum, specifically the courage to wade into the crud you've been running from.

Yes, the destination is real. But it cannot be forced by willful denial of the pain or pretended by putting on pretty, sunny faces that attempt to hide life's pain. It is only known by courage.

Are you ready yet?

May 25

**The great thing about getting older is that
you don't lose all the other ages you've been.**
-Madeleine L'Engle, American writer/poet

One of the silly games I enjoy playing with friends, particularly at small dinner parties, involves asking ticklish questions, such as, "If you *got to* go back and live one year from your life over again (implying a year you'd want to live over), which would it be, and why?" or "If you *had to* go back and live one five-year stretch of your life over again (implying a five-year period you didn't enjoy), which would it be and why?"

By possessing all of our past ages, we have the opportunity to gaze out at the rain or take a long drive while remembering different days, perhaps with wistfulness, perhaps laughter, perhaps just sheer joy at the majesty, craziness, and wonderful mess of it all. Whatever the effect that comes with it, there is so much memory food in the past, some bitter, some sweet. It is all right there to be touched, to be felt, and to be re-known.

That also means it's sitting right there, packed with so much learning and wisdom that we far too often run from because those gems of wisdom lay dormant, hidden inside shrouds of pain.

And, strangely, we often fear a memory even when it holds a gift. THINK about that. We fear a thought.

A thought.

A thought cannot be tasted, touched, heard, seen, or smelled. It has no mass, no nothing. It is literally only a thought, an idea, a grouping of chemicals and electricity in the brain. That's it! It's not even steam, smoke, or mist, which you can actually see and feel. It's literally nothing. Yet, that memory can be so extraordinarily powerful, crippling even. It's so odd to consider, isn't it?

And yet, we run from those memories despite the gifts they hold, precisely because they – well, ironically – *can* be tasted, *can* be touched, *can* be heard, *can* be seen, and *can* be smelled. Each and every one of us has had that experience many times with memories. They become more real than what is real, even if just to you, when no one around you knows of their existence, even in the moment you are reliving them.

Your greatest power, joy, and peace come from having the courage to allow those memories – not just the happy, pretty ones – and their emotional charges to be felt. It is to flush and flush them. We flush by allowing and by giving words to those memories and their emotional charges. Then, the day comes when the emotional charges are gone, just as they should have been allowed to flow by when they first came into your life. And all that is left is a memory with no charge, incapable of being triggered because there's no charge left to be triggered.

BADASS WISDOM

Underneath and beyond all of it is the wisdom they bear, the new peace they usher in, and the extraordinary power and happiness they bring forth.

Which ideas are you still avoiding? What wisdom awaits you? What are the biggest memories you most fear? Or, if you'd rather, what are the small ones? Start there. Start pecking away at flushing the small stuff. See what gets uncovered next...

May 26

> ### *The only tired I was,*
> ### *was tired of giving in.*
> -Rosa Parks, American revolutionary
> (on refusing to give up her seat on the segregated bus)

If ever there was a person in the history of humanity who had the right and experience to comment on being "tired of giving in," surely it was this fearless, fierce 42-year-old, work-worn, African-American woman in the segregated Deep South in 1955 America facing the full force of an egregiously racist country and all its powers.

Her words – so extraordinarily powerful, yet plain – echo down through the decades with the full reverberation of those who walked, sat, toiled, and ate it for an eternity. The motivation to move mountains can come from the strangest of places inside, including extraordinary fatigue.

What is the warm blanket this titan's words whisper to you? What does she make you see that you *so* don't want to see? What is the serum her courage injects into your veins as you face the forces of oppression in your own life? Why?

How tired are you?

When do you fully allow yourself to realize – really, truly *know* in its fullness – how tired you are of giving in?

The day that happens is the day old-you dies and new-you begins its passage through the birthing canal.

Happy birthday!

May 27

That which is original creates a new origin.
That which is original, by definition,
must stray off the previously worn paths.
It must wander; it must err.
-Blake Charlton, American Sci-Fi writer

Set in the parental agenda at a very young age, most kids (and later adults) spend so much life energy either conforming to what is expected to get praise, or doing the opposite as a giant "Screw you!" to those who've neglected them or the uniqueness of their needs, or who have sent underlying messages undermining their sense of worth. We are forever reacting to the messages, past and present, from those external power sources. Until we do the work of becoming more and more authentic, we spend much of our lives engaged in pursuits that bear the stamp of good boy/girl or rebel. The former is a path of shoulds and oughts, the latter a forever angry path of "NO!" Or, in some cases, the young person will toggle between the two, at times rebelling, at times conforming, but rarely operating from the center, from the authentic self. This begins to shape the personality and perpetuates well into and through adulthood.

However, there is a third path. The third path is the one where there is no path, where shoulds no longer matter and where you're no longer driven by some internal motor that needs to prove itself to others or scream your discontent and anger toward them.

Which path have you spent most of your life on, the first or second – shoulds or "Screw you's?" Which are you on now? Is your greater instinct to conform and do what's expected of you, or to rebel and take the path of the middle finger?

Do you have the courage to begin to cut a new, third path? What would the third path look like for you? What's the first scary step?

What's the scariest part about carving your own path where there presently isn't one? Why? Would you survive, anyway? Could it be glorious?

May 28

> *Remember that the best relationship*
> *is one in which your love for each other*
> *exceeds your need for each other.*
> -Dalai Lama

It's detachment vs. attachment, really.

It can seem so strange to think of love as detachment, since we almost reflexively conceive it to be the connection between two people, that which binds them together, whether as lovers, friends, or family. But the Dalai Lama seems to be saying (and I'm a bit hesitant to put words into his mouth, of all people), that to need is to possess, whereas to love is to enjoy, yet allow to be and allow to leave.

To need is to grip someone with a closed hand, to hang on; and to love is to hold them in an open hand, only to support, allow, and delight in their presence for as long as it shall last. Possession is using them for your own purposes and *needs* while they, perhaps, use you for theirs, *as if existence is not possible without them*, which means their existence owns you as much as yours owns them. But to love implies enjoyment and giving without possession.

What (or who) do you think you need such that it possesses you, while you falsely assume you possess it? What is it you cannot yet bring yourself to simply love with an open hand? What is the fear driving the behavior? Why? When did that fear first start? Where did it come from? And if this person does leave you, if the dreaded event comes to pass, will you be okay? Sure, you will grieve and grieve well, but will you be okay? Why?

At the very least we all lose each other, eventually, in death. That day will come and the heart and soul will grieve.

May 29

> *Believe in yourself! Have faith in your abilities!*
> *Without a humble but reasonable confidence in your own powers*
> *you cannot be successful or happy.*
> -Norman Vincent Peale, American author and clergyman

A.
- ☐ Computer stuff
- ☐ Car repairs
- ☐ Technical jargon
- ☐ Anything requiring physical endurance
- ☐ Cooking

B.
- ☐ Gardening
- ☐ Home repairs
- ☐ Investing
- ☐ Baking
- ☐ Camping
- ☐ Singing

What do you suck at? What are you mediocre at? Can you, off the top of your head, list five things you know you suck at or are middling, at best, at? Or, are you possessed with the rather fanciful notion that you suck at nothing and are an expert at everything you touch or even consider?

List A is a small smattering of stuff I'm truly awful at; B is the beginning of my mediocrities. As I've aged, I've realized how long those two lists truly are, and what a relief it is to no longer have to pretend to be knowledgeable or proficient at everything. It's so much more pleasant to sit back and let others teach me what they know. Plus, there's a playful delight when gardening, for example, which I'm only mediocre at, in knowing that my efforts could end up an absolute bust or complete mess. It definitely infuses my life with more laughter and drains the pressure.

And then there is List C, the one that delineates that handful of things for which you truly are touched by the gods – i.e. things that you're great at.

Which is harder for you to list, that which you are great at or suck at? Why? Is it harder to name what you're great at because you're conditioned to believe you're great at nothing or are immodest for even considering the thought that you might be great at something?

But, very often one's greatness, passion, and even joy is wrapped up in acknowledging and pursuing that which you know you have been gifted with. Sure, there are exceptions to that. But often life's greatest joy and responsibilities lie in recognizing and living that with which you've been graced.

May 30

All things must change to something new, to something strange.
-Henry Wadsworth Longfellow, American poet

One of the sadder interactions I have with people, young and old, is when they have aspirations, yet fear endeavoring them because they have pursued dreams or paths in the past, which seemed to come to no avail. Or, they fear beginning because they fear getting down the road toward that dream only to discover they now want something else. Because this has brought pain or scorn in the past, they see such changes of course as a curse, as something to be avoided. So, they don't even begin. It's sad for me to see them stuck and to feel the frustration and depression coming off of them, not to mention the agitation of wanting so much more, often even knowing they're capable of much more.

It is at this point that I tell them of something my wise old mother, Charlotte Evangeline Erlandson, said for decades, even well into her 90s before passing:

Sometimes, we have to pass through this door to get to the next door, which is revealed to us somewhere in that next room…when that next door is ready to reveal itself.

We long for all the answers up front. We believe we have to know the destination. Or we believe that the path we embark on must arrive at the destination we've envisioned, the vision that draws us forward. We worry, "What will people say if I don't end up where I said I was going?" So, we often don't even begin if the destination is not guaranteed, or at least highly likely.

Not knowing the end result is hard, as is allowing for a change of course to something even more enchanting to the soul. But the sage woman spoke from experience, not just her own but that of the thousands of people she had counseled over the years. The acorn cannot know, in advance, which directions its branches will grow in its 30th or 55th year, whether in response to winds, rains, or other forces; nor does it know which new water sources will beckon its roots to new depths. The evolution of the person is ever-unfolding. To allow for that is to trust, ultimately, that there is a path even when it cannot be seen; and that the slings and arrows of the naysayers and critics needn't derail you.

How much do you short-circuit your own growth, movement, and ongoing change into something new because you fear the sense of loss, fear the criticism, fear the unknown? At what point do you shift from seeing life as a destination to seeing it as a helluva journey, full of fun, pain, heartbreak, frustration, mountaintop experiences, and laughter? What would it take to finally let go of needing to control the results – i.e. to hold on loosely, to live with an open hand, passionately pursuing what you want yet simultaneously letting go of it, willing to forever live without it?

May 31

> *I mean, they say you die twice.*
> *One time when you stop breathing*
> *and a second time, a bit later on,*
> *when somebody says your name for the last time.*
> -Banksy, British street artist

Karen, my partner, spent a year and a half tending to her cousin, Vicky, with whom she had grown up in the same house in the Bronx, in the 1960s. Those two had always been thick as thieves. Their kids grew up together. They faced life's challenges together with laughter-filled, raucous Italian flair. That included, in Vicky's final year, the death of her longtime dog, Sierra, the death by overdose of her son, Nicky, and the consumption of her brain by glioblastoma. She also reconciled with her long-lost brother after 25 years. That year was sad, ugly, and beautiful. Yet, in some ways, Vicky had the most oddly peaceful year of her life.

And, day in and day out, Karen was there, holding her hand, stroking her hair, making her laugh her butt off with Roshawn, the amazing aide who lived with Vicky. Karen had found an apartment in the basement of the house of an old Russian man she had befriended years earlier. The house was a mile from our house so that Karen could be there daily, taking Vick for strolls in her wheelchair, and returning in the middle of the night when the night nurse couldn't work the Hoyer Lift so Vick could use the commode.

Karen gave and gave and gave love. She had to pull back, a few times, out of sheer exhaustion, because she was simultaneously running a multi million-dollar company in New York City. But she couldn't stop. Her adoration of her cousin, her sense of obligation to the family who had gone before her, and her innate spirit of self-sacrifice wouldn't let her.

We had a teary memorial service in our backyard. Since that day, Karen has many times wished she had done more. Though, I don't know how she could have. I miss Vicky and the laughter of her final year. Karen misses Vicky terribly in too many ways. Her sly, funny, pain-in-the-butt cousin is gone. But her name is still on Karen's tongue, and that of her sisters and daughters.

Are you giving of yourself? Who is dying in your life? Whom does your soul need to reach out to, to ease their pain? Whose passing do you grieve? Let yourself grieve, for as long as it takes.

June

June 1

Life is a balance of
holding on and letting go.
-Rumi, Persian poet

The whole 'manifesting' thing really exploded into popular culture in the 2000s with the release of Rhonda Byrne's book, *The Secret*. The concept had been around long before that, but with that book it took on a popularity it had not previously known. I had been experimenting with it for two decades prior to that, inspired by the work of Richard Bach and Shakti Gawain, in particular. But in the 2000s I definitely circled back to it. To this day, aspects of the whole idea that what you focus on will become your reality are still a part of my life.

However, they bump up against one other truth of life that I believe to be frustratingly inescapable. I've never met, nor heard of, anyone who has escaped without feeling the brushes and knives of life's pains, sorrow, deaths, and disappointments. I've not heard of anyone who has lived a pain-free life, regardless of what they've accomplished.

I absolutely believe the gods (or the universe, or fate, or luck, or happenstance) are more powerful than us and throw curve balls we can neither foresee nor control by any sort of Jedi mind manifestation. Furthermore, it has been my experience (and that of many I've known and counseled in life), that the greatest joys in life come not from what we want, manifest, and create, but from letting go of those very things. All too regularly, when we let go of that which we want most, the universe creates something quite different, yet still infused with elements of who we are and what we love, such that a new entity is built that could have, in no way, been foreseen or manifested intentionally.

Is it possible that you're holding on too tightly? Is it possible that the very vision you're holding onto so tightly is, in fact, obstructing the growth of something you cannot see that brings greater happiness than you've imagined? Is it possible that the real trick to life is not solely the visioning, but the ability to allow the universe to influence your path without viewing it as an obstacle to your success? Is it possible you can't even see your greatest happiness because you're blinded by the ego's wants?

June 2

Before you become a leader, success is all about growing yourself.
When you become a leader, success is all about growing others.
-Jack Welch, Former CEO, General Electric

It was the end of the first week of my senior year of high school. Always a bit flustered, Mr. Loo hustled into our senior literature class shaking his head while hand-combing his mop of wispy black hair. Standing behind his podium, he laughed devilishly to his seniors who loved him as a kind and playful intellect, "I just came out of sophomore grammar. Remember this, you always have to be mean in the beginning, so you can be fun and kind later. You can't be nice first and tough later, or they won't take you seriously."

BAM!!

He was kidding about the 'mean' part. He meant 'tough.' However, the point is spot on.

What are the areas of your life where you're leading with kindness because you're shying away from toughness?

Conversely, is your problem that you too often lead with toughness without infusing it with kindness, fairness, and just plain decency?

Which way do you err? If you were being honest, is it time to change that equation in your life? Is your toughness doing damage? Or is it your kindness that is ineffectual, because they don't respect you (which also frustrates you)?

The either/or thing doesn't work. When it comes to leadership, it's a both/and; a dance between both toughness and kindness.

June 3

The heights by great men reached and kept
were not attained by sudden flight,
but they, while their companions slept,
were toiling upward in the night.
-Henry Wadsworth Longfellow, American poet

I'm a firm believer that we toil hardest, yet most effortlessly, at that which naturally draws us forward in the directions we long to fly. There is no fulfillment in this life like laboring into the night at that which you love.

And, if you cannot engage the hard work of focus, over hours and years, even decades, it's not your deepest passion; or, when that love of the work wears out or the motivation feels depleted, it is that passion trying to point you in the direction of the next door you are to pass through to revive your life.

What could you grind at for hours, even years, and still not grow tired of it, or at least not for long? Have you ever considered creating a life built not on money or comfort, or at least not immediately so, but on just doing the stuff that moves your soul, the stuff that pulls up the grit, grind, focus, strength, and fire from your soul in ways nothing else can? At what point do you get sick of living life any other way than by doing what lights your soul on fire? What's the biggest obstacle inside you that you most need to conquer to live the impassioned life you dream of?

June 4

Be careful, lest in casting out your demon
you exorcise the best thing in you.
-Friedrich Nietzsche

I grew up in a far north, Swedish-American family. Five boys, one sister, and plenty of commotion. My parents were no shrinking violets. They had grown up on big family farms during the Depression and WWII and were used to lots of voices. To a degree, they encouraged it.

Nonetheless, my people and family in the north are generally quiet people. But I wasn't. From day one, it seems, I was a square peg in a round hole, at least with regard to volume and intensity. I stuck out for sure. I had one other intense brother, but even he wasn't as loud. And, there was definitely a feeling inside of me that I was too loud, too intense, later swore too much, and just had too big of a personality. It didn't help that I was an arrogant kid, too.

I was told to tone it down more by siblings than parents, which wasn't all bad because it taught me to learn different volumes and intensity levels. Teachers (some of 'em, at least), scolded me and told me to mellow out and quiet down. Yet, I had other glorious teachers and administrators in my blue-collar city that never tried to suppress me, they simply directed my energies into fruitful endeavors and helped me talk out my stuff.

We can so easily become conditioned in childhood to believe that who we are, or some aspect of who we are, is not welcome, not acceptable. The child then grows into teen years and adulthood with a learned dislike for those aspects of themself. The real shift in life happens when that now-adult stops condemning the aspects of themself that others do, or did, and actually welcomes and integrates them.

This is what I had to do. I had to stop fighting myself and seeing myself as flawed, even when in my preparation for ordained ministry some of those in power tried to convince me that I had mental problems, and a woman I was in a long-term relationship with tried to tell the world I was bipolar. (Later, I discovered she was doing that and making me the villain to keep the focus off of her and all that she had been told was wrong with her.) I had to integrate the part of me that I'd been taught was bad, or unwelcome, into my conception of myself, all of it good. I had to just finally let myself be me.

Now, 3-4 decades later, my friendships, love life, relationships with my own kids and siblings, and particularly my work are largely influenced by that formerly dark side of myself that was seen by many as a bad thing; a demon, so to speak. That loud, intense, swearing, at times obnoxious SOB aspect of me is part of who I am and I love it, whether others do or not.

You do you. But, do you have the courage to do you, especially when others would much prefer you to do *their* version of you? My demons weren't just loudness.

My demons were the fear of not mattering, not getting enough love and attention, never amounting to squat; the usual stuff we all have. But I had been coaxed to push out the wrong demons, until finally I put an end to that and the relationships that were pressuring me to do so.

When do you turn your thinking upside down and consider the possibility that the very stuff others have been trying to squeeze out of you is the real you; or the stuff they want to squeeze you into is not your real self? That you're being taught self-shame and that to be alive, free, and finally at peace and happy, you gotta welcome the parts of yourself that you've been most taught to hate?

June 5

You can't have a light
without a dark to stick it in.
-Arlo Guthrie, American folk singer-songwriter

There is a stimulus that often precedes the knowing of one's purpose, or dream, in life. It is the awareness of a problem outside of oneself, followed by the belief that you, yourself, are the solution, or a necessary part of it. It is not just to see the light inside, but to recognize the darkness where that light is needed most.

Then, it's about having the courage to actually go into that darkness with the goblins and terrors lurking inside. Yet, strangely, when possessed of a light – a 'why' for living – the darkness either isn't as scary or it still is but is waded into anyway.

Do you know your light? Do you know the dark to which you are called? Which of the ghouls in that dark frightens you the most? Are you gonna go into the darkness, anyway? Perhaps you're already doing it and have encountered plenty of bad things in the dark as you shine your light. What keeps you doing it? How has the original vision most changed since the beginning, or what has it morphed into? Are you allowing your soul to continue to change and pull you in new directions? If not, why?

June 6

Sadly enough, the most painful goodbyes
are the ones that are left unsaid and never explained.
-Jonathan Harnisch, American artist/author

"Sven, I have no problems with you leaving me. Just do me the courtesy of telling me you're done before you move on to someone else. Just do me that one decency," she said at the beginning of what would become a three-year relationship.

I was 33, and that was one of the most mind-blowing relationship statements I had ever heard. I had never, ever been with someone who stated from the outset that she was cool with us breaking up one day because, "Relationships often end. And that's okay." Boom! It was refreshing and oddly liberating. But she knew what she was asking of me. Courage. Too many times before, the other person had taken the cowardly way out and simply cheated on her. She asked only that I spare her that one pain and the accompanying deception.

Looking back, it's rather laughable how the relationship did end, just three years after her declaration. Ironically, she cheated on me with our next-door neighbor. When I called her out, we were standing outside next to my truck. No lie, she immediately stuck my hand down her pants. Hahaha. A master stroke of attempted distraction. I fell for it, in the moment. I mean, who says no to that? But, a day later, I started breakup proceedings.

She didn't have the courage she had asked me for. In retrospect, I get it, because it is so hard to look someone in the face and end a relationship. It just is. There's fear of backlash, hurting the other, being hated, looking bad, being alone, not having someone to jump to, an empty bed, no hand to hold or person to laugh with. It's just hard. Yet, life and just plain decency demand it. To do otherwise is the very height of selfishness.

But it's not just love relationships. Friendships. Family bonds. Long-time career settings. It just takes courage to do the hard things in life, even when we know they're right and necessary.

What's the hard stuff you know you gotta do in some life relationship that you so don't want to? Whom do you most fear facing, but know you have to and know it's time? Before you do, write a long, impassioned letter with all your thoughts and feelings in it; a letter you DO NOT SEND. (By not sending, you won't edit as you're writing.) Flush everything out. That will give you greater clarity and far less anxiety going into the conversation. Also, journal out all you're afraid of happening and how it would feel if those things did happen. Will you survive? What will be the hardest part? Will life go on? Flush it out.

Then go do what needs to be done. It's time.

June 7

To reach something good
it is very useful to have gone astray,
and thus acquire experience.
-Saint Teresa of Avila, Spanish ascetic and nun

Isn't it fascinating how, so often, parents and society want to curb a child in order to be normal, to follow accepted paths, to choose safe decisions, yet the true titans of history in all fields either never did that or weren't able/willing to do that for long? It's always the greats who argue for originality, mistakes, failures, quitting, and evolving.

Have you ever heard someone who achieved greatness, whether it be in industry or parenting, music or space, say that the path required being normal, safe, and predictable?

Why do we content ourselves to listen to the timid souls? Why do we raise our children to hold on to that which is secure?

Clearly, it is our own anxieties that get stirred up when others deviate or live their authentic lives. We need them to live within known boundaries so that we do not have feelings of agitation inside of ourselves. We manipulate the external to quell the internal. We control what is outside us and around us, including other people, as a way to control our internal voice and keep it from chewing away at us. And somewhere deep inside, we know that this is the same path that brings slow death to the spirit.

Do you, yourself, have the courage to go astray? More significantly, do you have the guts to encourage those who look up to you to follow their own original paths, rather than follow you? Do you have the ability to encourage them to go their own way, astray as they may seem at times, without your judgment? Do you have the ability to flush your own anxieties and allow others to become their real selves, essentially giving them power over their own lives rather than using them to meet your own longing for control?

As I regularly tell people, "The path to discovering who you are requires discovering who you're not, which requires the courage to both fail and quit."

June 8

Knowing it and living it
are two completely different things.
-Sven

He was a semi-neurotic, successful, very young tech up-and-comer in Manhattan. We had a standard 6-hour opening session. It was lively, deep, and impactful. Well, to a point. At the end of the session, he looked me in the face and uttered simply, "That's it? I know all of this."

"Do ya, now?" I responded. "Kid, knowing it and living it are two completely different things. And you ain't living it, as evidenced by your massive unrest in both demeanor and inner turmoil. You have all the answers, but you're terrified to live what you claim to know. That's the problem." He had no response.

As he walked out the door, we shook hands and he thanked me for my honesty. I shared one more thing with him: "One of the curses of being young is that for as painful as life can be at 26, you have no concept of how that same pain, carried another 20 years, can kill the soul. At some point you're going to have to do the work you say you know. Knowing differently and doing differently are totally different things. You gotta push through your fears."

What is it you claim to know, but aren't actually living? Write out all the things you know you're half-assing or avoiding, either because you don't fully believe it will work, or because you are honestly just terrified of the work, like my young friend. What's the biggest fear in leaning into the work rather than claiming it doesn't work and walking away? Whom are you most afraid of? Whose words and influence are still controlling your life, keeping you clinging to lower ground and an unfulfilled life? Do you have the courage to do the work, sooner than later, so you don't waste any more of your life?

June 9

Listening is a magnetic force.
-Karl Menninger, American psychiatrist

In every human interaction there is a transfer of energy. It's not just the words or touch that are exchanged. Some people lift us up, inspire us, cause us to leave with a kick in our step. Some people drag us down or are just *blah*. Sometimes, we know when we ourselves are being mopey or jacked, giving energy or taking energy. Those around us feel that and may even say so.

To bring more to life, the world, and humanity – more than you take – means to give energy in human exchanges. It means that people walk away from you feeling uplifted or even just a bit more energized.

How is this done best? Giving attention. Listening more than you speak. Having a positive, supportive response. When you do speak, speak in questions, not statements. Statements are *me* talking. Questions are the doorway for *you* to talk. Questions open doors for the other to be present, heard, understood, and seen. There is great power in the giving of positive attention and taking oneself out of the equation.

Do you create doors for others to walk through in your daily interactions? Do you listen, truly listen? Do you affirm and even sum up what you've heard? Do people walk away from you feeling heard, uplifted, and energized? Or are you the person who is always talking, always needing the floor, always putting your stuff out there, always siphoning attention but never connecting? You may like yourself, but do the people around you? If they don't, it may be an indicator that you're taking more energy and attention than you're giving? Maybe reverse that?

June 10

*You know you're in love when you don't want to fall asleep
because reality is finally better than your dreams.*
-Dr. Seuss, Children's author

Whether it be through:
- Excessive gambling
- over-working
- booze/wine
- unhealthy use of food
- cheating
- pills
- excessive exercise
- chaos addiction
- extreme busyness
- overuse of weed
- excessive gaming
- drugs
- incessant shopping
- over-parenting
- porn, or
- becoming reclusive, totally shutting down

...the quest to escape life can take on many forms, some clearly self-destructive, others more surreptitiously so, hidden beneath the cloak of cultural acceptability. But the desire to escape, whether the doer is aware of it or not, is because the life in which they exist sucks so badly. Thus, the inclination to numb themselves from it, or to finally feel something amid the numbness, takes over and turns into some sort of addiction.

Yet, as generally happens in life, that escape mechanism becomes more and more consuming, often to the point of either blowing up that person's life or grinding them down from the inside out. This is where getting clean, going to rehab, getting on a program, quitting the crazy job, or going on a serious new eating program are required. However, necessary as those can be, the real problem is not the escape mechanism, not the addiction, not the out-of-control behaviors any more than the sore throat and diarrhea are the problem during cold and flu season. No, those are just symptoms; the real problem is the virus creating those symptoms. *The real problem* in the life that has turned to obsessive behaviors, addictions, and the constant quest for escape, *is the life in which the individual finds themselves day in and day out; the life they are trying to escape.* The real problem is not the escape but *that which is being escaped from.* Change that and everything changes.

In a strange way, that compulsive escape has been like a best friend in that it seems like the only thing that can turn off your mind and make your inner pain go away. I had a 21-year-old female client tell me, "Sven, the three hours I'm bingeing and the three hours I'm purging are the only reprieve I have from all the pressures of my parents, school, and all the balls I'm trying to keep in the air." And, what she discovered as she went deeper into the root causes and messages she had received about herself and about life, and as we began to heal her past and present, is that the bulimia began to almost effortlessly fade away. The desire to escape left her because she had created a life from which she no longer wanted to escape.

Are you focused on the symptom or the actual virus in your desire to finally be happy and at peace? Is it possible that it's time to finally start deconstructing and recreating your world as you know it? Has the pain finally gotten bad enough? Has the high lost its ability to make you high? Do you seek to finally have a high, or happiness, that has carry-over rather than hangover?

June 11

Selfishness is not living as one wishes to live;
it is asking others to live as one wishes to live.
-Oscar Wilde, Irish Novelist and poet

Whether we're aware of it or not, we tend to call people 'selfish' when they are not acting how we want them to act. Our dislike stems from a sort of self-as-center-of-the-universe thinking and set of expectations in ourselves. This, depending on the amount of power we have over that person, can lead to controlling, condemning, and gaslighting behaviors on our part.

Or the opposite, depending on that person's grip on us, or the grip of the core beliefs we were taught about ourselves in childhood, we might allow another person to determine or too significantly influence our decisions, words, and life trajectory.

Thus, at its root, selfishness is the desire to live two lives, yours and mine. Conversely, selflessness can become an abdication of life to someone else, often (though not always) out of fear of truly living *my* life.

Yet, for better or worse, we are each given but one life to spend as we see fit. The willful thievery of another's life decisions is not okay. The willful abdication of one's own life is, indeed, your choice. But is it actually *your* choice? Wouldn't it be safer to say that the relinquishment of self-governance today was created by you never having the choice to begin with? Isn't it reasonable to say that you were conditioned to believe your life is not yours and that you must give your autonomy to some external power source? I mean, isn't that what your childhood was all about – not having a voice, not feeling heard or seen?

So, what's your task – to stop insisting others act as you wish, or to stop allowing others to coerce you into acting how they wish? What do you most fear in doing so? How about doing it anyway?

June 12

The grand mistake of life
is to have the experience,
but miss the meaning.
-T.S. Eliot, *The Dry Salvages* (paraphrase)

Shusako Endo, in his book *Silence*, wherein he tells of Christian-Jesuit missionaries first coming to Japan, explains how they would be tortured to death if they were caught proselytizing. There were posts driven into the sand at low tide, much the same as the posts sustaining a wooden pier. The monks were then hung from the top of that post so that as the waters rose, the waves would beat against their bodies, endlessly. No blood was shed. It was just the incessant pounding of the waves against the body that killed them, not drowning. They would die of fatigue.

It's a powerful, interesting thought, isn't it – dying of fatigue from life's poundings?

Perhaps the consummate pivot point of life where fates are unwittingly decided, is that ever-recurring moment when we choose, as individuals, what to do with our pain. It comes, again and again, minute to minute, hour to hour, year to year. We are constantly walking through life deciding what to do with not only the next prick from life's needle and pounding from life's hard press, but, often more importantly, what to do with the lifetime of past pricks and poundings that we ignored, stuffed down, and ran from.

The processing and disposal of pain is what separates those most *ALIVE* and at peace from those forever saddled with deep unrest and unfulfilled potential. The grand mistake made by far too many is believing that ignoring pain makes it go away. Few greater myths exist in human experience. It doesn't go; it just gets packed into a vault, deep inside. Vaulting it causes that pain to fester, like a colon that backs up and doesn't flush out, nor does it extract the vital nutrients from that which is passing through. The packing down of pain leads to what my very old father, well before he died, used to call 'spiritual constipation,' or impaction. Spread over decades, this is absolutely toxic to the soul, to life energy, relationships, careers, and actual bodily health.

The hard, ugly task is the allowing of pain. Vaulting is the disallowing of pain, thinking that trying to ignore it makes it go away. To allow pain means to recognize and physically express the pain in the moment when it happens, and subsequently as memories of it recur until it is gone (and it does pass!). But, the real moneymaker is when you simultaneously mine that pain – like the colon sucking nutrients from the food passing through – for what it is offering to teach you about life, people, the world, and, most importantly, self. The extraction of gems and rich minerals of insight and wisdom from our pain is where dross gets spun to gold. And only the wisest and most courageous do it. Everyone else just runs from it. This is where fortunes are won or lost, where fates are decided, moment to moment, over a lifetime.

Still running? Still believe that's the answer? Still living in fear of that pain overwhelming you, hurting you, wrestling your control from your hands? You think you're being tough. But instead you're killing yourself by neither processing nor disposing of your pain. You're losing your life, decade by decade.

However, worst of all, you're missing all that pain is trying to teach you about yourself and life. That's the real gold. You're literally running from life's great treasure, because you fear the dragons that surround it.

June 13

You don't have to specialize –
do everything that you love
and then, at some time,
the future will come together for you in some form.
-Francis Ford Coppola, Legendary American filmmaker;
Director of *The Godfather*

There is a forcing of life that happens when we become so possessed by the 'must' for a path. "I must go to this school;" "You must get such-and-such experience in order to end up where you should be;" "You must finish what you start. Never quit." There is an unwillingness to trust in the forces of destiny, in the flow of the universe, or the odd navigation of the soul.

As a teen, I aspired only to be a fighter pilot, after I aborted the dream of professional football because I simply wasn't good enough. By 17, I was in the top school in the country for becoming a United States fighter pilot. But, by 19, I walked away from that. It had lost its luster for me.

Despite where I would end up decades later, through most of my twenties the thought of writing anything other than in my journals was not even a blip on the radar, nor was speaking to large and small audiences or lecturing at the graduate level. Counseling was just a side gig I did.

Then, in my late-20s, speaking, writing, and counseling became my slow obsession, as would becoming a spiritual/religious leader. These new aspirations took turns through traditional routes, then began over decades to lead to new paths as new interests sprung up, such as NCAA coaching and being approached by Hollywood nine times, entirely unprecipitated on my part, to build a show around my life's work or plug me into an existing show.

All the while, the internal driver was simply to only do that which I love, or that which contributed to the doing of what I love. Life became play; serious play. I worked many a side job, usually waiting tables and tending bar. And I enjoyed that, too. But the lodestar was always only doing that which I loved. If I didn't love it, I gave myself permission to quit. Lost a lot of friends and family that way, which was something I grew to accept as the price of freedom and creative living. I was going to extract from this life joy on my terms. I'd rather fail my way than succeed someone else's way.

But then, in my 40s, it all began to congeal. All the disparate threads began to reveal themselves as this organic, gorgeous tapestry that was my life, and I loved it, even more. Sure, the successes, fame, and money came with it. But those were just bonuses to me. The delight was the 25-year path of becoming and pursuing that preceded the successes. Only the naive and the foolish think otherwise.

At the root, it's about trusting that your soul is leading you, trusting that you don't have to control the destination or even the steps, only the feel. It is to trust and be led by the feeling of love for this day, this action, this path, for now. Even on the ugliest of days, it is still a day on a path I would not trade, at least for the time being, 'til some new love seizes my attention and my heart.

Where are you at in this equation?

June 14

> *Your children are not your children.*
> *They are sons and daughters of Life's longing for itself.*
> *They come through you but not from you.*
> *And though they are with you yet they belong not to you.*
> *You may give them your love but not your thoughts,*
> *For they have their own thoughts.*
> *You may house their bodies but not their souls,*
> *For their souls dwell in the house of tomorrow, which you cannot visit,*
> *not even in your dreams.*
> *You may strive to be like them, but seek not to make them like you.*
> *For life goes not backward nor tarries with yesterday.*
> *You are the bows from which your children as living arrows are sent forth.*
> *The archer sees the mark upon the path of the infinite, and He bends you*
> *with His might that His arrows may go swift and far.*
> *Let your bending in the archer's hand be for gladness.*
> *For even as He loves the arrow that flies, so He also loves the bow that is*
> *stable.*
> -Kahlil Gibran, Lebanese-American painter/writer

My parents were 28 when they had my oldest brother, Kent. They then had four more children before having me, right as they were about to kiss 40 years old. Think about the difference between who you were at 28 and who you were at 40. Not only are those two significantly different ages, but the amount of change and growth that happens during those particular ages is huge. The career changes and expansions are big in those years. The settling hasn't occurred yet. The discovery of self often doesn't really kick in until the mid-30s. So much is going on over that 12-year stretch.

Thus, it's reasonable to assume that who my parents were for the oldest brother was radically different from who they were and how they parented me.

Every child growing up in the same household to the same parents experiences a distinctly different childhood and thus can turn out very differently. The experience of the oldest is very different from the experience of the middle child. The adults' parenting is very different when they have one kid in their twenties, then another in their late-thirties or even forties. The parents themselves are such significantly different people that it only makes sense that their parenting is going to be significantly different from one child to the next.

Now, also, factor in that a not-so-deliberate parent might favor one child over another. So now, you potentially have a Golden Child and a Forgotten Child. Or, there might be a Problem Child and a Child with Special Needs. Stamped with this new identity in the parent's brain, even if it's never explicitly stated, the child will likely forever be parented differently from the others and hence turn out differently. Makes sense, right? It's not necessarily a bad thing. But it can lead to problems. And, it can then take decades to unwind those problems, identities, and the inevitable fluctuations in parenting.

So, were you the Golden Child, the Loud Child, the Bad Kid, the Quiet Kid, or perhaps the Little Brother of the Golden Child? How did that identity impact how you were parented and, hence, your experience as a kid and perhaps even as an adult? Even more importantly, how has that label impacted, positively or negatively, your own identity or understanding of yourself? Was it ever actually true? Do you need to change it? How do *you* see yourself, if not as that?

June 15

It takes courage to grow up and become who you really are.
-e.e. cummings, U.S. writer/poet

The whole 'failure to launch' situation that often grips those in their 40s, not to mention their 20s (and which is not new to this generation but is definitely spotlighted), is influenced by a lack of courage that has not yet become inflamed by sufficient pain. It's caused by fear so gripping that it outweighs any courage.

Of course, this fear is of the criticisms, condemnations, and perceived loss of love and approval if one pursues an authentic life. This is what Cummings means by growing up. It is the infantile state of longing for the nipple of approval that brings warmth inside and satisfaction; that ever elusive nipple.

To grow up is to let go of needing the teat anymore, or perhaps even the outright rejection of it because of the vivid awareness of its price. And yes, this can last well into one's sixties and seventies when the longing for the nipple got driven so deeply in childhood, thus governing most decisions, in one way or another, throughout the full arc of life.

What nipple do you still long for that you cannot seem to let go of? The one that keeps you locked in submission, in fear of losing it forever? At what point do you open your hand and let it go because you realize that it's costing you your entire life?

June 16

> *After all, it is those who have a deep and real inner life
> who are best able to deal with the irritating details of outer life.*
> -Evelyn Underhill, English writer

There is a calming presence that naturally follows a life devoted to weeding out the anxieties, goblins, and tears that were never yours to begin with or that you were never allowed to flush out, from the weight of fighting parents to the seeming smallness of a stubbed toe. Those devoted to meditation, solitude, exercising, counseling, contemplation, self-reflection, journaling and the like discover new strength and the diminishment of fear, as their uprooting of weeds in their inner garden becomes more and more of a priority.

But these are spiritual disciplines. Like any other discipline – from saving money to eating healthy foods – they require deliberateness born of seeing the value in doing so and the dislike for life when not doing so.

Are you deliberate about cultivating the garden of your soul? Or are you simply hoping things, such as all that corrupts your sanity and happiness, magically change?

Bad news: They don't, not magically.

June 17

*There is something in every one of you
that waits and listens for the sound of the genuine in yourself.
It is the only true guide you will ever have.
And if you cannot hear it, you will all of your life,
spend your days on the ends of strings that somebody else pulls.*
-Howard Thurman, American author

In the quest for authentic living and *ALIVENESS*, one of the questions people ask me the most is: How do you know when a feeling or voice that's rising up from within is coming from my true self or from fear? I love this question, in no small part because it is a sign that someone is doing the work and asking high order questions.

The simple answer is this: If it produces calm, it's you. If it produces more anxiety, it's not. But I like to add, if it produces exuberance, it's you. It's your authentic self calling. There might be trepidation around executing it, which can be addressed and released, but there's a sense of knowing that this is the path.

What is the path of inner calm for you? What is your inner self calling you to? Does it scare you? Do you still know it is your path? Do you have the courage to execute it? Is today the day you finally do? And do you have the self-discipline to keep removing the inner blocks and anxieties, as they arise, through your journaling and releasing?

June 18

Boys bond bloody.
-Unknown

I have an older brother who, when we were kids, always roughhoused with me in a quasi-loving way, as boys tend to do. He played with me even though he was five years older than me. When he was studying in high school and college, David taught me memory tricks and how to study more efficiently. He took me with him to run wind sprints and throw him passes when he was training for high school and college football. Much later, he got me drunk for the first time...and a few times after. He was this intense, highly driven animal, whom I was and am so very innately like and connected to at a very deep level.

For so many years, and really in some ways even to this day, this brother inspired me to push harder, give more, unleash my full energy, be more focused, attack, and play and tease the hell outta people in a gentle way.

Even though we had hard years, he's easily one of the top five people who's most contributed, unwittingly, to my life's work. Easily. We went vastly different paths in life, but how we traversed those paths is oddly similar.

Who the heck inspires you? Whose teachings do you still use? Whose imprint on your spirit still fuels your engine? What'd they teach you, deep down? And what the heck are you doing with it? Got the guts and drive to do more? What about the discipline to do more? What're you waiting for?

June 19

An effective way to deal with predators is to taste terrible.
-Unknown, Immortal thinker and writer

It's a funny little quote; harmless, even meaningless, unless we take it as a metaphor. What if the predator isn't the mountain lion on the forest path you're hiking, but the one inside who has eaten away your sanity or sense of self? What if the predator is the one you're in a relationship with, forever consuming your autonomy and self-worth? What if you're still being eaten alive by a parent?

What would it mean to 'taste terrible' to that person, so to speak? What would you need to morph into, even if only temporarily, or do for them to lose a taste for your flesh? It's a bit of an inverted way to think, but what if the tool for your exit is not your self-improvement, at least for the time being, but your becoming distasteful in some form or another? What would that look like?

Change your dress, hide behind bulky clothes and a changed hairstyle? Use distasteful language? Change your career path, or shut it down completely?

I have counseled people married to abusers or control freaks who believed their only way to truly escape the prison of that relationship was to cheat on the abuser, thus rendering themselves disgusting to, and therefore unwanted by, the abuser. It's a bit of a sticky path because it inflames the abuse, at least in the short term. But in those rare times it is needed and used, it can work in facilitating the exit. Similarly, many a young person has broken free of parental grip and control by becoming so contemptible that the parent threw them out, setting the young one into a whirlwind of insecurity but eventually, a liberated life.

Interesting idea, ain't it?

What would make you most distasteful to those who regularly seek to eat you?

June 20

> *Good judgment comes from experience.*
> *Experience comes from bad judgment.*
> -Dr. Kerr L. White

If you are young or inexperienced and claim to possess wisdom, which of course is the basis of good judgment, you may be clever but you are likely a beggar, mooching off the experiences and insights gained by others before you. Until you've had the courage to endeavor your own paths – complete with its failures, fk-ups, and falldowns – you haven't had the experience, let alone the contemplation of those experiences, necessary for wisdom. Until you've taken other people's wisdom for a spin and possibly a wipeout to see how they ride, you've not gained any of your own true experience.

Bad judgment, which is the natural child of courage, or fool's courage, is part of a life well-lived, wherein there is growth and the constant evolution of self. Thus, bad judgment can be quite a good thing, particularly in retrospect.

Which of your bad judgments were the best decisions and greatest blessings of your life? Why? What fruit did they bear? When did you start seeing them differently? What causes you to see them differently now?

June 21

Sven, we're always selling ourselves.
-LeRoy A. Erlandson, My father

I can recall numerous times in my life when Dad would say that to me. It always struck me as odd, because these words were coming out of the mouth of a pastor whom you'd think would always be selling God, or something. Yet, from the first time he said it to me in my teen years, I understood the profound logic of what he was saying. The salesman is a conduit for the product. Hate the saleswoman or find her bland or off-putting, and you're far less likely to buy the product, right? Dad understood the precursor necessity when wanting to get your point across or getting through to people, whether your product is bottled water or lawnmowers, artificial hips or God. You're selling yourself first.

But if we transfer Dad's idea across platforms to the realm of Self, it becomes even more true. We're forced to confront the reality that the salesperson and the product are one in the same. So, the obvious question becomes: Do you believe in what you're selling – i.e. in who you are and who you are putting out there into the world? Is the product – or Self – you're selling consistent with who you really are? Is it a product you're proud of and eagerly put forth?

Or, are you whoring yourself out, becoming whomever you need to be, just to get some need or want met, such as the need for affection, affirmation, approval, acceptance, or attention? Have you become some factory-generated clone widget designed solely to yield some (emotional) profit for the salesperson and manufacturer?

Does your longing for kind words and having someone stay with you and love you outweigh your need to be real and love the product?

When do you get tired of selling crap you don't believe in because you're so afraid of not getting buyers and hence, the smidgens of love in return?

June 22

It takes a lot of time to be a genius.
You have to sit around so much doing nothing,
really doing nothing.
-Gertrude Stein, American author living in France

See, this quote really digs deep. First off, there are many types of genius – intellectual, creative, political, social, engineering, parenting, musical, etc. Thus, the point isn't just that inaction, per se, is necessary for the actualization of one's greatest potential. Though, for many types of genius that is precisely what is needed.

The larger point being made by Stein, at least as I see it, is just below the surface. The reason this quote jumps out at the reader is because it seems to make no sense. It's selling the idea of doing nothing, which goes completely against the ethos of so many people, and certainly many cultures around the world, particularly the United States. The reader's immediate response would likely be some version of, "Well, that's just ridiculous. I can't do that. I'd be a laughingstock!"

Therein is the deeper point: Excellence, greatness – the craving to fly at full wingspan as who you really are – comes at some very high prices, not the least of which is the madness to go against everything we are wired to believe is the ticket to success. Genius and greatness might require, for some, that they stand against an unyielding corporate system. For other forms of genius it might require risking life itself. For others, the fullest expression of massive potential might demand turning previous notions of art upside-down in the face of scorn and ridicule. To bring deliberate excellence to parenting/leading a young family, it might require the courage to stand up to the ostracism from parents and family-of-origin.

What all of those have in common is that genius, greatness, and flying at full wingspan demand the ability and willingness to suffer withering criticism from others and do it, anyway. It's always the fear of others that stops great dreams and accomplishments.

What is the insane thing you know you'd have to do to accomplish, or at the very least usher in, your genius? What are the crazy ideas you bring to your sector of life? Whose criticisms do you fear most? What is the grand challenge in front of you, and do you have the audacity to do what you, and perhaps no one else, know needs to be done?

So get after it!

June 23

With age comes the inner, the higher life.
Who would be forever young, to dwell always in externals?
-Elizabeth Cady Stanton, American suffragist

Boy, that's insightful.

Stanton almost takes it as a given that this migration from externals to internals is inevitable. While for some that movement comes much later than mere age. It might be absent, or avoided, 'til well into old age. For, the shift of focus brings painful epiphanies, not the least of which is that much of one's past has been a grand waste – 'full, but unfulfilling' is usually how it goes.

Nonetheless, if that transition and concomitant pains can be weathered and not avoided, the settling calm and sense of reconnection to the real texture of life – to the feeeel of it all – is experienced as 'higher,' to use her word. It is "to feel the soil in my fingers and on my knees as I stoop in the garden, like back on the farm as a kid," as my mother used to describe her own sense of *ALIVENESS*.

That's really what Stanton is talking about: that sense, or feel, when connected to life, as opposed to the high when acquiring experiences, trinkets, and ego-satisfiers. It's what's going on inside, and discovering that peace, calm, reflection, and solitude, and feeling the breath of the universe itself which matters. It is a greater experience and feeling than all the acquisitions from the past.

Have you experienced that inner life yet? Or are you still running from it out of fear of that transition period with all its pains?

Well, perhaps the day will come when you're ready to do it anyway.

June 24

*Solitude is a way to defend the spirit against
the murderous din of our materialism.*
-Thomas Merton, French-American Trappist Monk

Once you have gotten past the fear of silence and being alone, once you have done the work to quiet the voices inside and around you that kept you pushing, driving, ever in motion, yet never good enough and never 'there,' there comes a calm that is both welcome and refreshing. There comes a yearning for release from stimulus, noise, and even motion. There is something profoundly settling and resetting about a quiet evening alone, an early morning in a garden, a bench in the woods, an innertube on a lazy river, a deep sofa after a long stretch of work, and just the joy of being alone.

I have always enjoyed road trips alone – sun-scorched, seemingly endless ribbons of highway lull me into a trance of deep thought, occasional dips into boredom, but always the freedom and peace of the self in solitude.

Solitude. It's very different from mere aloneness. Solitude is chosen willingly, eagerly. It is savored deliciously. It is the reconnection of the self to the soul, to the center, to the voice of the universe reverberating inside, on the skin, and around.

Have you reached the point yet where solitude is a joy and bringer of peace? Have you moved through the fear of what you formerly thought of as aloneness into the very different space of solitude? What really triggered the transition? And what was the biggest obstacle inside that you had to overcome to reach a place of embracing solitude?

It's nice to be here, isn't it?

June 25

Screw it!

I very much enjoy the stories of people who cast aside all fear, criticism, and certainty of loss in order to go after what they felt called to go after....and lost. I love those stories. I love the sheer audacity.

The stories where they emerge triumphant in the end are, of course, glorious and easy to like. But God bless the ones who *fail* gloriously. There is a sheer majesty in the human spirit that is willing to accept that if failure be the outcome, so be it.

Though, even the ones who succeed tacitly accept the possibility of abject failure. Their choice is made all the more fantastic by the lionesque souls who endeavor greatness and go down in flames.

Oh, the humanity of being willing to embrace death and thereby embrace life itself, rather than making slow love to the decay of endeavoring nothing, clinging instead to safety.

What is your greatness calling you to? Do you have a "Screw it!" in you? Do you fear glorious failure and death? Are you good, if you do? Got the crazy in you to do it anyway? If so, I raise my SKOL to you!

June 26

*To have doubted one's own first principles
is the mark of a civilized man.*
-Oliver Wendell Holmes Jr.,
Former Associate Justice of the U.S. Supreme Court

Our core beliefs – the deepest stuff we were taught about ourselves, our identity, and life itself – drive more of our lives than anything else in or around us. Though, those same core beliefs – or first principles, as Holmes calls them – were almost invariably planted by someone(s) outside of us, usually a parent, when we had no power to stop it and sought only to gain the attention and approval of the one selling it. Just as importantly, those core beliefs are generally unknown to the bearer and invisible to the naked eye – i.e. awareness of them, not to mention their extraction, requires a helping hand in looking inside. This is why I wrote, *There's a Hole in My Love Cup*, and created *The Badass Counseling Show* podcast; to help those unfamiliar with their inner world to see what's really wrong and what's been driving them the whole time.

This doubting of first principles is a deconstruction of what your parents and society built. For, creation is invariably preceded by destruction. Some of your new self will, in fact, include segments from your parents, things you were taught about yourself and life. However, so much of who you are to become will not include that, or certainly not to the same degree. But in order to know where your parents stop and you begin, you must crack it all open, deconstruct it, then reconstruct it your way. The birth of your real, original self demands it.

Ready?

June 27

Great minds have purposes;
others have wishes.
-Washington Irving, American novelist

There's a difference between fulfillment and fun, between walking through life with a sense of satisfaction, not because you've accomplished your goals but because you're working toward what you're passionate about, and happiness, wherein you're ever striving for the next high or the one big high after which you can finally be happy. The men and women we exalt most in life are those who are enraptured in something greater than themselves, a purpose which sweeps up their energies and focus.

On a piece of paper, make two columns. At the top of the first write, "What do I most want, at least as far as I can see, today?" And, at the top of the second write, "What might my purpose be?" Then play with it. List bullet point answers in each column. Ask other questions within this exercise, such as: What's my highest dream; what path would light me up; what would make me most proud on my deathbed to have done with the decades I have left? How do your answers to these questions inform, or determine, your lists in the two columns?

Don't write as if your lists are permanent or must be acted on. Just play with it. There's no need to rush it. In fact, you can't rush it, no matter how impatient you may be to have the answers right now. The soul reveals what it will reveal when it is time to do so.

Then, as you continue to mull over this, over time your answers will become clearer. At some point in the future, you will be pressed by your own senses to make a decision between the two lists. Truth is, you may, at some point, have both, but you can't pursue them both simultaneously, at least not honestly. Will you be a person of purpose or a person with wishes? Will you be a person in it for himself or for far more than himself? Who are you, really?

June 28

Dare to be wise.
-Unknown

It seems an odd thing to say. Why would wisdom require daring?

I came to understand the reason in young adulthood. For whatever asinine reason, when I was 22, I prayed that I would be given two things in life: a woman who would be with me forever, and wisdom. (Little did I know that the former would take me a good stretch down the path of bringing the latter.)

Well, I got the former, had two kids together, and divorced. Yet, by the mere existence of those two kids, she is forever linked to me on every Erlandson/Johnson family tree that gets written. (It seems the gods have a bit of a sense of humor...or know my destiny better than I do.)

The latter, I quickly grew to discover, is the sum of only two things. Only two elements, one accidental and one deliberate, can make that perfect cocktail of wisdom: pain and self-reflection. If there is no pain, the thoughts and words are inexperienced and thin. They do not stir the souls of men and women; boys and girls, perhaps, but not adults. If there is pain, as many of the aged, or middle-aged, have experienced, there is knowledge but no depth; the power is in having survived, which is no small thing. But, lacking the reflection on the experiences and exploration for the gems of insight they bear in their talons, there is no learning for the hearer of the story. Without exploration of the pain (what caused it, how it felt, and what it was sent by the universe to teach oneself), there is no waymark for those who struggle on their own paths.

Pain and reflection. Both demand courage, for the pain often comes from venturing into the unknown or forbidden – those paths you've been told not to take but your own soul knows you must. That is a courageous act. And, self-reflection requires the courage to relive it, again and again, through the lens of mining it for what it's trying to teach you about life and about self.

That is the price of wisdom: to see pain as a gift and to find the blessed teaching inside it.

June 29

Is love really blind?
-Don Santo, Kenyan rapper

We so often say after breakups, "Now I see him for who he really is." But what if the opposite is true? What if it is only through the eyes of true love that a man or woman is finally seen for the self that is their true soul?

In breakups, sadly, we see the masks, the pains of the father/mother, and fears re-consuming them, as they were before they met your love. And they see yours. You also see yours, again.

Worse, what if those masks, pains, and fears were all there when you first met them (which they were), and you saw them but didn't want to see them? What if the indicators were all present (which they were), but you ignored them? What was going on in that past iteration of you, that old you, that caused you to poke your own eyes out, to choose to make your love blind?

See, it's not that a breakup reveals who a person really is. No, it reveals the rest of who a person is that you didn't want to see in the beginning.

Is it possible that you wanted the love so badly – because of your own fears, parental pains that got transferred surreptitiously onto you, and tragic beliefs that were pressed into you – that you allowed yourself to ignore the unhealed half of who they always were? You can claim love-bombing made you not see it. Nonsense. No person can fully hide who they are. It was there revealing itself. And you gotta own your share of the equation, or you'll carry that crap into your next relationship and the next one after that.

Yet, the beauty of this story is that the glorious cocktail of your love with theirs enabled two people to more fully express the truest part of who they were, at least for some brief window of time. And it's hard to let go of that when you've experienced it for the first time or in a massive dose. For that matter, it's similarly so easy to simply hate someone with whom you shared that cocktail mix, who no longer wants the more-revealed self you've become.

What a lovely opportunity for growth. For, now the hate inside that you must flush out is revealed to you. And should you have the courage, the fears, parentally transferred pains, and self-beliefs are revealed to you. Now, you can get about the business of extraction of them, lest they corrupt what is ahead for you. Which part do you most fear touching and flushing out first? Why?

June 30

Whatever makes your soul happy, do that!
-Unknown

Having grown up on a farm during the Great Depression and WWII, my mother spent most of her 93 years with her hands in the dirt, growing flowers, vegetables, and as I'm sure she'd say, quite a few weeds, 'til it all started to hurt her joints too much in her nineties. It was all for the pursuit of beauty. A beautiful salad; a beautiful bushel basket full of harvested, brightly colored tomatoes, carrots, raspberries, zucchini, pumpkins, and wax beans; the beauty of geraniums, marigolds, morning glories, African violets, and Moses in the Bulrushes; and, above all, the beauty of lush, black Minnesota topsoil in her increasingly arthritis-gnarled hands.

Beauty stirs the soul. Beauty has the power to grip our attention, mesmerize us, and stir us to focused action. But of course, the particular beauty that stirs one oftentimes falls flat for another.

The beauty of a powerful or elegant piece of music. The beauty of a particular face. Beauty of character or a person's actions. Beauty in the cuteness of a puppy or kitten. Beauty in design or turn of phrase. Beauty of a particular movement.

Where do you find beauty? What, at the level of perfection, is most likely to stir your soul? Or, what genre of life is so innately compelling to you in its beauty that even gross imperfection in it is still astounding to your hypnotized soul? Is it possible that you need more of that in your life?

It's called 'tending soul.' Like a garden. You gotta nurture it. Feel that soil of your soul in your fingers.

July

July 1

Change will not occur,
until the pain gets bad enough.
-Sven

Is it killin' ya, yet; I mean, just hammering the heck out of you? Are you so beaten down that you don't even fear the consequences anymore? Are you so beleaguered, weathered, broken, and dismayed that no change scares you, anymore, that you no longer give a crap? If you're not there, then you haven't reached, what I call, the 'F**k it!' point. You may be close, but you ain't there yet. Whether slowly or quickly, it keeps getting worse. But, it hasn't reached the breakthrough point.

Here's the thing. Your pain will get worse, because pain – whichever flavor it may be – doesn't magically heal itself. Your soul will conjure even more pain, so as to finally break you of the curse of your fears, infusing you with the power to finally create new life. Thereby, the door is finally opened to walk into authenticity and a true *ALIVENESS*.

The 'F**k it!' point is this glorious place where all the pain of life finally gets so doggone bad that today, for the first time ever, you have the *courage* to do what, just yesterday, you could not possibly have done. Yesterday, the fear was too great. Today, you have the *clarity* to know precisely what the path is, when just yesterday it was fog and uncertainty.

Are you still not quite there? See, you cannot force the 'F**k it!' point. If you're still thinking about things, you're not there yet; still apprehensive, you're short of it; still wringing your hands, your pain hasn't gotten bad enough. The clarity and courage when you're there are unequivocal. It's not words, thoughts, belief, or hope, it's knowing. And, knowing is very different, particularly when coupled with no longer caring. It's a wicked cocktail.

If you're not there yet, there's still a fear or two. What do you fear that keeps you in this horrible situation? What would new life look like to you, if the universe, or soul, were to bless you with enough pain to push you to and through the 'F**k it!' point? What's the vision? Have you written it out? Maybe today is the day you do that in granular detail.

July 2

> *The reasonable man adapts himself to the world.*
> *The unreasonable man persists in trying to adapt the world to himself.*
> *All progress, therefore, depends upon the unreasonable man.*
> -George Bernard Shaw, playwright

When was the last time you were conscious of what you really wanted to do in a situation but pulled back from doing so, for fear of backlash, condemnation, or being seen as something bad? More pointedly, in what area(s) of life are you most inclined to be reasonable, get along, or go with the expectations of others, or society, when your own heart, or inner voice, is calling you to something very different?

Why do you choose the reasonable path? What do you fear? What is the one sentence you most fear someone saying to you or about you, or most fear someone(s) thinking about you? Who is the person most likely to say that to you? That's the person who still, to a greater or lesser degree, owns you.

When do you start living a more gloriously unreasonable life?

July 3

How strange when an illusion dies.
It's as if you've lost a child.
-Judy Garland, American actress/entertainer, Minnesotan

One of the hardest-hitting, kick-the-living-crap-out-of-you experiences that many clients of mine experience is when we explore their childhood and discover that the way this parent or that, or both, treated my client falls nowhere under the definition of 'good parenting,' often not falling under any definition of parenting, except 'horrible.' What comes next is the realization, "I never had parents or family, to begin with. I've been alone the whole time."

BOOM!

Very often, this same client has spent a lifetime trying win a parent's praise or even acknowledgement, spent a lifetime trying to stitch together a family, only to be met with frustration and fraying. Holding on and holding on to the belief that he or she actually had a family, the client gets hammered when seeing that it has been an illusion the whole time. What follows is the grieving and odd liberation that comes from allowing the illusion to die. It brings tremendous grief and yet a feeling that they no longer have to keep trying to maintain something that never existed. It also brings a reckoning with a profound sense of aloneness. That can be hard. But, at least it's sure footing, because it's finally truth. Life can now re-begin based on truth.

What are the illusions you've been keeping alive? Are they regarding self, family, love/relationships, life, career, health, or something no one can see? Are you ready to face them, allow them to die, and go through the grieving? Are you ready for liberation and new life based on truth?

July 4

*When you feel in your gut what you are and then dynamically pursue it
– don't back down and don't give up –
then you're going to mystify a lot of folks.*
-Bob Dylan, Poet, Minnesotan, Nobel laureate

The most mysterious people in life are those who are just damn happy and have an energy that is different from and greater than others. You can see it in them. You feel it. It comes off of them. We say things like, "What's his secret?" and "I want what she's got!" They're mysterious, because they seem to have mastered life, or found that *ALIVENESS* that eludes so many.

It's not just putting on a happy face. That's fakery. The forced smile and pretend happy. Nah, this is something different. It's someone who burns clean energy. You can just feel the difference.

And yet, the poet says there's no secret to it, at all. It is simply to unrelentingly live who you really are. Of course, knowing 'what you are' – i.e. your authentic self – requires cutting out all that you've been taught you 'should be' or all that you've been taught sucks about you or is unwanted. It takes the courage to reject the diminishment of your real self. It is to choose your own truth and worth, when it means potentially losing those who want you to be who they want you to be, or who you've always been.

Maybe that's the mystery the Minnesota man speaks of. For too many people, the courage to choose self over others is unfathomable, too difficult, against everything they've been taught they should be.

Do you stand in wonderment as you gaze upon those who live freely, aggressively attacking life and dreams, savoring it, or energized in a way you've never been? So, is the hardest part of the quote (above) the inability to feel what/who you are? Or, the not backing down? And, what is it about that part that so terrifies you? What do you fear seeing, experiencing, hearing, feeling, if you do it? Is it possible *that* is your biggest obstruction to experiencing a life of *ALIVENESS*? How bad do the pain, frustration, lethargy, unease, anxiety, depression, and feeling a sense of waste have to get before you finally have the courage you never felt you possessed, that you only admired in others? How long before the pain outweighs the fear, and your courage bubbles up within you? How long will you sit on your hands?

When do you finally set yourself free to be the freak-ass, interesting, self-driven, fascinating, on-fire person that you were created to be?

Free to be authentic. Free to pursue your own happiness, on your own terms, at your own killer speed, or slow speed. Free to even enjoy your own screw-ups and failures as much as your successes, because for the first time in your life you are on your own path, truly and fully *ALIVE*!

216

July 5

You can't connect the dots looking forward.
You can only connect them looking backwards.
So, you have to trust that the dots will somehow connect in your future.
-Steve Jobs, Founder of Apple

Before the age of 20, I had:
- [ ] quit college twice, including one that had me on track to be a fighter pilot;
- [ ] quit a Division I, Top Ten ranked NCAA football program; and
- [ ] turned down an admissions offer to an Ivy League business school.

By age 30, I had:
- [ ] two kids;
- [ ] been divorced once;
- [ ] quit college again, before graduating from a tiny fourth school;
- [ ] quit seminary/graduate school twice;
- [ ] co-authored my first published article;
- [ ] been kicked out of the ordained ministry track by my religious denomination; and
- [ ] plunged into what would become a 12-year suicidal depression.

By age 40, I had:
- [ ] attempted suicide (bled for an hour before calling it quits and asking a passerby to call 911);
- [ ] written four books that pretty much no one read, including the very first book ever to name and flesh out the 'spiritual but not religious' movement in America, now the largest spiritual-religious movement in American history (No one keeps writing 2, 3, and 4 books when no one is reading them.). Though, my first book was critically reviewed and acclaimed in two scholarly journals;
- [ ] a second divorce;
- [ ] been thrown out of ordained ministry two more times for my controversial books, my stance on gay rights, and what was thought to be my generally offensive personality;
- [ ] had my rights to, and relationship with, my kids stripped from me by my ex;
- [ ] been villainized in much of my own family by my first ex;
- [ ] been a successful NCAA head strength coach, but quit out of boredom;
- [ ] lost two parish pastor positions for my stance on gay rights, long before my denomination ratified the ordination of gay clergy;
- [ ] lectured at the graduate and undergraduate levels in the fields of early

childhood spirituality, sociology of religion, sports psychology, and fitness coaching;

☐ watched countless efforts at growing an online presence, in the earliest days of social media, fall flat.

By age 50, I had:

☐ been railroaded out of one more large church as a pastor, because of my stand on gay rights and my writings;

☐ given up on ordained ministry;

☐ given up all of my life possessions and small bank account to minister to the homeless and live among them, sleeping on concrete every night for 2 ½ years, on the streets of Oakland/Berkeley, CA;

☐ written two more books and, while having gained representation by the largest literary agency in the U.S., watched them sell a mere hundred, or two, copies, per year;

☐ had a few articles and commentary pieces published in magazines and newspapers;

☐ continued to attempt to create an online presence with my work and ideas, all to no avail;

☐ created online DIY video courses that almost no one was buying;

☐ developed a counseling practice of some repute that I had moved to Manhattan, NYC;

☐ re-established a relationship with my now adult-children, in their twenties;

☐ experienced formerly critical old friends and family coming to me for private counsel.

By age 55, I watched:

☐ my online presence explode globally across many social media platforms;

☐ skyrocketing sales of my last book, which details my counseling method as a way to help people heal themselves;

☐ my soul counseling practice go global;

☐ the soul counseling podcast I host and executive produce go instantly viral, hitting over one million downloads in 12 months;

☐ my love life begin to extend into its second decade with a woman who herself had built an $80M company in NYC;

☐ my relationship with my children had become better than I had ever dreamed.

Today, though the immodesty of saying so pains my Swedish-American piety, my work in the fields of soul, suicide, infidelity, motivation, and happiness are respected by millions around the world.

There is no way on earth any of the success and global influence I have been entrusted with, today, could have ever been predicted even 10 years ago. Several of the social media platforms my work has exploded on didn't even exist. Certainly, it couldn't have been predicted 30 years ago, back in my twenties. Social media, as a whole, didn't exist back then. For most intents and purposes, personal computing, itself, barely existed.

There's no way any of the success happens if I hadn't had the constantly wavering belief in what I brought to the table! Yes, constantly wavering. There was ample doubt in me, often driven by withering criticism from external forces. Plus, I had no idea where the hell it was all leading. All I knew is that I was going to win or lose based on one thing, one voice, one intuition: MINE! Screw it! I'd rather fail following my own voice than succeed following the prison of someone else's. And either you're on board for that, or you ain't in my life.

But, I had to go through the excruciating depression. I had to find my own way out, because no one really was able to help me. I had to experience the loss of my kids; the gaslighting; the two divorces; the suicide; getting thrown out of individual churches and my larger denomination many times; the slow drag of decades of zero success and no professional support from anyone; the abject failure of countless books and ancillary career pursuits; the brutal denial by social media to go anywhere for a decade and a half; and lack of money (though I worked countless restaurant jobs to always pay child support and my own bills).

I had to go through all of this, as well as all the failures and pains I've forgotten, as my 55 year-old mind forgets more than it remembers, nowadays, in order to be precisely positioned where I am today. We can only connect the dots in reverse. All of those failures and hardships enable me to speak knowingly to the pains and struggles of those I'm trying to reach. It was all necessary.

Has it occurred to you that all the misery now is in preparation for the influence and joy you'll have later? But, you must have the courage to continually mine for the gems of wisdom and great gifts your suffering, loss, and failures hold in their hand. You must constantly be open to the movements of the universe, holding onto your vision loosely, allowing the universe to infuse your life with new elements you could've never predicted.

July 6

Our bodies communicate to us clearly and specifically,
if we are willing to listen.
The more willing you are to surrender to the energy within you,
the more power can flow through you.
-Shakti Gawain, Author, *Living in the Light*

Fully grasping and embracing this concept by Gawain requires a rewiring of the cultural mindset that says everything smart, every good choice, all best paths originate in the mind. Turning that notion on its head, the intuitives and those connected with soul know that both peace and real power come from somewhere not in the head. Intuition, which is the voice of the soul, is sensed not in the brain but deeper in the body. 'Trust your gut' is such a common phrase as to be almost cliché. Yet, its commonness reveals the universality of the experience of real knowing of one's truth and path, or real knowing what the choice is in this or that decision.

Unfortunately, we too often infuse that trusting of gut with distrust from the brain, which has stuck inside it the voices and fears from others.

But, life truly begins at the point of surrendering to the voice of the body, the soul, the gut. Previously unseen power begins to flow, the more you listen and bank on that voice. It is power that is not conjured or contrived, just effortlessly flowing in fuller and fuller force.

It's time to start listening, trusting, and surrendering. It's time.

July 7

*The single biggest mistake people make in trying to get happy
is they do more things that make them happy.*
-Sven

If you're reading this book, there's a chance you read the precursor to this one, *There's a Hole in My Love Cup*. One of the pivotal concepts of that book, really the fulcrum on which the book turns is the quote above. Society sells the bill of goods that having and doing more will naturally bring greater happiness. We venerate the rich and famous. We look up to those who are constantly working harder. We strive to have more and do more.

However, having spent the better part of my career as the personal counselor to those very same rich and famous, I can tell you as a matter of absolute fact that neither riches nor fame bring immunity from pain, unhappiness, and severe unrest of the soul. No matter how powerful the will that brought those acquisitions, the soul (when filled with debilitating messages from childhood and countless pains) will eventually grind to a halt even the greatest titans. Thing is, we as the public will never see it, unless it becomes so out of hand that it splashes into the tabloids. But, it's there.

What's the point? Happiness, peace inside, genuine fulfillment, and true *ALIVENESS* are not dependent upon the acquisition and experience of more happy things, more diamonds, so to speak, but infinitely more dependent on the removal of more people, places, plans, purposes, principles, and self-beliefs that suck the life energy out of you. It is the removal of the raw sewage of the soul that brings about happiness and fulfillment. If you have a handful of diamonds in your hands, it doesn't mean a thing if you have giant pipes dumping raw sewage onto your head. All you will be able to see, taste, touch, smell, and hear is that sewage. Until that is gone, that sewage is the ever-dominating reality.

What is often most difficult for many folks to understand is that the most toxic sewage ain't the stuff outside you, such as hurtful people and life-sucking careers. Nah, it's the internal stuff that has been there since ages 2, 6, 9, and 13. Believe it or not (and a great many don't), that's how powerful that childhood stuff really is. It can last for and near-completely undermine an entire life.

So, one of the most critical exercises you can do is to take a piece of paper, draw a line down the middle, creating two columns. At the top of the left column write: 'Diamonds: That which actually gives me energy;' and the right column: 'Raw Sewage: That which sucks my life energy out of me.'

Now, list everything, small, medium and large that falls under each heading, both external and internal. Under Diamonds, also list the energy-bringers in your life presently, as well as things you've done in the past that energized you, and things you've considered doing in the future. When it comes to that Raw Sewage column list anything, whether externally or internally, that bleeds your life energy or is just killing you. Be particular about looking at what the notions are that you've been taught to believe about yourself, life, and the world; list them under the appropriate column. Have the courage to name the people (and their messages) that belong in that right-hand column. List everything.

Consider and journal, as you go about this exercise:
- ☐ Who or what are all the people, paths, or possessions that have power over me?
- ☐ What are the internal demons and external power sources that I have not yet named that still have influence over my life?
- ☐ Why do I keep giving them power over my life?
- ☐ Am I ready to take that power back and start running my own life more? How, specifically?

Then, if you want to up the ante, start doing and going after more of the left list – saying 'yes' to them, finally – while simultaneously reducing or eliminating the people, things, and beliefs in the right column that you doggone well know are bleeding the life outta you. That's where life really begins – at the courage to finally, bit by bit, say 'no' to all the raw sewage in your life.

July 8

It is not the strongest of the species that survives,
nor the most intelligent,
but the one most responsive to change.
-Charles Darwin, English biologist

Holy misquotes!

Darwin's words and ideas are seemingly always misinterpreted into, "Only the strong survive" and "Survival of the fittest." Yet, here he makes it explicitly clear that strength is not the linchpin of evolution. Rather, it is willingness to adapt and change. Well, that's a beast of a different stripe.

Overlay that concept onto the realm of finding happiness, peace in the soul, true purpose, and *ALIVENESS* and it still rings true. These ultimate life pursuits are not acquired by the strong, but those willing to change when the pain gets bad enough, those willing to shed life-draining paths and people, those willing to see new doors opening in pursuit of a vision that is not quite manifesting. Toughing it out has little value in the evolution of the soul, and more often than not tilts toward slow internal, and even physical, decay.

The soul is talking. Where is your soul calling you to adapt? Which changes need to be passed through next? What doors need to be closed?

The real challenge isn't grabbing the next vine as you swing through the jungle, but letting go of the last one. We grow so attached to the security. And, as you've heard me say a million times, change will not occur 'til the pain gets bad enough. 'Til that old vine has withered in your hand, you ain't never gonna let go. So, has it?

When do you start letting go sooner in life, rather than waiting until all is dying inside you and around you?

July 9

He keeps me in his pocket
for a rainy day;
he swears I'm not an object,
as he yo-yo's me away.
A friend is what we'll call it,
but my friend, he does not know,
each time it rains I love him —
so to his pocket, I must go.
He thinks he's being clever,
but I am not a fool;
his love ain't worth a penny,
so to my heart I must be cruel.

-Coco Ginger, American poet, *A Pocket-sized Girl*

One of the harder things to do in life is to look a human being in the face and tell them that you don't want to be with them anymore. Whether it's a family member, a longtime boss, a friend, or a lover, breaking things off, or breaking up, is so fear-inducing for some people that they will string out what they know to be dead or highly toxic, rather than simply euthanize the relationship.

One of the things that I see and hear quite frequently is the reluctance people have to end a relationship that brings a feeling of security, or just familiarity in having the lover, safe job, or family member around, even though deep in this person's heart they know that they don't want to stay in that relationship. They just like having them around. So by not breaking it off, one person is fundamentally using the other person to get the comfort in familiarity, using them under the illusion that there's hope for a richer or continued relationship.

It is not fair to perpetuate hope in another person when you know inside of you there is no hope. Whom are you using because you like the security of having them around or because you are afraid to look them in the face and simply tell the truth, afraid to hurt their feelings, afraid of the potential backlash? At what point in life do you begin living with greater integrity, including doing the hard, uncomfortable things like ending relationships that need to end.

Who is keeping you in their back pocket? How extraordinarily painful is it for you to admit that, not to mention truly face it and move on with your life? You cannot fear being alone or fear the voices of criticism from your past that rise up against you when you are alone. Liberate yourself. Heal. Take your life back!

July 10

"A leader is best when people barely know he exists,
when his work is done, his aim fulfilled,
they will say, 'We did it ourselves.'"
-Lao Tzu, Chinese philosopher

Before my second year of college at the US Air Force Academy, as with all cadets, I was expected to take flight training in glider airplanes. In the training aircraft there are two seats in tandem, front for student, rear for instructor pilot, or IP (who were upperclass cadets, who had hundreds of hours in glider cockpits, and some flew high-performance sailplanes). Each seat is equipped with identical hand and feet controls.

One of the very first commands that a glider student learns is, "My plane," which is accompanied by the response, "your plane." Simply put, the IP would get the plane up in the air and stabilized, then say, "your plane," thereby instructing me to put my hands and feet on the controls, at which point I respond, "my plane." In doing so, the IP is handing control over to the student to learn basic maneuvers and, inevitably, screw things up, until the IP instructs, "my plane." At this point, the student (me) would take his hand off the joystick and feet off the rudder pedals, and respond, "Your plane." The IP would right the plane and hand it back with, "Your plane."

Clear leader. Clear follower. Clear demarcation of power. Clear communication. No scolding. No wrath. Even when lives were at stake, flying in a plane with no engine. Clear, cool heads.

The goal was to get the student to the point where, after many flights, it was her plane from pre-flight to taxi, aerotow to release, nose-high stalls to recoveries from spiral dives, held off landings to post-flight, all while on the student's "my plane." The culmination of this process is when the student is ready to take their first solo flight with an empty backseat.

Any truly effective leadership position (company boss, parenting, captaining or coaching a team, leading a band, or general contracting the building of a house) is little different. There is a constant toggling between 'your plane' and 'my plane.' The goal of the time together is the student, employee, son/daughter finally able to solo, because they were taught by someone well-accomplished, cool-headed, driven not by their own fears and anger but their desire to build a skilled, confident person ready for solo flight. But far too many parents and leaders hold on to power and control, unwilling to hand the plane over, convinced the student is incompetent and untrainable. These are amateur leaders; non-leaders, really. They are people who are neither qualified, nor possessed of sound mind to lead and cultivate young hearts and minds.

Are you cultivating talent? Are you constantly giving power back to the student, after righting the plane? Or, are you scolding, mocking, and criticizing? Are you teaching in an atmosphere of respect and calm, even kindness? Or, are you misusing your power? Have you done the work necessary to be a qualified IP of employees, subcontractors, kids and other people's lives? Are you trying to grow others to be strong and able? Or, are you withholding control and power for yourself?

July 11

The surest way to corrupt a youth
is to instruct him to hold in higher esteem
those who think alike
rather than those who think differently.
-Friedrich Nietzsche, German philosopher

If you were to spitball it, what percent of teachings that you've been inculcated with by adults, peers, and culture have fundamentally pushed you toward normalcy and what percentage have encouraged you to be different? As you've moved forward with those values put in you by others, how much life do you feel you have wasted trying to fit into the boxes of normal?

Second, if you were to assess your own truest belief system, inside of you, what percent do you believe in normal/acceptable and what percent do you believe in being different? Are you okay with that percentage?

What percent of the change you know you (still) need in your life swirls around too much normal and not enough willingness to be different? Is it possible that choke of normalcy is what's slowly sucking the years from you? Is it possible that now is the time to break free of the box of normal?

July 12

Never fight an inanimate object.
-P.J. O'Rourke, American satirist

When I was an NCAA Head Coach for Strength and Conditioning, I knew doggone well that the biggest determinant of failure or success on the playing field, rink, or court (and life, as a whole) was not the strength of my athletes, but the stuff going on in their heads and, even more importantly, in their guts – the messages that were churning in them, driving them, subverting or expanding their best efforts and intentions.

I seldom saw this in more stark relief than when a young man full of frustration, rage, and pain would punch a brick wall that we had in the weightroom or somewhere in the athletic facility. (It was always a young man; never saw a young woman or non-binary individual do this.) It wasn't a frequent occurrence, but enough seen as to be notable. The blood and broken bones I've seen it cause is tragically laughable. Embarrassingly, I think I did it once – once! – as a kid.

Chalk the young guy's actions up to testosterone or uncontrollable inner pain taking mad turns, if you like, but it's a cautionary tale for the rest of us. While your walls may not be made of brick and mortar, what walls are you foolishly raging on and bloodying your fists on? If, in the quote above, we think of 'inanimate object' in terms of something or someone in your life that is inflexible, intransigent, or immovable, it cracks the quote wide open.

What the heck are you wasting your life energy on? What do you keep pounding on or trying to chip away at that shows no evidence of yielding, compromise, or movement? Is it career-related, family, friends, love, parenting, health, money-related, or something else? Why do you keep bloodying yourself? Why have you not gotten the message that this thing, or person ain't changing? Why is it so darn hard for you to realize what is really so bloody obvious? What is it you just so refuse to let go of?

My father used to kid, "Sven, why does a moron keep beating his head against the wall?"

"I don't know, Dad. Why?"

He'd respond with a wry smile, "Because it feels sooo good when he stops."

July 13

> *Will my eyes adjust to this darkness?*
> *Will I find you in the dark —*
> *not in the streaks of light which remain, but in the darkness?*
> -Nicholas Wolterstorff, American philosopher, *Lament for a Son*

There can be little argument that the death of one's child is at or near the top of life's most grievous events, one every parent fears. But what gets tragically, quietly lost is that the nature of the death can be unseen, unforeseen, or completely foreseen, each with its own unique daggers. For example:

- A parent's child can die in a tragic accident; gone instantly; goodbyes and hugs never exchanged; the return never coming, day into day, year on top of year;
- The light can go out of a child's eyes at a very young age; body and traces of soul so present, but so much gone;
- One's child can fall tragically into the abyss of drug addiction, occasionally coming out, but ever slipping further into its grasp and the known, inexorable destination, wherein for some of the survivors there is decades-driven, guilt-ridden relief;
- A child can disappear without a trace; the parents and family left wondering if the child is even alive and racked with the extraordinarily painful hope that they are;
- An adult child can be overtaken by mental illness with no insight in the adult child (no awareness that they, themselves, are even sick), where the parents are left grieving a person that is now forever gone, though still alive, never to return as the person they once were.

And, the guilt. The sorrow. The enormity of pain. Each day, the decisions must be made and remade...and remade again. Can I let go? How can I even consider letting go? I can't let go. But I must let go. But I can't.

Worse are the feelings and questions around the survivor/parent's own mortality, now that such a gaping hole has been created in their life: Should I stay or should I go? How can I keep living? How can I go? I can't do either. This feeling caught in between is killing me.

And, the soul eventually forces you to grieve. And to grieve. There is no end around. There is no busyness, no drug, no nothing that can wash away the pain or keep it at bay forever. Eventually, it demands to be dealt with. There is but grieving. Only the path through it is the path past it. And each heart-wrenching, soul-crushing step down that path is, itself, the choice to live. It is that Divine Spark — that pilot light — deeeeeep inside, still flickering. That desire to live, rising up from the soul. Because, if you didn't want to live, you surely wouldn't go into that pain, unless you were flagellating yourself with the pain, out of guilt or self-hatred. But even then, the soul longs to live and if we allow the grief to flush out of us, it too does pass, eventually.

Finally, it is that desire to live that is ever life's greatest act of courage. To live amid death, amid loss. It is to walk, sometimes limping and broken, at times even just crawling toward that day you cannot see – that day when there is sunlight again, when against all odds there is laughter again, without guilt. It is to one day walk differently in this world, to walk joyfully amid the sorrows of the world. It seems heretical to even say, but it is out there, waiting. It is true. Many who have allowed the pain to purge and purge and purge some more, have discovered that day out there and the new life that comes with it, always with the memories, but no longer the deep pain.

Do you have the courage to grieve, today? Do you have the courage to take one more step? Or, perhaps, today is a day to just rest. Trust your soul.

July 14

The world's greatest teacher is pain.
The world's greatest university is life.
-Matshona Dhliwayo, Zimbabwe-born Canadian philosopher

One of the most controversial, yet uncomfortably true things I learned in all of my years studying world religions, the works of Joseph Campbell, James Hillman, Carl Jung, and Martin Luther, among others in related genres, is that pain holds gems of wisdom in its hands. Inside the dark forest of the soul there are cascading waterfalls of epiphanies, sparkling hidden jewels of deep truth, and depths of peace and new power.

I have become an absolute believer that pain is life's greatest teacher, even our greatest friend. Lives are transformed by pain, broken into new depth, wisdom, and strength. Often the question most fraught with trepidation inside of me is when I ask a client, if the time is right, "What was this horrific event, or time of life, sent to teach you?" Or, for those who are not inclined to think there's an entity sending things our way, "How is this grand hell you're in the greatest blessing of your life? What is the colossal truth your soul can extract from this vastness of pain?"

This is what it means to courageously mine our lives for the wisdom life bears, often in the most gruesome of areas – life's pain. This is when our perspectives on ourselves, on life, on others are often flipped on their head. Perhaps death no longer brings fear. Relationships are felt more deeply. Worry slips away. We begin to walk more calmly and see more deeply, understand others more deliberately, give more richly, and simply hide less.

What are the gems of wisdom hidden inside the pain you're experiencing? Is it possible that the gratitude you keep trying to focus on is achieved not by giving thanks for the good but seeing the blessings in the curses and the hells?

July 15

> *Every saint has a past and*
> *Every sinner has a future.*
> -Oscar Wilde, Irish poet

I think the inclination in reading this quote is to focus on the second clause and read it as giving us hope, which clearly seems to be part of Wilde's intention. Each of us has the opportunity to be happy, no matter what crud we've done in the past.

For me, the quite beautiful part of it is the first clause. Isn't it fascinating how we tend to over-venerate the people we look up to, almost desiring to whitewash their past or, if we don't know their past, assume there is nothing questionable or outright bad in it. *Yet, it is often that very wayward, hurt-filled past that later informs and, in no small part, creates the saint.* Read that again. It is that walk through life as a normal person, replete with struggles and failures, heartbreak and sorrow, people we hurt and penance we must do that shapes and drives the person whom we look up to later.

That means that when we're going through the 'past' Wilde refers to, when the past is in fact our present, we have to be forgiving of ourselves, but also, more importantly, understanding that this present is shaping us, breaking us down, breaking us open, deconstructing that inside which isn't us, teaching the us that is to come. In other words, where you are today is not the final destination. It is all transformative and experience-gathering, in service of what is ahead. The guilt, the hardship, the owning of the pain you've caused is intended to destroy and to create. We simply must always be mining it for what it is trying to teach us about self and life, the world and people.

Here's the really tricky, even offensive part. The harder the now, the more powerful the insights and the greater the depths of wisdom it can bring. Thus, the harder the now, the more life-giving you have the potential to become for life and for humanity, not to mention yourself(!), when you come out the other side.

What are your humiliations and guilt trying to teach you about self and life that you have been running from for a very long time? How is it trying to grow you from within? In what way will those lessons most change things in your life ahead, if you were to speculate?

July 16

The more I study the world,
the more I am convinced of
the inability of brute force
to create anything durable.
-Napolean Bonaparte,
Iconic French Emperor and military commander

It seems ironic, doesn't it, to read those words from a man who is universally known throughout history as a fearsome general intent to expand the reaches of his empire? This, of course, shows our own limitations, thinking that military leaders have but one means to accomplish their ends: brute force and tactics.

Yet, here we are with what can only be words born of long experience in the games and wars of life. It's notable that at Bonaparte's death France was little bigger than when he began his life's campaign to grow it, thus giving credence to precisely his point above. It seems to indicate that he leaned on brute force, but tragically discovered that it really didn't work.

I see this often when working with presidents of companies, leaders of teams and organizations, and others trying to make their way up to the top roles. I see many people believing in their own abilities and willpower driving their vision forward, fixing, making things happen, which is often what it takes to build a business. However, the mere fact that they end up coming to me for counsel indicates there are problems, often well beyond the office or business setting. Very often, the brute force approach is one of the problems. Because, that same approach rarely works in personal relationships and becomes increasingly less constructive in parenting their own children. Lastly, they discover that it ceases to work effectively as their work world grows.

But, it's hard to shut off president-of-the-company mode when you walk in the front door at night. It's hard to not fix your friends and children. It's hard to keep your mouth shut and listen. It's hard to believe that someone might actually know better than you. It's hard to allow room for the universe to work, rather than always forcing your agenda, convinced "If I don't do it, it won't get done." And yet, that is precisely what this great French leader is teaching us – the brute force method is far less effective than we think, and, I would add, creates immense collateral damage, backlash, and ill will.

And so, if they have never learned or employed it before, brute forcers have to begin to relearn and use a softer sell technique for moving through life, or even a much more frustrating one for them: a farmer planting seeds. My father and mother grew up on farms during the Great Depression and WWII. Dad would regale us with farm stories 'til we were bored to exhaustion. But those stories stuck with us and became the foundational wisdom for our own lives. And that planting and slow growth of ideas is the farmer's way of living: planting seeds, tend the soil, water, sunlight, care, water, sunlight, care. The seeds take root and slowly begin to grow, even when you can't see them because they're still below ground. This creates durable plants that produce fruit, grain, and vegetables.

Where do you tend to fall: a brute, a soft seller, or a farmer? Is it possible to learn all three, appropriating them individually where the situation calls for it? What situation, right now, are you trying to force your way through that you might be far wiser and savvier to take a softer or subtler approach? Most importantly, what is the biggest stumbling block inside your own self that keeps you forcing your way through life, rather than becoming more nuanced and less aggressive in your pursuits?

July 17

Let go
or be dragged.
-Zen quote

When I was in late elementary school/early junior high, the dad of one of my two best friends bought a boat, a little speedboat. Every weekend or so, in summer, Mr. Hughes would take us three boys out to one of Minnesota's billion lakes and patiently tow us as we learned to ski, then learned to slalom, and eventually learned to do some tricks. In all of that learning, we swallowed a lot of water and had our trunks yanked off plenty of times, while the boat dragged a boy who had not let go of the tow rope. We quickly learned.

Then after a few hours of that, Mr. Hughes would go sit on the beach with a small cooler of Schaefer beer and enjoy his afternoon in the sun, as us boys swam around in the water.

Over the years, few things in life exhilarate me more than water skiing. I am an old man now, but I still like getting out on the fresh water of the Housatonic River or a lake when I am back in the far north. Getting old, I still eat some water, as I ski far less frequently. But, waterskiing gives me energy in ways not many other hobbies do, even though it's physically demanding. Writing does the same for me, as does my work at counseling and my heavy workouts in the weightroom. Time to myself gives me energy, too.

What gives you energy? What breathes life into you? What's dragging you that you refuse to let go of?

Stop asking the question what makes you happy, at least stop for a little bit. That's a head question. Get outta your head and just feeeel the answers. Start asking questions that force you to read your own body and read your own energy: what actually gives you physical energy? What makes you feel light? Do more of that.

What makes you feel small? Do less of that.

What are 10 things that give you energy? For each one, state why it gives you energy? What it is about that place, action, time, or purpose that is so energizing?

As a twist on those questions: What are those things that fatigue you, but fatigue you in a good way, in an exciting and satisfied way? On the flip side, what are the things that fatigue you by just sucking the life energy out of you? And do you see the distinction between the two different types of fatigue? Strive for the former!

July 18

> *A man should never be ashamed to own*
> *that he has been in the wrong,*
> *which is but saying in other words*
> *that he is wiser today than he was yesterday.*
> -Alexander Pope, English poet

I may be alone in this, but for me there are few things in a human personality more unbecoming, more likely to cause me to distance myself from someone than their need to always be right and never concede mistakes or fault. It's one of the earmarks of a tragically frail ego. It's a person who cannot bear the thought of others being critical of them, questioning them, or seeing them as anything other than great, perfect, or better than. That is definitely not a healthy ego, but rather one living in fear.

Are you a know-it-all or, perhaps, someone who never concedes fault or being wrong? Have you ever correlated that to why you maybe have fewer friends? Ever thought about going into that and healing it?

Or, who is in your life that is that sort of person – never wrong, always in the right? What is it in you that keeps tolerating it? Or, maybe you like it. If so, why?

July 19

> ***There is no greater sorrow than to recall, in misery,***
> ***the time when you were happy.***
> -Dante Aligheri, Italian epic poet

How much do you voluntarily torture yourself by staying stuck in, or constantly reverting back to, the past when you were happiest, or happier? How is today's pain made worse by this backward gaze?

Maybe it was the happiness in a love you once had, while today you don't. Maybe it was before your family member fell so deeply into the mental illness, and you long for the old them. Maybe it was back in the glory days of your career, which preceded this time of paucity and longing.

This is one of those situations in life where the love we hold onto (for people, position, places, purposes, etc) actually causes pain, where it behooves us to release our feelings of love, at least if we desire to live free, happy, and *ALIVE!*

What would it take for you to begin to let go of the love(s)? Has the misery of today, heightened by warm memories of the past, gotten bad enough that you're ready to do that work of letting go of love? Or do you need to stay here for a while longer?

When it's time, you'll know.

July 20

*I have found the best way to give advice to your children is
to find out what they want and then advise them to do it!*
-Harry S. Truman, U.S. President

Look again at who said that. Harry S. Fricking Truman! Definitely one of the tougher SOB's in American presidential history. He ended WWII in definitive, if ugly fashion. A leader you would think to be forceful speaks in this quote of a very different approach to parenting than what you might expect.

When I speak to parents, I flatly tell them that one of the most important things they can tell their own children is, "You make good decisions." This is an enormous message for a child to get, because it teaches the child self-trust. That alone both honors the child's own inner voice and gives them permission to follow it, two things I see so little of in troubled or struggling adults. Instead, I see lots of wavering, uncertainty, and lack of clarity, because they've been taught to either distrust or outright reject their own inner voice, feelings, and wants.

Teaching a child, then teen, then adult-child that they make good decisions and to trust their own intuition and wants, especially when they've made mistakes, is to give them the power to self-correct and get to adulthood confident in themselves. Otherwise, that young-adult will be forever leaning on you, or whomever they love next, to tell them what to do with their lives, which creates generations of infantilized adults. It may feel good if you're the one they're coming to, but it's in no way healthy for their long term happiness, because they're forever dependent.

What's quietly lying below the surface of President Truman's thoughts is the wisdom that when the child/teen/adult-child is allowed to trust and learn from their own paths, they often come to the same realization the parent might wish to force on them now. That's the depth of Truman's wisdom: let 'em learn on their own. If we're being completely honest, there's also the very real possibility in many situations that the kid creates a new path, success, or insight with greater depth and nuance that either proves parental advice wrong or expands what the parent thought they knew to be true.

So, is it possible the best advice for you, as a parent, is to stop selling advice to your kids and to set them free and empower them to trust their own inner judgment, even when they make mistakes? What fears or enjoyment of power over the child do you need to overcome internally in order for you to not only do that but follow through on that, time and again?

July 21

> *If a kid asks where rain comes from,*
> *I think a cute thing to tell him is, "God is crying."*
> *And if he asks why God is crying,*
> *another cute thing to tell him is,*
> *"Probably because of something you did."*
> -Jack Handey, American humorist, *Deep Thoughts*

I really can't resist including humor when it comes to considering the deeper things of life, particularly the work of Handey. And, while this one is a good laugher, it also opens the door to a deeper gem of insight in this work of self-care.

From the moment the child is born, the parent is, for all intents and purposes, God, endowed with total power and authority. The child's dependence on the parent is absolute.

And, while Handey's quote is comical, it belies a deeper truth that the child will believe the self-shame taught to him/her, if the all-powerful parent-God says it to be so. Tragically, far too many parents do exactly that, even from a very young age. "You're a bad boy." "Stupid girl!" "You're such a disappointment." "I don't care what your feelings are." These messages teach the child that parent-God does not like them and that it is their own fault that parent-God is upset.

Does it really require some grand leap of imagination to grasp how powerfully those messages will embed in the child and, then, how far into adulthood those messages will cast their long shadow? Are you able to see that the messages you received were as if from God, itself? Is it possible that you even took that on as your own voice, believing it is you who are your own worst critic? Are you able to understand the intensity, then, of the work you must do to be healed of that powerful internal God-message?

What are the messages you were taught about yourself by the parent-God? Is it possible those messages were never true to begin with? What do you speculate it would most take for you to move through, release, and move past those very God-messages?

July 22

Don't worry that children never listen to you;
worry that they are always watching you.
-Robert Fulghum, American author

Have you ever had it said to you, or thought it about yourself, that you married your mom/dad? Maybe you've thought it about someone else?

Truth is, we all marry a parent, so to speak, to some greater or lesser degree. But where the realization hits like a ton of bricks is when we're in a relationship or marriage where we're particularly unhappy and the mistreatment by our partner is heightened, because, we're so searching for a 'why' in those situations. Why, why, why? Then when it hits, it just clobbers us, "Holy cow! I married my mom/dad!"

But, what does it mean to marry a parent? It's pretty simple, really. Generally, you were raised in a home where you were conditioned to act certain ways, particularly around the parent(s), and also believe certain things about yourself – your core beliefs – and about love. That usually included some repercussions if you didn't act and believe accordingly. So, you then go into your dating relationships where you, at some deep unexamined level, choose someone who treats you precisely the way that parent did, or very similarly. The love is there, as it was with the parent, but it is in larger doses it seems, which is sensory overload for you (or maybe a surprise or completely unbelievable), because you've never experienced that. So, you're convinced this is your forever love.

However, the problem is that all the negative crap that was there in childhood with that parent is there with this person, as well. Maybe it's neglect, the harsh or abusive language, the high expectations that never get met, the extreme taking (narcissism). But, because you're so overwhelmed with all the immense good (or so it seems, but it's merely more than you've ever experienced) and you are so opened up that you ignore the bad. "Oh, it'll go away," or "It's no big deal."

Obviously, it doesn't go away. Therefore, as the problems of life and relationships arise, as they always do, the other side of your partner comes out more, and your old, subservient, fear-filled self comes out. The cycle that began in childhood now continues into the next generation.

Why does all of this happen? Because, it's familiar. Back in childhood you were taught that this is what love is. This cruddy treatment became your everyday life. Also, if you were raised by one parent in some crappy way and the other parent allowed it, then not only did this form of love become your reality, it was normalized by the second parent. You received no significant counter-messaging through the other parent's actions, even if their words were consoling when Parent #1 was being cruel, neglectful, abusive, or harsh. Their actions still normalized all of this crud.

You okay with that? At what point do you do the work to unravel all of this and finally heal?

July 23

Success is the necessary misfortune of life, but it is only to the very unfortunate that it comes early.
-Anthony Trollope, English novelist

Few things are more common among the young, at least in America, than the desire for success. It's not that it is absent among the older, but it does get tempered and more transparent as we age.

Starting in 4th grade, I played football. It was hard to grow up in Minnesota in the early 70s and not love football, despite four Super Bowl losses in my young lifetime. I played Pony League, PeeWees, Cubs, junior high, senior high, NCAA D1 and D3.

Yet, as I aged, I began to think about success and sports, specifically I realized what a curse it must be to play in the NFL and have the good fortune to be on a Super Bowl-winning team your rookie year. I mean, sure, how ecstatic to accomplish so many life dreams at 24! But, then what? Do you know how few players in the entire history of professional football ever got to hoist the championship trophy? That means that 24 year-old kid who got the early championship is now cursed with the Sisyphean task of playing to reach the top again, but likely never getting there. Further, what will he do when he gets out of professional football? It's not that he won't have a lovely, successful career. Plenty do. It's that, at least for a very long time, the likelihood of anything ever measuring up to that level of mountaintop satisfaction and sheer ecstasy is radically diminished. In fact, there has to be a long period of recalibrating what happiness is.

The idol-veneration that persists today, just as it always has, causes young people to listen to the young words of young idols, which is, as it generally always has been, filled with blandishments about the glam life, success, fame, and money. So, the young grind themselves down when considering relative success and their own lack of it. To the older folks, the 20-something and 30-something idols from music, film, fighting, gaming, sports, and business all seem a bit thin in wisdom.

For those who do not get success early in the 20s and 30s, they begin to see the beauty of it by the time they reach their 40s and successes do finally begin to come. You had to grind, grow, love, fail, make hard decisions, fear, succeed in small doses, keep attacking, fall back, address new fears, learn, grow, etc. Long down the road, the successes came a bit more, then possibly a bit more. There is a deeper satisfaction that exists in successes and joy that come later, rather than earlier.

Are ecstasy, joy, peace, and fulfillment all possible after early success? Of course, but it requires a lot of rewiring of the brain, in terms of what future success is not only going to take (because if you got it early, you likely see it as a natural course of life – i.e. easier than others might see it) but even look like.

Is it possible your disappointment over not having found success yet is skewing your ability to see the possible long term gain of it and the potential for the future successes? Or, if you're a parent, is it possible that pushing your kid to succeed young is a mistake? Or, a bit tangential (and a bit obvious), is it possible that your version of your child's success is not their version?

July 24

> *...The sins of the parents*
> *shall be visited upon the children*
> *unto the third and fourth generation.*
> -Deuteronomy 5:9, Hebrew Bible

Whether you believe in the religions that cite this verse as part of their sacred scriptures or not, and whether you believe in a God, at all, is your business and not necessary when considering this point. For, it doesn't take a religious person to see how fascinating this verse of the Jewish/Christian Bible is in light of healing past pain in childhood. For, it points to the notion that even thousands of years ago people had intimate experience with generational trauma, even if they used different language to describe it. They saw family crud get passed down and passed down. They simply chose to ascribe the source of the problems to their God and his wrath, where today many would call it both DNA and generational trauma. It's real stuff. We are not the first people to discover it or have a name for it, nor are we the first to believe we have a solution for it.

Nonetheless, awareness is still the first task and the one thing that has the power to change it. Seeing the problem and acknowledging its impact is required to begin to create any formidable change. It's the first step in changing you, and hence your future generations, or even those you might impact should you choose to not have children.

So, what is the crap you carry in you from your past, from your family of origin? And, can you go deep into the question: How is the generational trauma inside me impacting how I walk through life, the decisions I make, the career ideations and choices I have had, the relationships I've had and helped to destroy, the children I am raising, and so forth? Am I really looking honestly at all of it, or am I wanting to hide from the real truths?

July 25

> *Anytime you're gonna grow, you're going to lose something.*
> *You're losing what you're hanging onto to keep safe.*
> *You're losing habits that you're comfortable with.*
> *You're losing familiarity.*
> -James Hillman,
> American psychologist and founder of archetypal psychology

It can be in career, love, family, parenting, friendships, avocations, physical/mental health, habits, finances, or any aspect of life. We have all had the experience, many times, of holding on desperately to one thing or aspect of life, even when we know it is deteriorating, has gone bad, or has reached the point where it's just destroying us....and yet we hold on, still. We *know* it's bad. We *know* it. But we cannot bear to let go. It's the devil we know vs. the *potential* devil of what we don't know.

It's familiar. That, and that alone, is what keeps us holding on, even clinging for dear life. It's fascinating to note that 'familiar' has the same, rather obvious, root as 'family' – the Latin *familia*, which means 'intimate.' We've become so intimate with the life we know and choices we've made that anything outside of that familiarity box is terrifying as hell, even when the life inside that familiarity box is painful as hell in its own way, which is why the pain has to get so profoundly bad in life (inside the box of familiarity) before we finally break outside of the box.

This is rarely more true than when it comes to the intimacies of going deep inside to hunt and actually look at the real truths of your past, the myths of your family-of-origin, and the beliefs you were taught about yourself. Sooo much of your very identity, as you've known it, is rooted in those beliefs and stories of your childhood. To consider even looking at those, let alone adopting new beliefs and a new life, based on actual truth, is bone-shaking. The price seems too egregiously high.

What are the familiars that you're clinging to that do not serve you and have not for a very long time? What is it you most fear in the realm outside of the box? Has your pain gotten bad enough that you're ready to explore outside the box?

July 26

The best index to a person's character is
a) how they treat people who can't do them any good, in return, and
b) how they treat people who can't fight back.
-Abigail 'Dear Abby' van Buren,
American 20th Century advice columnist

Think about this quote. Re-read it. I mean, is there anybody who disagrees with it? Isn't it fascinating how it's basically a universal human attribute to admire those tragically rare individuals who are generous to those who can give nothing back or benefit them in no possible way, and also those individuals who have power – be it physical, political, economic, force of character, or title – but do not use it against those with less power, but in fact use it to build up and help the powerless?

What is it about those two attributes that are so powerfully moving to all of us? And, why is it that we see those two attributes as exceedingly rare, at least in large doses?

Really, the answer to both of those questions is the same. It's because we all innately recognize the greater human trait of putting and keeping our own individual selves, and those who are but an extension of our self (kids, spouse, family-of-origin, closest associates, the businesses or careers I myself have built), at the center of the universe, deserving of and receiving all first fruits of the harvest, or perhaps even all the fruits and benefits. It is so insanely hard, especially in certain cultures, to extract ourselves from the center of the universe. To that end, it is so sadly easy to use others, particularly our progeny, to keep us at the center of the universe and continue to benefit me, even at their expense. There is a universal realization of how selfish and self-centered the human animal is. The human ego is a virus which plagues us all.

Thus, it leaps out at us when someone seems so damn foolish, yet so doggone admirable, when they give of themselves to someone *for no good reason*, except the betterment and/or building up of the other. It's beyond beautiful. It's sublime.

How do you need to most push yourself to step out of your own ego, which, by the way, includes your own fears that consume you?

And yes, there is a flip-side to this. Those who give and give, but deep down – so deep they may not be able to see it – the giving is done to get love, in return. There are those who spend their lives giving to others, trying to win affection, at massive expense to their own self. This is out of fear of the voice inside that says they have no value, at all. This person needs to exorcize those voices.

For in the end, what is needed is humans who do love themselves, and thereby give of themselves to others, but out of abundance, not out of longing for scraps of love.

Where do you fit in this whole equation? What most needs to change?

July 27

There are three things all wise men fear:
the sea in a storm;
a night with no moon;
and the anger of a gentle man.
-Patrick Rothfuss, American author

There are certain people in this life who are genuinely gentle souls. They may even be very large, physically powerful people, who, either by design of their parents or by the result of a life that carved them to be this way, are incredibly deferential and exceedingly gracious. Interestingly, they've been endowed with a fuse so long that you can push them and push them and push them with no adverse response. You can be repeatedly thoughtless or unkind, and they will see you with understanding eyes.

But eventually, long down the road, should you foolishly persist in your selfishness or inflicting of pain, you push them across a threshold you do not want to push them across. It is the point at which they know that that's enough. They know they've been dragged so profoundly far above and beyond reasonable treatment that they simply no longer feel even the slightest sense of obligation to be gentle or kind. It is that point at which they know they have permission from themselves and from every god, parent, or star that has written the course of their character to step outside of that character to defend themselves or stand unabashedly against the uncouth tool who pushed them this far.

A gentle man/woman/person pushed beyond what any person should be continues an ugly scene that they are fully at liberty to write.

So, who are you pushing beyond their limits, or who is pushing you? What is it that's going on inside you that causes you to endure so much, when you're certainly under no obligation to endure all of that? Is it possible that someone, somewhere taught you a self-neglecting version of love that has you eating too much crap; and that maybe you need to do some healing work to stop allowing it to such a degree, because of the inner pain it causes you? When do you finally stand up and shut that offensiveness down?

246

July 28

Good is the enemy of great.
-Jim Collins, American author, *Good to Great,*
Professor, Stanford University's Graduate School of Business

Settling.

So much of life becomes settling, if we allow it or, perhaps, if we actively choose it. I don't mean settling for less than riches, success, fame, or greatness. I mean, settling for less than whatever it is you really want out of life. We so often in life choose to settle, both in the large stuff and the small stuff.

Here's an odd story. My mother, many times, told me of reading about CT Studd, as a child growing up on the farm prairie of southern Minnesota during the Great Depression. Profoundly impacted by Studd's life of missionary work in India and Africa, that young girl dreamed of becoming a global missionary, just like him. Among many other poems and Christian writings, Studd wrote such things as,

Some want to live within the sound of church or chapel bell;
I want to run a rescue shop within a yard of hell.
-CT Studd, British missionary and cricketer

It requires no grand leap of imagination to see how a young girl of faith, whose own mother told their one-room church country pastor to, basically, "Stick it!" and founded her own house church, could be moved by such words and the actions that followed them. It's easy to see how she would idolize and want to mimic his life. His courage and commitment so inspired that little girl that she dreamed of, too, becoming a missionary to China, Africa, and India. Two of her brothers later became clergy; one a missionary to Quenca, Ecuador, for 20+ years.

Yet, by the time the story was relayed to me, the youngest of her six children, the settling had already been written and executed. She would candidly admit so. While there is a possibility her youngest, now an adult, might misread her story and meaning, it seemed quite clear in tone and energy that the story was told with wistfulness. Her WWII-generational default to seeing and focusing on the good in all things would rarely allow her to verbalize actual regret, at least not to anyone other than in privacy with her own spiritual counselor. But, her "message behind the message," as she used to call the thing we must always listen for when someone speaks, spoke of settling. And foolish me for never pressing her to dive into the why and when exactly the settling happened. But, it was there.

She became a pastor's wife for decades and a mother of six, including a few miscarriages. She would later go on to accomplish greatness of a different stripe as an adjunct professor at the largest Lutheran seminary in the world, as a published authority on children's education/development in theological journals, as Director of Education developing entire education programs, rooted in a "cradle to grave" comprehensiveness, in some very large churches, and as a very quiet, wise old woman with her own spiritual counseling work with pastors and pastor's wives.

She settled and later recovered, then rewrote the story. But, there is little doubt in my mind that she settled. Did she ever achieve the greatness or accomplish the great things her childhood self dreamed of? No, I think her answer would be 'no.' Was she fulfilled by her life? In many ways, yes, for sure. Though, at 92, she told of being excited about a new book she was reading about goal-setting! 92; goals! She wanted to write more articles and start a podcast, for Pete's sake. No lie. This was a driven woman, who just wanted so much more from life, both when she was a child and as an old woman with the spirit of a child.

Sure, you can recover and rewrite the script of your life. No doubt. But are you settling? Why? And are you okay with that?

July 29

What if it's not 'love-bombing?'
-Sven

One of the bigger cliches in pop psych culture, besides 'narcissist,' is the term 'love bombing,' which refers to the act, early in a relationship, of showering someone with love, gifts, time, energy, attention, praise, etc with the intent to delude the receiver into thinking the love is real and lasting, and to cause the receiver to not see red flags present in the bomber, which are always there.

However, in seeking to fully disassemble bad situations to find the deeper causes, I find myself dissatisfied with such a simplistic answer to why someone missed and allowed mistreatment, early in a relationship. I do this not as a mechanism to blame the one who got hurt, but as a way to help that person change what he/she/they can inside, so that they don't let it happen again. Recognizing that the receiver of the love bombs did not *cause* the bomber to later mistreat them, the receiver did *allow* that person to mistreat them. That 'allowing' is nearly always the result of what an individual has been conditioned to believe in childhood about him-/her-/themself and about love.

So, what might someone have experienced, or been taught, in childhood that would cause them to be susceptible to said bombing and all that bombing can cloud in a relationship?

It's pretty simple, really. If you grew up in a home where there was little affection shown, or where there were no kind and encouraging words, or where there was no listening, or where "I love you" maybe wasn't spoken, or where supportive actions were never seen, then you grew up with the belief that a love famine is normal, which further means that anything you experience beyond a famine is an oozing smorgasbord of loveness and ecstasy.....and all rational thought, critical thinking, and self-defense mechanisms are out the window – ie you're screwed! The power of feeling love in a greater dose than you've ever received (which isn't much) can override all rational thought and self-protection mechanisms.

Or, if you grew up in a 'good' home but the love message was that you had to keep giving and giving love to keep someone else happy, even at your own expense, then you became conditioned to believe that receiving love is rare and completely contingent upon you giving more and more, which creates a core belief that you don't matter. This sets you up for chaos when you meet someone you desire who treats you as though you do matter.

Thus, it's not that you were being bombed, per se, with some astronomically huge amount of love and displays of affection, care, and interest. No, it's just that this person was doing more than you had ever experienced, even though that same amount might be considered baseline for someone growing up in a home where displays of genuine appreciation, kindness, and mattering were quite everyday.

The implications of this are that it's much more possible to fix it for your next relationship, because the blind side, so to speak, exists in you, not in having to be wary of predators. By exploding the myth you had been taught and by doing the deep inner work, you no longer have a sensory overload when such love happens, thus making you far less vulnerable to mistreatment. By realizing and owning that you were taught a very messed up version of love, and by fully disassembling that, you become much more powerful walking into future love and friendships, as well as career, family, friendships, and your relationship with your own self.

Is it possible that you were taught an abnormal version of love, and that myth has corrupted far more of your life than you realize? What were you taught about love? Have you really fully explored all of the messages you received about love and about yourself? Perhaps, it's time.

July 30

I was an overnight success all right!
But thirty years is a long, long night.
-Ray Kroc, The man who built McDonald's into a global colossus

While I have been inspired and guided far more by the writings of men in my field, there is no one whose career trajectory I more identify with than Ray Kroc. He toiled his butt off for 30 years to no acclaim. He was 52 when he first visited the hamburger joint/malt shop of the McDonald brothers in San Bernardino, CA, in 1954. But, he was 59 before he bought them out and began his worldwide expansion of what would become, inarguably, the very biggest and most dominant fast-food chain ever.

To toil for 30 years, unsatisfied, yet still hungry for more is impressive. But, to be 52 or 59 and still be gutsy enough and intense enough, especially after having never seen the summits you've dreamed of, to climb brand new mountains is absolutely unheard of. To never have the success you long for yet keep driving for it into your 40s, 50s, and 60s is so inspiring!

For 30 years, I wrote six books no one was reading, built my own formal and personal education in my field, counseled thousands of people, fought with little success to get my voice and ideas out on fledgling social media, and toiled and toiled. I was 53 before my career finally popped. Fifty fricking three! Yes, it was a long, long night.

I had long since let go of needing success to be happy. I mean, I gave up my life possessions to minister to and live among the homeless on the street, sleeping on concrete every night for 2 ½ years. Somewhere in me I still wanted success, sure, in some small way. But I had simultaneously let go of it. I was finally playing fierce, but loose, just going where my heart and soul called me to go.

If I'm honest, in hindsight it was precisely as it was supposed to be. I simply could not have been or done at 34 or 45 who I am and what I am doing now. I wasn't ready. I had neither the full skill set, nor the full wisdom, born of more hard experience, that I would need in order to do what I do in the ways I now do them. I had to endure the slings and arrows, and the slow grind of time. I had to come out the other side of the furnaces of life. I had to plumb it all for the wisdom it all bore. It had to be precisely as it all was. I unequivocally believe that.

How much stick do you have? How much grit, grind, and just plain doggedness do you have? Is there anything in the world you want badly enough to toil 30 years without getting it, but toil anyway? Really? So, are you doing it?

July 31

> *I pray to God within me that He will give me the strength*
> *to ask Him the right questions.*
> -Elie Wiesel,
> Holocaust survivor & author of the international bestseller, *Night*

Now, there's a question: Is it possible that your lack of fulfillment, peace, happiness, greatness, or *ALIVENESS* is because you're asking the wrong questions?

What the heck does that even mean? What's the difference between the right and wrong questions when it comes to that big stuff you dream your life to be, or the small and medium stuff you so wish would change?

Well, I have no doubt that others would counsel you differently. But, alas, you're not reading their book. So, I'll share simply what I believe. I, both personally and professionally, believe there are only two fundamental questions that matter in life, two you've encountered at another point or two in this book and, for sure, in the predecessor, *There's a Hole in My Love Cup:*

Who the hell are you, really?
and
Do you have the courage to be who you really are?

That's it. End of story.

If you relentlessly throughout your life keep asking those two questions, again and again, of your deepest voice/god-voice inside of you, and if you just as relentlessly live your authentic self, bit by bit, you will experience power, purpose, persistence, peaks and peace the likes of which you've never known, ever. There is no deep and lasting happiness outside of the living of self as it feels right only to you at your deepest soul level. No amount of success or external love can make up for the emptiness of a life that is not your original self. No other person can tell you what moves your soul. Nor is anyone else the ultimate 'permission source' that grants you the right to live authentically; that comes solely from you.

If you'd like to follow it up with the questions 'why?' or 'what's really standing in my way?' great! That will help you immensely in staying true to who you were put on this earth to be, whether by the universe, fate, or your DNA and upbringing.

Are you asking the wrong questions or the right ones? What pre-formed identity and authorities in your own head and past keep you asking the wrong questions? Tired yet of the discontent those wrong questions continue to bring you?

August

August 1

There are two questions that we have to ask ourselves.
The 1st is, "Where am I going?"
The 2nd is, "Who will go with me?"
If you ever get these questions in the wrong order, you are in trouble.
-Howard Thurman, African-American theologian, author

I love this quote by this great thinker, not just because it's about prioritizing your life, but because he nails through ominous implication the effects of choosing poorly. I see the effects of this decision in people's lives and relationships, all the time. They prioritize the partner they choose over the path they choose. Down the road, it leads to all sorts of struggles, both in the relationship and in their souls, because they often sell the farm (in the form of lost opportunities, severely compromised dreams, and loss of self) – i.e. sell out the path – to keep the person and/or keep the person happy.

The truth is, there's nothing inherently wrong with that choice. It's your life, your choice. But, as Thurman states, there are mighty consequences, and they ain't pretty.

However, what's most poignant about his words is that your path you choose, done rightly, comes from self, comes from soul, from your sense of your own identity. Thus, committing to that is a lifelong statement of your worth and movement in and toward your own happiness. Then, it's a matter of finding someone (or trusting the Fates to bring the right person), whose path aligns, somehow, with your path.

In sum, it's a primary orientation to the inner life (soul, path) with secondary orientation to the outer life (partner, lover). To invert that equation and make the outer the driver of one's life, seldom ends well. Or, at least, it goes through massive upheaval before ever ending well.

But there's one last twist in this outer/inner discussion. Often the person we take with us is not the lover or partner. It's the person we're carrying with us in spirit, often quite unaware. It's the voice of the critical mother, the absent father, or the abusive person from our past. Often we are making our choices of path because we're still answering to this person who takes up real estate in our brain and infects our whole body. Their voice is the one we're forever answering to, seeking approval and acceptance from, or saying, "I'll show you" to. And so, we bond to a path of proving ourselves, acquiring ego stuff – money, success, titles, fame, trips, fine clothes, fine dinners, more and more outer stuff. Quite unwittingly, we're bringing that person with us, even if they've long since passed away, on our journey of life. It is their voice determining our path. Everything becomes a response to that voice.

So, are you getting the questions right? Do you truly know the voice of your soul? Have you been oriented to the outer rather than inner? Is your life driven by fear, anxiety, and longing for someone you've never had closeness to? Or is it rooted in a deep sense of knowing, of calm, and of real purpose?

August 2

Be wary of those who seek to steal your dream.
Be even more wary of those who seek to tell you
what your dream should be.
-Ralph Marston, American author

"Sven, I never really got any negative messages, as a kid, from parents or otherwise. In fact, I distinctly remember my parents saying to me, time and again, 'The world is your oyster' and 'You can do anything you want to do with life," he told me.

I laughed. He looked at me, perplexed. "Dude," I said, "I hear that stuff all the time. Supposedly idyllic childhood, positive namaste parent messages, all that. But, invariably, somewhere hidden in the gold is the dross, the poison. It's always there, hidden."

For example, I had a guy, ten years ago, counsel with me for three months. His parents told him he could do whatever he wanted, as long as it was in the fields of medicine, finance, or politics. I had another guy tell me he got the 'oyster' message. But at age 17, confronted with the biggest decision of his life, to date, of whether to accept Harvard admission to study literature, which was his grand love, or play lacrosse at the Naval Academy and subsequently fly jets, his father stepped in and effectively made the decision for him – college athletics and jets! The biggest decision of his young life got taken from him, which implies that if dad took that major decision, he had been making, or influencing, the son's medium and small decisions prior to that. The papa didn't all of a sudden change his nature and act out of character. A youngster trusted with lesser decisions would be trusted with this one, because the parent sees the value in teaching the son/daughter to trust their own decision-making, even if the child changes their mind later, as that, too, is part of life.

I have had countless other friends and clients who've seen, after deep diving with me into their past, that it was often the well-timed, perfectly placed question, comment, or raised eyebrow (or even the forceful 'no' or stomping of feet and raising of voice) by the parent that caused the person to turn from their own oyster to falling in line with parental expectations or nudges.

It's in there. All of those nudges, subversive questions, override comments, and insidious doubts that were deliberately, or accidentally, placed by mom, dad, or whomever was most powerful in your life. Very often, the greatest power over those messages infecting your life comes from awareness, or, as my Depression-era mother always said, "Naming the beast is half the problem." Once you are aware, once you see the parent doing it, you can't unsee it, and you realize that the onus is now on you to act.

Can you begin to spelunk the recesses and forgotten memories of your past to unearth counter-messages to the oyster mantra? How were the counter-messages delivered? What was the substance of those messages? Can you bring yourself to admit that the very people who claimed to love you most potentially undermined the very message they were selling? And why; why were they doing it? How do they benefit from selling the oyster message, or claiming to have sold that message? What fear was causing them to dissuade you from actually following the oyster?

What were the explicit positive messages told to you by the primary power sources and love sources in your life? What subtler messages or events came at other times that either completely undermined those explicit messages or chipped away at their truth? What are the parameters your parents have set for your life that you can't transgress without retribution, no matter what oyster you're pursuing?

Worse, are you selling the oyster to your child, yet short-circuiting it, because of your own fears? How do you justify it? Is your justification substantive or simply born of your own fears? Whose life is it, really? Is that answer reflected in your actions?

August 3

*Over the years, I have come to realize that the greatest trap in our life
is not success, popularity, or power, but self-rejection.
Success, popularity, and power can indeed present a great temptation,
but their seductive quality often comes from the way they are part of
the much larger temptation to self-rejection.
When we have come to believe in the voices
that call us worthless and unlovable,
then success, popularity, and power
are easily perceived as attractive solutions.
The real trap, however, is self-rejection.
As soon as someone accuses me or criticizes me, as soon as I am rejected,
left alone, or abandoned,
I find myself thinking,
"Well, that proves once again that I am a nobody."
... [My dark side says,] "I am no good...
I deserve to be pushed aside, forgotten, rejected, and abandoned."
Self-rejection is the greatest enemy of the spiritual life
because it contradicts the sacred voice that calls us the "Beloved."
Being the Beloved constitutes the core truth of our existence.*
-Henri J.M. Nouwen, Dutch professor and writer

He sets up the battle lines pretty simply, yet accurately. Our lives are dominated by this constant movement between self-rejection and honoring of self, even loving self. We spend so much time in the world of success and power in their many forms, including career, parenting, certain friendships, money, things, and how we walk in the world. But all are a response to that voice of self-rejection. All are (or can become) a constant living in tension with that self-negating voice inside.

But, to live the life of soul, of authentic self, one must reorient daily to seeing self as beloved to you. It is to see yourself as a gift to life itself. It is to walk humbly in a recognition of your divinity, your innate goodness.

To not do so is a corruption of self and of the happiness inside that is waiting to spring up and calmly permeate every piece of your life.

Can you hear it, that sacred voice of your own soul that says you are beloved? How well do you hear it? If you were to be totally honest, what percentage of your thoughts are dominated by that belief in your own goodness, and what percentage are dominated by the self-rejection and hating on yourself? Is it 30% good and 70% self-rejection? Or vice-versa? Or something else? Does it need to change?

August 4

Argue for your limitations
and, sure enough,
they're yours.
-Richard Bach,
Illusions: The Adventures of a Reluctant Messiah

I've always enjoyed the challenge of Bach's quote, because it pushes in two directions. One, it squares off against those who say, "Well, I can't this..." or "I have this limitation, so I just can't that..." He argues that those things you see as your grand inhibitors – your parents, your diseases, your society, your physicality, etc – aren't. It's simultaneously offensive and enlightening.

Yet, there's another way he pushes in this quote. What if it's not your perceived lack of power, agency, or ability that keeps you small? What if it's A) your lack of imagination, and B) your clinging to something you think you really want? In other words, what if your crime, your limitation is small thinking – i.e. you're not dreaming big enough?

Now, there's a mind-blower!

What if the reason you're not getting the success you want in the areas of life you desire is because the universe is screaming at you, **"DREAM BIGGER!"**

What if your affliction is lack of imagination? And, what if that's quickly accompanied by lack of guts to pull the trigger on it?

What if you don't have the success you want because you actually, deep down, want something bigger? Got the guts?

August 5

What is to give light
must endure burning.
-Viktor Frankl, Holocaust survivor

How do you frame your pain and the hardships you have endured or are enduring in your life?

The simple fact of the matter is there are times in life when we get so overwhelmed by grief, loss, lack, sadness, frustration, hopelessness, absence of success, prolonged misery, and more that we simply cannot persist, when life refuses to let us do anything but shut down. There are periods, sometimes years, when the pain is unrelenting. I have lived it, 12 years in a suicidal depression, and the movement out of it was not immediate. That hard stuff can last a very long time.

Amid it, there are days when we simply have no choice but to power through, to go hard-nosed and perform to get the job done.

But, whether it be the up days or down years, we lose an opportunity when we create no way to frame the pain and depression. Framing pain, or giving it context or reason, changes it. You don't have to. In fact, there are a whole lot of clergypersons who've performed a whole lot of funerals who explicitly state that there is no 'why' to death, for example, and that searching for a why, or reason, is an exercise in futility. But I disagree. I believe the human mind forever searches for, if not a reason, a way to frame it, even if it only makes sense to the bearer.

I happen to very much believe Frankl's quote. Everything is a setup for later. I believe in this in no small part because I'm a former competitive powerlifter and NCAA Head Coach for Strength. No one lifts heavy weight or leads championship teams without first lifting small weight and middle weight and leading losing teams, middling teams, and highly competitive teams. He who is faithful in little will be entrusted with more. AND, we must build strength of spine, strength of character, to be prepared for what is ahead. Then, we must simply keep moving forward, mining each experience for what it is trying to teach me about life, the world, humanity, and, most importantly, self. This loss is preparation for future battles and victories.

What are you enduring? What's the hardest part? What has this been sent by your soul to teach you about life and self? Are you getting the message? What are you being asked by life to let go of? What's the hardest part about letting go of that precise thing?

August 6

*If you truly want to be respected by people you love,
you must prove to them that you can survive without them.*
-Michael Bassey Johnson, Nigerian author and poet

One of the great dilemmas facing many families today is young people who are into their early-twenties and stuck, often at home with their parents. These young people have not begun the process of stepping out into the world, either by living on their own or getting a job that they're working hard at to begin the transition to independence. What exacerbates and, in fact, causes the phenomenon in the first place is the excessive criticality of the parents. Interestingly, for all the sturm and drang surrounding this, it's not a new phenomenon.

Another great dilemma that bears great similarity is a lover caught in a relationship that they cannot bring themselves to get out of, because they fear being on their own, having to do it by themselves. They may also fear breaking their lover's heart or enduring their partner's anger for their leaving. Yet they stay, miserable inside the relationship. Again, this is not new.

Still another great dilemma that bears similarity to the previous two are the massive amount of people longing to be loved by their siblings and/or parents, yet forever getting the short end of the stick in that regard. They forever feel unloved, unwanted, mistreated, or outright maligned by those who have known them longest and claim to love them most. Yet, because the longing for that familial bond and, subsequently, familial love is so great and long-standing, they keep holding on, despite all evidence in a decades-long pattern of behavior from the family. They're terrified to extricate themselves, for fear of never getting that love and for fear of possibly realizing, "I've been alone the whole time." This is a tale as old as the hills.

What these all have in common is that there is a power imbalance. The parent has the power over the 20-something; the partner has the power over the stuck lover; the family has the power over the adult-child who feels caught in this ugly web. The person stuck wants something that they have and won't give: acceptance, affection, approval, acknowledgment of what they've done, and apology. And so, the person stays stuck, because the thing they fear most is letting go of getting that from the parent, other lover, or family.

Thus, the only real solution, given that the other entities won't change and, in fact, have no incentive to change, because they already are getting all the perks – i.e. you wanting them and their approval, is for you to walk away, to let go of ever getting that love, acceptance, and release from their disapproval. It requires, ultimately, you proving to both them and yourself that you can live without them. They still may never give you what you used to want. But you will have proven it to yourself.

See, what really keeps you stuck in this horrible position is that *you do not believe* that you can survive without them and their love. You do not believe there is life outside this relationship. You do not believe you will ever find love, family, or even food, water, and shelter, if you leave. And, you're wrong.

One of the greatest superpowers in life is to know you'll be okay on your own, and even be happy. What keeps you stuck is the fear that you won't. Can you do it? Will you be okay? Can you survive...and thrive!...on your own?

August 7

Just because something isn't a lie does not mean it isn't deceptive.
A liar knows that he is a liar,
but one who speaks mere portions of truth in order to deceive
is a craftsman of destruction.
-Criss Jami, American poet & essayist

At the end of a long day, Susan was telling her husband, Jay, about an interesting encounter she had, that morning, at her coffee shop, while getting some computer work done. "I saw that man I was telling you about with the intriguing life. It was fascinating" etc. She then regales her husband with everything they discussed, and even answers her husband's jealousy questions. She's very relaxed as she tells him everything.

Unbeknownst to Jay, however, Susan left out two seemingly infinitesimally small details: 1) she chose to work at the coffee shop rather than at work or home, because she hoped to see that man; and, 2) she deliberately put on lipstick and mascara, when she normally would not on a workday morning, because she was hoping to run into him again. Susan knew that telling those two details would tip her hand. Jay would know definitively that she was, basically, trawling for that man. She was attracted to him in a way that was not benign. She knew Jay would know that, if she revealed those two key facts. She told 95% of the story, but left out that critical 5% that really told the whole story. She created, what I call, "The illusion of transparency."

Having written about this in a previous book about cheating, I had a pretty good feeling this was exactly what was going on. So, in our couples session, I pressed her and she stood fast in her story. However, as fate usually has it, further down the road, she accidentally showed her cards to her husband. He knew the interactions with the man had expanded into full-blown cheating, based on some of her other deviations from long-established patterns. He refused to relent in holding her feet to the fire, and she eventually told him everything. He shattered her illusion of transparency. The marriage was now toast, and they both knew it, despite her bleating and pleading to get him back.

What is the illusion of transparency you are creating? Or, is there someone creating one with you, even though you smell that there is more that is not being told? Do you have the courage to stick to your guns, even if it means the relationship ending? What do you fear?

August 8

Just between us
I think it's time for us to recognize
The differences we sometimes fear to show.
Just between us
I think it's time for us to realize
The spaces in between
Leave room for you and I to grow.
-Rush, Canadian rock band, *Entre Nous*

One of my very dearest friends calls her older sister "the witness to my entire life." That means something to her. This older sister is the one person who has been there, through it all together, witnessing her life, and in total appreciation and awe of her. It's not just that big sis has seen it, but she understands it, or understands her, as best any one person can.

I have a brother like that. John. He's my sympathetic witness. He most definitely has not always understood me, nor I him. And, we've had our brotherly quarrels, over the years. Though, with him they've been rather small. But, he carries my story, and I his. And, we each willingly and proudly tell the other's story, blessed to have each other, even though he and I are so roundly different.

Do you have a sympathetic witness to your life? It doesn't have to be family. Maybe they've not been there from the beginning, or been there lately, but it's in their gaze that you feel truly seen, understood, appreciated, or just plain smiled upon. Who is it? Why that person? And in what esteem do you hold them? Why? What do they represent in your life? Have you told them?

August 9

> **If you want to find the secrets of the universe,**
> **think in terms of energy, frequency, and vibration.**
> -Nikola Tesla, American inventor

"Sven, what the hell is wrong with me? I sit outside my office, every damn morning, just trying to get up the energy to walk through the doors and do my job, one more day. Why am I so unmotivated? The job pays well. The people aren't bad. I just cannot seem to get motivated."

I couldn't even count the number of times, over the years, I've heard this complaint. Very often, as with this person, the individual sees him-/herself as the problem. In their own eyes, something is wrong with them or their motivation, rather than seeing the depletion of energy as a clear sign from one's soul.

See, as we tune into our own soul, more and more, our energy talks to us. We stop seeking answers from our head and lean increasingly on our own body, skin, gut, heart, throat, and chest. Our own energy talks to us. It reveals the truths of the soul, or intuition.

I used to really struggle, as a young adult, with trying to discern what my path was, both in the micro and macro decisions of life. I would try to imagine which path was the path of light and which of dark. I would make pro/con lists. I would give weight to the arguments or rationale of those around me, whom I trusted, or whomever had power over me, or whomever just spoke loudest.

But, at some point, I began to realize that my own energy seemed to talk to me. As I gave myself permission to filter out those external voices, I could feeeeel my own body. And, when I trusted it, it either led to greater exuberance, greater calm, or greater growth. Most importantly, it always felt good and right for me, even if it was very hard. There was a natural infusion of energy when I took the path that felt right. Or, very often, there was a release of tension/anxiety and a sense of relief that came with it.

I began to read and trust my energy, more and more. Now, I trust only it. I still accept input from those I trust, but always go with the feel inside, in the end. Anything that bleeds my energy, bores me, numbs me, sucks the life out of me, or that I have to conjure energy to do is definitely a path of not-me, and I abort as quickly as possible. Any path that breathes life into me, energizes me, or brings relief/calm is my path. And I trust it, no matter if it scares me or is looked down upon by others.

What is sucking the life out of you or suffocating you? What paths, pursuits, people, places, purposes, or plans in your life do you have to conjure energy to keep doing? What have you become totally numb in?

When do you begin to listen to the preponderance of negative energy welling inside you regarding x or y in your life? More importantly, why is it that you don't trust your own energy? Where were you taught to distrust your own feel? Is it possible that whomever taught you to not listen to your own voice was wrong and is, perhaps, controlling you even still today?

What are the five scariest things you would have the most trouble letting go of in your life? What is the scariest part about trusting that, no matter what happens, you'll be okay? Why? What are the ten parts of who you are that you most fear revealing to others and to life?

August 10

One believes things
because one has been conditioned to believe them.
-Aldous Huxley, English writer and philosopher

20 years ago, I had a twenty-something client in my office, who had come in to help me better understand his sister, who in turn was suffering from drug addiction. Through the course of our conversation, as I pulled on the occasional loose thread that just didn't make sense, it became clear that there were some secrets not yet on the table. As I pulled, more and more, stories of incest perpetrated against this young man arose. Secrets came to light, for the first time ever.

This led to ongoing counseling for this young man, during which he remarked, at one point, "Y'know Sven, I may be totally wrong for saying this, but I blame my other parent more, not the one who actually did this bad stuff to me."

"Oh wow! I gotta hear this. Why?"

"Well," he continued, anger and tears rising up simultaneously, "not only did [the other parent] know it and allow it, but they didn't shut it down. By not denouncing and stopping it they fricking *normalized* it, as if this is okay. They taught me this is what a normal family is. Now, even though I'm 27, I have no idea what a normal family is. I am terrified to have kids or even go near kids. I'm so scared of becoming a parent, not because I'd ever do anything so grotesque as that, but because I know, I just know, I'd screw them up. I hate [that parent] so much for teaching me that this heinous [expletive] was normal. I [expletive] HATE IT!"

What was normalized in your childhood home that should not have been? What's been the price you've paid and torment you've endured by having that normalized? What was the hardest part?

Worse, got kids? If so, what are you normalizing for them? Maybe it's not incest, but is it something destructive to your child's soul and/or future relationships and life? Are you proud of it? Has it occurred to you that the stuff you're normalizing for them is somehow woven into what was normalized for you? And yet, have you actually changed it? What could possibly be more important than stopping the normalizing of something you know to be detrimental to your child?

August 11

There is no birth
without blood and the tearing of flesh.
-Joseph Campbell, Mythology/religions scholar

I am reminded of one of the images from the birth of each of my children. In both cases, after the mother and I had each held the baby and the nurses were now taking the baby through their checklists, I recall glancing down at the floor for no particular reason. Splattered all around the birthing bed was a massive amount of blood. It was a lot, at least to this layman. If memory serves, an episiotomy was also necessary in one, or both, cases to facilitate the movement of the child out of the birth canal.

It's funny, in all the decades I've counseled people and moved them from old self to new, I've never had a situation where there wasn't pain in the birthing process of the new person, and where I didn't have to make cuts, as it were, to the old vessel, because there was some greater or lesser resistance to the process, itself. There are cuts to be made and always blood on the floor in the spiritual birthing of a new self. Always.

If you have begun your movement from old self to new, what blood of the old you, what blood in your relationships, work, family, finances, and health has been spilled? What cuts have had to be made? What unexpected tears came about? What pains have you had to go through?

More importantly, what blood is ahead? What cuts need to be made to facilitate your further movement to a new self and a life that reflects it? As you consider the blood, tears, and cuts ahead, what do you fear most? Is it necessary to do, anyway, despite the blood? Is it time yet?

August 12

> *When I was 30, I cared what people thought.*
> *When I was 40, I stopped caring what people thought.*
> *When I was 50, I realized nobody gave a sh*t, to begin with.*
> -Unknown

We spend so much of our lives worrying about many things. Yet, so few things exceed the human anxiety pantheon like the god of fear of what others will think of me. It drives how so many people think of themselves, attack the world, choose their career path, dress, walk, bathe, and every odd thing in between. Different people weigh different parts of life heavier, based on their own fears of scorn from others. Thus, everything has the capacity to bear a dagger of pain of criticism from others.

Very often, those fears start very young. So many are conditioned to forever fear the harsh or critical words of others. Too many have installed a security system of microphones inside their own head and cameras around them, pointing inward, at themselves, forever self-monitoring for even the slightest hint of a gaffe, misstep, possible future offense. This is on top of the cameras facing outward, monitoring everyone around, forever reading people for potential threats or what they want, so that one may get love from them. We become experts in reading people and hiding self.

Until. Until we realize, eventually, everyone else was so damn worried about themselves and how they were perceived that they seldom gave more than a moment's notice to us. The few number of minutes most people, even family, spend thinking about us in any given year is so small compared to the number of hours and months we are with ourselves in that same year. But, we far outweigh their minutes with the amount of time we spend worried about their thoughts of disdain and words of put-down. Too late in life, too many realize that they've wasted so much energy and time in the frivolous and painful pursuit of the nothingness of avoiding criticism.

What percentage of your life, if you were to spitball it, have you spent fearful of what others think of you? What would it take to liberate you from giving a crap, anymore? Or, what amount of courage would it take to liberate yourself from even 50% of the anxiety you continue to waste on stuff that doesn't matter? What would it take for you to finally change what consumes your time and thoughts?

August 13

If a person can't control you,
they'll attempt to control the story about you.
-Unknown

I've seen it in extended families, friendships, work settings, teams, and relationship breakups. A family will create a whole narrative around the black sheep kid and all he/she has done to hurt the family. Work teams will complain to management and demonize a particular coworker who thinks outside the box. A person will bad-mouth an ex lover to their kids, friends, family, or even their lover's family.

We create stories about others as a way to maintain control of our own image or as a way to simply hurt the other person. By creating a storyline about the young adult son or daughter who fails to launch, the parent keeps the focus on the villainy or irresponsibility of the young adult, thereby reinforcing the parent's own image and belief, "I'm a great parent. The fault is not mine." No longer able to get their child to do what they want, the parent builds and fortifies the artifice of the child's badness. The parent needs to believe and needs the child to believe that the child him- or herself is the problem, likely precisely as they've always done. The story also manages to hurt the young adult, which feels good to some parents, because they're upset at the kid for not doing what the parent thinks they're supposed to be doing. This for some parents is a nice little byproduct, even if they'd never admit it.

Then, if at some point later, be it 2 or 20 years, that 'problem child,' now a full adult, has the courage to stand up to and attempt to destroy the false narrative created about him, as well as the one that the parent(s) is not the great parent she pretends to be, the parent will often heighten the use of power to protect the false narrative.

I had a former lover/mate who went out of her way, both in the relationship and to our families, to paint herself as always the hero or victim, and me as always the villain. After she broke it off, she doubled down, turning much of my own family against me and even harming my career. Years later, I would realize that she did all of that to hurt me for not doing what she wanted me to do. But also, and perhaps more importantly, she did it because she was terrified of people seeing her as she saw herself, thanks to her mother and father. She couldn't bear even one drop of criticism, as it would only reinforce the message of not being good enough and not being wanted, which she had been hearing her whole life. So, she hid behind the lies she told about me.

So, what are you hiding? In what ways do you create narratives about others as a way to keep the focus off yourself? Do you demonize your mate? If so, why? What are you afraid of? What's the biggest accusation you use to keep your partner/spouse looking bad and you looking good? Are you a hypocrite in this?

What family myth are you a part of believing/reinforcing, or perhaps inventing, so as to keep someone (yourself?) looking pristine and out of the gun sights of the critics? Whom are you throwing under the bus? Or are you doing it in a work setting?

Are you ready to start being honest and own your crap and the pain you're sowing? Are you ready for radical honesty about your own failures and insecurities in your close relationships? Or are you going to keep using and manipulating people you claim to love? Or, are you going to keep endorsing someone else's myth (a parent's myth) they've erected to protect themselves, and keep reinforcing it so that you won't draw their wrath?

What's really going on inside of you that you're not admitting and getting out into the open?

Lastly, who is creating a narrative about you? What is the story? Do you see through it? If so, when will you have the courage to dispel it or stand against it, even if doing so comes with loss?

August 14

To the kid who just did a dumb or bad thing:

You're not a dumb person. You just did a dumb thing.
You're not a bad person. You just did a bad thing.
-My mom, Charlotte Erlandson (she said this a lot...to me)

Tell a boy he's a bad boy, and he believes it. Tell him enough times and he starts living the part. Keep telling him, and he believes it forever. Tell a girl she's dumb and she'll believe it and live it.

But here's the kicker, a child's brain will believe they're bad, even if you just tell them they did a bad thing, even if you don't tell them they're a bad person. A child's brain (and often even an adult's brain) will naturally, and somewhat understandably, make the not large leap from "I did a bad thing" to "I must be a bad person," if it happens repeatedly.

However, telling a child they did a bad thing, but they're not a bad person, divorces the action from the identity. A child will learn, with time, into the teen and young adult years, that purposefully engaging in repeated bad actions does, in fact, make you a bad person in the eyes of society and many others. But in the young years, getting the message that you're not intrinsically bad, just because you screwed up or are still learning the rules and learning to follow them, is a massive shift from believing in your own innate lack of worth.

Taking steps like these are what it means to parent deliberately, rather than just reflexively, such as just doing the same or opposite of what your parents did.

But also, often we lash out or speak recklessly, as parents, because we are so caught up in the speed of our own lives that we fail to slow down and be in the moment, particularly in those critical moments when the child is in a vulnerable situation in our own hands. The undisciplined parent speaks with an uncontrolled tongue. The parent with self-discipline can slow himself down and be present, or even stop his own emotions on a dime, so that they don't clutter the parenting process.

Are you parenting deliberately? What is it you know you're screwing up in your parenting? What do you know you need to change to begin to parent more deliberately? From what to what?

Do you see the value in and have the courage to execute contrition and full, real apology, where you've caused pain or done damage? Never underestimate the power of acknowledgment and apology for what you've done wrong by another, particularly when it's accompanied by changed action.

Do you have the wherewithal and presence of mind, in the moment, to convey to your child that he/she isn't a bad person but just did a not-so-good thing? Or, are you undisciplined in the heat of the moment, such that you lash out or say something potentially hurtful to the soul of your child? Do you need to widen the amount of time between stimulus and response, so that you can slow down and calm down?

If you are in business, lead people, are a teacher, or have people under you in the chain of command, do you see the value in simultaneously calling out the wrong behaviors yet keeping the integrity of their character intact? Further, do you see the potential damage of not doing so?

August 15

> *You've got to play with that killer instinct, man.*
> *You've got to hate that guy across from you.*
> *Then after the game is over, tell him what a nice guy he is. Shake his hand.*
> *Especially if you win.*
> -Chuck Bednarik, NFL Hall of Famer

As a former NCAA Strength Coach and long-time counselor in the sports field, one of my favorite things about coaching high-level sports, athletes, and coaches is the extreme intensity in them for what they do and how they live. It's part of why my work resonates across platforms to people on Wall Street, in the arts, in the military, and other similar high cost/high payoff fields. It's what we used to call the 'killer instinct.' It's the capacity to shift into full attack mode, on a moment's notice, and stay in it, till the task is accomplished. It's a state of absolute focus and the conjuring of all of one's life energy to go full speed in the right direction of that focus.

> *It was like Mama suddenly realized I was good,*
> *that she didn't have to apologize for me.*
> *It was the strangest feeling.*
> *One minute I was on the stage with my mother,*
> *the next moment, I was on stage with Judy Garland.*
> *One minute she smiled at me, and the next minute*
> *she was like the lioness that owned the stage*
> *and suddenly found somebody invading her territory.*
> *The killer instinct of a performer had come out in her.*
> -Liza Minnelli, American actress/singer,
> on her mother, the legendary Judy Garland, Minnesotan

In what directions do you have the capacity to light it up with the killer instinct? What fires you so much that going killer is almost effortless? Do you have the courage to attack your areas of killer instinct even more, to vehemently go after what you feel called to go after?

> *You got to have the killer instinct.*
> *If you do not have it, forget about basketball and go into social psychology*
> *or something.*
> *If you sometimes wonder if you've got it, you ain't got it.*
> *No pussycats, please.*
> -Bill Russell, American, NBA Hall of Famer

On the flip side, when and in what ways does your own killer instinct get in the way in other fields of life? Do you lack the ability to dial it down, to make it more appropriate to the situation at hand? For, it can get just as unwieldy as any other ability, left unchecked.

Do you get how great a gift it is to be able to light it up inside you at that level, and how you've likely honed that ability, over decades? Are you using it for honorable work, or only self-serving work? There's got to be a good dance of both to feel fulfilled in life. That's just how the human code was written. We need both. And, the killer instinct is one tool that enables both.

> *Now that I'm losing some, I can see how tough I was –*
> *the killer instinct, the single-mindedness, playing like a machine.*
> *Boy, that's what made me a champion.*
> -Chris Evert, American, tennis Hall of Famer

August 16

> *Art is the ability to tell the truth,*
> *especially about yourself...*
> *What I am saying might be profane,*
> *but it's also profound.*
> -Richard Pryor, American comic/actor

I was in my first year of seminary in Berkeley, California. One of the core requirements of Lutheran seminarians was that, in addition to their schooling, they spend a minimum of 10 hours per week working under a pastor-mentor of a church in the area. Seminarians are paired with pastors that seem like a good fit. I got paired with a pastor who looked to be right out of the rock group, *ZZ Top*. He had played nose-guard for Purdue football in college, rode with a motorcycle gang in his 20s, and had an iron clasp grip of a handshake. He also happened to have, in addition to his standard-for-all-pastors Master of Divinity degree (in addition to his undergrad degree), his masters and licensure as a Marriage and Family Therapist. He was this odd-looking, oddly gifted, short giant of a man (think *Lord of the Rings'* Gimli, but a few inches taller), who had a louder laugh than any person you've ever met, and swore with the best of them. His preaching was insightful and deep, and the people *loved* him in his congregation, which brought folks from the Navy base, as well as retirees and young people in the small community. He was a badass because he was so incredibly well-rounded, fully integrated.

His name was Roger Bauer. By his mere existence, he shattered my notions of what a godly person, let alone a pastor, were. I had grown up the son of a pastor and four of my uncles were Lutheran pastors, too. And among the Scandinavian Lutherans of the north country, teetotaling, modesty, and piousness were seen as the hallmarks of being Christian. Roger's mere personality construction, having grown up among the German Lutherans of Michigan, completely blew that up for me.

Best part? After the service and disrobing in the sacristy on Christmas Day morning, he and I walked over to the parsonage where we met his wife and mine. She poured up shots of schnapps and we toasted a successful morning and a blessed Christmas!

But the real best part was that he taught me by how he lived the fusion of sacred and profane, holy and secular. He was this wonderful collection of seemingly contradictory parts that gave permission to me to be my fullest self, without judgment – i.e. to live my truth in its fullness. Everything changed, after that, for me.

Have you integrated your profane and profound, your sacred and secular? Or, do you still judge some part of you, still keep some aspect of you in the shadows, because you suffer from some childhood person's voice, or because you're constricted by religious views that no longer fit you? Do you still have judgmental voices in you, condemning you for this or that, even though your authentic self does not see your shadow side as bad? Is it your sexuality, your personality, your pursuits, your dreams, or what? What do you need to pull out of the shadows and fully integrate into your character and personality, so that you can finally live in the freedom and *ALIVENESS* of authenticity.

August 17

Glorify who you are today.
Do not condemn who you were yesterday
and dream of who you can be tomorrow.
True masters are those who've chosen to make a life rather than a living.
-Neale Donald Walsch, American author

"Sven, I've spent so much of my life, most of it really, striving to get there, to make more, to achieve more, to get happier," he said to me.

"Would you do it differently, if you could do it all over," I asked.

"No, I don't think I would," he reflected. "But, I would've infused it with a regular reminder that I'm exactly where I'm supposed to be. Even though I wanted more and still do, it would have reduced my anxiety and my discontent with the present, if I had reminded myself regularly that this spot on the journey is perfect and right where I'm supposed to be at."

Has it occurred to you that you're right where you are supposed to be? There's nothing wrong with longing for more, whether it be more peace, influence, income, success, happiness, time with family, or what have you. But if that longing is robbing you of the ability to enjoy today, as well, then you're holding on too tightly and you're wasting and missing a lot of life. Or, if your shame over your past, even if your past was not shameful but someone taught you to shame yourself, grips and chokes you, you need to do the work to free yourself of that suffocating voice, or you'll never be present to the gloriousness of *this* day and who you are.

What would it take for you to see and appreciate this? Do you have the ability to throttle down, a bit, and see your trajectory as beautiful, just as it is? Do you have the willingness to go into the painful voices of the past, so that you can finally recognize and release them?

August 18

There is no greatness where there is not simplicity, goodness, and truth.
-Leo Tolstoy, Russian writer

What does it mean to walk through life with goodness? What does it mean to be an instrument of love, kindness, generosity of spirit, and a hearty dose of laughter in life?

It's to give energy. Ultimately, all human interaction is a transference of energy from one person to the next, and sometimes back. Every one of us has had the experience of feeling drained after an interaction with a particular person. It's because that person's pain, need for attention, or hijacking of the conversation took energy from us. Every one of us has had the experience of not wanting to be a burden to someone else with our hurts and sadness. Every one of us has had times when we simply cannot carry others and need to allow ourselves to be tended by others instead.

But, spiritual mastery means having ways to release that heaviness, means having self-disciplines for replenishing my energy when it has been given to, or taken by, another person.

Goodness is about willingness to give energy to others, in one form or another. Yet, it also means being willing to be vulnerable and even lean on others, because at times trusting others and being vulnerable are their own form of giving energy to another.

On the balance, do you give more energy than you take? Do you have mechanisms/tools for replenishing your own energy, when you've given it to others? What do you need to be doing more of (or less of) to ensure the flow of love into your own love cup, as well as the routine cleaning of the accumulated crud therein?

August 19

*The privilege of a lifetime
is being who you are.*
-Joseph Campbell, American scholar,
whose work was a large inspiration for the *Star Wars* movies

The goal of life is *ALIVENESS*. It is to feel the mad rush of life, the crippling fear and pains. It is to experience the sublime calms and ferocious tempests, to embrace it all, characterizing none of it as bad, but all of it as life itself, all part of the experience.

But there is only one path to doing so, and that is the path where there is no path. It is the carving of one's own path, not for the purpose of being original, per se, but for the purpose of being self. It was said in Arthurian Legend that, when departing Camelot to begin his Grail quest, which is, in the end, quest for self, each knight would walk his horse along the edge of the forest, ducking in to begin the journey where the forest was darkest, only where there was no path already. For, if there were a path, then it is not his path. The courage at each tree, rivulet, mountain and new crossing is to feel the calling from within oneself for which direction to go next. For, to live the fully self-authored life is to evermore tune into self and make each passing decision based on the feel of self, rather than the attempt to be anything, even original. Original happens. It is the result of authentic. But authentic only happens as a result of moment-to-moment authenticity.

To give oneself permission to live this way, to endure the slings and arrows of those who would call you foolish and persist anyway, is your greatest gift to yourself. It is to give yourself room to breathe, create, expand, contract, dial it up, pull it back, and read/live the self, moment-to-moment. But giving oneself permission to self-author requires seizing it back from those who stole it from you in the first place. Ahhh, there's the rub, isn't it. The toll for being, saying, doing, and becoming who you really are is the courage to say 'NO!' to your gods – the people who've run your life, condemned your decisions and often your very existence, and the people you've just always assumed held the keys to the kingdom that is your life.

Pro Tip: They don't.

Whom do you continue to abdicate your own power to? Who are the gods you still give your life, your decisions, and your self-authorship over to? Why do you do it? What do you seek from them? More importantly, what do you fear? That one fear is the great wall standing between you and your living authentically. Each day you choose to allow that, you *choose* to allow that. Each day, you choose to hand your life over to someone else. Are you okay with that?

August 20

> ### *Stay hungry;*
> ### *Stay foolish.*
> -Steve Jobs, American genius & billionaire

This is one of my all-time favorite quotes, which, upon first hearing it in the late-2000s, became one of the lodestar mantras of my own journey.

Why?

Because, it powerfully reinforces my commitment to trusting and executing what my own voice is saying, moment-to-moment. It reminds me that to fear how others might see me, were I to fail in this or fall flat on my face in that, is dumb and an utter abdication of my life to something so completely arbitrary and meaningless. It grounds me in the sheer power of being willing to be thought stupid. For, once that Rubicon is crossed, the enormity of self-belief is profoundly empowering.

This quote pushes me to play lean and to keep pushing myself to pursue the next fire in my belly, the next passion project, the next brilliantly insane idea, because my soul hungers for it. It reminds me to live aggressively, to attack what I'm jacked up to really go after.

Do you fear playing hungry? Do you fear looking foolish? Which do you fear more? What percentage of your life, your ambition, your standing up for yourself, your career, and the relationships you really want (vs the ones you're just tolerating) is short-circuited by your fear of playing lean or looking dumb, or irresponsible?

What would it take for you to finally move through and past these two powerful fears? Are you sick of not going after your dreams, yet; I mean, really going after them? Whose scorn do you most fear, if you were to play hungry and foolish as you attack the life you want?

August 21

I love to see a young girl go out and grab the world by the lapels.
Life's a bitch. You've got to go out and kick ass.
-Maya Angelou

What is it that you can see in a young person that inspires you? So often in life we look to those older, wiser, or simply those who came first as sources of inspiration. But, one of the delightful flavors of aging is seeing in youth some quality, some action, some something that lights a fire inside to watch it, some something that gives you goosebumps.

I love seeing excellence and courage in young people – someone young who has mastered something or who has the fire inside, attacking life with sheer force. I love it. Also, creativity in youth tickles me, conjures up and lights my own creativity.

What is it for you? And, what can you do to clear the way for it on a young person's path, or support it? Are you obstructing or facilitating the pursuit of greatness and passions in those younger or less powerful than you? What more can you do?

August 22

> *Be ready to revise any system,*
> *scrap any method,*
> *abandon any theory,*
> *if the success of the job requires it.*
> -Henry Ford, American automaker

Wow! That's a beast of a quote.

Ever tried not just bucking the system, but actually trying to change it, not to mention *radically* change it, whatever that system might've been? Ever tried scrapping an old way you, or others, have methodically done something? Ever tried aborting a myth system, story, or theory you, yourself, have been living by or working in?

This is egregiously hard stuff to do. The powers and persons who crash their vitriol down onto you can grind your will to a halt, even to shreds. And, often, we walk away from the suffocating inertia, feeling as if we've lost, when really we've won. Because, we've cut ourselves free from our own old inner forms that kept us married to obstacles of progress. Walking away from, or even exploding, old forms and theories is precisely what you need in order to create progress.

And yet, if those efforts to transform outdated systems and beliefs actually begin to bear fruit, well, that can be an incredibly exciting experience. When the powers that be haven't fully ground you down, yet, but have opened to your vision, even if only a bit, there is a window of hope, an infusion of energy, and a sense of living on the edge of innovation that fires the soul. *This* is *ALIVENESS!*

In your journaling, bullet point the top ten things, both externally and internally, that stand in your way of going boldly toward new systems, theories, and methods; ten in your personal life and ten in your professional life. After each one, list your fears. After each one list any other feelings that arise as you consider it. Now, continue to journal on the whys, whos, hows, and whens of all of this. Keep flushing it all out.

August 23

Can't no man play like me!
-Sister Rosetta Tharpe, Rock and Roll Hall of Famer

Rosetta Tharpe was raised by her very religious mother in the American South. Picking up the guitar at a very young age, she became known as the girl with the guitar, which was unheard of, in those days. She traveled on the Gospel/evangelical traveling circuit with her mother, shocking and entertaining crowds at a very young age with her gospel lyrics performed in bluesy/secular style, which had basically never happened before. She invented it! She made the leap into popular culture by performing on radio, signing a 10-year recording contract, and performing at both the Cotton Club in New York City with the legendary Cab Calloway, as well as Carnegie Hall, all the while singing spiritual rock and roll in clearly secular/popular settings. And, secular audiences loved it.

To many all time rock and roll greats like Chuck Berry, Elvis, Eric Clapton, Bob Dylan, Little Richard, and Keith Richards, Sister Rosetta Tharpe is known as *The Godmother of Rock and Roll*. She is also cited by other music greats such as Johnny Cash, Muddy Waters, Aretha Franklin, Beck, Neil Sadaka, Karen Carpenter, Meat Loaf, and Tina Turner as being very influential in their lives and music. In 2017, she was elected into the Rock and Roll Hall of Fame.

But, the ugly twist of the story is that this African-American woman watched her legacy be erased just as surely and frantically as she was writing it. Her style of bluesy, gospel-infused rock and roll, which she clearly pioneered, was being credited to young white boys, such as Elvis, who clearly pilfered her substance and style and openly admitted it; Jerry Lee Lewis; and the Rolling Stones, who admit their lineage tracks through Muddy Waters, cites Tharpe as one of his giant influences. Popular culture, right up until 2017, couldn't bear to accept that a woman – let alone an African-American woman! – was the genesis of rock and roll, yes even before Chuck Berry, who also openly credited her. By the 1970s, her memory in popular culture was – poof! – gone.

While there was the occasional posthumous mention or award, her name was rarely, if ever, spoken. Then in 2007, Gayle Wald, a woman, came out with the book, *Shout Sister Shout!* Tharpe went on to be inducted in the Blues Hall of Fame, have a BBC documentary done on her, as well as a PBS special. In 2017, another woman, Bev Ragovoy, herself the wife of the deceased Jerry Ragovoy, who was the founder of *The Hit Factory* and writer of such songs as *Time is on My Side* and *Piece of My Heart*, championed her story. She and her production company turned *Shout Sister Shout!* into a musical that has been performed at the legendary Ford's Theater in Washington DC and, as of the publication of this book, appears to be making its way to Broadway. These powerful women are un-erasing Sister Rosetta Tharpe's extraordinary legacy.

And to think, back in Tharpe's day, in a racist and exceedingly patriarchal, religiously driven society, she was heavily demonized and subjected to withering criticism, because she was a woman who played guitar (that alone was all but unthinkable). More than that, she did it at such a phenomenally high ability, while creating rhythm and blues with spiritual content. This had never been done. Oh, and she was a closeted bisexual. She was a courageous visionary in every aspect of life. "Women can't do that and shouldn't do that" was the refrain shouted at her, and she did it anyway. Now, other women have sprung up to make sure her voice and influence get the proper due.

So, what do they say you can't do?

August 24

*Success consists of going
from failure to failure
without loss of enthusiasm.*
-Winston Churchill, British leader

Which draws you in more, a biography of a person where you hear only of successes, or one where there is setback and failure, success and pitfall, re-emergence and screw-ups, failures and more growth?

Is it real to live a story of only success? Surely not. So, failure, then, is woven into the fabric of every single human life, even the most guarded, fear-driven life of hiding and avoidance.

If that be true, then the big differentiator between the scared and the *ALIVE* seems to be the attitude toward failure. Real success, according to Churchill, is not the incessant drumbeat of achievement, but the willingness, perhaps even eagerness, to fail. Failure keeps us young, fresh. Fear of failure is the beginning of old age. Being right is old. Failing repeatedly and unabashedly is vibrancy, an embracing of the adventure of the human lifespan, it is this odd spiritual coitus with the soul of the universe, itself.

Do you fear failure and cower? Or, do you look it in the face and say, "Rock and roll, hoochie-koo! Let's fail big, baby! Let's swing for the fence!"

What, or who, do you most fear if you do swing for the fence...and don't hit it? And, please don't say yourself, because no baby comes out of the womb hating on themselves. You were taught that self-criticism. Someone taught you that voice; it's not native to you. So, you may think it's your critical voice you most fear, but that's only because, as a kid, you so sought approval that you adopted someone else's critical voice as your own to avoid the pain if you disappointed the one who taught you. You did it to survive.

So, again, whose voice do you most fear if you do fail? And if that voice were to come to pass after a failure, would you be okay? Sure, you'd grieve and have to flush out a lot of other feelings, but *would. you. be. okay?*

Once you realize you would be and that life would go on, well, that's when everything changes and you start swinging for the fence.

August 25

Harmlessness is the only true religion.
-Mahavira, Father of the Jain religion

How heavy is your footprint in your daily interactions and over the course of your lifetime? Do you walk with gentleness and kindness, or the dull thud of indeliberate bumping and bruising, hurting and scraping of others?

What I mean is, do you actually look at how you walk through life? Do you actually see how you impact others? Do you even recognize the value of doing so?

Conversely, for the meek and timid, are you harmless because you fear coming out of your shell, because you've chosen harmlessness as a defense mechanism against criticism and being left to be by yourself? Or have you chosen harmlessness, though fully capable of conjuring the energy to do otherwise, because it is what you value, knowing damn well the impact of your past thuds?

What has driven you to greater harmlessness in life? Why do you do it? What is the satisfaction, the accomplishment in doing so? Or, are you the person who needs to become more harmless? Is it time to reassess?

August 26

If you're still coping,
you're not healed.
-Sven

A great amount of counseling that clergy, therapists, and other healers do is helping people to cope with internal pain in their heads, hearts, minds, bodies and souls. At times, this is a very necessary course of action that can provide tools for assuaging hurt and hardship, so that daily functioning is even possible.

However, in my work I'm geared to one thing and one thing only: healing. Results! My work is about getting the damn virus out, so to speak, not just trying to make your symptoms go away. What that means is going deep into your origin stories – what you've been taught to believe about yourself, the messages you heard, picked up, or were incessantly told about yourself and life, growing up. It also means exploring the feelings that accompany those messages and memories, as well as what the presence of those messages and beliefs in your past says about the people who delivered them, which is often the scariest part of the work, as I discuss in "There's a Hole in My Love Cup," the precursor to the book you're reading.

Healing the soul is not about 'managing' anything or 'coping' with life. It's about going deep to look at, discuss, and flush all the crud you've either been running from or mired in your entire life. And, an easy way to start, for some, is to first begin flushing out all the feelings, even the ones presenting in your day to day. That makes way for the messages to be visible. It also makes room for the amount of energy and feelings you're going to experience as you see more clearly *who* taught you and what they *really* taught you.

Are you coping or healing? Is your therapist taking you deep or letting you just skim the surface with your weekly recounting of life's dings and dents? When do you tire of not going deep, of not having lasting healing and peace, of simply coping? What's the fear driving the behavior? Are you ready to finally pass through that fear and do it anyway?

August 27

Pain (any pain – emotional, physical, mental) has a message.
The information it has about our life can be remarkably specific,
but it usually falls into one of two categories:
"We would be more alive if we did more of this," and
"Life would be more lovely if we did less of that."
Once we get the pain's message, and follow its advice, the pain goes away.
The more severe the pain or illness,
the more severe will be the necessary changes.
-Peter McWilliams, Author *Life 101*

Your own soul (or, if you prefer, God/Universe/the gods/spirit/Higher Power) is always talking. Chiros – the perfectly timed hand of the universe – is always now. There are no messages you have to wait for, because there is always a constant bombardment of new messages, just likely not the ones you have been waiting for or want.

But life – the *soul* – is always talking. Always, and in a blessed, beautiful, serene way, the soul is whispering to us. More often than not your soul whispers through your pains, your hardships, your failures, and your sectors of discomfort and resistance. Any place you lack calm, relief and/or exuberance is the place where your own soul is calling you to new paths, change, and greater loveliness, joy, and laughter.

Are you listening to your pain, your falldowns, your failures, your screw-ups, your discomforts, and your embarrassments? What are they whispering to you? Why do you keep resisting? What are the severe changes you fear? Or, rather, what is the price you fear in those changes? Why do you fear that?

What is underneath it?

August 28

Give what you have.
To someone, it may be better than you dare to think.
-Henry Wadsworth Longfellow, American poet

I have a brother, who has spent decades quietly toiling to no fanfare in the hushed rooms of the dying. Specializing in cancer hospice social work, he has held the hand of more dying people and their families/friends than any person should ever have to. He has helped countless people navigate the labyrinthine healthcare system to meet their physical, psychological, and spiritual needs as they, or their loved one, are dying. He has whispered gentle words of reassurance and sat silent to just listen when words would be clutter.

There will be no statues erected in his honor when he passes. For, on one hand, his gifts are humble, though infused with a monster intellect, profound love for people, and a durable spirit. But his seemingly small gifts (or so some might call it) have changed and comforted thousands of lives at life's most critical and painful juncture – the terrifying movement into death. If that is not the touch of the gods themselves, then what is?

Every gift you bring to the world has a profound impact when it meets precisely the right need rising up in someone else or something else. To what degree is your life held back by your belief that you bring little to the table of life, that you have little to contribute? Does that cause you to withhold that which you do bring?

Is it possible you're wrong?

August 29

> ### *The soul is more powerful than the will.*
> ### *It wins every time.*
> -Sven

Every time someone hurts you in word, non-verbal, or deed, it's as if they have put a hand-size rock in a large burlap sack on your back. When we're young, we have lots of strength and can carry lots of rocks. But, as time goes on, the amount of rocks in that child's sack grows and quickly becomes too great. Even a child or teen begins to feel weighed down. This is depression.

The problem then expands as that teen gets stuck with more rocks, handed more wounds and pains moving into and through adulthood. Put hundreds of pounds on anyone's back and that person will start to make decisions which compensate for or are directly determined by that heavy load and the fear of taking on even one more rock. Further, the knees, hips, and back will start to give out, over time. The heart will be taxed heavily as it tries to feed the body. The willpower grinds down, because the demand for strength and one more step of endurance is unrelenting. Eventually – eventually! – even the strongest is ground to a halt.

Have you ever thought about how many of your life decisions, even down to the most minute, were influenced by or the direct result of the messages you were burdened with at a young age? Has it occurred to you that your lack of peace and happiness are a direct result of the messages you were taught about yourself?

If you have kids, have you done the deliberate work of demanding back any rocks you put into the sacks of your children? Have you fully owned the damage you caused, or have you just cursorily said, "Sorry. Now lets move on?" What is gained by you not claiming and owning the hardship you've caused your children with your words and messaging? What soul-sucking damage do you cause by not retrieving the rocks you put in your childrens' bags? Are you merely protecting your own frail ego at the cost of soul pain and heavy loads for your children? Is it really worth it? Why wouldn't you want them to fly at full wingspan, unburdened by the pains you placed on them and in them?

When do you finally set your child, or grandchild, free of the pain you caused? Can you maybe do it before you die? And, what if you die tomorrow?

August 30

It is not the critic who counts;
not the man who points out how the strong man stumbles,
or where the doer of deeds could have done them better.
The credit belongs to the man who is actually in the arena,
whose face is marred by dust and sweat and blood; who strives valiantly;
who errs; who comes up short, again and again;
who spends himself in a worthy cause;
who at best knows in the end the triumph of high achievement,
and who, at the worst, if he fails, he at least fails while daring greatly,
so that his place shall never be with those timid and cold souls
who neither know victory nor defeat.
-Teddy Roosevelt, American President and war hero

Life should not be a journey to the grave with the intention of
arriving safely in a pretty and well-preserved body,
but rather to skid in broadside in a cloud of smoke,
thoroughly used up, totally worn out,
and loudly proclaiming,
"WOW! What a ride!"
-Hunter S. Thompson, American journalist and author

I'll just leave these here. You likely don't need my help ruminating on or journaling on them. You know exactly the questions these raise in you. Journal them out!

August 31

> **The difference between a student and a master is**
> **the master has failed more times than the student has tried.**
> -Multiple attributions, including Mac Duke, Branding strategist

Old Johnny Johnson was a disheveled man who used to sit on his ratty bench out front of the cafe and to the left on the main street in our 600-person town, when I was younger than six. He'd put a Life Saver candy between his thumb and forefinger for me. Then when I went to take it, he'd slip it back behind his forefinger, so I couldn't get it. He'd chuckle, then hand it over. I liked him. He was slow, with a cane. But he was nice to me.

Richard Silverstein was a dear family friend and retired schoolteacher. He and his family were members of Dad's church and his house was on my paper route in my pre-teen/teen surburb, after we moved from that small town. This older gentleman flat-out said he saw me as unique and asked my parents if he could give me special tests and mentor me, a bit. I loved being around that man, just down the block, as he'd watch the Mets, or listen to me when I talked, or tell stories of sleeping with his weapon as a warrant officer in the Army.

Lenny Samuelson was the happiest man you ever met. I was a 6 year-old preacher's kid and he'd take me on his lap during worship service, my legs dangling between him and his effervescent wife. He and his wife would invite the preacher's family over for Christmas season party/meals in his big house. When I was 17, he was the first grown man to take me to lunch and a beer, as I had just gotten into the US Air Force Academy and he had been an F-86 Sabre pilot in Korea. I always felt seen, special, and happy around him.

Patrick Wisniewski, Sr., was the father of a girlfriend in 10th grade, who would sit in the breezeway of his house, smoking cigars, talking with me for hours. He was the one who introduced me to the vision of going to West Point or one of the academies. He could laugh and make you think, at the same time. Loved that guy!

Joe Frank was the wrestling coach in his early-40s in high school, who taught us physical and mental toughness at levels none of us blue collar boys knew. We laughed at his almost-caricature drill sergeant personality, but we respected his intensity, depth, ability to create champions, and his love for his wrestlers. Other than my father and my brother, he was the biggest male influence on my life.

Roger Bauer was the 40-something pastor who revolutionized my idea of what spiritual really is in my first year of seminary, and did so with a laugh bigger than Santa, himself.

Who has mentored and molded you? What did they teach you? More importantly, what did they make you feeeeel? Were you heard? Seen? Special? Are you bringing it full circle in the lives of young people you encounter, giving more than you're taking? Is it time?

September

September 1

The more powerful and original a mind,
the more it will incline towards the religion of solitude.
-Aldous Huxley, English writer

How can you hear your soul if everyone is talking?
-Mary Doria Russell, American novelist

It has been said to many folks who are considering moving to get away from their problems – whether it be pains from their past, people who are negative, or present experiences that are dragging them down – "Y'know, you can't move away from your problems. You take them with you."

There is truth to that, to be sure. But it clearly implies that creating distance, be it geographical or even distance created by hard boundaries, doesn't matter or help. I disagree. Oftentimes, the very thing needed for healing is space, room to breathe and not feel suffocated by the voices and memories of others. Room alone can be a healing tonic, not to mention an opportunity to hear one's own voice, unjudged by those assailants who've perhaps forever sought to squelch that voice rising up from within. The hearing of one's own voice is absolutely critical to both healing and happiness.

Is it possible that the very thing you need most in life is just some doggone room to breathe? Space can be so extraordinarily freeing and so impactful in clearing the head. Do you need new geography, or perhaps stronger boundaries? Maybe it's not a physical change in geography so much as a pulling away from a person, group, or place? Do you need to block someone? Perhaps you need to completely stop listening to someone. Do you have the courage to execute that need, to honor the need of your soul to breathe?

September 2

> **The pain will leave you**
> **once it has finished teaching you.**
> -Unknown

What so many people don't realize is that life is fair, very fair, when it comes to one big thing. No one – quite literally no one – escapes life without pain. It may hit shockingly late in life or tragically too early. But, no one escapes life unscathed. Not just by pain, but wretched, soul-searing pain through seemingly endless hells of fire. Those hells look very different from one person to the next. And, it is a fool's errand to begin comparing whose is worse. But, it is unequivocal that pain is ubiquitous. No heart goes unbroken or body unbeaten.

Thus, one of Life's Top 5 Biggest Questions becomes, What do I do with the pain?

This one question, perhaps more than any other, determines the story arc. It writes itself into every decision subsequent to it:

Do I run from the pain in the myriad forms one can (from gambling to boozing; working upon working upon busyness and busyness; pills to addictive gaming; or swiping and scrolling; sex to smoke; over-parenting to chasing chaos or the new adrenaline rush); or

- Do I stop and allow it to wash over me and overwhelm me in the myriad forms it can?
- Do I run from the pain or face it and sit in it for as long as it lasts, going ever deeper to understand its roots, mining it for insights into self and life, until it all passes and the calm comes, that peace that passes all understanding?

Running from my pain means its innate sorrow scares me; the fear creates a persistent drumbeat of anxiety inside, which then is infused into every decision, major and minor, after. Running from even one ounce more of pain becomes the story's leitmotif, hidden but ever-present.

Do you see it? Are you finally aware of not just your running from the pain, but how anxiety and fear have driven your decisions? Do you realize, particularly, how your fear of others' criticism, questioning, and scolding – or your longing for their assent or acceptance – has driven so much of your life, and how none of it may actually be your authentic self?

Are you tired yet? Are you ready to finally allow the grief? Whether to stop running is one of life's hardest decisions. Have the running, distracting, and powering through gotten bad enough yet that you're just plain exhausted and ready to finally face it? If not, it will.

September 3

> *The path to discovering who you are*
> *requires discovering who you're not.*
> *That subsequently requires the courage to quit*
> *that which is not you,*
> *which in turn requires the courage to no longer care*
> *about the inevitable criticisms that surround quitting.*
> -Sven

The ground we walk on rests on top of giant tectonic plates below the surface of the earth. These plates are thousands of miles long and deep. When they shift, deep below the surface, they cause massive rumblings up here where the sun shines, rumblings we call earthquakes.

Deep inside you are the tectonic plates of the soul, into which are written the very code of your authentic self. But, throughout your early life, other messages got rammed down your throat, embedding somewhere inside you. Cheap cement got poured over those massive plates and cheaper lies got written into them: you're unwanted and unwantable; you're not good enough and you suck; you don't matter, not the real you.

Traveling through life, the unrest, anxiety, and turmoil you've felt on the surface find their roots in the grating of those two forces – that which has been shoved down your throat meeting that essence rising up from your soul. All of your loss of liveliness is because of those two forces battling inside. And, until that which was forced upon you, even by loving people, is jackhammered and extracted by you, there will be no peace in your soul.

Even the slightest shift in core beliefs is a shift in the tectonic plates underneath your life, creating wonderful, long-awaited earthquakes of change in your life principles, actions, and relationships. Which of yours are changing or need changing? Why? And what are the overdue, likely earthquakes ahead in your everyday life?

September 4

On the journey of the soul
there is nothing more important than solitude, courage, and openness.
And the greatest of these is courage.
-Sven

As I see it, there are 3 basic steps in the ongoing spiritual journey of life. The fundamental first step is creating the solitude and silence to *hear* your own inner voice. But that requires slowing down, which means your pains and feelings you've been running from will wash over you and need to be flushed out. For they are what is blocking you from hearing your own inner feel, or voice.

For many, the idea of facing and feeling it all from the past is a pain too great to even consider. They fear solitude because there is no silence in it, only the thundering of the past inside of them. They need the noise, noise, noise of life outside of them as a constant distraction. However, for those who begin to clear out the inner storms, they finally begin to feeeel with clarity the calling of their soul.

Thus, the second phase of the spiritual journey is summoning the courage to *heed* that voice. And, what makes heeding that voice so terrifying is that it requires taking it from inside and pushing it outside you. It means exposing your real self to the world, no longer living in the safe shell of your persona or fake self.

That means running a great risk. For, what has kept you in that shell is the fear of incurring the wrath of the people and voices you've been kowtowing to your entire life; the voices of criticism that sear so badly. This fear is so powerful for a great many people, because they've been wounded so badly by these people in the past, that they would rather keep their new vision inside, rather than ever going after it. Being criticized by these people when living the persona is bad enough. But, being criticized or mocked by them when showing your real self would be a fate worse than death.

Nonetheless, should you have the courage to hear and heed your soul's calling, the third step is, for many, the hardest. It's a master-level step. To doggedly pursue the vision that possesses your soul is big. But, it is so easy for that vision, particularly the waiting for it to come to fruition and the allowance for new visions to grow out of it, to be a source of immense unrest, impatience, dissatisfaction, despondency, and hopelessness. We tend to grip a vision so tightly that we choke it, or its squirrelliness and slow gait choke us. Thus, what is required to live a life of imperturbability, where you are on top of life, rather than life controlling you, is *to live with an open hand.* Mastering life means loosening your grip, living in a state of openness. It is to simultaneously pursue with drive and vigor that which possesses your soul and to also let go of it everyday. It's to be okay if it never happens, or even excited if it morphs into something very different.

To live with an open hand is to let go of trying to control results. It is to hold on loosely. It is to allow the forces of life and the universe to infuse our vision and path with new life, exciting new twists, and things formerly unseen and unimagined. But we lock our identity into the initial vision, the results we seek to achieve. Thus, not achieving those results is felt as a grievous loss. But to live in a state of joy, openness, and play is to enjoy the ride, possessed of the vision, but not consumed by all the ways it can make me feel when it is not coming or when things aren't 'just right.'

Lastly, we are always cycling through the *hearing*, *heeding*, and *opening*. We are always calling up more solitude, more courage, and more openness as we loop through life.

What is in you that you refuse to slow down and hear? What past pains do you need to drain out, so that you can hear and feel that inner calling? Whose voice and criticism do you most fear, if you were to have the courage to actually voice and pursue that calling? In your pursuit of that vision, can you begin to let go of the thing you want most? What would it take for you to return to a state of play, so to speak, and enjoy the ride in this new grand quest you are on?

Doors open doors open doors.
-Sven's mom, Charlotte Evangeline Erlandson, Parenting master

September 5

Transformation can be immediate,
if you go deep enough.
-Unknown

There are few things in life I believe more than the words of this quote. My entire life's work is predicated on this pillar of truth. Yet, we've been lulled into stony sleep, believing that inner transformation must take years, even decades. Some even believe it never actually happens.

If your healing is taking forever, you're not going deep enough, and likely for one (or both) of two reasons. Neither is a reason for shame. Either, 1) You don't know how; or 2) You're terrified of what's down there.

Well, the 'how' question is solved simply by asking two questions, and *writing down the answers*: A) How are you feeling either right this minute or about that thing you've been thinking about/remembering; B) Why?

Now do it again, How are you feeling, now? Why?

Again. Deeper. Again. Relentlessly deeper.

You can add into the mix other questions, as well, which you then write down the answers to:

- When did it start?
- What were the circumstances?
- What was/is the hardest part about it?
- Why?
- What are the implications of looking at the truth?
- Who would disagree?
- Do you have the courage to look at and live your truths, anyway?
- What is the gift this pain/experience is here to teach you about self or life?
- If you can't answer that, take a guess, knowing you could change your mind tomorrow.
- What's the scariest part of all of this?
- Why?
- How do you feel? Etc.

Now, if the issue is not knowledge of how to go deep, then the issue is courage. Nothing on earth will terrify you more than all that is inside you. The enemy is within, and you weren't born with that enemy. It is all that you fear. All that stuff is the terrifying ticket to your healing. All of it.

Everything else, every other person is secondary or next. But first are the demons of inner self, the ugly truths and fears you're terrified to face.

So, then the question becomes, How fast do you want to heal? And yes, it really is that simple. The speed of your growth into new life is pretty much completely in your hands, a function of – derivative of – your own courage and willingness to go into the ugly. Everything else is an excuse. That's all.

September 6

> *We do not choose love;*
> *love chooses us.*
> -Riann C. Miller, American author

> *You're everything*
> *I never knew*
> *I always wanted.*
> - Katherine Reback & Joan Taylor, *Fools Rush In*

Have you ever had the experience of finding yourself in a great relationship with a sort of someone you never thought you'd see yourself with, someone so far afield from anything you had ever imagined? It can be a shocking, revelatory, disorienting experience.

Yet, it is so easy to strangle love before it ever arrives. We do it every time we adamantly insist love must look the way we imagined it, when we leave no room for the infusion of the gods or whimsy. Too often we seek to control outcomes so fiercely, our grip so tight, that there is no breathing room for serendipity and amazing surprises. Control, of course, is always driven by fear of pain. So, we cling tightly to what we've envisioned, insistent we cannot be happy, unless the future (or future person, as it were) looks precisely thus and so.

One of the grand beauties of life is that the gods, or Universe, or the depths of your own soul, have a stratospherically bigger imagination and understanding of what will make you happiest than your conscious, rational mind does. But you'll never experience that, unless you have the courage to take it for a spin and trust it is so, unless you have the courage to live with an open hand – simultaneously driving toward your highest aim while allowing for the possibility it may never come and the possibility that what does come will be infinitely better.

How open are you to the flow and infusions of the universe that you cannot control? How able are you to trust that, no matter what comes, you'll be okay and you'll find joy in new ways? Because, the desire to control, the tight clinging, is driven by the fear that if you don't control it, you won't be okay? Ultimately, it comes down to playing loose vs playing tight. Fear and longing for control cause us to play tight, thereby choking off wonderful new possibilities for greater joy, peace, and *ALIVENESS!*

September 7

*It is only by risking our persons from one hour to another
that we live at all.
And often enough our faith beforehand in an uncertified result
is the only thing that makes the result come true.*
-William James,
19th Century 'Father of American Psychology'

Few things in life get derided, spat on, put down, undermined, and doubted more than passions, beliefs, and dreams. The often ugly furnaces of society and even those who claim to love us can just as easily torch a dream to ashes as burn off its impurities, thereby strengthening it.

But, it is that willingness to walk into the fires – to *risk* in things that are not yet seen – that is the difference between greatness and hiding in mediocrity and a life undone. It is the difference between the erection of massive dreams into reality and living with regret or quiet mocking of those who dare.

The thing that hamstrings dreams is fear – of derision, of failure that leads to derision, of poverty that leads to hardship and derision.

Do you risk for that which you believe in and are passionate about? What's the next risk? What's the great fear that makes this next risk a risk, at all? Whose derision do you fear? And if that great fear comes to pass, will you be okay? Will you grieve, adjust, learn, and move forward?

September 8

*If you end up with a boring, miserable life because you listened
to your mom, your dad, your teacher, your priest,
or some guy on television telling you how to do your sh*t,
then you deserve it.*
-Frank Zappa, American musician

One of the highest-grossing movies of all time is the blue, James Cameron sci-fi flick, *Avatar*. Uniquely, in this movie, love is expressed among the warrior, alien people not with the words, "I love you," but with the words, "I see you."

How powerful a thought – to be seen for who you really are and to be wanted for that. Isn't that what we all want – to be truly seen, understood, accepted, and wanted? This person sees me *and stays!* Wow! What a concept.

But being seen for who you really are is dependent upon one extraordinarily powerful and terrifying thing – the willingness to reveal yourself, which of course is predicated upon you even knowing who you really are. Revealing your true self takes mighty courage.

How can someone love you for just plain old you, if you won't show that person your original self, warts and all? Are you still hiding behind your walls? Has your pain gotten bad enough that you're willing to risk and open up? Has your longing to be seen and accepted, even wanted, grown powerful enough to overcome the demons inside holding you in fear, mediocrity, unrest, and even lethargy?

Have you done the work to even know your authentic self? What is the scariest stuff to look at, the stuff you're most afraid to sort out in the quest to know self? What is it about you that you most fear showing, even to someone who loves you? What do you most fear happening if you do?

September 9

If we possess our why of life,
we can put up with almost any how.
-Friedrich Nietzsche, German philosopher & poet

Over the decades, I've worked with a great many people who've been captivated by a vision for their lives, and they're either living it and busting their hump in building it, or they ain't. Those that aren't going after what they truly feel called to do with their lives aren't somehow inherently flawed. Rather, almost invariably, they are still being sucked down by the pain, fears, and BS beliefs they've been taught about themselves, in the past. All that deep crud zaps motivation. That stuff has to all be flushed out before they'll ever have the inner power to bring their visions into reality.

But, this quote is looking at a different aspect of being consumed by a dream. It's the person possessed of a reason for living, for attacking life, for waking up and running hard, each day and year. And to be consumed by such a why is the craving of so many people struggling to find self and find life. So many people want to know their purpose, or "God, what's your will for my life," or what would make them most feel energized by life. That longing for *ALIVENESS* runs through all human existence. To not have that 'why' is most commonly because of precisely the same reason mentioned in the first paragraph – the crud of the past is packed inside you, on top of your authentic self. The more you get that crud out, the more your individual, original calling rises up effortlessly from within. With that comes a seemingly endless motivation to attack life.

There is an extraordinary power that comes from being lit on fire by your why. When I was writing my earliest books, which almost no one was reading, I would wake at 3am or 4am and write, some days, until 7pm, with only the briefest of breaks to eat a sandwich; or perhaps I'd write only 'til noon. I'd lose track of time while writing. I'm a big-time morning person. Yet, strangely, I'd be more energized at the end of a day of writing than I was at the beginning. I couldn't wait to wake up and do it all over again. I lived in poverty, literally on the street, while writing two of my books. I didn't give a crap. I was just totally focused on what I felt was my work, my calling, my passion. I've endured all manner of criticism, put-downs, and humiliation for my work, including losing a lot of family and friends. It hurt at the time, but in the end I knew I valued my work more than the people who wanted me to conform to their arbitrary expectations. One or two people encouraged me in blazing my own path. Several people applauded, even though they didn't understand what I was doing. But, no one supported me in my career. Except for the most minor of things, I was and am a fully self-made man. And, that's true only because I had to believe in my why, 'cuz ain't nobody else doing it.

What was my why? Same as it is now: just be who the heck I am in every moment and only do that which I love or that which facilitates my building a life based on what I love. If it doesn't meet those criteria, it's not in my life. I went hardcore, and I'm happier for it and laughing my way through the ups and the downs. But first you gotta get used to the downs, to the point where they no longer intimidate you.

What's your why? Are you ready to get after it?!

September 10

A conscience is what hurts when all your other parts feel so good.
-Unknown

How much of your truest self do you, or did you, sacrifice to feel good, to be happy, at least on the surface? How much of your own 'feel good' came at the expense of others? And how does that sit with you, inside...deep inside?

That's your conscience talking – the part of your own soul that knows it's calling got co-opted by ego – that desire for more and for me, and me some more. See, I believe the soul in its truest expression does not compromise others to help self, unless others are destroying your self. I believe that at our essence we are all good, not desiring to lift up ourselves if it means others don't have better, too. Thus, it's a violation of our own soul/conscience when we compromise another so that we might have more or be more. In our most silent times, we know it, deep inside. This, of course, is part of why so many people cannot bear to sit alone with only quiet around them. For it is in those moments, or hours, where we cannot deny the muted voices inside that spring from our own self.

What seems on the surface like the pleasuring of self is, at much deeper levels, a betrayal of self. And, we know it. You know it. You know when you're betraying your own real truth.

So, are you? Got the guts to face it and maybe even fix it? Write it out. Don't stop. Going deeper, what's the wound in you, from your past, causing you to take from life so that you may not have to feel that wound that never healed?

September 11

It's fine to celebrate success,
but it's more important to heed the lessons of failure.
-Bill Gates, Co-founder of Microsoft

There are fewer states in the US that have franchises of all of the major professional sports, yet have fewer championships than Minnesota. Minnesota ranks with Arizona as down near the very bottom of the list of championships accrued by any state possessed with teams from all of the major sports leagues. I personally have lived through four Super Bowl losses in my lifetime, as well as two Stanley Cup finals, and countless miserable seasons, with only the smallest number of bright spots. So, being from that state, one becomes accustomed to losing. And, it sucks. It forces you to develop one helluva sense of humor!

Yet, there's a lot to be learned from losing and setbacks. In fact, it is in losses that you see the areas where the most improvement is possible. The inclination in our own lives is to run from the loss, heartbreak, and pain, because it's too much to bear. However, as with any team that reviews film after losses, eviscerating the performance to see what needs to be done, we have the opportunity to look deeply at our own lives to see potential for massive growth. Instead, too often, after pain and loss, we eviscerate the person or organization that we believe caused us that pain. This rich opportunity to grow slips through our fingers, because it's so much easier and less painful to run from the pain by scapegoating someone else.

Do you wonder why you keep making dumb career mistakes, or just can't seem to take off with your career? Wonder why you keep picking the wrong people in your love life, again and again? Can't figure out why, in your parenting, your kids pull further and further away from you?

It's because, to some greater or lesser degree, you're avoiding the necessary self-reflection, even evisceration, to see what is going on inside you and how that may be adversely impacting what's going on outside of you. How am I making my problems worse? More importantly, is there stuff operating inside of me, driving me, that I'm missing that is causing or somehow allowing bad sequences of events?

Failure is gold. It holds in its hand the most valuable gems of wisdom. But the price for uncovering those gems is the fires of the smelting furnace. You have to possess the courage to endure the pain that comes from looking at it, all over again.

Are you running from your failures, utterly ignoring the gems of wisdom and cascading waterfalls of insight and new growth they bear? Has it occurred to you that you'll never enjoy the championships of life without doing so? Further, has it occurred to you that you've never lost those failures, nor the opportunity to learn from them? They're just sitting there inside you, waiting to be mined and submitted to the intense heat of analysis, so that they may finally give you the new life you seek so desperately.

September 12

> *Isn't it funny that they say most girls have daddy issues,*
> *when really, every dude does?*
> -Amy Schumer, American comic

She was dating the older guy for a year or so. She could hear the whispers behind her back. Friends and family would say under their breath, "Daddy issues!" She was happy as the dickens and enjoying the relationship, but couldn't shake the internalization of all the stuff she knew people thought. Eventually, she came to me and asked, "Do I have daddy issues, Sven? What does that even mean, if it's true?"

It's her second question that is the real issue. What does mommy (or daddy) issues even mean, other than just being a meaningless, throwaway slander of someone else?

At its simplest, parent issues means to be interacting with someone similar to mom or dad (not just in age, but in character, temperament, or any other aspect) as a means to meet a deeper need. But, even that is a simplistic, surface-level understanding of the issue. And, by that rendering, really, we all have daddy and mommy issues. We all have stuff, as we move into and through adulthood that we're trying to get resolved inside, stuff that is influencing our decisions, stuff that we really can't even see with the untrained eye, stuff that finds its origins in childhood.

I was deliberate about conveying to my client that dating someone older or younger than you is in no way inherently wrong. If it makes you happy, go for it. But, if you have doubts or concerns inside yourself about yourself, it never hurts to address those, even while you stay in the relationship.

But when those inner voices are so big that we're engaging in behaviors as a means to heal or compensate for past pains and issues, that's when it's time to get serious. What we discover, when doing so, is that if you had a relationship where the same-gender parent was mean or neglectful and the opposite-gender parent was a source of refuge or when the opposite-gender parent was hurtful, it is only natural to seek or find an older person who treats you in a way that provides you the feelings you never got or the feelings that felt so good from that opposite-gender parent. The person you're in a relationship with becomes an avatar for that opposite-gender parent. Still you seek to get the approval, acceptance, acknowledgment of the past pain they caused, and/or an apology. Until you heal your own stuff, you'll keep seeking to get your needs met through someone else. And, that's the crap that undermines otherwise good relationships.

Then, there is the simple fact that very often our parent issues have nothing to do with which gender they are. As Schumer's quote points out, often the biggest issues are with the parent with the same gender as me.

So, you can have that relationship with the older person. Nothing wrong with that. But if you're doing it, unwittingly, to heal some past wounds, the relationship will splinter.

What are your daddy issues? Mommy issues? Both? Worse, in what ways are you creating mommy and daddy issues in your child(-ren) that are bigger than they need to be?

September 13

The way you motivate a football team
is to eliminate the unmotivated ones.
-Lou Holtz, American football coach & analyst

What drives you? What gets you out of bed? What inspires you? What has the capacity to give you goosebumps, focus your energies, and draw in the full force of your character?

If you can't get on-fire and sustain that, there is something blocking you from within. If you can't get motivated or keep it going through to completion, something serious is off inside. Either the direction you're wanting to go isn't actually your innate GPS talking, or you have messages inside you that keep dragging you down. In the case of the former, that happens when we're still answering to someone else's expectations or fearing someone's reprisal (see: parent). In the case of the latter, the BS beliefs you were taught about yourself ("I'm not good enough," "I'll never amount to anything," "Nobody wants me or what I have," etc) keep pulling you down to the ground when you're trying to soar.

To extract all of those debilitating messages demands identifying them, first, then having the courage to simultaneously determine their origins and explore all of the feelings you have toward the people who implanted those messages. This can be quite difficult insofar as it often requires seeing family myths in new light – i.e. that mom and/or dad were not what I've always seen them as, and that they did damage. And *that* stirs feelings, often extraordinarily powerful ones, that must be given the light of day to be released.

Do you have the courage to not only face hard truths, but welcome to the surface ugly truths and accompanying feelings that you long ago buried deep out of sight? Do you have the fortitude to feel that which you never knew you felt? Do you have the courage to see, stand up to, and possibly destroy the family narrative and myth?

September 14

> ### *Train yourself to let go of*
> ### *everything you fear to lose.*
> -Yoda

Why? Because, you may still pursue whatever you like, but once you let go of needing it, as if your very existence, or happiness, depended upon it, you're no longer living in fear. Once you allow for the fact that you may never have it, and that's okay, you're no longer gripped by the anxiety of "what if I don't get it" or the depression of "it's not coming, and that makes me sad." Once you're simultaneously letting go of the very thing you want most, you're living with an open hand, able to create happiness and have fun with life, even without the thing you think you want most. That is power. The lack of having is no longer this inner weight, dragging you down. The notion of never getting your heart's desire, but creating a life that oddly makes you wonderfully happy, anyway; well, that's power!

So, what do you fear to lose, or fear never having – a lover, money, success, fame, happiness, peace, a particular career, hope, respect, family, acceptance, children, the American Dream, friends, God, health, security, control, calm, time? What is it for you?

Now, challenge yourself to begin the process of letting that very thing go. The more you let go of that which you think you can't let go of, the less you're driven by fear; the stronger and more at peace you become; the more life becomes about play, laughter, and lightness.

September 15

> *When I am .... completely myself, entirely alone....*
> *or during the night when I cannot sleep,*
> *it is on such occasions that my ideas flow best and most abundantly.*
> *Whence and how these ideas come I know not, nor can I force them.*
> -Wolfgang Amadeus Mozart, Composer

That's a pretty damn good argument for authenticity from one of, if not the greatest musical composer of all time. "...Completely myself...entirely alone" is a common thread as the formula for strong creativity, not just in the arts, but business and medicine, and all other pursuits. The root of the fullest expression of one's greatness, regardless of field, is commitment to communication with one's own soul. How much more convincing do you need?

What's lovely is Mozart's little add-on, at the end, "...nor can I force them." We can't force ideas and creativity. We can cultivate them by tending our spiritual disciplines of rest, solitude, freedom, quiet, exercise, diet appropriate to your own self, and the like. But, as with all things from the Muses, the Fates, and especially Cupid, we can neither predict nor precipitate them. We can only be receptive when they are sent.

Thus, it would seem the task in facilitating the fullest expression of self is to keep removing from inside and out all that hinders authenticity and aloneness, and to keep tilling the soil that the seeds might take root and become shoots, when the forces of the universe ordain.

Are you removing and tilling? In what ways have you not, yet? What is the greatest obstacle you most fear removing? Why? What's the price, or the feared price, if you do?

September 16

> *If people have time and patience,*
> *they will be able to count the number of seeds in a watermelon.*
> *But not one person can tell you*
> *how many watermelons will grow by planting one seed.*
> -Evelyn Murray Drayton, American author/speaker

The father of my very first girlfriend, Missy, owned a produce grocery in our suburb. It was big, popular and had the best produce. This man, Bob, was active in the community. Every year, when the high school football team finished its two weeks of late-summer, two-a-day practices, Bob would provide, at no charge, a full spread of Black Diamond watermelons, cut and on tables, for the boys, the cheerleaders, and coaches, right as the team was coming off the practice fields on that Friday before school started. Nicest guy doin' a darn nice thing for some boys and girls. As players, this little event, every year, meant that we had cleared the hardest obstacle of training all year. We got to stand around, sweaty, dirty, and bloody, eating sweet melon, spitting seeds, and laughing our butts off.

This was just one of the many things Bob did for our community. We loved it. Sadly, Bob has been dead for well over a decade, but it's a tradition that continues from the 1960s to this day, as the store is now run by his son.

Where do you give? What is the delight for you in giving? How does it make you feel? What opportunities, in the past, do you wish you had taken for giving of yourself more?

Or, perhaps you give too much? Do you give and give, hoping people will then like you, or at least not be mean to you or reject you?

So many people fear that if they're not constantly giving, they're not lovable, not worthy of love. So many other people create a facade of giving to others, but use it only to make themselves look good.

To live a badass life is to both fill your own love cup and give from that love cup to others, so that they, too, might know peace, joy, love, and laughter. It is, in particular, to give to those who have less, to the weak, the afraid, the outcast, the alone. It is to be a good steward of your abundance. Those are the people we respect most in life – the ones who give of themselves.

September 17

> *Turning and turning in the widening gyre,*
> *The falcon cannot hear the falconer.*
> *Things fall apart. The centre cannot hold.*
> -WB Yeats, Irish poet and politician

Yes, you've read this quote in the book before. March 12. Why?

It is my all-time fave line of poetry. And, like all great poetry, it bears metaphor and meaning in multiple directions. So, the read today is very different from the previous one, because these are words so radically tragic – all things spin in entropy; greater chaos leading to greater equilibrium. (Pro tip: Most think of entropy as chaos when it is actually chaos leading to greater equilibrium as things settle. The chaos is the transitional, not permanent state.)

Everything falls apart and dies. It's the code writ large on nature and the universe, itself.

But, we so hold on to existing forms, so fear lack of control, so fear insecurity. Beneath that, what we really fear is the anxiety that wells up inside when things outside us are not just so. Thus, we attempt to control people and situations to assuage our own inner turmoil. That control is a tight holding on.

What are you holding on to? What is it really? Is it the person? The dream you had? Or is it the sense of security that was baked into that path or relationship (or you thought it was)? Is it possible for you to simultaneously hold on to things and people while letting them go? Can you allow the butterfly to alight on your finger without needing to touch, grasp, or contain her; instead allowing her to fly when she will? Is not the tragic beauty of it in the ending, as much as the beginning? Isn't that when we feel most alive, when we feeeel most intensely – when the heart has been scored, as a steak on a grill?

We fear losing that which we hold on to, because we fear that if I lose this, I won't be okay. What is it you fear happening inside if you lose this thing you're clinging to? Is it possible that, yes, you will grieve, but life will go on, and that happiness and peace will one day return? Is it possible that the tenuousness of your inner life (and the concomitant fear) is driven by the belief you need something outside you, perhaps some person or acquisition, in order to have worth, peace, and acceptance of self inside? And, is it possible you're wrong? Is it possible that self-value and peace are quite independent of anyone outside you or anything outside you, because those things and people all eventually fall apart, decay, and die? Can you accept the inherent alone nature of life?

September 18

> *Just play. Have fun.*
> *Enjoy the game.*
> -Michael Jordan, NBA GOAT

If you had the chance to share a burger or beer with the person who is literally the world-renowned, very best in your career field, and they offered you advice, would you take it? Would you, at least, listen?

Now, what if that person were, instead, the unequivocal greatest in a field completely unrelated to yours, would you take their advice, not on your specific line of work but on life and some of the larger concepts outside of your field?

Maybe yes, maybe no. Irrefutably, it's pretty hard to say 'no' to those questions. You'd kinda have to be a damn fool to reject wisdom from the best of the best? There's always some metaphor across platforms, some transferable truth.

> *Play is the highest form of research.*
> -Albert Einstein

And, here we have the best of the best, or certainly one of the three best basketball players of all time saying, "Play and enjoy the game." We have the best of the best, or certainly one of the three best scientists of all time saying, play is the ultimate research method. It's an interesting statement coming from the player and scientist who worked harder than anyone else. So, their seriousness for their work is indisputable. Yet, here they are saying to just play and make it fun, as if the work and play are so interwoven that to remove either robs the other.

Has your life become so serious that you've lost the play? Why continue to play tight? What are the underlying fears causing you to do so? Whose criticism do you fear if you change the game? Would you survive the criticism and, then, finally have a life far more consistent with who you are and, therefore, one much more playful? When it's our own authentic path, even the work is play. It flows. It's effortless, in its own way. And that's the beauty. That's when we become light as air.

September 19

One of the pitfalls of childhood
is that one doesn't have to understand something to feel it.
By the time the mind is able to comprehend what happened,
the wounds of the heart are already too deep.
-Carlos Ruiz Zafron, Spanish novelist

In many homes there is a parent who is actively engaged in some form of abuse, neglect, or the delivery of overt negative messages to the child, such as:

- You're fat
- You're skin and bones
- You'll never amount to a damn thing
- You're the pretty daughter – i.e. you're not smart
- You're the smart daughter – i.e. you're not pretty
- You're dumb
- Bad boy!
- Loser!
- You're such a disappointment, etc.

The long term negative impact, protracting well into middle- and even old-age, can be profound. Those messages can insidiously infect every aspect of a person's life, while the person remains unaware of their existence. A person can feel they are forever fighting themselves, fighting some inner problem they cannot even see. It's as if they have one foot on the accelerator and one foot on the brake.

But what makes that crappy parenting even worse is when the other parent, if there is one, is not shutting that message down in the first parent, or, at the very, very least, conveying a counter-message, either implicitly or explicitly, that is equally robust and persistent. For, if the parent renders no counter-message, then that parent is doing something almost worse – normalizing this crud! By not fighting the message of the first parent, the second parent is saying that the first parent's message is normal, right, and good. Therein is the problem.

(Usually, this is an indicator that the second parent lives in fear of the first. The first parent has the power and the second knows it. Often, the second parent will secretly give weak counter-messages to the child, because they fear doing so openly and robustly, knowing they'll receive backlash. So, their fear of the first parent keeps them normalizing negative messages toward you – i.e. they're protecting themselves at the expense of you.)

Confirmed by the second parent, that message embeds so deeply that the young person, and later the adult, defines his or her life by it, even if they carry a veneer that proclaims, "I'm great! I'm wonderful. I love me," as well as "I had a great childhood." Deep down, the most powerful messages of their life, driven into them by the most powerful people in their life, run the entire operation, unseen, unknown.

Which parent committed the greater crimes in your life? Which parent delivered the messages? Which parent normalized them? What was the role of the 'other' parent in your life, the coward? Who had the power between your parents? How did that power differential impact your childhood and life? What messages got normalized that never should have? What has kept you alive amid a lifetime of being taught to believe these messages about yourself?

September 20

"Don't be ridiculous," said Maya. "You can't fail at a relationship.
That's like getting off a roller coaster
and saying you failed because the ride is over.
Things end. That doesn't mean the experience wasn't worth it."
-Hazel Hayes, Irish YouTube filmmaker and author

I was in a long term relationship, or two, when I was a young adult, and I recall them both being exceptionally tumultuous for a number of reasons, not the least of which was the crap I brought into the relationship, particularly because I had not nailed down a clear career path. I was sort of flying by instinct, letting the path unfold in front of me. I wasn't following society's expectations of what a married man should be. Now, it worked for me, and largely still does, but it created loads of headaches and fights in the relationship, as did our naturally emotional, loud personalities.

In that context, I recall one of those women saying to me, "Sven, being with you is like riding a roller coaster. I love roller coasters – the twists, turns, jerked this way and that, spun upside-down – just not every day of my life, all the time. You're fun but you're also exhausting. But do you know what the hardest part about being stuck on your roller coaster is?"

"No, what?" I asked.

"It's somebody else's roller coaster. I'm not in control of the twists and turns, and being turned upside-down. I have no say."

She wasn't wrong. She brought her own massive share of BS to the relationship, no doubt. But, I could plainly see how right she was, how hard it must be to trust, or just allow, your own life to be largely impacted by someone else's life, especially when my career was totally being flown by the seat of my pants.

What was the impact of that insight on me, particularly moving forward in subsequent relationships? When dating got serious with someone, after that, I went overboard in detailing the nature of my life. I made it clear that they need to be secure in their own self, so that they're not thrown off by the way I live my life. Some would say I should become more stable and less roller-coastery, so that it's easier for another person to be with me. That is, indeed, one solution. But that wouldn't have been authentically me. So, I chose to, instead, shrink my pool of potential love candidates by simply being my weird-ass self, who flies my life my way – i.e. largely unpredictable – but simultaneously being completely, and I believe refreshingly, honest about it to potential consorts. It went something like this, "I love ya and think you're great. And I'd love to keep moving forward with you. But x, y, and z is how I live my life, and that's not for everyone. If that doesn't work for you, I totally understand. I have no beef with that. If you need to walk away, you go only with my blessing and gratitude for the nice times we've had together. And,

I'll still pick up the check. But, if you stay you can't try to contort me to your model of what I should be, or I will have to walk away." It was that simple. Many of the times, they did walk.

However, for the past nearly 10 years I've been in a lovely relationship. Is there more predictability as more of my life has evolved? Yes, absolutely. But it has been on my terms, and there are still large swaths of my life that continue to unfold, delightfully unpredictable. And, the partner I am with enjoys it because she is secure in herself and delights in people who hold her attention, not the ones she has to hold and control.

Whose roller coaster are you on? Are you okay with the parameters, with their twists, turns, and upside-downs? Who is on your roller coaster? Are they willing participants? Is your life dragging them down? Are they dragging you down? Got the courage to create your own life roller coaster?

September 21

I lay it down as fact that if all men knew what others say of them,
there would not be four friends in the world.
-Blaise Pascal, French mathematician

The wife of an old friend reached out to me, years ago. I didn't know her. And, while I did know him from church, way back in grade school, and I liked the guy, we weren't close. She had seen pieces of my work on social media. Turns out, her husband had cheated on her. He admitted to aspects of it to her, but she feared he had done more than that.

I get hundreds of people reaching out to me weekly for advice, help in desperate circumstances, affirmation, and so much more. I try my best to get to some each week, at no charge to anyone. I try to help in what small ways I can, to the degree I can. In this case, I fast-tracked her to the head of the line, because I knew him, and gave her a day of my DM-ing, off and on. I was plain with her in telling her it put me in a helluva hard spot. But, I try to just play the ball as it lies, helping people who are hurting, regardless of personal price, oftentimes. So, I helped her. Gave her my insights, which I knew perfectly well were damning of him. I knew he was lying, because I have a 30-year history of counseling on this subject; have written a two-volume book on it; and have experienced cheating from all sides of the equation, personally. My knowledge ain't just observational and theoretical. It's that AND coming from significant professional and personal experience.

I knew he was lying and covering-up. I told her so, where and in what ways. I also told her he'd continue to deny and she'd never get the evidence she thought she needed for closure or certainty. I told her she can heal herself without this, and can save or walk away from the marriage without this, as well.

What did she do? She weaponized my words and my name against him. Predictably, he continued to deny and say I was off my rocker, precisely as I told her he would do.

Now, I knew there was a possibility of this, before I ever waded into this with her. And, I'm okay with any small old friendship with him then becoming toast. I accepted that potential price before I ever opened my mouth. I was just in shock that she furthered my discomfort and bad position by weaponizing my name and words. I have had this happen with strangers, but never an old friend. I never regretted what I did in trying to help a person in distress. However, as it was her right to use my words and name as she saw fit, since we were bound by no agreement of confidentiality, so too was it my right to walk away. And I did, at that moment. I felt taken advantage of and betrayed. So, I walked. She did what she had to do for her. I did what I had to do for me. I regret none of it. I begrudge her nothing, and I de-charged all of my feelings toward her, at the time. I just didn't want anything to do with her after that.

What do you do when you feel betrayed or taken advantage of, or when someone hurts you in some way? More importantly, did you know there was a possibility of that happening, going in? Recognizing that you knew there was a possibility, do you now harbor a grudge against that person for doing what was within their rights to do, even if it made you feel bad? Isn't the wiser and more honest course to acknowledge their right to have done what they did, as well as your feelings, then do the simple work of flushing them out of you (by allowing them and giving them words, perhaps through journaling or letter-writing)? Isn't that better for you, long term, than holding onto animus toward the other person and carrying that negative energy around inside you?

September 22

> *People will do anything, no matter how absurd,*
> *to avoid facing their souls.*
> -Carl G. Jung, Swiss psychiatrist

I have known friends and acquaintances who admit to paying therapists obscene amounts of money, over years and even decades, while they knowingly lied to their therapist, terrified of touching their own deepest stuff. Sometimes it came in the form of artfully dodging deeper questions. It's similar to the patient who doesn't want to tell her doctor how many packs she really smokes each day, or the athlete who hides steroid use.

Similarly, I have had as my own clients people who spent decades numbing themselves in over-working, booze, gambling, incessant busyness and chaos, pills, over-family-ing, extreme exercise, endless cascades of food or grass, and helicopter-parenting, to name a few, all with the underlying motive of running as fast as they can from that tidal wave of the pain, fears, and garbage beliefs they've been taught about themselves, in their past. Often the running is done unwittingly. But it drives their life, nonetheless.

Yet, for all the willpower expended in that decades-long marathon, the slow grind of the heaviness of the soul always overpowers that will, always grinds a life to a dead stop, forcing the person to finally face the truths of the past. Seen thusly, depression is not a curse but a gift, a calling from one's own soul to finally go inside and heal. It's a squinting of the eye, a peer into the future that can be, if one but have the courage. To run from or numb the depression is to miss the opportunity it holds for new life. As with all things, the pivot point from depression-as-curse to depression-as-gift is courage – the courage to go inside, self-reflect deeply and face the hard stuff, flushing and flushing all the crud.

Yet, that's the fear – facing it, becoming overwhelmed by it, perhaps it even killing you. That's why the fulcrum on which growth and authenticity turn is courage.

Are you still running from your own soul, your own truest identity, and all that is required to wade through in order to see and live that authentic self? What are the absurd lengths you've gone to in an effort to avoid your soul and it's beckoning to you? Have the pain and exhaustion of it all finally given you the courage?

September 23

Sin...is not what it is usually thought to be;
it is not to steal and tell lies.
Sin is for one man to walk brutally over the life of another
and to be quite oblivious of the wounds he has left behind.
-Shusako Endo, Japanese author

Do you know your footprint? I mean, do you truly know and see the breadth and weight of your being as you walk through the world? Do you see the lives you touch and how softly, or harshly, you touch them? Do you have awareness, full cognizance, of your bumpings into others, the toes you step on? Or, are you only aware when you crush a soul, if even that?

Awareness of self and your own impact are not binary – knowing or not knowing. It's all measured in degrees, not just on or off. And, as we age, we discover that the most revered souls are those who have full capacity to dial up the intensity to slay dragons, but nonetheless walk through life with a kind, aware touch, a soft footprint. The evolved man is one who has no interest in doing harm. He can light it up, should the rare situation call for it. But he long ago aborted that as a primary story arc for his life. The true warrior is the one who can fight the bad, when necessary, but has a gentle touch and a kind soul.

In what way do you sin by brutally walking over the lives of others? In what ways have you still not fully fine-tuned your awareness meter? Why? What do you fear sacrificing if you were to touch more gently, give more freely, and walk more lightly? Or, do you most fear dialing it up in those rare, necessary times? Why?

September 24

Sven's First Rule of the Gym:
"Shut the [bleep] up and
do the work."

My daughter was about 8 or 10 when she got her first lesson in gym etiquette. I had my kids for that summer day. But, I desperately needed a workout and my gym had no room for young kids or for my 12 y.o. son. So, I left the kids with my brother nearby, while I went for a quick self-hazing.

When I picked them up, I was steaming. In between sets, I had witnessed some guy go over and start telling some young woman what she should be doing differently in her lifts. He was obviously hitting on her, which in and of itself, is nothing new or particularly wrong, even in a gym. It was the how. I let my daughter know about it.

"Sweetheart, if someone ever comes up to you in the gym and starts telling you how to lift, here's what I want you to do" as I raised both of my middle fingers. "Do that and say, '[Expletive] off!' So, do it, right now. To me. Fingers and '[Expletive] off!'"

She hesitated, giggling nervously. My son watched from the backseat with a big grin. She raised one middle finger tentatively.

"Come on," I said.

The other finger came up. Both up, she said sheepishly yet with a big smile, "[Expletive] off!"

"Good. One more time." Again.

"Good" I told her. "There's nothing wrong with approaching someone else and initiating conversation, even asking them out. And, you're going to have plenty of people do that in your lifetime. You too, son. But, it's how they do it, and how you do it. If some jerk has to fundamentally insult you by presuming to tell you how to lift, or do anything, unasked, then that ain't someone you want to be with or be around. It's condescending. You don't have to take that. You shouldn't take that. Every gym has those dips who tell others how to lift, even if they're not hitting on you. There are plenty of them outside the gym, too. I was that guy when I was 19. Don't be a jerk and don't tolerate them, whether they're asking you out or anything else."

They both got the point.

What's good for the gym is good for life. Don't tell people what to do, unsolicited. Nobody likes that guy. Are you guilty?

Ps. No, to my knowledge, my now 29 year-old daughter has never had to do this, at least in that way. And, I highly doubt she ever would, even though she knows she can.

September 25

***Wisdom is seeing truth in
opposing sides of the same argument.***
-Unknown

My father was an extreme contrarian. The most positive person you've ever met, but also the most playful. He loved taking the opposite position, just to mess with you. If you posed a theory or argument, he'd instantly go to showing how there's truth in the opposite of what you're saying.

You want to frustrate the heck out of your teenager or know-it-all twenty-something? Do that. Watch their head explode. For, it sooo makes that kid feel unheard. I know. My dad would pop that huge pimple on my shoulders all the time. And it drove me nuts.

It wasn't until my 30s, when I had settled down and also come to terms with the realization I had to let go of needing to feel heard by my 70-something father, that I began to hear his contrarian crap as something more. I began to see the wisdom. I had always known him to be possessed of insights, but this was different. I could finally hear and see the brilliance of his ability to immediately see the other side. And I got it. I got that it was precisely that skill that gave him the common touch, the relatability. He could connect with anyone, precisely because he could see the truth in their experience, their life, their choices, and their words. He could be contrary to his own biases, contrary to his innate human belief in the invincibility of his own positions, and contrary to his own better-ness.

The humility in the position and the wisdom that it gave birth to became rather breathtaking to me. And, it is one of the greatest gifts he has given me. It's that eternal spanking of, "Don't get too full of yourself, boy." And, I like it. Keeps me humble.

Do you see the truth in those who oppose you or are different from you? Are you even open to considering it? Do you see a correlation between your unwillingness to do so and your aloneness or perhaps your disconnection from others? Do you so desperately need to be that right, all the time, unbendingly, even when you're not completely right? What's the childhood programming you received which that action is a response to?

September 26

> *The hardest thing in life*
> *is having feelings in your heart*
> *that you can't put into words.*
> -Unknown

There is so much loaded into this quote.

The reason children act out is because they have feelings inside them that they can't get out of them. Those feelings cause such inner turmoil that the only release they often have is physical: slamming a door, yelling, crying, screaming. While that physical act releases the pain, in the moment, the messages that accompanied or created the initial wound, which in turn created the feelings, lodge deeply. Children don't have words for their feelings. Good parenting is about helping the child or teen to find words for their feelings, as well as creating safe space for the child to verbally express what they really feel.

Precisely the same is true of adults. The angst, sadness, anger, rage, frustration, jubilation, lethargy and so forth that we feel, or have likely accumulated over a lifetime, we have never developed the vocabulary or safe space to eject. So, when we finally give ourselves permission, we go to therapists, rabbis, psychologists, good friends, or anyone who will both honor our feelings and help us find words for them.

Why does the adult or child need words? Because, as the quote intimates, it hurts to have feelings stuck inside, unable to get them out. It's spiritual constipation, or constipation of the soul. As that constipation continues or increases, it creates toxicity in the heart, soul, mind, and spirit.

This is why great songs can be so transformational. Through music and lyrics they can name your experience. Thereby, the song conveys you are not alone in this world, while also helping you better understand what you are feeling.

This is why journaling is such a powerful tool, as is writing letters that you do not send. It gives words to feelings and thereby pushes them out, which also enables you to more objectively *see* what's going on when it's outside of you, rather than just experiencing it inside you. It's the act of giving yourself safe space to talk about your feelings and the why's for as long as you need to.

How constipated are you? Does it hurt yet? Do you need to further cultivate your feelings vocabulary? Do you need to be more deliberate in creating safe space for the extraction of your feelings? Is there a child in your life who is aching with unexpressed feelings? An adult? Can you help them find the words? For, naming the beast is half the problem.

September 27

Let's be friends.
-Said during far too many breakups

Yeah, doesn't work, at least not immediately. The friend thing. Usually, if one person is pushing in a breakup for friendship, the other is settling for friendship. One is wanting to pull back; one wanting to use it to get closer. That's why the friendship doesn't work, not right out of the gate. One is using it as a tool to get away, the other to hold on. It's not mutual enjoyment. It inevitably will lead to pain and a hard discussion in 3-6 months, when one just won't let go or starts acting creepy.

Friendship just isn't possible, immediately. There's too much longing for more and longing for less. There's no mutuality. Wants are imbalanced.

Just give the ending of the relationship and potential friendship room to breathe and die/grow organically. Make a clean break. Don't try to fake a friendship as a sort of means to let someone down easily (at least easily for you; at least until you realize they are still holding on and you have to have the not-so-easy hard talk you should have had, long ago).

Whom are you holding onto? Whom are you trying to escape from? Whom are you avoiding cutting it off from completely, or at least till two people can move in new directions and create a bit of breathing room before starting a new relationship form? What needs to happen inside of you in order to have the courage and clarity to have the hard discussion and walk away, for the time being? If you're on the receiving end, what do you need to have the courage to let go of and face, so that you are not clinging and creating likely discomfort later? Do the work of introspection and getting it all out in your journaling.

September 28

It has been my experience that folks who have no vices have very few virtues.
- Abraham Lincoln, American President

What is your level of earthiness? Or, how much of your life is spent trying to be pure, or at least perceive yourself as better than others; or have them perceive you as such?

When I was young, I believed that goodness and purity were interdependent, even mutually exclusive. Then I met people, as I slowly aged, who broke that mold, whose goodness and commitment to serving humanity were unquestionable. They were everything I admired. And yet, they were openly flawed individuals, or impure, or simply not perfect and not striving to be perfect. They accepted themselves as broken, and weren't afraid of those flaws being seen, regardless of people's perceptions of that. I admired that. The fearlessness – the willingness to be real – was enchanting. More than that, it was their rejection of belief that they could somehow overcome their humanity that gave them an utter absence of pretense. Rather they accepted their brokenness, even capitalized on it, as they worked, unwavering, to be a gift of light and life in the world.

In my life, I have been a drunk, a bad father, financially irresponsible, a loud and obnoxiously offensive person, and have in my 20s and 30s been involved with the wives of countless men (and a few women). It's just part of the fabric of who I am, or have been. Not proud of it; not ashamed of it, anymore. I accept it, even enjoy those parts of my past, at times, if for no other reason than those experiences give me the opportunity to speak to the humiliations, embarrassments, and shame of others in a compassionate and perhaps even wise way. No pretense, just one more flawed human stumbling through life, trying to be a little bit of a help to others. Yet, I've simultaneously strived to reduce the pain I bring to the lives of others, to be as harmless as possible, because every one of us already has our own pain without Sven adding to it.

Those unattractive parts have kept me down-to-earth and far more understanding of the struggles of others. Without those, or if I were to hide those, it would be very easy to stand above others or act as if I have a right to judge from above rather than come from underneath to support them.

If you were to be totally honest, do you stand above, at times? How easy is it for you to forget your humanity, your own failures, your brokenness, and falldowns, your own impurities, and your unshakable impurity?

Each person is different, but I choose earthiness over perfection in the people I admire and am inspired by. What do you choose?

September 29

It is a funny thing about life;
if you refuse to accept anything but the best, you very often get it.
-W. Somerset Maugham, English novelist

It's the time aspect of that last clause, isn't it – "very often"? It ain't "always," just very often. If it were "always," well, everyone would do it. It ain't a sure bet.

Nonetheless, when I was in my decades of struggle and building the work I believed in, decades of no success, I ran across this quote. It inspired me, even with that time clause. I was already living the risk of simply going after the work and purposes I believed in and most enjoyed. So, the risk that I wouldn't get what I was striving for was already implicit in my continuing down this path without any guarantees. I understood the potential to come to the end of my days and have nothing to show for it. I chose it, anyway. Thus, when this quote came across my path, I doubled down. Someone else had been where I am, right now, and discovered upon continued pursuit that they ended up getting their heart's desire. So, I persisted another decade, and it all came....in spades.

The point is that the axis on which this maxim turns is the aspect of it not being guaranteed. And, this is the risk of life, of authenticity, of boldness: Do you accept the innate risk?

For me, the innate risk was mitigated, nearly eliminated by the fact that I just wanted to do what I do in this lifetime, success or no. I let go of the results, largely if not entirely. It's a total cliché, but it really became, after decades, about the doggone journey and not ultimately the destination. Even though I still fancifully dreamed of the destination, I let it go and made life about the work I love and the laughter of it all. Man, did I lighten up! It changed everything, in terms of how I looked at life and walked through it.

So, the risk in the time clause is really subservient to whether or not you can let go of needing results, successes, and outcomes in order to feel fulfilled. Can the joy of the path, the play of the journey, and the joy of the work itself that you love so much be enough to fill your heart? Or do you just need, need, need those doggone elusive results. Because, when the latter is the case, we tend to cling too tightly, choking life and ourselves of the ability to play loose, thereby often choking off greater results. If we don't give the universe room to work and infuse itself into the journey, we lose massive opportunities and things we cannot ourselves create.

Is your happiness stitched tightly into achieving it, whatever it is? Is it time to rethink that need? Will life have been a waste if you don't ever achieve it? Might there be a flaw in that thinking?

September 30

In taking revenge, a man is but even with his enemy;
but in passing it over, he is superior.
-Sir Francis Bacon, English author/philosopher

I cannot know if Bacon was approaching these words from a moral vantage point or something else. However, as I read these words and taste them in my mouth from the vantage of middle age, I experience their truth not as a moral position, but a position of freedom of the soul.

I had such profound animus toward my wife, post-divorce. I had been cheated, had my kids stripped from me, had my family-of-origin poisoned with her words, and obstructed at every turn. For 10+ years, I patiently waited, knowing I might have to wait 20 more, for the day when justice would come. My vindication would come in the form of my adult-kids wanting to know the truth, or to know my side of the story. I knew that kids become adults become parents become wiser. I knew there was in them an innate human longing to know themselves by knowing their own real history and who they really came from. I silently held on to all of the stories, all of the memories of the pain she caused and lies she told, just waiting.

With time, I began to see that a cloud followed me, inside my heart – the pain, the anger, the desire for vindication. I knew that same cloud subtly impacted my children. So, cognizant of all of this, 11 years after the divorce, I tired of the cloud. I realized she was winning without even trying; stealing my happiness. So much of my own life joy was siphoned or squelched by years of clinging to the injustices and the desire, if not for revenge, for the truth to be known by my children.

So, I chose to deliberately lose. I quit the fight and the holding on to everything. I let go of the pain, anger and ego. It's like that scene in the movie, *The Mission*, in which the native in utter befuddlement at the nonsense of it, cuts away the long rope tied to Robert DeNiro's character, at the end of which were tethered the remnants of a lifetime of sins. His penance as a monk had been to drag around the detritus of his past sinful life. Released from the burden, my life became lighter.

I did it for myself, and for the children, though they did not know. I paid a price for a good long while from that decision. But the freedom and joy, finally, were more than worth it. She no longer had any power over me. Let them hate me, if they will. I decided to come alive. And, I won. I won my life back and, incidentally, completely cut off her power in my life, whether she was aware of it or not. That's when life began. The hate and desire for vindication, or anything, were gone. She no longer owned me. By their twenties, my kids and I began to regrow our relationships, which now flourish.

What enemy owns you by the mere fact that you desire to exact revenge? When does your desire for *ALIVENESS* outweigh your desire for justice, or vindication? When do they stop being your focus? When do you become your focus?

October

October 1

Wanna fly?
You gotta rise above the shit that weighs you down.
-Toni Morrison, American novelist

One of the most common comments I get from people who feel stuck in their lives is some derivative of, Sven, I can't figure out what I'm supposed to do with my life; or, I don't know what my purpose is; or, I don't know what I want to do with my life.

My response always comes back to this fundamental truth: the only thing keeping you from the life you dream of is the crud inside you that you were taught about yourself, about life, and about the world, but mostly about yourself. That crap is packed so deep and heavy on top of the calling of your soul that the calling cannot be heard, like layers and layers of leaves, snow, dirt, ice, and mud packed on top of the forest floor and the roots below that long to spurt through to see the sunlight and bear fruit. It's not that the yearning of your soul is not there. It simply lies dormant, quietly waiting for you to clear the decades of snowpack, leaves, mudpack, and icepack. It's heavy lifting to do so, but it needs to be done.

The more you do it, the more that little shoot comes out of the ground *effortlessly*. Roots give birth to shoots. That's what roots were made to do. It's written on their very DNA to do so. Your dream – the calling of your soul – doesn't have to be sought or found. It's not 'out there' somewhere. It's nothing you have to figure out. It will become abundantly obvious to you, the more you have the grit to remove all the crud packed on top of it.

Further, just as the seed/root does not need to summon strength to push that shoot upwards, you don't have to conjure energy to attack your dream. All you have to do is remove the pack, the inner obstacles. Do that and your energy increases exponentially from day to day, effortlessly. Spontaneous, increasing energy comes seemingly out of nowhere. Why? Energized is our natural state. Thus, your problem is not that you can't generate the energy to go after your dreams. It's that you still have pain, fears, and BS beliefs you've been taught about yourself that are keeping that parking brake locked in place. Remove those and the vehicle can finally run the way it was built to.

What inner crud is still there? What have you still not gotten off your chest? Who is still dragging you down?

October 2

Until you make peace with who you are,
you'll never be content with what you have.
-Doris Mortman, American author

"Sven, he wants to put our son on Adderall for sports," the ex-wife said to me. "I don't know if that's a good idea."

Her husband, who ran a semi-large East Coast corporation, remarked, "Yeah, and do you know why? Because he's 15 and he needs to up his game to a whole new level. He can't get into a top college just on his grades but with his ability in hockey, he has a real shot. But he needs the focus and intensity. And, he has to get into a top college if he's going to get into a top-level field and be successful, which he has to have to be happy."

"I so seldom see such brazen stupidity," I thought to myself. "I mean, so wrong on so many counts. Ack! Where do I begin? You need a top college to succeed? You need big success in order to be happy? Never mind the question of whether this young fella actually wants all this crap, which I happened to know, having counseled the boy, that he didn't. However, this oldest child was so desperate for his father's approval."

"Jim, just so I'm clear, you want to put a 15 year-old on a performance-enhancing drug for sports?"

"Yes."

As a former D-1 athlete and NCAA strength coach, who has also coached Olympic and professional athletes, I could go into the flaws in Jim's thinking (or lack of) and parenting philosophy here, not the least of which is all the people I have known at high level colleges and careers who were only there to please the parent, even though the son/daughter actually hated it. But the real issue is that Jim neeeded his boy to succeed. It had nothing to do with the boy. He was a sweet, teen kid just sorting out his way in life and hoping to get a girlfriend. Pretty standard stuff, except that he was also very intimidated by his father and wanted his approval.

Jim was so insecure that he saw his son as a projection of himself into the world. If the boy didn't succeed, Jim feared people thinking less of himself. He, himself, was worth nine figures plus, and had spent his life trying to prove himself to a mother who had criticized him since childhood and a father who was emotionally absent and let his mom tear him apart. Now, in his late-40s, he was so insecure that he needed to control his son, to the point of drugging him...*for sports...at 15!*

I worked with Jim about a month before he bolted, convinced that he knew better. Did I mention that Jim was several years younger than me, at the time, only in his mid-40s, but was 60 lbs overweight and had severe health problems, all of which he and his doctor both attributed to extreme overworking? Jim didn't know better. He had sacrificed even his own health for money and prestige. Jim believed that image is everything. Self is irrelevant, in Jim's thinking. The notion of healing self was too scary. And so, now, he was destroying his own son, year by year.

What are the aspects of yourself that you've still not made peace with? How are your own personal issues bleeding into and negatively impacting your interactions with others, perhaps even harming them?

October 3

The desire for safety stands against every great and noble enterprise.
-Marcus Claudius Tacitus, Roman emperor

We spend so much life weighing risk. We spend so much time and mental energy attempting to determine, in advance, what the (good) outcome we hope for might be against what the (bad) result we fear could be. We then assess how bad the bad might be, and then, very often, pull back. For some, that process is a never-ending cycle through every possible option in every aspect of life, searching for every possible pain eventuality.

Call that 'overthinking.' For the overthinker, the incessant fears are their own sort of safe cocoon, which never has to be ventured out of, even as the cocoon brings its own death. Because the butterfly was never meant to stay inside the cocoon, but to kick its way out of it, thereby strengthening its wings.

We so cling to that which is safe and so fear losing it that we will endure all manner of hardship or just plain mediocrity and boredom. This is how dreams get tossed onto the junk heap of life. Too risky. And somewhere in the fears is always the dreaded line, "What would they think" or "What would they say?" Always the fear of others.

This is how bad relationships stay bad. This is how people end up staying in climates that don't agree with them. This is how health and financial situations flatline. We choose careers that are safe and won't incur scorn. We choose people to be around us, whether as lovers or friends, who are predictable or even tedious, when perhaps we long for more. We might even allow someone else's strong opinion to run our lives, because we can't bear the thought of standing up to them and the kerfuffle that would follow, can't bear the thought of standing up for ourselves at the price of being hammered with their questioning or criticism. It's safer to live meekly.

It is that doggone desire for security. It lives in each one of us. That safety is a warm blanket, no doubt. Yet, there is another fire burning deep inside the human animal. It is that vision that keeps us looking out at horizons. It is knowing you're meant for more. It is that longing to accomplish something with one's life. It is that burning zeal to feel fully *ALIVE!*

Even as we clear the hump of middle age, there is still that hunger in there. It doesn't go away. Hence, the human condition is that feeling of forever weighing one longing against the other – safety against passion. And, as we age, it is so easy to become enfeebled by fear, more and more, to cling to safety, more and more. But the desire to have that fire in the belly pushes us. For our own fight against mortality we have to choose it. Knowing we only get one dance on this earth, the bold ones do choose it, do choose that path of *ALIVENESS!* By whatever means possible, they overcome or simply push through the fears the overthinkers cannot shake, refusing to be trapped in lives of safe decay.

The question is, what do *you* choose? What passions grip you and call you to break free of your secure prison? Has it occurred to you that the keys to your jail cell are in your pocket? What is the primary fear that has to be overcome so that you can finally live, accomplish, fail, try again or try something new, feel on fire, again and again?

October 4

The grand mistake of life
is to have the experience but miss the meanings.
-TS Eliot, American essayist,
The Dry Salvages (paraphrase)

Pain sucks. No doubt.

Yet, one of the top three biggest mistakes people make in life is they run from pain. Because it hurts (obviously), people reject pain, avoid pain, deny pain, put pain on others in order to not feel their own pain. People engage in all manner of mental contortionism and relationship gymnastics to not have to tangle with pain. Unhealed people will do anything – ANYTHING! – except allow it, allow themselves to feel it when it comes, and allow themselves to purge and release it, which is the body's natural cycle and self-healing mechanism, when it comes.

Worst of all, people don't allow themselves to mine it, like gold miners swing the pickaxe to dig, hack, and then sift for that priceless commodity that has stirred kings and commoners for millennia. Pain, and the experiences and memories they emotionally charge, are life's greatest teachers, indisputably. They bear in their clutch that other grand commodity – wisdom, depth of experience, and that abiding peace that follows in their wake. By running from the pain and meanings every experience bears, people become stagnant in life, never growing. Too, they become overrun by anxiety – the anxiety of avoiding new pain and the consumption into the pain that already exists inside, slowly pulling them down, despite their best contortions.

Life is trying to force you to expand from your smallness of self, but you're resisting, because the emotion is too great for you, too fear-inducing. Every experience bears wisdom, even ones with only a small amount of pain affixed to them.

What wisdom might you be oblivious to because you can't bear to feel even a trace of pain that is attached to the experience? File this mining of experiences under 'awareness.' It is to actively choose to see all life and soul are attempting to reveal to you. What are the pains and memories you're running from that are nagging you, beckoning to let them teach you? Plainly put, if there is pain, anxiety, depression, fear or any other heightened emotion there is gold. It's that simple. The high emotion is the dragon guarding the riches, trying to scare you off. Slay the dragon, keep the gold. Your choice.

October 5

> *A master in the art of living draws no sharp distinction*
> *between his work and his play;*
> *his labor and his leisure; his mind and his body;*
> *his education and his recreation.*
> *He hardly knows which is which. He simply pursues his vision of*
> *excellence through whatever he is doing, and leaves others to determine*
> *whether he is working or playing.*
> *To himself he always appears to be doing both.*
> -L.P. Jacks, English educator/philosopher

By the time I was six, we had moved from a 600-person town where dad had been the pastor of a 3-point parish to a very blue collar suburb with a 1,500-member church across the street from the parsonage in which we lived. I very much loved growing up in that church, especially as the youngest of the preacher's six kids. I got away with murder.

Funny thing is, just as they say 'charity starts at home,' it would seem murder starts at home, too. It was dad allowing and at times encouraging our 7 and 10 year-old murdering of the rules of what preacher's kids ought to be. Saturday mornings, for instance, dad would walk across the street to the very large church complex and let himself in to spend hours in his office, studying the lexicons, Hebrew scripture, and Greek concordance in solitary preparation for the next day's sermon and teaching. But, he'd also let my brother, John, and our friends, brothers Darren and Glenn, and my close buddies Jon and Dave, slip in, locking the door behind us. We'd then play hide-and-seek, running around for hours in all of the church's attached buildings. Or maybe we'd bring in our walkie-talkies and explore closed-off passageways and hidden rooms, whether above the sacristy or deep in the furnace room. Or, maybe we'd climb around on the flat roof over the education wing or the one over the youth room/annex. We had free run of the joint, as long as we stayed out of the offices, so as to not disturb him in his studies.

Sometimes, it'd just be brother John and me launching balsam glider planes from the church roof or paper planes from the balcony in the large sanctuary, seeing who could hit the forward-most pew, turning God's house into Kitty Hawk proving grounds. Many a time, we'd string 8-pound test fishing line from the railing at the edge of the balcony of the nave all the way down to the communion rail at the front of the church. We'd then duct tape paper clip hooks to all manner of weighted objects to get them to zoom down the line from stern to stem, forever adjusting angles and weights for maximum speed. (Though, we were always largely respectful in or around the altar....well, unless, of course, the mini-container of finishing nails that just came rocketing down from the sky broke open at its terminus and scattered its contents hither and yon. At that point, we became penitent supplicants on all fours, suitable to the area we found ourselves in, foraging for every last nail that people kneeling at communion, the next morning, might find stuck into the bottom of their shoes; also knowing old Mr. Pound, the head custodian, would know exactly how finishing nails found themselves embedded in the chancel carpet.)

John and I were the final two of the Erlandson six. Dad knew damn well by that time that boys left unattended would get into shenanigans. They will murder the rules. He was a boy with three brothers on a farm in the 1930s and 1940s. He knew, and I think a part of him enjoyed knowing his boys (and even his daughter) were just being boys. Murder starts at home. And so, church was always a place of play, laughter, ease, comfort, fun, and happiness for me. It was God's house and God *clearly* loved kids! My own father, the WWII-generation pastor, taught me so.

Pretty cool, right? I frickin' love my deceased dad for that. Think of the message that teaches kids without ever saying a word. Pastor in deep study; kids screwin' around, at play in the house of the Lord. The sacred and the nearly profane (at least to many parishioners, if they had known) co-existing, dancing under the same steepled roof.

Do they dance well together in your life? The holy and the secular, the sacred and the profane, the serious and the playful. Or has life become all seriousness? Or perhaps you've made no room for deep thought and meditation amid the running around of life? Where's the yin-yang flow between sacred and secular, quiet and playful in your life? How much of life do you cut off, and for what damn reason?

October 6

When hit by boredom, let yourself be crushed by it; submerge, hit bottom.
In general, with things unpleasant, the rule is:
The sooner you hit bottom, the faster you surface.
The idea here is to exact a full look at the worst.
The reason boredom deserves such scrutiny is that it represents pure,
undiluted time in all its repetitive, redundant, monotonous splendor.
Boredom is your window on the properties of time that one tends to ignore
to the likely peril of one's mental equilibrium.
It is your window on time's infinity.
Once this window opens, don't try to shut it; on the contrary,
throw it wide open.
-Joseph Brodsky, Russian-American poet

Boredom is the one curse and blessing I have struggled with most in my own life. While pride/vanity is my greatest sin, boredom is my greatest affliction. I have lived a crazy dance with it, over 5+ decades. I can recall, as a three or four year-old, when all five of my older siblings were off at school, being home alone with mom. After Captain Kangaroo or The Electric Company were done on TV, or perhaps in the afternoon after my nap, I might go to mom, who was in her office studying if she wasn't doing another of what must have been incessant loads of laundry. I'd ask, "Mom, I'm bored" (question posed as a statement).

Her responses, born of wisdom from raising many kids and her field of master's study (early childhood development and education), always orbited around something like, "So, be bored," "savor it," "what's it trying to show you or teach you," "don't run from it." I'm sure I'd occasionally pitch a fit when she said that, because I wanted her to make my boredom go away, which she deliberately wouldn't. And my fit would morph into distraction by something else, the boredom seemingly solving itself. Though, occasionally, if my whining grew loud and unbearable, she'd offer some odd idea or entertainment, perhaps it was by giving me a thimble, a few tiny boxes, some string, or a darning egg and maybe three paper clips and a magnet, or some such koan of oddities, always followed by something like, "Now are you bored?" or "Go escape your boredom!" Off my little mind went, gently shoved into a creative state.

Thus, I've always known, even since childhood, that boredom is my friend and, other than soul pain, my greatest teacher. Yet, as life sped up in junior high and beyond, the rush and the desires seeped in and became more of a factor, turning boredom from old friend into old friend who has become annoying. I'd still escape to it, or find myself in it, but the proclivity to distract became more common. Though, it caught up to me in my own failure-to-launch 20s and much later in my unhappy-with-life late-30s. I'd get stuck in inaction and the boredom it brought.

BADASS WISDOM

It was somewhere in those 30s that I began to re-acquaint myself with my old friend, not as annoying, but as gift-bearer. No longer did I seek to distract from it, but instead would deliberately go further into it. I'd simply lay down and close my eyes when I felt most bored. I had discovered the mind-blowing insight that boredom is driven by anxiety, an agitated mind – that is, the longing to do, to have, to experience more, rather than to be content in this moment. That's the very definition of agitation. Once I allowed the boredom and the anxiety to come up, and then journaled about them or simply collapsed into them, they both passed. And, I returned to a state of inner calm. That calm brought creativity, as always, but it also brought a re-centering and happiness.

The anxiety that would lead to distraction, compulsive behavior, addiction, or reckless action had been removed by going into it, welcoming it. For, it, like any other feeling, passes. If allowed to be felt, it comes and goes, like the breeze.

Is it possible that the boredom you're stuck in is trying to teach you lessons about your life that you don't want to look at; so you run, you distract? Is it possible that the problem isn't the life ennui you feel but the anxiety under it, the restless discomfort of longing, and the answers to the path ahead are found in non-movement of body or mind? Is it possible you're choosing the incessant dance of boredom and distraction because welcoming and looking at what's driving it all scares the bejeebers out of you; or perhaps because the thought of creating a new life out of your own box and string is terrifying? When does the boredom get bad enough that you finally collapse into it or solve the full equation of what's behind it all?

October 7

In so far as the mind is stronger than the body,
so are ills contracted by the mind more severe than
the ills contracted by the body.
-Cicero, Roman author, orator, and politician

The loads of crap plunged onto young men, nowadays, are mercilessly dumb in their over-weaning macho blandishments. Young men buy that garbage, hook, line, and sinker. Yet, it's no less volume than the messages the young received 20 or 60 years ago, only different in how it's packaged. And, of course, there's no shortage of garbage heaped on young women and non-binary folk. The infections that plague teens and young adults only exacerbate the multitude of infections pressed in there by parents and family, when they were preteens and children. The accrued giant jumble of stored external messages can destroy lives, joy, and purposes for decades subsequent.

The ills contracted by the mind, and pressed into the soul, are infinitely more powerful than anything contracted by the body, no matter the force of your willpower. The soul always wins in its desire for an authentic life. So, the soul, weighed down with suffocating infections, calls, even *drags* your life down into depression, lethargy, and inescapable inertia. To purge the symptoms of pain, laziness, boredom, failure upon failure, and misery upon misery requires finding, naming, and flushing the very infections of messages that caused it all. Or, the mind will never be free and its misery will also drag down the body itself, into decay, illness, and finally destruction. Don't doubt it.

The infections. The infections. Either you keep trying to run or you turn into it all, welcome it, accept it, and begin the purge.

What do you choose?

October 8

When I'm trusting and being myself as fully as possible,
everything in my life reflects this by falling into place easily,
often miraculously.
-Shakti Gawain, American writer

This is usually when I get most clients looking at me sideways. It's something impossible to truly believe, not to mention count on, until you've experienced it.

In my book, *There's a Hole in My Love Cup*, I discuss how the spiritual journey is really about the process of creating integration of inner life and outer life, because the life of depression, anxiety, and unfulfillment finds its origin in living in your outer world as a very different person from who you are inside. The messages you've received, over decades, have conditioned you to trust only those who embedded those alien messages inside you, and distrust your own inner voice rising up from your soul. The journey toward a life of the peace of integrated authenticity comes from having the courage to be, say, do, and become on the outside who you really are on the inside, ejecting the alien messages.

Three things happen the more you be, say, do and become who you really are, integrated outside and in:

1) You start to lose people, close people, some you thought would be there forever. You lose the people married to the idea of who you used to be. That is scary stuff and often the biggest thing that keeps more authentic selves locked inside people than anything else;

2) You start to gain people, to effortlessly attract, more and more, people who say, "I love who you're becoming," or "If you went back to being who you used to be, I wouldn't be the least bit interested," or "I just love that you have the courage to become." A whole new world begins to creep into your life, because your energy has changed. You've shed increasing amounts of that which you never really were, the malformed appendages to your life from those alien messages.

3) Stuff starts to fall out of the sky. Stuff you can't even begin to imagine with your conscious mind. Magic starts to happen. If I've seen it once, I've seen it countless times in the lives of those who do the work of ejecting the aliens. Yet, this idea is the sticking point for many folks. They just can't believe it to be more than contrived hokum....till they engage steps 1&2 fully and completely. You effortlessly attract that which is just right for you. And, contrary to what the folks selling the idea of 'manifesting' would have you believe, it's not done by just imagining. It requires the ugly work of rooting out those foreign messages that corrupt even your ability to imagine. For, when those voices and messages are still present in us, the

dreams we aspire to are often only in reaction to the foreign messages. Thus, unlike the manifestation folks, if you get out that which is not you and never was, then the magic that comes is often not what you imagined, or not always in the form you imagined. Instead, in the long run, well after it has come, you grow to realize it is *better* than you imagined, better suited to the who-you've-become than anything who-you-were ever could've imagined.

Still, it's all contingent upon the trusting and being of self, as Gawain articulates, which demands flushing out all that undermines that trust with doubt and fear. To this end, Gawain has one more thought:

> *The process of change does not occur on superficial levels,*
> *through mere 'positive thinking.'*
> *It involves exploring, discovering, and changing*
> *our deepest, most basic attitudes toward life.*

You ready to start taking your real being for a spin, letting it out in bits and pieces, at the very least? What areas of life do you most want to begin to trust and live your original, real self? In what ways? You also ready to start eliminating and changing your most basic attitudes and core beliefs, many of which were never yours to begin with?

October 9

It only takes one move to get to State.
-Joe Frank, My high school wrestling coach,
who had produced numerous State Champion teams and individuals

You can't get to State with just one move!
What are you thinking?!
-Joe Frank, the next day or week

You can imagine the quizzical looks and snickers that shot across the wrestling room when Joe, our wiry, fierce, iron-headed coach would unwittingly create such jigsaw puzzles. Yet, oddly, not a one of us simple-minded high schoolers doubted or failed to see the truth of both statements. We got it. It became yet one more lesson in wrestling *and* metaphor for life that we knew we were being taught. We knew it. There was such accessibility and pith to his wisdom.

The life lesson? More often than not, life is a 'both/and,' not an 'either/or.' Both this and that, not just x or y.

Unfortunately, though, nuance makes us uncomfortable. Not being able to just have one clear and absolute right choice, robs us of being able to take and maintain the self-righteous high ground. It disappoints the ego, and blurs choices, muddying life as no longer better than everyone else.

What are the both/ands you're being forced to accept, or at least face? What's the hardest part? What does it require you to let go of? How's the ego doing, as you consider doing that? How much more difficult does it make things, knowing you don't have the clarity of an absolute right choice or position?

October 10

The future happens, no matter how much we scream.
-Derek Walcott, Saint Lucian poet and playwright

The terrible things of our life have to become woven into the meaning and story of our life. But, it takes time and effort, not to mention a whole lot of opening up, tears, facing helplessness, giving words to our pains, allowing the guilt to come and to pass, then letting go. The desire to be happy eventually outweighing the sense of obligation to feel bad, we push, unknowingly, toward acceptance.

And what is acceptance? It is to one day, after years of wrestling with the angel of pain, accept its horrible blessing. It is to finally let go of the sense of guilt demanding that we stay miserable, out of tribute to this loss, whatever it may be, and to the person we once were. Acceptance is when the story and the interaction with it, day to day, are no longer laden with powerful negative feelings. The experience and memory of it all becomes de-charged, all the high anxiety now gone. It becomes part of the fabric and story of your life, be it a divorce, a death, a gigantic failure/loss, or what have you. With diligence and willingness to change and grow oneself, the fuller tapestry of your life and identity reveals itself.

Here you've reached a whole new level in your ability to walk joyfully amid the sorrow of the world. The sorrows, losses, and miseries do not scare you like they used to, nor do they cripple you so. More and more, they become woven into the very fabric of life, expected, sadly welcomed, felt, addressed, and moved through. This is the aging of the soul into vintage.

Has your desire to be happy or at peace yet begun to outweigh your need to hold on to the pains and sense of obligation to them? How does your sense of self and identity change when you stop resisting this and begin to accept it as your inescapable new reality? Why? What do you know you need to finally let go of?

Oftentimes, the greatest peace comes of surrender.
-Richard Paul Evans, American author

October 11

A bad beginning makes a bad ending.
-Euripides, Greek playwright

When it comes to dating, whether dating a potential lover or potential career, there are always red flags. No path or person is without them. The question becomes what we do with them, or, hell, whether we even see them or allow ourselves to see them.

For some people, their past is so miserable and also so normalized that when they come to a new relationship they literally don't even see red flags. What might be a red flag to someone else can't even be seen, because the past causes today's problems to be seen as just part of life.

For others, there was such a love famine in their childhood where they got, at best, a smidgen of love, that to receive any, at all, even a mere triple-smidgen, is seen as an absolute bomb of love, when in fact it's nowhere near and nothing even remotely resembling a normal amount, let alone a bomb. And such a huge perceived love causes one to be blinded to any red flags. Or it causes one to ignore them, hope they'll change, or believe they're not really a big deal.

Rather than addressing the red flags, talking them out, and working toward them becoming non-issues, they are ignored or missed. Tragically, ignored little red flags become un-ignorable massive problems, which, the longer they're given unobstructed oxygen, become the very preventable downfall of the relationship or path. Small things invariably become big things.

And what is a red flag, generally speaking? Anything that doesn't feel good. Sounds silly, but it's true. If it doesn't feel good, and it's small, it will persist and grow. This is why the ability to feel one's own feelings and be accountable to them are paramount to happiness in relationships. For, then you will hold others accountable to them. For, if you don't, those little don't-feel-goods eventually become an aggregation into a giant this-sucks!

What red flags are you ignoring or not seeing? Or, in the case of the latter, what in your past might be obscuring your vision? Is it possible there's more work to do?

October 12

You've never seen rage like a narcissist accused of something they definitely did.
-Unknown

I'm not a big fan of the term 'narcissist', because it's soooo overused and diluted in meaning. But, that's just frickin' funny!

So, whether the person you've dealt with is an actual clinical narcissist or what I call an 'extreme taker,' we've all had the experience of dealing with someone who is so profoundly full of themselves and convinced they are the very center of the universe that they are happy to extract every bit of love from their nearest and supposedly dearest – i.e. you. And, we've all experienced their self-righteous, over-blown responses when called out on even the remotest or most minor of offenses.

But, why?

Everybody in life is just trying to get their love cup filled, whether it's the extreme taker or the extreme giver, or anyone in between. Everything goes back to whether that love cup got filled in childhood and if it got a hole poked in the bottom. Some extreme takers grew up in a home where little to no love was shown, where there was abuse, where things like "I love you" and hugs were withheld, and/or where criticisms or neglect were constant. Others grew up in homes where there was an ample amount of love for them, because they were the Golden Child, who could do no wrong, as long as they kept being golden and doing all the right things – i.e. all that was expected of them, causing them to never be allowed to be authentic, but instead a bastardized version of themselves, hence causing them to feel unloved for who they really were. In either case, the hole in the love cup is from the underlying message from the parents that your truth ultimately doesn't matter. So the child becomes an adult forever needing constant love shown to them, because any that is given to them keeps draining out the bottom.

Ultimately, extreme takers continue to act as narcissists to someone, because the other person allows it. This isn't to blame the victim. This is the simple fact that at some point in the relationship, likely very early, you started allowing them to take more love than they gave, to be irresponsible with your feelings, to not apologize when they wounded and not own when they were wrong. So, their power and abusiveness in the relationship with you went unchecked, and hence grew.

So, while the quote is funny that no one is more self-righteous than an extreme taker, it's also tragic both for them and for the person who doesn't get out.

What's your experience? Have you journaled out all of the pain from your extreme taker, as well as the self-loathing you were taught young that set the stage for you to allow such a situation to grow in your life? Or perhaps the message that got implanted is that if you're only lovable when you're giving; that if you don't keep giving and giving and giving and giving more love, the other person will not like you anymore and leave you. Perhaps that is what needs to be journaled out of you?

October 13

Sometimes a bully has to be punched in the nose.
-DaMon Vann

One of the ugly truths of life is that there are times in life when there's dirty work to do – clean toilets, shovel manure, scold an unruly child, correct a beloved employee, or say 'no' to a needy parent, to name a few. Yet, for as much as we don't want to do that work, somebody's gotta do it. This ugly thing has to get done. Somehow, we know it has to be us, whether because no one else is stepping up or because we're the leader and this is what leaders do, at times.

To compound the discomfort, there are those times when that which must be done is something that isn't only distasteful but scary. Be it physically frightening, fear-inducing because of the inevitable verbal fight or denial, or because of the potential to lose position, there are those rare times in life when we have to stand up to and shut down a bully, or try. There are no guarantees of change, but there is definitely a high likelihood of conflict. And man, do we largely as a species hate conflict. So, we avoid and avoid, which is how bullies become bullies, in the first place. No one wants to push back or to shut 'em down. Too risky.

Maybe it's a bully co-worker, parent, adult-child, in-law, friend, spouse, or employee. Eventually, it reaches the point where action has to be taken.

So, it falls on the giant-slayer, you. Fear courses through you, to some greater or lesser degree. If you've done it before, perhaps it's not as scary. But if there's potential for loss or conflict, there's fear. In the end, you do it anyway, if for no other reason than you're just terrifically sick of the BS, the misery, the arrogance of the bully, and that this one person or entity is robbing your joy in life. You screw on your courage and do what must be done.

And, that's the difference between coasting and accepting responsibility in life. Yes, we're ever striving to create lives where joy and peace are maximized, but that means not just always being a peacekeeper, placating others to keep things calm. To truly create peace and happiness in the kingdom of your life means to be a peacemaker, which means *making* something from what it presently isn't. When it's not peaceful, fulfilling, and joyful, the peacemaker makes it so. That's leadership. That's taking control of your life and responsibility for the joy of those around you.

But, because it's so scary to stand up to bullies, we back down in life, until eventually we can't, anymore. Avoidance ceases to be an option.

You done running from what you know is no longer an option, done avoiding? Are you ready to screw on your courage? Can you articulate in one sentence what you most fear in doing this? Do it. Can you articulate in one sentence precisely what it is that most needs to be said or done? Do it. At what point in your life does *making* peace and joy become more important to you than running in fear and maintaining a sucky status quo?

October 14

> *The best way to find yourself*
> *is to lose yourself in the service of others.*
> -Mahatma Gandhi

My neighbor, John, is one of the harder working guys I know. Works long hours running an honest, small business. On the weekends, he's out clearing land, working on his property, and improving his family's life. This guy hustles, is a vigorous dude, and is several years older than me.

But, interestingly, every time there's a snow, John is pushing his snowblower over to my other next-door neighbor, an elderly couple, to clear their rather long driveway. John loves helping but also just loves pushing his two-stage snowblower. I think he's actually having fun. He's also the first to help yet another older neighbor move her heavy flower pots and the like. It brings him joy.

Ann, his wife, is a schoolteacher, who when not educating our city's youth is volunteering at her church and fighting in local politics to save community centers and other things that enrich our community.

They're stellar reminders for me that life is simultaneously about filling our own love cup and giving voluntarily of ourselves to others, particularly those in need and those who can benefit us in no possible way. We each have different ways we can give, but also different ways we enjoy giving. There can be such joy in giving, such deep fulfillment, especially when the act itself is something you already enjoy doing.

How can you push yourself harder to give of yourself more? Or, what is the shift that needs to happen inside of you, from a mentality of mostly serving you and yours to giving of yourself back to humanity, this earth, and this life we each walk for only a brief moment? How are you holding yourself back from all you could be doing to help those in need? Are you ready to stretch yourself? And, can you do it in ways that you actually enjoy?

> *I slept and dreamt that life was joy.*
> *I awoke and saw that life was service.*
> *I acted and, behold, service was joy.*
> -Rabindranath Tagore, Bengali polymath

October 15

As soon as you trust yourself,
you will know how to live.
-Johann von Goethe, German writer/poet

I am of the absolute belief that the three biggest mistakes committed by parents are teaching a child:

1. Who he is, apart from the function he serves for the shallow parent, doesn't matter;
2. She is not actually loved, but is only appreciated when she's doing what's expected; or she will be punished when going against the controlling parent;
3. Not to trust her own inner voice, the calling of her soul, but to forever yield to either the parent's will or wrath, long into adulthood.

A great many friends, family, and therapists focus on helping others learn to love themselves. That is important, no doubt. But you can love yourself some, particularly after good therapy, but still not trust your own voice, because you've been so conditioned, your entire life, to always listen to and seek out external power sources – first parents, then spouses, bosses, friends, and, well, parents yet again and again. The implicit message you've been taught is that you can't be trusted with life. And so, the grand fear becomes doing so, inch by inch, failing and succeeding, but continuing to trust a little more. For, living on another's agenda has never been a recipe for happiness and peace.

Fully immersing a child in the words, "You make good decisions," when 'good decisions' means something other what the parent wants or expects, teaches him to trust his own voice. To do so, especially after that child or teen has fallen flat on her face, rather than to retract the power from her, is to teach that young one that you fully trust her voice and that she can, too. And so, with continued encouragement, she will. (As an aside, the further benefit of teaching the child to trust their own voice is that in doing so you teach the child that failure or loss does not equate to diminishment of either worth or boldness.)

We teach a person the power and strength of trusting their own inner voice in childhood, so that when they come to adulthood they can function and move, avoid pain (yet sort through it when it inevitably comes), choose bold action, and live free. When we teach them, as children, to trust the voice of the parent over the voice of themselves, we teach them to doubt themselves, hesitate, stop and start, move tentatively, never go after the brass ring in relationships, personal lives, hobbies, adventures, career, and health. We breed cowards. Strength, because it comes from within, is at its max when it comes from the core truth of who that individual is. Otherwise, it is false strength, because it depends forever on someone else telling them what to do, which is inherently a position of weakness. Most importantly, you will not know how to live *for you*, only how to live for them. And, that ain't happiness. That ain't self-love.

Whom do you need to teach to trust their own decisions? What's the hardest part for you about letting go of control of this other person? Is it your life or theirs?

Who taught you to distrust your own inner voice? Do you still? Is it time to begin to truly trust and love your authentic self?

October 16

> *Only in the depths of his loneliness,*
> *when he has nothing to lose anymore*
> *and does not cling any longer to life as an inalienable property,*
> *can a man become sensitive to what really is happening in his world and*
> *be able to approach it without fear.*
> -Henri J.M. Nouwen, Dutch priest and professor

I once heard a simple quote, "The ego, like the egg, is of no use, until it is cracked." Until we are broken, bruised, beaten down, alone, we still cling to our own sense of mastery of life. We still cling to that which we believe can and should happen, still cling to life as our own, to be determined by us with us at the center. Ego.

But, to be destroyed to the point of being unable to raise ourselves out of it is to finally realize that life/universe/fate/luck/God does, in fact, at times give us more than we can handle, so that we'll finally need something outside of ourselves, so that we'll finally have our grip on the center of the universe wrested open. Finally, I realize it's not all about me.

Oddly, in that same transitional moment out of my own immortality and ultimate importance, I no longer fear losing life. I no longer fear losing the immortality, importance, and my former need to be seen as the center of the universe. I become, in a word, fearless, because I no longer cling. It's what we cling to that we fear losing. When we fear losing, we play tight or fear really trying or fully engaging. We obstruct flow.

How is your misery your greatest gift, long term? Has the fearlessness come yet? What longing do you still cling to that keeps you in fear of losing it?

October 17

Follow your inclinations
with due regard to the policeman 'round the corner.
-W. Somerset Maugham, French-English playwright/novelist

The way to know the calling of the soul is not to think but feel. The body speaks. Your energy on your skin, in your solar plexus rises up to speak, constantly attempting to direct your steps and choices. Even its silence is a message to stop, shut down, and be silent.

The soul-filled, true badass life is one governed by the movement from head down to intuition; the movement from a life of thinking to a life run by feeeeel. The mind too easily becomes cluttered with messages from the past, from society, from the expectations that seem to never end. Thus, we become unable to feel, to hear the speaking of the soul conveying our deepest truths, longings, and paths. Removing all those judging, controlling voices increases lightness and the courage to act on one's own inclinations, regardless of the judging words and sideways glances from others, living or dead.

The mind becomes subservient to the feeeeel, the voice of the soul, no longer vice-versa. For, that old way didn't work, in the end. Now, the soul takes over as GPS, and brain and body become its vehicle for getting there and also just for enjoying the journey itself. Further, yet again, the determinant, the gasoline for driving that vehicle becomes courage, alone.

Got the guts to just fricking *be you*? How bad does the path of life have to get before you pine for your own life, your way, so much that you finally make it happen?

October 18

A sincere and warmly-expressed apology
can produce the same effects as morphine on a suffering soul...
Be the hero of hearts; learn to say 'I'm sorry.'
-Richelle E. Goodrich, American author

If you were to be totally honest, when it comes to saying "I'm sorry," which is harder for you:

To say it when you've done something wrong, bad, and hurtful; or to say it when someone else is hurting for reasons that have nothing to do with you?

Is it harder for you to say, "I screwed up. And, I'm sorry;" "I am so sorry I hurt your feelings. There's no excuse;" or, is it harder for you to say, "Honey, I'm sorry your boyfriend left you," as she cries uncontrollably for weeks, or "I'm so sorry your wife left you," or "Tom, I loved Skeeter, too. He was the best hunting dog and sweetest soul"? See, the former is about yourself; the latter is about the other. The latter is when you know someone you love is hurting badly, you did nothing to cause it, and there's nothing you can do to make their pain go away.

One is about fear and shame. It's knowing you need to apologize for something you did that you're ashamed of, don't want to admit, or maybe fear backlash for. It's about repairing the breach you created. And, you really, really don't want to do it.

The other is about compassion and helplessness. It's feeling someone else's pain, and knowing there ain't a damn thing you can do to make their pain go away. It's the consoling, "I'm so sorry," that comes from the heaviness of my heart feeling the heaviness of your heart.

Of course, the easy answer to the question is that the former is harder, because it's so humiliating. It is a place of extraordinary vulnerability. It gives someone else power over you – the power to kick you in the teeth, to reject you when you're down, when you've deliberately humbled yourself. It's one of those things in life that no one particularly enjoys. And so, few people do it.

So, yes, it's very honest and very easy to say that apologizing for something you've done is the harder task...

...'til you've loved someone sooo much who is hurting;

...'til you have the child with the illness that requires yet another surgery or transfusion;

...'til you have a best friend dying of cancer;

...'til your loving father, or sister, is wasting away and knows it.

...'til

...'til...

And this is what it is to be alive, to be responsible to the other. It is to no longer run from the fear of pain in its myriad forms. It is to make the pain of the other person, whether you've caused it or you haven't, more important than your own fear of feeling their pain. It is, in the end, to realize that both "I'm sorry's" are the same. Both are about feeling the pain of the other so powerfully that you carry it and/or do all you can to make it go away. It is to experience their vulnerability for them or with them. It is the willingness to feel the heaviness of the other's heart.

This is an act of the tenderest courage. This IS badass.

October 19

> *...the scarlet letter ceased to be a stigma which attracted*
> *the world's scorn and bitterness,*
> *and became a type of something to be sorrowed over,*
> *and looked upon with awe, yet with reverence, too.*
> *And, as Hester Prynne had no selfish ends,*
> *nor lived in any measure for her own profit and enjoyment,*
> *people brought all their sorrows and perplexities,*
> *and besought her counsel,*
> *as one who had herself gone through a mighty trouble.*
> *...Hester comforted and counseled them, as best she might.*
> -Nathaniel Hawthorne, American writer, *The Scarlet Letter* (paraphrase)

Are you of that later stage, having endured the slings and arrows of an original, torn, and difficult life where you've been stripped of so much ego, where you've weathered it all and come out the other side with little more, yet nothing less, than the ability to hear and truly understand the troubled others only now walking through it?

We each have gifts we bring, some earlier, some later. But that full-circleness of life calls the busted, humbled, and stitched back together to give of themselves, not out of obligation but opportunity solely to give of their understanding what little they may. For, that is so often enough.

Have you aged and healed into full-circle? Are past pains your gift to the hurting? If you're not there yet, can you do the self-care work and can you trust that day of full-circle giving will come when it will come? Or, perhaps, even as you continue to heal now, you are already a gift to those just a few steps behind you?

Blessings to you on the journey, as you too are a blessing to others.

October 20

Val: Why do you go out there?
Sandra: Because dead people give such good advice.
Val: What advice do they give?
Sandra: Just one word – LIVE!
-Tennessee Williams, American playwright

Both of my parents died during Covid, though not because of it. Dad at the beginning; mom nearly two years later. They were in their 90s.

With those two deaths came the realization that nearly every last person whom I've drawn the most inspiration from in life is now dead. There were others. Joseph Campbell. A couple of dead theologians/thinkers. My high school wrestling coach. An old Jewish fella from down the street. A mentor-pastor from my seminary years. An uncle. A gregarious Finnish friend of my dad.

Yet, they still inspire me greatly. It's odd to consider how much of my life energy comes from beyond the grave. I don't even mourn not having them. Their lives carried so much force, so much wisdom and depth, so much meat as fuel for thought and spirit that I am still feeding off their existence, even in their deaths. I still need them – less in everyday life; more in the foundational concrete blocks of who I am, how I think, and what forms the trajectory of my life pursuits. Mostly, their existence, words, and paths gave permission to, and thereby struck, vibrated, and resonated with the strings deep inside the piano of my original self. By still doing so today, they bestow to me both energy and deep peace. What sort of power source produces energy after its death?

From whom do you still draw inspiration, energy, and trajectory, even though they're dead? Have you told them or the spirit? Have you thanked those who've gone before? What do they tell you? How do they challenge you? Which fires do they stoke? And who will draw fuel for life, after you are gone? In what ways? Have you thought about how you are a contribution to inspiring others' lives?

October 21

*The main sign that you are following your intuition in your life
is increased ALIVENESS!
It feels like more life energy is flowing through your body.*
-Shakti Gawain, American New Age writer

In the end, there is but one metric of the fulfilled, happy life, only one: *ALIVENESS*. It can come in many forms, from relief to exuberance, from poverty to prosperity, from purpose to release from obligation, love to finally letting go of love, calm to clarity. The odd complexity of life dictates that there are so many twists and turns, unexpected wrinkles and delightful surprises that what was *ALIVENESS*, a decade ago, is for the same person now life-sucking. What is inspiring for one person is the very definition of death for another.

While *ALIVENESS* is an animal of a thousand faces, by definition it always results in the same thing: more life energy. That's experienced in major leaps and, especially, in the day to day. If you're waiting to win the relationship lottery, get that career title you've been driving towards for so long, finally reach retirement, or whatever your grand life goal is *and then you'll be happy*, you're living life wrongly. For, the need for that acquisition in order to feel fully *ALIVE* indicates you don't feel fully *ALIVE* now. And, the simple fact that it's such a big thing you need in order to finally feel alive (at least for awhile) is, itself, a clear indicator of how great the longing and need inside you are – i.e. how great the hole in your love cup actually is. This is critical; do you see that? Let me say it again, the mere fact that you need something so damn big in order to finally feel fully *ALIVE* indicates how dead you really are inside; else, why would you need such a colossus in order to finally feel that way? There is some dragon inside you that you believe will only be slayed with the largest of swords swung in the largest of strokes. That, alone, is a clear indicator that you have huge past crud that needs to be dealt with; for, that dragon is those voices, pains, fears, and BS beliefs about yourself from your past.

Yet, if the overwhelming desire for that massive acquisition sat inside a life where there was great joy already, then the longing for that acquisition could still be present but not degenerate to the level of an absolute *requirement* for happiness and *ALIVENESS*. It's such a cliché but *ALIVENESS*, happiness, and peace are built in the mundane, the everyday, the small, bit by bit, 'til over time a life of happiness is created. That is not the same as a rejection of still swinging for the fence, so to speak. It is, instead, a falling in love with the small and medium, while simultaneously working toward the large pursuits that move the soul. There need not be rejection of the large. In fact, many of life's greatest contributions to humanity were done by individuals *ALIVE* in the small and medium, who felt powerfully compelled to chip away at the giant.

There is one last thing begging for attention: that new car smell. Why, when we can finally afford it, do we buy those season tickets we've always wanted? What is it we gain when our kid has a steady good-paying job at 20 or graduates from college? What is it about finally getting that lover that we crave so much? What is it we get internally from getting that promotion into the C-Suite?

We get that feeeeling. It's the feeling we chase in everything we do. It's the rush, the high.

But that new car smell fades. So, then, it's on to something new. Always some new drug, new success, new expectation we tell our kid to do, new thing we need our lover to tell us to prove we're loved, new baby, dog, or outfit to make us feel that feeling.

But what if we attacked the root, rather than the fruit of that root? What if we were to go inside to dig for where that longing is coming from, what unfulfilled need, what voices from the past still echo forward? What are the questions and messages, from long ago, you're still a living answer to, trying to make go away with your efforts and mad runnings? How would life be different if you were to finally extract those questioning voices that were never native to you, to begin with?

What if the focus of life no longer became the thing but the feeling you desire to feel? What if there were more than one way to get that feeling, and perhaps to even make it last much, much longer? What if you're using a screwdriver to pound a nail? What if you're using the wrong tool because of a lack of full comprehension of the problem?

The stuff that lasts, the feel that endures, is not the one that comes in one fell swoop, but the ones we build into the everyday. That's it. That may include eating habits, exercise, meditation, friend time, nature, ocean/lake, laughter, alone time, reading, long drives, music (concerts), a warm bed, and hot baths. But, it often also includes the building of some new life, something bigger than self and my own mere daily happiness. The joy is in the doing and building, not the having and achieving. And so, we end where we started this daily thought, that daily life and what it's building; and how it looks to you is very different from how it looks to me. *ALIVENESS* is defined differently for each of us. Do you truly know yours?

October 22

Feeling stuck?
You haven't asked the right question yet.
-Jaya Bhateja, Executive coach

So often in life, we come to a place or a period where we just can't seem to decide. Life has us caught between two very difficult choices, each with its own benefits and price.

Are you there now? Stuck there awhile?

Get paper and pen; don't just do this in your head. Getting things outside of us helps us see them clearly and more objectively.

Write out each option. Then, next to each one write out *in one sentence or less* what your single greatest fear is in choosing that option or if you don't choose the other option. Be as clear as possible. Which fear scares you more? Is it the option you want more? Very often it is.

If that most feared thing came to pass, would you be okay? We so often think we won't be, if it happens. We think, if that feared thing were to come to pass, I won't be okay. But is that true? Would you end it all, walk away from life? Or, would you grieve, go through a long period of recovery, then move on with life? Likely the latter, right? So it's not as scary as your inaction indicates. All of your over-thinking is unwarranted.

Here's one more fun little trick. Flip a coin. Heads is one thing you want. Tails is the other. As the coin is in the air, before landing in your palm, what's the hope that shoots through you? Heads or tails? That's the one you most want. That's your heart's calling.

Is your life more governed by fear or happiness and passion? Are you okay with that?

October 23

My fear of being real, of being seen, paralyzes me into silence.
I crave the touch and the connection,
but I'm not always brave enough to open my hand and reach out.
This is the great challenge:
to be seen, accepted and loved, I must first reveal, offer, and surrender.
-Anna White, American author

The grand longing in relationships is that deep need to be seen for who I really am, and then liked for who I really am; not my facade, not my persona, not my ego stuff, just me. It's the need to be loved for just being me, to be heard, to be felt on a visceral level...and the person stays, even though we fear them leaving.

"Wait a minute, I showed you who I really am – like, really, really am – and you like it? You really do like me?" That is crack! There are few experiences in life more powerful, peace-bringing, and joy-inducing than that, right there. And what happens when we have that experience? We, hesitantly, want to open up a little bit more, to see if it's real, to see if you'll still like me, to see if it really is true that I'm okay. Then a little more. Then a little more. Then with time we learn more about ourselves that we didn't even know was there, because this person created a safe, loving, accepting space. And that was balm to the soul. Few things heal and bring new life like that.

Yet, the price of that peace and joy is guts. To be seen and loved for who you really are demands having the sheer courage to show who you really are, to reveal a bit of yourself, then a bit more. And there's no guarantee it is safe, until well after the fact. They can swear, up and down, that it's safe to reveal yourself and you will be loved, but what do they do with your self-revelations after you show your belly? Do they ignore it, perhaps minimize its importance, or belittle it? Do they weaponize it in the next argument? Or, do they accept it with compassion and a kind heart, ever after protecting the sanctity of who you truly are? (Of course, it doesn't mean they won't make mistakes and will never hurt you. The myth of the pain-free relationship is precisely that, a myth. But there is acknowledgement and contrition if they do hurt you, or you with them.)

Is it possible you've been wounded so much in the past that opening up terrifies you to your bones? In that case, the real courage comes not in revealing yourself to another, but to yourself. It means accessing inside you and allowing to rise to the surface all that hurts inside you. Then it's necessary to flush all of that out through journaling, writing letters you don't send, and other methods. It's getting out those memories that have emotional charges, because it is those memories and charges that are causing you to disbelieve in your worth and importance. The path to being accepted and loved by another for who you really are demands revealing your authentic self to yourself, and accepting compassionately who you really are, warts and all. This is me, and I like it.

What parts of you are you still not wanting to see, allow, and accept? Is it possible that the greatest obstruction to your healing and having life-giving relationships is not outside you or the other person, but inside you? For, they cannot see, accept and love you, until you see, accept and love yourself. Otherwise, they'll always be loving a false version of yourself...and you'll know it. And it'll feel good but never be that deep inner peace and joy you seek.

October 24

Do not go where the path may lead.
Go, instead, where there is no path and leave a trail.
-Ralph Waldo Emerson, American writer and poet

We get so many voices in life encouraging us to take the normal path, the path that'll make the surest money, the path that'll guarantee stability and, hence, security. But, one of the interesting things about human interaction is that people speak from a position that reveals their own values and beliefs.

So, that may mean that what they're saying is absolutely true...*for them*. It does not mean those are universally and absolutely true. In fact, it's silly to assert so. For, those same people are using phones and computers that were invented, developed, and designed by people who absolutely did not follow the same beliefs that they did. The Starbucks they go to was created by a man who believed, back in the 1970s, that Americans wanted a coffee shop they could go to for high quality coffee, which barely existed in America (tip of the hat to Peet's Coffee of Berkeley), and a place to find a bit of community outside of church, Knights of Columbus, or the bowling league. He made a trail where there wasn't one.

Pretty much any product used by the person hewing to the secure path was created or brought to market by people who had the courage to pursue design and the arts. The books he/she reads and podcasts he/she listens to were created by people who believed in their passions, even though the creator's journey stood a very low likelihood, at its inception, of ever turning any profit. But they went that way, anyway, creating a path...and now the naysaying user follows the creator's lead. The movies and TV shows they watch were brought to life by people who went against the odds and created a path out of the value system they were raised in. Likely most of the athletes and musicians you idolize were told by family or teachers, friends or uncles/aunts, "You can't make a career doing that. Get a job. Be realistic." But they didn't.

They said, "F**k off." They had the courage to live outside of someone else's comfort zone. It's not our own comfort zones that keep us trapped, per se. It's that we allow ourselves to stay trapped in someone else's definition of a comfort zone. Because we seek that person's approval or acceptance, or because we're scared of their condemnation, we sit fearfully inside their comfort zone, 'til we don't.

The difference between staying in that person's comfort zone and following your wild dreams, crazy-ass visions and ambitions is pain and courage. When the stultifying drudgery and oxygen-less belief system of theirs gets painful enough, you'll be imbued with the very courage you lacked yesterday. Pain is a brilliant teacher that way. It takes us where we never thought we could go. And so, you'll stop needing their approval and stop fearing their inevitable criticism. You leave the expected path and begin to blaze a trail. In doing so, you'll give courage to the next timid soul to do the same.

What do you dream of? What are the visions you have for your life, regardless of your age, or especially because you feel time slipping away? When do the fantastic ideas and importance of your own life matter enough?

Whose comfort zone are you trapped in by your fear (of criticism) and longing (for their approval)? Has your pain gotten bad enough, yet? Do you, at least, feel it getting worse? Is it possible your day of release is finally coming or fully upon you? Is your courage rising? Why now?

October 25

The hardest time for writers is
that dead space between projects.
-Jay Bland, American author and professor

Jay is an old friend of mine. We were dear friends, back when we both lived in LA. He had eschewed a Harvard PhD in literature and a fellowship from Harvard as a poet-in-residence at his alma mater to move to LA to write young adult fiction and screenplays. To pay his bills, he taught at a nearby college, including poetry classes wherein he dissected the works of Atmosphere and other great hip hop/rap poets. Cool dude! We were poor as hell, but we were *ALIVE* and felt the struggle. Despite the struggles of daily life, searching for new love, and the pasts that each of us were fighting, we were most assuredly *ALIVE*! It was awful and beautiful, at the same time.

One day, I recall one of us was between writing projects and it was somewhere between Jay's daily habit of a Cheerios breakfast and lunch of white rice and tuna that he lamented the words above. It's the disorientation, the boredom, the itch to be working again, the lack of purpose that afflicts the writer between projects. It's in no way unique to writers. Hunters, salespeople, soldiers, actors, firefighters, bullriders, even waiters and athletes all long for the rush, the utter focus of doing what you most love to be doing. It's the hunt, the kill, the adrenaline, the calling day in and day out to something bigger than yourself. It's incredible to be in that zone. To not be there, to be robbed of it as a writer 'til the Muses bless you again with the next project is hellish. Will it ever come again, is the question that plagues the brain, churning and churning.

For my mother it was gardening. Nothing on earth made her heart sing more than having her "hands in the soil," as she would say. Nothing. Not time with her grandkids. Not counseling people. Not daily prayers. Nothing. She and dad were farmers at heart, master gardeners who loved the earth and utter majesty of what lies below the surface. Thus, it makes me tear up, even now, at 5:47am on a Thursday morning at a Starbucks writing, when it is dark outside, knowing she'd be out in her gardens this early. I get wetness in my eyes, this still morning, as I consider when she was in her late-80s and she finally conceded, "I can't garden anymore. My arthritis hurts too much." A very life-giving piece of her went fallow that day, autumn of life moving slowly into her last winters.

The universe gives and the universe takes away, be it seasonally, from project to project, or eventually permanently. We are all at the whims of the gods. To ashes we return. And when we try to force what the gods have not ordained, we force it and it shows: fakery, garbage, over-weaning effort, desperation. And so, the task of life becomes opening our hand, letting it go – our looks, our loves, our passions, vigor. It becomes learning how to purge the anxiety and quiet the mind when the project, the sale, the hunt, the grand love is fading, then absent. Mastery of life requires mastering the screaming silence when not consumed by the next endeavor.

Are you purging the anxieties when between projects, when not doing what you most love to be doing, or are you forcing it? Does the low-level crap you're producing when forcing it make you realize maybe it's a better idea to face your own fears and the fact that you do not control your path? In other words, when do you begin to actually master yourself and trust the movements of life, rather than forever allow your anxiety and the underlying fear to run your life?

October 26

> *For it's not the light that is needed, but fire;*
> *it's not the gentle shower, but thunder.*
> **We need the storm, the whirlwind and the earthquake in our hearts.**
> -Frederick Douglass, Former slave then leading American abolitionist

It's hard to imagine a person more worth listening to and learning from than a former slave who became a leader in the fight to abolish one of the most heinous aspects of any nation's history. Here his words ring down through the ages admonishing us for our quiet dance through life, making slow or timid changes

Are there times when the hard attack doesn't work? Of course. But that's not really his point. Surely one can simultaneously have the thunder in the heart yet apply different methods at different times to accomplish the grand callings of the heart. The point is that the thunder, the fire, etc are there; right there; at all times, informing or driving all action. When we stifle, doubt, or undercut that thunder we deny the purpose written on our hearts. And, each person is assigned a different set of callings, for their life. But, each person is given the energy, the power to execute that. It's just that too often that energy gets suffocated by the messaging and pains from early life. As a result, we question the calling, itself, precisely as we were taught to doubt or dismiss everything that came from within as a child; pushed, instead, to always heed the beck and call of those around. Thereby is the message, "Don't do what you feel compelled to do. Don't listen to yourself?" pressed into the wet cement of the child's soul, forever after running that person's life, until it grinds to a halt, demanding destruction and new creation.

But, the people who change the world, the people who live lives of greatest exuberance, thunder and *ALIVENESS* are those who not only hear their call from within, but they heed it, and have tapped the fire and storm needed to drive, to push, to grind, to attack. Without those elements – the hearing, the courageous heeding, and the high-powered engine of fire inside – dreams wither on the vine, the fire turning to light to flicker to a wisp of smoke as it dies.

The world needs your fire, your thunder! We need your authentic, powerful self courageously running in the direction of your dreams and calling, whatever that unique path may be that you carve.

What's your calling? If you don't know, have you had enough pain that you're sick of running from it all and are ready to finally create the solitude necessary to flush all the pain, so that you can finally hear your inner voice? If you do know the deepest calling of your soul, what's the single biggest fear that inhibits your courage to execute? Lastly, do you have the thunder in your breast and the fire in your belly? What's suppressing them? What's the grand fear keeping you from expressing your power in all its fullness? When do you begin to finally have the courage to unlock all this stuff and live the life you were meant to live?

October 27

I haven't a clue as to how my story will end.
But that's all right.
When you set out on a journey and night covers the road,
you don't conclude that the road has vanished.
And, how else could we discover the stars?
-Nancy Willard, American writer/poet

On this courageous journey you are considering or already on, do you see the full road stretching in front of you for miles, or do you see the next step?

It is the next step that we are called to, that which we know we have to do, if we're going to finally start listening to ourselves and living our lives our own way. No, you can't see all the twists, turns, mountains and dark valleys ahead. No, you can't prepare for all eventualities. Yes, it is scary. Yes, a ton could go wrong. Yes, it will be embarrassing and humiliating if you fail and fall down, which you will.

Then, eventually, the further along you go, the less and less any of that stuff will bother you. You'll start to have a love affair with the unexpected twists, mountains, valleys, and the stars and glowing moon of night. You'll fall in love with the journey, itself, quite apart from whether you ever reach any destination. For, you will finally be *ALIVE*! Nothing on earth beats that feeling. That is the one we all seek. Every drug, every affair, every title, every raise, every sexual encounter, every win, every relationship we cling to – all of it is the pursuit of, the hope for that feeling of being *ALIVE*!

October 28

Here's to the end of this chapter, to all the late nights,
early mornings, learnings gained and experiences shared.
Here's to the hardships that became our teachers, to the heaviness that
taught us how to rise again. And to the people who would stop their world
to sit and celebrate our presence.
Here's to the times we chose feeling over disconnection,
freedom over perfection,
courage over what's known and certain, and doing the work.
Here's to releasing what wasn't ours to keep.
Here's to holding our palms wide open to our blessings.
And here's to taking one step forward
into the hope and possibility of tomorrow.
-Danielle Doby, Author

As my parents were aging into their late-80s and Dad's Alzheimer's began to slowly kick in (less in the gutting of his mind than the slowing of his ever-vigorous, farm kid body) and Mom's heaviness of having to tend to Dad became oppressive, my sister, Karla, moved from her decades-long home in sunny Texas to, once again, take on the brutal winters of Minnesota. Her heart for Mom and Dad guided her path back home to do the one thing she had always been best at, handling multitudes of details and all while bearing a never-fading upbeat spirit. A few of my brothers and their wives had been covering their medical, financial, and spiritual needs for years. But, the return of Karla was like getting a long-needed contact hitter with solid defense and speed on the bases in baseball, or the speedy winger in Rugby when fly-half and hooker are solid, right before the playoffs. She just brought this infusion of energy and severe attention to detail.

Then she stayed. It has been a couple of years since the folks passed, her self-imposed duties complete. An old life chapter closed, a new life chapter has begun with not nearly the sunshine of Texas. But, she has embraced it, laying down new roots, revivifying old relationships. And, life goes on.

What passions and yearnings call your heart? Do you trust and follow, or resist and fear? Are chapters needing to be closed? Where are your talents able to serve your passions and loves?

October 29

Some men die by shrapnel,
and some go down in flames.
But, most men perish, inch by inch,
in play at little games.
-Robert D. Abrahams, American lawyer and poet

If you were to be totally honest, even if just for a moment, what percentage of your life is spent in pettiness? I don't even mean pettiness by what the world might say is petty or the critical, doubting, and scolding voices in your life might say is petty. I'm saying by your own reckoning. If you were to list all of the elements of your life on a piece of paper, then put a check next to all of the ones that even you, yourself, consider petty, what percentage of them would have a check? I'm not saying you can't justify those small and large pursuits by some other metric, but it's still the pursuit of a small person, as you see it?

For me, it has been as high as 80%, particularly in my younger years. Even when I was pursuing things socially acceptable and desirable that looked so big to me or to others. There are plenty of small things that look big. I quickly outgrew them, not knowing the path ahead, only that this path no longer fit for me. I chose the big feels of peace, purpose, *ALIVENESS*, even though I had no idea what they would look like in practicality. I chose a commitment to near-total authenticity, no matter how it looked to others and the world; to be me, warts and all. Within that commitment to self is, innately for me, this huge love for saving the world and individual human lives in the small ways I'm able.

So, really, this quote is no grand conundrum or jigsaw puzzle. Are you playing small with this one life you've been given?

Is it fear that keeps you in this small sh*t? Are the little games you're playing being determined by the messaging you received as a pup? What are the grand visions that are the fullest expression of your most authentic self?

October 30

I'm not feeling very well. I need a doctor immediately.
Ring the nearest golf course.
-Groucho Marx, American comedian

One of my favorite activities is going on extended road trips, particularly in the American West. Only on road trips do I allow myself those giant 44oz Diet Cokes from the machine at the giant truck stops. I love nothing more than endless miles of ever-undulating roads and the next turn in the road that reveals unexpected and ever-changing scenery exploding in front of me. I love the inevitable boredom and how it yields ridiculously creative fruit. Mostly, perhaps, I thoroughly revel in the hypnosis of the road, the trance in which I can spelunk the deepest recesses, memories, thoughts, and feelings inside me. Just miles and miles of calm exploration. It's absolute gold.

In stark contrast, and completely unrelated, I hate golfing (though I enjoyed watching Jack and Tiger on TV). Truly, hate. Not only do I generally suck at anything in life that requires finesse, whatsoever (and golf is the ultimate in demanding finesse), but there is no definition of 'fun' under which I can find the words "carry a heavy, unwieldy bag on a five-mile walk while also engaging in extremely frustrating activity." Yet, some strange birds consider golf the greatest gift of the gods to humanity. The combination of exercise, nature, and mental focus is for them a delight.

While it's cliché to say, we each have our own odd joys, our own sources of inspiration and regeneration, our own ways through which the gods speak.

How does God, or soul, or Universe, speak to you? What activities inspire you? What breathes life into and regenerates your soul?

Equally as important is the question, Do you prioritize your own regeneration? And if not, why so? Do you wait for things to get really bad before you make your sources of inspiration a priority, again? Or, do you incorporate those things that breathe life into you, large or small, into the disciplines of your everyday or weekly life? What needs to happen in order for you to take the health of your own spirit more seriously and treat it with much more deliberateness?

October 31

Always read stuff that will make you look good
if you die in the middle of it.
-P.J. O'Rourke, American journalist/satirist

The purpose of a funeral service is to comfort the living.
It is important at a funeral to display excessive grief.
This will show others how kind-hearted and loving you are
and their improved opinion of you will be very comforting.
-P.J. O'Rourke, American journalist/satirist

I couldn't resist. That's just doggone funny. Both. There's a nice little truth question in there, too.

How much of your life is being spent looking good to others? What percentage?

But here's the twist, concern for how we look to others isn't, at least in my reckoning, innately bad. In fact, a whole lot of good has been done while influenced by the desire of someone, some organization, or some country to look good. Thus, the real question is not, "Am I doing it to look good" but "Is my quest to look good to others coming at the expense of my real self and the authenticity of my soul. Or, are soul and vanity working in symbiotic tandem?"

How can you channel your passion for looking good into great stuff for others and life? Can you do it while making sure you're not suppressing your authentic self?

Go for it!

November

November 1

How lucky I am to have something that makes saying goodbye so hard.
-Winnie the Pooh, courtesy of A.A. Milne and E.H. Shepard (illustrator)

Parents dead yet? Lost any close college or high school friends? God forbid, has a sibling died? A lover pass away, perhaps? A child?

Sounds odd, but death kills. If you have not gone into, sat in, and allowed your pain from those deaths to purge and flush out of you, it is killing you from within, ever so slowly. You can play all sorts of games with yourself, distracting yourself in a myriad of ways, "I'm fine. I'm fine." But, that death sits there, deep inside, waiting to be given the light of day, taking its pound of flesh, each passing week and year. Unflushed pain is a plugged toilet. It only gets worse, ruining everything surrounding it.

I had a client quit counseling with me after 3 sessions. "Sven, I've put in 11 hours with you and you haven't changed me," he kindly, yet firmly stated before exiting.

I patiently responded, "That's actually true. But I've spent 11 hours with you and you have not truly opened up once, particularly regarding all the death in your past. I can't heal you if you don't open."

"I don't know what you're talking about. When my 32 year-old brother died, I cried all night, then woke up the next morning and went back to work. I distinctly remember it," he retorted, utterly oblivious to the idea that massive loss demands massive grieving, and similarly oblivious to all that pain from the death of his brother (and earlier his mother) likely driving his addictions to both food and work.

I know you're afraid of the pain overwhelming you, if you even go near it. I know you're afraid of losing control and that you spend so much energy, right now, trying to keep a lid on all the pain. It will overwhelm you. You will lose control, at times. And that's okay. You can move through all of it.

But you're not ready, until the pain, frustration, comfortable discomfort, chaos, sadness, or what have you get bad enough. Change will not occur, till the pain gets bad enough. Does your life suck badly enough yet? Don't worry, it will. This crud doesn't magically heal itself. Keep holding on to your tenuous control and sanity. Your soul is trying to lead you to higher ground. But first it must break your grip on security.

November 2

> *"He recognized with authentic realism*
> *that anyone who permits another to determine the quality of his inner life*
> *gives into the hands of the other the keys to his destiny."*
> -Howard Thurman, American author & philosopher

One of the big mistakes I see people making when doing soul work is in assessing the parenting of their own mothers and fathers. Specifically, they mischaracterize a parent who constantly told them what to do, how to dress, what career moves to make, what they think of their partners, etc. "It's all about control," they'll say, as if that perfectly summarizes the parent and cuts down to the real issue. That's a problem, because calling the issue control, as if that's some grand epiphany, creates the feeling of having drilled down to the root, when in fact there's a deeper issue driving the control. And, if that deeper beast is not named, there will be no true release of the pain, fears, and messages it bears, nor will there be release from the control itself.

At the root of control is fear. It's always fear. A controlling parent is terrified that you will:

- embarrass them or not make them proud
- pull away from them, leaving them alone (perhaps in an unhappy marriage/life)
- take your power back
- hurt yourself (this is an insidious one, because it enables the parent to justify withholding power from the child/teen/adult, claiming, "It's for your own good")
- make them sad by not doing what they want, which implies *to them* that you're not their child anymore, or that they don't always know what's best for you, which in turn undermines their belief that they're a great parent, which in turn undermines their whole identity.

Everything is fear. That means that the trajectory and quality of your life is being determined by someone else's fears, and you're complicit in allowing that to happen by not getting at the root of the problem. You are making your parent's fears more important than your happiness. You okay with that?

And, and, and waaaaayyy back when you were a kid you got the message that got near-permanently implanted deep inside you that mom's/dad's feelings and wants are more important than yours, and to go against them makes you a bad child and hurts mom's/dad's feelings. So, even now as an adult, if you go against their wishes, control, and fears, you're bad and you're hurting them. This, of course, is total crap! You're bad for becoming your own man or woman? You hurt someone else for owning your own life and dreams? How weak must that parent be that they need you to live your life their way, otherwise their precious feelings will be hurt? Rather than address, own and excise their deepest fears, it's far easier to use you as their tool to band-aid those fears.

Further, if you *allow* their fears to drive your life, rather than allowing your own passions, fires, needs, and feelings to swell up from within and drive the arc of your life, then you have forfeited your bliss, your inner peace, and your sense of purpose and fulfillment in life. You can make that choice – to give up your life for mom and dad, but it's a horrible choice. It is living death. You've already taken out the shovel and are digging your grave.

Of course, that's not the worst part. Even more life-sucking is that if you can't seize your own life, you'll raise your own children in reaction to or lock step with your parent's fears swirling inside you. Thereby, your parents and their controlling fears will be raising your children, even if it's only those fears dominating you from inside, because you never broke yourself free. You did not break the generational trauma. You did not do better by your kids. Nah. Your parents are very much alive and well inside you, impacting every last decision...

...because you allow it.

November 3

*The most important thing that each of us can know
is our unique gift and how to use it in the world.
Individuality is cherished and nurtured,
because, in order for the whole to flourish,
each of us has to be strong in who we are,
and carry our gifts with conviction, so they can be shared with others."*
-Robin Wall Kimmerer, American 1st people, decorated professor

Pressure to conform is nothing new. In childhood, we are taught to play on teams, conform at home, and fit in at school. And, truth be told, learning to live and work together in human community is a necessary trait. However, routinely, we squeeze the originality out of children, out of others, and out of ourselves. It is so easy to demonize the different.

Yet, the wise realize that individuality is necessary not just for the long term happiness of the individual, but for the health of the system, itself – family system, school system, societal system. Each person brings special gifts, talents, insights, and "the power of a million new ideas" (*Chicago*).

Whom are you squelching? Where has the pressure come from in your life to silence your individuality? Has it occurred to you that the world neeeeeeds your original voice, ideas, strength, and courage? You owe it to me and everyone else, as much as you owe it to yourself. We need you to have the courage to be the real, unvarnished you!

November 4

SKØL!

-War cry of ancient Vikings as they ran into battle, essentially meaning, I will meet you, comrades, at the end of this battle when we will drink from the skulls of our dead enemies, thereby releasing their souls to Valhalla and celebrating our victory

I grew up in the 60s and 70s. That means I lived through all four Super Bowl losses of my childhood football team, the Minnesota Vikings, not to mention other significant losses, later in the 80s and 90s. Every Sunday, I would read the Sports section, memorize jersey numbers, sizes of players, schools they came from. I used to dream about them coming to my house to play snow football, and later become one of them. By my teens and twenties, I would remember phone numbers, license plate numbers, and other random sequences using decades of Vikings jersey numbers. The Vikings are, to this day, my all-time favorite team, any sport, any level, deeply embedded in my sense of identity, dumb as that sounds.

That said, I'm simultaneously the consummate fair-weather fan, if I'm honest. All of those soul-crushing losses, all those years, after pumping so much energy into my Vikings, became just too unbearable, especially when the losses were mixed with beer, in my 20s. The sadness doubled. Eventually, I stopped investing. Stopped watching games, preferring to track scores on my phone. Only really investing, a bit, if they made the playoffs, which came with the inevitability that they would lose (likely in the first round). It was just too much of a repeatable, predictable energy-suck. It took the fun outta the game, for me.

I look at all of life that way. Every aspect of my life has to be its own form of net gain, in terms of energy. Even all the people I've served without a charge provide me a sense of just being me and doing my part to make the world better, which is its own gift of energy.

If this minor, medium, or major action or activity does not somehow give me energy, I just don't do it. Thereby, I have so much surplus energy. The real task of happiness, peace, and *ALIVENESS* is ultimately not found in what you do, but in what you no longer do, what you refuse to do, say, and believe. The beginning of new life is found in the no. That takes guts.

What are the paths, purposes, plans, and people that have proven, over time, to be net losses, energy-wise, in your life? Can you list them? Can you identify, specifically, how each is a net loss? Write it all down. Have you reached the point of reducing, or cutting out entirely, those elements that no longer breathe life into your soul? When does it become a gift to yourself to give less to that which you used to love most?

November 5

Passion is energy.
Feel the power that comes from
focusing on what excites you.
-Oprah Winfrey, American tycoon

One of the more frequent, impassioned questions of longing I hear, particularly from young people, is, "Why can't I find what I'm passionate about? Sven, what's wrong with me?"

The sister of this, which I hear with almost greater regularity, is, "I have huge dreams, but I just can't seem to get motivated" or "Sven, I'm always starting and stopping. Why can't I sustain the motivation to follow through on the stuff I wanna do with my life?"

While it seems like two separate issues – one an issue of finding one's true destiny/dream, the other an issue of motivation – the problems and solution are identical. In both cases, the person harbors here so many pains, fears, and BS beliefs they've been taught about themselves that they cannot hear/feel their own authentic voice buried underneath it all; nor can they sustain the strength to move forward, because those bring such an inner heaviness with them. The problem is the past utterly crippling the present.

The solution is the scary, ugly removal of those pains, fears, and BS beliefs you've been taught about yourself. Until that happens, every path is a bastardized version of a small amount of authentic self mixed with massive crud from your past – i.e. it ain't nowhere near what the hell you were put on this earth to do or dream of doing.

When that solution is engaged, what grows is a clarity, power, and grit that simply never existed before. The dream becomes obvious, the motivation endless. We naturally and rather effortlessly pursue that which we're most passionate about. When on our authentic path, motivation is not an issue. We naturally work hard and deliver the grit when we're excited about what we're doing with our life. If you ain't jacked up to do the work, it's either because you've got too many pain, fears and BS beliefs weighing you down, or the path you claim to want ain't your real, deepest passion.

Do you struggle with either of these two issues? How long will you keep running from the heavy, hard work of removing all the crud that is blocking the expression of your most authentic self? How bad does the pain have to get? What is it you most fear that keeps you stuck in this state of not doing the work to heal and finally come alive?

November 6

A living thing seeks above all else to discharge its strength..."
-Friedrich Nietzsche, German philosopher and poet

Having been a pastor and, for a brief time, hospital chaplain, I have been present at many a death bed, holding the hand of the dying, as did my pastor father and spiritual counselor mother. More so, I have counseled those not yet in the final grip of death, but experiencing the years of slow movement toward it. Additionally, I have a brother who spent an entire career as a cancer hospice social worker. He is truly a death and dying expert.

I cannot speak for them, but I have been around their stories and have my own experiences. I do know this, end of life regrets, when they exist, boil down to a power unexpressed – a deep aspect of self that was never given release and expression, allowed to bloom into full fruitfulness.

Individual power comes in many forms. Some are given physical power or extreme physical endurance, others the power of immense creativity, to others the power of compassion or of fierce intellect, to still others the power of grit and intense hard work, or to break apart a complex problem into manageable steps. None better than the next, just different.

The constipation of the soul that manifests in forms of dissatisfaction, anxiety, unrest, boredom, fatigue, depression, and the unscratchable itch finds its roots in some power. Down deep it is something unique to you, longing to be expressed. Failure to discharge leads to extreme discomfort and dissatisfaction. It is a slow death.

What inside you has been longing for expression? What inside you most blocks the discharge of your power and authentic self? What would it take for you to finally take the bull by the horns and attack it, plunging into it to discern and release its grip on your soul?

November 7

Football is entertainment. It's not life or death.
If winning or losing is going to define your life, you're on a rough road.
-Bud Grant,
NFL coaching legend & the only person to ever play in both the NFL & the
NBA, winning two NBA championships with the Minneapolis Lakers, four Grey
Cup Championships as coach of the Winnipeg Blue Bombers in the Canadian
Football League, and losing four Super Bowls as coach of the Minnesota Vikings

What is it in your life that you treat as life or death, when it really isn't? What
are you taking far too seriously? As a result, how much of your happiness and peace
is tied to something that, in the big scheme of things, really doesn't matter, or at
least not very much?

Or, how much of your identity is tied to winning (or just not losing)? Now, this
is quite a bit more common, isn't it? Hell, I'd be lying if I said there isn't some of
that in me, too. Winning kicks ass, at times. But, like everyone else, I've been in
enough 'for fun' games and leagues to see plenty of people who take winning
faaaarrrr too seriously, as in they can't ever play just for fun. As a result, they're no
fun to be around. They kill the fun for everyone else. I grew up with a guy whom
we'd often let win, or sometimes never invite, because he was such a baby/a-hole
when he didn't win.

In human interactions the people who can't ever see someone else 'win' or can't
bear to see themselves as anything other than #1 are often just unbearable people.
They'll diminish others, including spouses, children, co-workers, siblings, and even
friends. But, alas, no one likes a dickhead. Thus, they often become isolated because
of their own need to feel superior.

Is this you? Might it occur to you, at some point, that this really is no way to go
through life, and that this trait is such an obvious indicator of your own massive
insecurities? When do you maybe do the work to change that?

Are you close to someone like this? Are you exhausted yet?

November 8

Do you want to be heard, helped, or hugged?
-Robert H. Friedman,
American entertainment executive
& producer of *The Badass Counseling Show*

Wanna forever change the quality of your friendships, family, love relationships, and parenting – *especially* parenting? Just ask this question anytime you're in a conversation with someone where they seem serious, it's clearly important to them, or where you know the conversation is heavy.

Why? It immediately orients you out of your own world and onto them and their needs. It takes you out of the center of the world and puts them there, even if only for a small moment of time. Further, it helps you better meet their needs. It is so easy to forever live in fix-it mode with others, if for no other reason than it can be hard to be silent and listen without actually *doing* anything. But fix-it doesn't work when someone just really needs to feel heard, seen, loved, appreciated, or understood.

Can you step out of the comfort zone of being in motion and fixing, and move into being present, listening, and making it about their agenda, rather than always your own? Your relationships will never be the same.

November 9

There is no need to control and force things to happen.
You are right where you are supposed to be.
Start flowing. Stop forcing.
-Kylie Francis, Social media influencer

One of the more advanced and more difficult to execute bits of wisdom I've encountered in middle age is:

Effort = Ego

The more effort you are putting into something – anything! – the more ego you have wrapped up in it, which, in turn, means you have massive fear wrapped up in not accomplishing it. For, the construction and maintaining of one's ego edifice is unequivocally sewn up in one's fears of lack. We pursue and pursue to fill the hole, often exquisitely large, inside. This crater was formed by the confirmations of worth and ability we did not receive in the past or the ego poundings we did.

Therefore, the cure to the sense of lack that hole creates is either to fill it with the ego's cravings and drives, or simply allow, and allow to pass out of you, the extreme feelings of fear it gives birth to. The former creates a life full of anxiety and running hard toward the filling and away from the emptiness. The latter gives birth, eventually, to a life of peace and fulfillment without the extraordinary external efforts of energy, time, drive.

What if the answer is not outside you? What if the need is not for filling but for allowing the fears to come up and come up, until they go? What do you lack or fear lacking? What ego edifices have you created, or long to create? Do you see how the edifice is a clear pointer to the lack you fear most?

November 10

Your time is limited.
So, don't waste it living somebody else's life.
-Steve Jobs, Apple Founder

Have you ever known someone well enough that you trust them, where they respected you and your boundaries so much that they didn't try to force their own agenda on you or tell you what to do? Have you known someone who so loved you and you trusted them so much that you gave their words and thoughts more weight than you would give to other people?

In contrast, do you have, or have you ever had, people in your life, perhaps for a long time, who were often telling you what to do, expecting you to do it their way, even though you chafed under their forced direction and, perhaps, deep down, did not trust them, at all, even though you would still do their bidding?

The former is a person you have given real estate in your soul and life, because they've earned it with respect and trustworthiness. The latter is someone who has taken real estate, claiming it and you as their own, to do with as they see fit. Do you see the difference? Do you see the problem?

It raises the question, how did the latter person acquire the real estate and how do they retain it? More often than not, it was stolen, because they had power over you, either actual power, such as one might have over a child; or, they had power over you in your own head, because you had previously been conditioned to unwittingly trust and keep giving trust – conditioned to give away your power, long prior in life by someone(s) who never gave power back to you. More often than not, they retain the land by fear – you fear them harming you with words or more, if you stand up and take back what is rightfully yours by birth.

Power given vs. Power taken.

Do you give away power to anyone? I know I do. I have a very small handful of people I give trust to, whose words I weigh heavier and stronger than anyone else's. But, it is a complete, 100% choice on my part, out of no sense of obligation to do so. I long ago engaged eminent domain and retook all real estate inside me, tight-fistedly giving only the tiniest parcels in the subsequent decades, and occasionally leasing slightly larger tracts, which would be quickly rescinded if contracts were breached.

Has your power been given away, or was it stolen? From whom do you want to, or need to, reclaim land inside you? Who demands land, as if it is their own?

You're still on someone's agenda, either in big, small, or medium ways, whether you can see it or not. So, the question becomes solely this: Is it voluntary? Did you actually choose to be on this person's 'shoulds' as the plan for your life? Or, do you still choose it, today? If so, why?

Why the heck are you continuing to choose – *choose!* – for your life that which someone else wants from you or for you? Why, at such an advanced age, would you continue to willfully sacrifice what little time you have left, just to make someone else happy or avoid their wrath or blowback? Why? Especially if that person is long dead. What possible justification could you have, other than you've given up, long ago? Why not create an ending worth living?

November 11

Passion is one great force that unleashes creativity,
because if you're passionate about something,
then you're willing to take risks.
-Yo Yo Ma, Chinese-French-American cellist

All great acts, discoveries, work, and creations begin with excitement – the igniting of the fires of the soul. It is something quite remarkable to meet someone who has met their own destiny, or next destiny, as it were; to meet someone on fire. It is something altogether awe-inspiring and extraordinarily powerful to be the one on fire, to experience that sheer volume of strength and enthusiasm inside. People spend years waiting for the touch of those fires, desperately searching and longing for their passion to arrive.

But here's the thing. It's been inside you the whole time. It's not out there to be found. It's underneath it all, under the crud, pain, fears, and garbage beliefs you were taught about yourself that got written into the cement that got poured over the rock bottom of your soul. The message and that cement have to be jackhammered out of there, destroyed for good, so that the real messages written in the gorgeous bedrock in the depths of your soul may finally, effortlessly rise up and fill your life with impassioned new directions.

That requires courage. For, the messages, the origins of that cement, and the pourer of it all have to be faced. This inner work has to be done.

The passion is down there. The calling of your soul is down there, waiting.

Ready? What's the one thing, person, or belief that most needs to be jackhammered outta ya', so that your volume of power may be unleashed?

November 12

Have you heard that it was good to gain the day?
I also say it is good to fall.
Battles are lost in the same spirit in which they are won.
-Walt Whitman, American poet

A simple question for you; there's no right or wrong answer; but, if you were to be totally honest:

Would you rather lose following your own plan and purpose
or
win following someone else's plan and purpose for your life?

I have spent a great many years helping people unhook their trailer from the truck of someone else's designs for their life. I have had many people come to me unclear why they were so unhappy, and invariably it is tied directly to this. It, then, does not take long before they are confronted with the question of whether they'd rather potentially win externally on someone else's agenda, but lose internally, because they're not living their own true desires and dreams; or, potentially lose the external accomplishments but gain the joy and exhilaration of living from their source inside. It's no easy choice. For, going against someone else's designs comes with the criticism of unhooking from them, but also the potential onslaught of double the volume of those voices, if they fail.

More often than not, anyone who has been working with me for even the briefest time chooses the latter – the unhooking – because they've spent too long, too much life energy, and too much misery trying to be happy by making others happy with their choices. To unhook and make life work demands a willingness to lose the day, as Whitman discusses in the quote. It requires the realization that a day or life lived on one's own agenda and for one's own purposes is, in itself, a life well-lived, quite apart from the results. Even as success is still striven for, it is being vigorously on one's own path that is the source of deepest peace and energy. That is what differentiates the fulfilled from the unfulfilled, those with peace from those who are ever searching, never finding their way.

So, what's your answer? Has the pain of living on others' agendas sucked enough life out of you, yet? Are you willing to fail standing up for and traversing down your own path? That's really the question of life, isn't it?

November 13

Excess on occasion is exhilarating.
It prevents moderation from acquiring the deadening effect of habit.
-W. Somerset Maugham, English novelist

This quote bumps up against that cliché we've all heard, "Moderation in all things." Clearly, they're saying two different things, even if they're not totally opposite. So, which is it? Which is the right path?

Well, my challenge to any person when faced with the decision of which of any two paths is right for them is to take them both for a spin and feel along the way which feels right for him or her. In my case, I'm a huge believer in "moderation sucks," which is a twist on the Maugham quote. I do not and have never striven for moderation, middle of the road, temperance in any form, or especially balance. Screw balance, which is usually just a euphemism for moderation and the temperate life. Balance, to me, is like holding onto the steering wheel as you go down the road, trying to keep it perfectly still and unchanging, at all, despite the undulations of the road as it comes at you. Balance is striving to stay in the middle. I definitely enjoy the middle, at times, but I also adore the rush, the exhilarations, the unknowns and the undulations.

I believe in ebb and flow, yin and yang, utter slavish focus on selfishness and utter loss of self in selflessness, and every point in between, the choices determined by the calling of my energy, and that alone. Perhaps at the end of my days, when the reckoning happens, the overall balance on the chit will be somewhere near the middle, near a balanced life. But, it will not be because that middle was ever sought, but because the goal of the life I live is *ALIVENESS*, which means extreme excess and extreme self-abnegation, moderate quest for more and moderate self-denial, mild taking and mild giving, all dependent upon the moment, the year, the chapter of life and the undulations of the roads they bring. I loathe the timidity of moderation for moderation's sake, but that's just me for my life. I choose to not be governed by the fears that are the natural precursors of moderation and dull habit, unless, of course, the madness of a particular path has grown weary, such that in that one sector of life the calm of the middle road is a lovely respite. Yet, we each must choose our own path.

What do you choose? Why? To what degree is that choice of yours fear-driven or forced? Are you okay with that? More, is that choice reflective of your authentic self? If so, go for it! If not, you gotta ask yourself why the hell you're choosing something other than your authentic self, and if you're okay with reaching the end of your days, reading that long receipt of your life, and realizing you have never lived your real life that your soul longed for.

November 14

> **We cannot change anything unless we accept it.**
> **Condemnation does not liberate; it oppresses.**
> -Carl Jung, One of the Founding Fathers of psychology

There are so many things we cling to in life:

- things we think we need
- people we cannot imagine living without
- beliefs we hold to
- results we want

We spend lifetimes trying to change something or someone, only to repeatedly be banged back and forth, against the walls of life, jostled, bruised, denied and shut down, never accomplishing the results we so long for, no matter how long or ferociously we try the proverbial 'break down the doors.'

I've discovered in my own life and those I've worked with that letting go of the very thing we want most, or even just letting go of the results, often later leads to the most startling results. And it's a doggone relief. I just accept that this is the state of my life, and I build and grow in new directions, only to discover, later, that those old things are now changing, because I let go of trying to force them. My desire to change them implied a dislike for who or what they were. With that dislike gone, the pressure was released and the change came organically.

What do you cling to so tightly that there's no room for organic growth, or perhaps there's even resistance to the change you push for? Do you realize that the resistance to the change you want may be the direct result of your condemnation of it, implied in your desire to no longer have it be as it is? At what point in life do you accept, allow, let go of the change you think you must have, or embrace the change you fear, and move on in new directions?

November 15

The only cure for grief
is to grieve.
-Rabbi Earl Grollman, American writer

The reason your energy feels heavy and your soul is not light is in large part because you have pain inside of you that you have not yet grieved. It can be related to anything, not just death. You have experienced loss and hurt. And those demand to be both grieved and given words and deeper understanding. Else, they drag the soul down, drag the life energy out of you, and, with time, drag you along, despite your silly claims of being over it or on top of life. Like giant rocks in a huge burlap bag on your back, slowly but surely, over time, they push you into the ground, driving you into an inexorable depression.

One of the secrets of finally becoming light, finally pulling the rocks from the bag, finally living in a state of effortless energy is to grieve and reflect. In your journaling today, list all of the pain and hurts you have experienced in your life that you know still have an emotional charge attached to them, that you know you still need to de-charge. One by one, you must begin to allow that pain up and out of you. We flush out the pain – effectively emptying the bag of any rocks – and increase our energy by allowing the soul to grieve, by finally turning and facing the very pain we have been running from for far too long. What do you need to grieve, reflect on, and give words to? Do you have the courage to finally face it?

November 16

From goblins and ghosties
and long-legged beasties
and things that go bump in the night,
Good Lord deliver us.
-Old Scottish Prayer

My pastor father had an old prayer book from 1963, about the size of your hand, that he kept, along with others, in his office library, whether at the churches he served or in his final years as a chaplain at the Veterans Affairs hospital in Minneapolis. It now rests on my office shelf, along with other books of the trade that he frequently referenced. This particular prayer book is full of highlighted prayers, dogeared pages, and occasional notations. Inside the back cover, in his signature minuscule cursive writing was this prayer, clearly one he had picked up somewhere and found so ticklish that it had to be saved with the pre-printed ones in the book. It was just the sort of prayer he would like – playful, poetic, yet packing an underlying punch. I actually read it as my siblings scattered mom's and dad's mixed ashes on the old Erlandson family farm in Hallock, MN, way up north in Kittson County, one of the northern-most and coldest counties in the contiguous United States, where dad had grown up, during the Depression and WWII.

I include it here, not because I'm selling religion or its god, rather because I like the underlying punch. It's a beautiful metaphor. We are all, every one of us, seeking both refuge and security from the things that go bump in the night, from the unknownies and scaries in life, whatever they may be, unique to each person. We seek security not just from the ones that go bump at night time, but the ones that scare us in the bright light of day.

We strive for and cling to money, family, position, land, privacy, anesthetics, and any number of pursuits, principles, people, and the like that promise the securities we seek from the ghosties we fear, whether inside us or out.

What are the beasties you fear most? How much of your life, energy, and time is spent striving for that ever-elusive security? How much do you seek security from the grand ghostie of them all, death? And, does that fear of death immobilize you or energize the life you're living?

November 17

> *Everyone thinks of changing the world,*
> *but no one thinks of changing himself.*
> -Leo Tolstoy, Russian author

This quote really has nothing to do with changing the world, per se. Instead, it is a bit of Tolstoy throwing down the gauntlet, challenging each of us to shut up about our big dreams for everyone and everything else and just fix *ourselves*.

What do you use daily as a way to avoid going inside and changing yourself and your life? What stories do you tell yourself and others? Do you state things about yourself as immutable facts, so that you don't have to do the inner work of changing those things about you? What is the life that you run to as a way of not having to change yourself? Are you tired yet?

November 18

*The act of taking something that's really hard
and putting enough energy into it so it melts...
It's like playing with the sun.*
-Dick Polich, American artisan and foundry founder

Mr. Polich made a long career out of helping world-renowned artists turn their visions into giant signature sculptures. His expertise, as the quote indicates, was subjecting the world's hardest metals to the extreme furnaces of his massive foundry, turning them into malleable entities the artist could work with.

I like this as a metaphor for spiritual life. The gods, or the universe is forever subjecting us, each one, to the fires of life, melting our hardness, burning off our impurities, refining us into something more usable for the organism that is life, itself. This simultaneously brings extraordinary pain and, through/after the fires, fuller joy and a peace we had not known, if only we allow ourselves to be bent and hammered into something new. This is something we discover, as we age – so much of who we were, back then, we don't miss. It was nice while it lasted, but what was burned off allowed for such a different life to be solidified.

Similarly, there are times in life when we are called by our own soul, really, to be the fire which melts hard things and people from what they were, into something new, usable, and more beautiful. Sometimes, we are the ones called to burn off the impurities and refine something or someone, whether by teaching a new truth or standing against something formerly immutable. Sometimes, we too are called to play with the sun. And that can be fiercely intimidating work, which comes with no small amount of uncontrollable fires, mistakes, and burns. Nonetheless, the work still has to be done. And, sometimes, we are the ones who are called to do the work of making hard things soft, so they can become hard, again, and even more spectacular.

What is the sun that you play with? What are the metals you melt? What are the burns you've endured in your work? Proud of those scars and scabs? Do you enjoy your work?

How has life subjected you to the fires? Did you allow yourself to be melted? Did you seek the questions for your growth that the fires brought? Did you allow them to take you deep? How have you been re-formed? What were the aspects of you that got burned off? How is life better, since they've been gone? Which are you, at times, wistful about?

November 19

Championships are won and lost in the off-season.
-The guy who wrote this book

It's not in the testing moment that the victor is decided or the results determined. That happened months, even years prior.

You want achievements in your career? You hustle when no one's watching. You want a body you can be proud of? You care for your teeth, skin, innards and eyes assiduously.

Similarly, do you want a spirit that is finally relieved of a lifetime of pain, fear, and heavy burdens? You gotta do the work between counseling sessions, when you're experiencing strong feelings that don't feel good, when old tapes start playing in your head, and when you're bumping into issues in your relationships. It's the off-season. It's when no one else is watching.

What motivates the off-season work of growing and strengthening the soul? The same thing that drives teams to work harder out of season: hunger, desire, fire, intensity, drive to win at this game you've been given to play. It's the game of self in life. And, if your hunger for a life of greater peace, happiness, fulfillment, and *ALIVENESS* is not consuming, or at least powerful, you'll not do the work and, thus, not get the results you claim to want.

Are you doing the work? How hungry are you? Has the suckiness of life gotten bad enough that you're finally – *finally!* – one motivated individual? If not, how much worse does it have to get before you are? Why, what do you fear?

November 20

Do not consider painful that which is good for you.
-Euripides, Greek tragedy writer

Do you begrudge life, the universe, God, or some other person all the pain you're experiencing or have experienced? Are you angry by it – the unfairness of it all?

The badass, elite level of wisdom and inner peace comes when we make the slow, loathed movement from pain-as-curse to pain-as-blessing. On lower levels, such a thought is beyond unthinkable, even outright offensive. Alas, life teaches us, especially if we have the courage to allow it rather than fight it, to sit in it rather than run from it, to mine it rather than bury it. It is to be in it as long as it takes for it all to pass and teach all the truths in its horrible grip.

Everything is different after that. The shift is felt in every segment of life, from carriage to countenance, from dreams to desires, from vulnerability to vulnerable-by-choice. Everything changes when pain and the fears of it no longer consume our thoughts and life.

Is your pain still a curse, an anomaly to be avoided? What would it take for you to finally allow and accept? How would you be different if you saw this mad pain as blessing rather than curse, as mineable rather than requiring burying?

It's fascinating to consider, isn't it, even if it's simultaneously horrible to consider?

November 21

When I die,
I want to go peacefully, like my grandfather did, in his sleep;
not yelling and screaming, like the passengers in his car.
-Jack Handey, American humorist

Go ahead; take a minute and laugh. I knew you'd like that one.

Just a lighthearted one, today, to apply to a heavy topic – death. My question for you, today, is not how do you want to die, but what do you want your life to have been about? Will you be proud of the ride you took, content with your decisions, happy about it all?

What if that day is tomorrow? Ask yourself those questions, today, knowing you may well die tomorrow. You may have not accomplished all you wished to accomplish. But, the timing of accomplishments is usually out of our hands in life. The real question is, Do you strive for what you want to strive for? Are you driven today by your dreams and excitements, or by someone else's expectations? And, are you okay with that? And if you aren't on the journey of *your* life and passions, what the hell is it gonna take for you to finally start doing so?

So, what's the dream? Write it out. And, starting today, force yourself to look at it every day, because now the genie is out of the bottle. Now you have to acknowledge what your dream is and, if you're not following it, you have to feel the pain of knowing you're not following it. You have to be consciously aware that you're abdicating your life. And for what? What do you fear that causes you to not want to look, each day, at what your dream really is *and pursue it?*

November 22

When love beckons to you, follow him,
though his ways are hard and steep.
And when his wings enfold you, yield to him,
though the sword hidden among his pinions may wound you.
And when he speaks to you, believe in him,
though his voice may shatter your dreams
as the north wind lays waste to the garden.
For even as love crowns you, so shall he crucify you. Even as he is for your
growth, so is he for your pruning. Even as he ascends to your height and
caresses your tenderest branches that quiver in the sun, so shall he descend
to your roots and shake them in their clinging to the earth.
Like sheaves of corn, he gathers you unto himself.
He threshes you to make you naked.
He sifts you free from your husks. He grinds you to whiteness.
He kneads you until you are pliant.
And then he assigns you to his sacred fire,
that you may become sacred bread for God's sacred feast.
All these things shall love do unto you
that you may know the secrets of your heart.
And in that knowledge become a fragment of life's heart.
-Kahlil Gibran, Lebanese-American poet and painter

Poets and painters, moviemakers and magazine publishers, songwriters and the salespeople schlepping all of it have long sold the idea of full immersion into love for the person or purpose that seizes your heart. And there is a certain naivete and willful ignorance of the immense pains that come with blind, immersed love. Certainly, any and all loves require some measure of temperance, at times.

Yet, Gibran, while beckoning us to love, as poets and troubadours have always done, is sorta stating something different. He's teaching us, not just coaxing us. He's so profoundly and deeply telling us of one of, if not the ultimate human inevitability. Love, to which every one of us is called, at one time or another, will quicken the heart like nothing else on earth, yet will simultaneously destroy you...like nothing else on earth or in human experience. Gibran is echoing the great Roman philosophers' exhortation, *Amor fati*. 'love your fate, love everything precisely as it is, precisely as it was always written to be.' To fully dive into love is to dive into life and become what we are all consigned to become, ground down to wheat in the very bread of life, eaten by life itself.

What are the loves that consume your heart? Have you embraced them fully? Is it your children, your life's work, your lover, your art, your journey, your deep inner caves? What beckons you? What holds you back from embracing it passionately?

November 23

People often say that motivation doesn't last.
Well, neither does bathing – that's why we recommend it daily.
-Zig Ziglar, American author and motivational speaker

One of the phenomena I see very frequently in my clients is that after a few months of working with me and clearing out a lot of the crud that has been bogging them down their entire lives, and learning new skills for living, they end the counseling and go off on their own, ready for life – high, exuberant, eager to attack life with new skills and a sense of liberation. A few months later, I get an email. They've crashed and need to figure out what on earth is going on.

Here's the thing, when you've been down a long time, that being down feels awful. But, when you've gone up and kissed the mountaintop, no longer burdened by that stuff that held you down for so long, and then crash, for whatever reason, that low feels infinitely lower than that exact same low did, just months prior. That low stands in stark contrast to the high they've known from our work. So, they come back needing a life correction.

Invariably, the problem is that they stopped bathing, stopped doing the daily disciplines I taught them that got them to those heights in the first place. It's similar to the guy who is 40 pounds overweight and out of shape, who hires a trainer and start going to the gym. Within 3-6 weeks, he starts losing some noticeable weight and even sees a few beginnings of muscles. Feels great. Looks better. Perhaps his wife even wants to have sex with him. With that head of steam, he one week, one Wednesday, calls his trainer to say he won't be able to make it for their appointment Thursday; "work-related stuff." As it always does, one Thursday then becomes a Tuesday and a Friday, becomes multiple days and the sweet taste of steak and potatoes, not to mention ice cream while watching *Law and Order* reruns. Soon he has gained that 40 back and the old misery has crept back in, but worse.

Self-care is a discipline. And, like going to the gym and monitoring your food intake, it sucks. It sucks to have to do this crap, or to simply be disciplined. But, that's the price of greatness and feeling wonderful. Everything in life has a price. Everything. So, shut up and do the work. That's the first rule of the gym, be it the gym with cast iron or the one of books, pens, and sheets of paper. Nothing motivates like experiencing the suckiness of a life that has degenerated to such a level of misery, day in and day out.

So, has your life gotten crappy enough for long enough that you're ready to not only start but *maintain* the soul disciplines necessary for happiness and fulfillment? Are you ready to finally pay the price, day in and day out? Or, have you grown comfortable with that strong measure of misery you hate?

November 24

Here I stand.
I can do no other.
-Martin Luther, Leader of the Reformation

Few words in the history of humanity have more shaken and changed the world, yet are less well-known than these eight. Google them; read the story and the impact. It's riveting. One man stood against the most powerful organization in the world at the risk of losing his own life and the freedom of millions of others, and issued a hearty 'Kiss my ass!'

It's no small thing that four of history's other world-changing words, "I have a dream," were spoken by a man named after the man above.

Listen to Luther's words. There's no fluff, no poetic flourish, just the straightforward German statement of sheer resoluteness. With those words the very foundations of Western civilization began to crumble, slowly but surely.

What are the words and truths of your very existence that you cannot recant, on which you live and by which you are willing to die? This is where real power comes from – people knowing the handful of words and truths at the very bedrock of who they are, and having the courage to live them, daily. There is no power more immovable and immutable than a person who knows who he or she is and has the balls to live it, moment to moment.

What percentage are you living that core truth of who you are? Does it permeate every act, every day, every interaction, every pursuit, and every decision, one way or another? Because, if it doesn't, you're wasting your life, because you ain't being you. And that, above all else, is the grand tragedy of being given but one life.

November 25

Everyone has his own specific vocation or mission in life;
everyone must carry out a concrete assignment that demands fulfillment.
Therein, he cannot be replaced, nor can his life be repeated.
Thus, everyone's task is as unique as his specific opportunity to implement
it.
-Viktor Frankl, Holocaust survivor and author of *Man's Search for Meaning*

The purpose of the work of drilling down into self and flushing out all of the pain, fears, and BS beliefs you've been taught about yourself is to discover, below it all, the very bedrock of your identity. It is in finding and living in your identity (no longer in the safe shell of who you were expected to be or who you had to be to survive) that you move into a state of peace, power, freedom, energy, and joy.

But also, inside that center of who you really are is the purpose written on your soul of what you are called to do next with your life. Whether it was written by some greater life force or simply by your own soul, itself, inside of there is the very DNA of your greatest joy and highest calling. It is the one for which your particular confluence of interests and abilities are perfectly suited. It is the one that simply brings you the greatest joy and challenge, creating in you a true sense of fulfillment.

That is how we know our purpose in life – or, as Frankl calls it, our meaning. It is that path which brings with it the drive to accomplish it, or at least doggedly labor at it. Every odd strand of your life weaves a thread into the cloth of the calling of your soul – the flowers you like, the sounds you hate, the personality types you gravitate to, the pains and frustrations you have a particular gift for letting roll off your back, the failures, the insecurities, the favorite sweater or pair of shoes, the exercises you despise, the memories of certain teachers you treasure; everything is woven into that grand tapestry of your life and your purpose. EVERYTHING!

Thus, to not labor toward the dreams and in the work to which you have been called by your soul is to deny the world of a uniqueness that will never exist again, and therefore also deprive the world of the unique expression only you can bring. The world needs you, whether you believe it or not.

Have you been clearing out the crud blocking the full expression of your authentic self, rising up from deep in your soul? What are you beginning to see more clearly is the purpose for which you have been designed? What is the calling that would give you joy and deep fulfillment to pursue and toil at? What would just be fun to build or work at? Don't doubt that energy, that fun-ness, that excitement. Don't belittle a path, just because someone's old voice inside you calls it frivolous or less-than. This is what it means to have courage – to hear and heed your own truth, rising up from deep within, beckoning to you, even when others (be they outside of you or inside you) mock, doubt, or undermine you. It is courage you will need to live a life of meaning, if it is the meaning you choose, rather than simply gobbling up the one that has been force-fed to you.

November 26

Marge, it takes two to lie:
One to lie and one to listen.

-Homer Simpson, cartoon philosopher-father

Delightfully idiotic as Homer Simpson has been for decades, he hits it outta the park and gets a free beer for this one. If someone lies to you the first time, you're a victim. But, if they lie to you a second time, and most certainly a third time, you're a volunteer, a participant, if you know they're lying to you.

Who's lying to you? And, why are you still listening to them? Most importantly, what the heck is going on inside you that you knowingly and willfully continue to listen to someone, potentially someone who claims to love you, whom you know either is lying or has lied to you in repeated or egregious ways? What need is being met by staying in the conversation with this person; or, what do you fear in walking away from this conversation and this person? What is the fear driving your behavior? And, has it occurred to you that, until you are willing to accept that which you fear happening or let go of that which you think you cannot live without, they will continue to lie to you, because of the permission your presence tacitly gives them?

As a fun little bonus to start your day with a chuckle, here's another Homerism, "Just because I don't care doesn't mean I'm not listening."

November 27

I don't know what your destiny will be, but one thing I know:
the only ones among you who will be really happy
are those who have sought and found how to serve.
-Albert Schweitzer, French polymath & Nobel Prize winner

In my work with individuals, corporations, couples, law enforcement, athletes, politicians, entertainers, educators, young people, and so on I consider it my most sacred duty to help others hear and heed their own individual, inner voice, which no other person on earth can know for them. That requires extracting all the other voices and pains blocking the messages from their own soul.

But, I also believe that there are universal aspects to our individual identities rising up from the soul of each person. I believe it to be a foundational, inextricable aspect of human identity to desire to be an instrument of good in the world. I really believe that. How that good takes form for Billy is very different for how it is executed by Susie or Polly or Jeffy. I believe it's in our nature to desire to bring love to the world and that there is more in the human soul than self-interest, acquisition, and the desire for security. I also believe humans are at their happiest and most fulfilled when moving as a love instrument in the world, be it toward other people, or animals, or nature, or space. This may sound too soft for you, but the truth of it is unequivocal: we are love-beings, just as much as we are pleasure-beings, power-beings, safety-beings, and just plain animal-instinct-beings.

What are the ways your soul most enjoys or longs to give love to humanity or to the earth, or animals, or what? In what ways does it most delight you to be of service and reduced self-interest? Or, do you over-give, to the great diminishment of self; are you an extreme giver for reasons that may not be the healthiest? What is your present relationship with the part of your soul that longs to be a force of love and goodness in the world?

November 28

Men decide far more problems by
hate, love, lust, rage, sorrow, joy, hope, fear, illusion,
or some other inward emotion, than by
reality, authority, any legal standard, judicial precedent, or statute.
-Cicero, Roman philosopher

In my last book, *There's a Hole in My Love Cup*, I discuss how the quest to change behaviors never changes behaviors long term. The focus on behaviors as either the problem or the solution to life is silliness. For, actions are invariably driven by the core beliefs, longings, and fears down in the soul of the individual. If the core beliefs are not changed, the individual will, inevitably, revert back to the actions that grow out of those core beliefs and drivers, such as those listed by Cicero.

Yet, there's another interesting little piece to the equation. Right in the middle, between surface behaviors and core beliefs of the soul there is a layer that we call our principles, laws, values, reality, and the "right thing." We all claim to run our lives by those, and that our actions are smart, sound and determined by savvy principles. But those principles in the layer between behaviors and core beliefs are no more than backfill – socially acceptable justifications for the longings, movements, and determinations of the soul. Without the good logic they appear to convey, we feel foolish, naked in the face of detractors and critics. In the fear of looking foolish, we too often allow our principles, right thoughts and shoulds to trump feel, intuition, and bald honesty of intentions.

And, the unhappiest of people live a life of backfill, forever justifying themselves, forever stuck in the middling realm of socially prescribed shoulds and thou shalts. The nakedness of having no justification but one's own inclinations and calling is just way too much to bear for the common person and many of the great ones, too.

What percentage of your life actions, behaviors, and choices come from the realm of deepest self and what percentage from the backfill of justification and seeking acceptance? How's that working out for you? Who's voice do you most fear in living from the soul rather than fear of their judgment?

November 29

> *The grand benefit of going through hell*
> *is that it's not as scary the second time,*
> *and certainly not so the third time.*
> -Sven

My first divorce ripped my fkng heart out. I had been madly in love with her since I was 22. I was in my late-20s when she ended it, two kids later. The thought of my kids not having a 2-parent home and me losing her were too much. It took me 2 ½ years to get over her.

But, as life goes, I met someone who was, at the time, infinitely better suited to who I had become through the trials and growth of life. By now I was in my early-30s and she was celebrating her 40th birthday. Totally different woman. Totally different relationship. I was madly in love, again. Remarkable woman. Though, in the end, similar result – I divorced her.

However, there was one distinct difference this second time. I was just as broken up (though for different reasons). Missed her just as much. Cried my eyes out for a year or more. But I had been through it once before. So, it wasn't as disorienting. I knew the waymarks. I knew what to expect in the process between us, what to expect might happen inside me, how long it might take to grieve, how heavy and hard the pain would feel. My dance with the pain, 10 years earlier, prepared me.

Moving forward from that 2nd divorce being finalized, I was never intimidated by the thought of losing someone, as I had been for the first 37 years of my life. I would go on to love just as hard, give just as intensely, and be just as much of an idiot in love. But I didn't cling, at least nowhere near as much, because I wasn't afraid of being left. I wasn't intimidated by hardship and pain. I knew what that sector of the dark forest (or hell, as it were) looked and felt like. I knew it was doable and I'd survive. The sun would shine again.

Whether it's love, career, family, kids, friendships, mental or physical health, is this your first time through this sector of hell? Second? Third? What doesn't scare you anymore? What do you still run from? Are you able, yet, to see things coming before they do? List the things in this situation that you're still most fearing or have anxiety over? Now journal out, for each one, why you feel that, what that's coming from, what other associated feelings you have? Assume those things will all happen; will you be okay? Will life go on? Can you work your way through it all or will it end you, somehow? Keep flushing out all of your thoughts and feelings through more journaling.

November 30

To err is human;
but contrition felt for the crime
distinguishes the virtuous from the wicked.
-Vittorio Alfieri, Italian dramatist

My mother died on this day, in 2021, at the age of 93. She left a rather strange legacy, well, a few actually. But, one that she was particularly deliberate about, most notably in her last 10-15 years, was going to each of her adult children and asking each to share with her, please, any remaining ways we could think of that she had hurt us, disappointed us, or fallen short. She wanted any pain she had caused to be returned to the owner, her. To the very end, she was parenting deliberately, owning her sh*t, insisting that her children carry no rocks on their heart that she had put there.

There was no ego there. Or maybe there was, but she defined it differently. To be proud of herself as a parent, or at least to feel good about her parenting, meant to do no harm and to repent for any harm she had done. She would listen, say back what she had heard, apologize, and yet sit even longer with reflection on what she had done. And, though anything she might've done was decades in the past, she would strive to still change and do better.

That's called deliberate parenting, even though in their final 20 years, each of us kids joyfully took on different roles of taking care of our parents. When you consider that deliberateness was how she parented, is it any wonder why we were so eager to serve them, as they aged, each in our own individual ways?

Is it possible your idea of good parenting is skewed? Is it possible it's not about the idea of you having made no mistakes, but you continuing to own and take back from your children any pain you caused? Is it possible that good parenting isn't about getting a sense of worth from your children, but a feeling of serving them, to the end – giving and not receiving? What do you need to go back and own, neither defending yourself, deflecting, or denying? Can you give that gift to your children? Or is there still so much of your own ego sewn up in not admitting mistakes, failures, and hurts you caused? Now, when their lives should be flying, they are still bogged down by the pain you caused and that your ego refuses to own and take back from them. Are you seriously so frail that you're okay with choosing your own ego over their happiness and fulfillment?

December

December 1

It's on the strength of observation and reflection that one finds a way.
So, we must dig and delve unceasingly.
-Claude Monet, French painter

Without reflection, we go blindly on our way, creating more unintended
consequences,
and failing to achieve anything useful.
-Margaret J. Wheatley, American writer

When I was a kid, striving to get attention, one of my go-to ways for getting it was to pretend to know something about everything. So hungry for praise and to be seen, I was the classic arrogant know-it-all. Somehow, I thought that was a good thing.

Well, as we all know, it doesn't take long before we realize there's always someone smarter, stronger, tougher, faster, richer, etc. Bump into enough of those people and the arrogance goes out the window. (Small men have to keep small worlds.) In retrospect, I'm so glad I did and it did. Of course, now, I can't stand know-it-alls; the man or woman who has to (always pretend to) be the smartest man (or woman) in the room. He'll couch opinions as facts, have something to say on every topic, and listen only till he thinks of what he wants to say next. It's so exhausting and so unbecoming. Yet, that guy never realizes how much he repels people.

As I've aged, I've grown to both respect the hell out of and love people who have the decency and courage to say those three precious words, "I don't know." They have no problem being silent and can speculate answers, and offer such as speculation (rather than knowledge), but they're not ever-striving to seem right and sound smart.

So, let's play with that idea, a bit. Let's turn the notion of "I don't know" onto your own life. If you were to set your *future* aside and only look at your *present* and *past*, what are the three biggest "I don't knows" in your life? That is, what are the three biggest things from your past and/or things you still think or do in your present that you have no explanation for, or that you have always answered "I don't know" when queried about why you do that? What are the great unanswered questions of your life?

Now, if you were to speculate what the answer to one of those questions is, what would you say it is? Just if you were to take a wild guess, knowing you could change your mind tomorrow or next week, what would you say is the real reason. I often have people say to me, when I press this, "Well, I don't know. I've never thought about this before." I know you haven't. I'm asking that you both think about it and stay focused on it. Then, throw out the answer it might be, just off the top of your head; or the possible answer.

Next, do the same for the other two. After doing so, to test for veracity, sit on those answers for a couple of days or a week. Dwell. Come back to it in a week and feeeel it. Does it feel like this really is the answer. If you have to think about it, back and forth, let it go. When something is right, you just feel it. There's a sense of knowing.

Another way to test its veracity is to ask, Does this answer bring an epiphany? Does it feel like a "Holy Crap" moment, like "Wow! Wow! Wow," like you just stumbled upon something very real, very powerful. If not, it's likely not it. When you hit the answer to a long-held "I don't know" you know it. You feel it.

If it be a new epiphany, then the trippy part is spinning out all the ramifications and sub-epiphanies that grow out of it. What is it you now realize you need to be/say/do/become? And, how does this re-write the story of your past and present? If you can dive into your own "I don't knows," you can do some serious soul-spelunking!

December 2

There is no failure, except failure to serve one's purpose.
-Henry Ford, American 19th/20th Century tycoon

There are three phases to the living of one's purpose: 1) hearing it rise up from within, 2) having the courage to heed it, and 3) letting go of it simultaneously while you're pursuing it.

1) If you don't know your purpose, it's because deep down you're terrified to slow down, create some measure of solitude, and allow all the pain, fears, and truths you've been running from to wash over and out of you. For, under those three terrifying things are the truths of your authentic voice – i.e. your life purpose. Remove those and the voice of your soul rises up effortlessly, showing its face after decades of dormancy.

2) If you know your purpose but aren't going after it at 100mph with your hair on fire, it's because of the known. It is not the unknown, but the known that scares the bejesus out of you. You know *exactly* what your brother or deceased mother will say; you know *exactly* what your old buddies or father will say; you know *exactly* what society or your spouse will think of you. In the face of that, you'll keep your vision inside, thank you very much.

3) If you've courageously pursued your purpose, despite toils and mockery, but you've not brought it to the fruition you are convinced it must become, it's because you're scared of living with an open hand – simultaneously pursuing what you're passionate about, yet allowing it to morph into wildly new ideas, allowing the Universe to lead you in new, strangely unexpected directions. You're frightened by the idea of new dreams stirred up in your soul, if it means letting go of old ones.

Your grand failure in life is one of three things:

- avoiding seeing your deepest passion, because you're afraid of all that will be revealed to you about your past; or
- avoiding going after it, because you're afraid of what the most powerful voices in your life will say or think; or
- avoiding allowing it to look differently from what you imagined or allowing it to morph into something new.

Your grand failure has been that you've chosen security over self; fear of others over an authentic life; control over openness. And, you know precisely the misery you've been experiencing, as a result, year after grinding year.

Ready to finally do the work of going solitude to flush out the crap; or going balls-to-the-wall, regardless of what others will inevitably think; or letting go of this iteration of your dream, only to be open to it morphing into something bigger and brighter? What's your biggest fear in this whole process?

December 3

Follow your bliss.
-Joseph Campbell,
first scholar to synthesize all of the world's past/present myth systems

In so many ways, life boils down to one very simple question, Are you going after the calling of your own soul – your bliss, as Campbell would call it? If not, why? What do you fear so much that you dare not go after the yearning of your own soul? To whom have you abdicated your entire life, joy, and brief walk on this planet?

For the record, when Campbell speaks of your bliss, it's not the momentary high or escape. Though, those have their place and time as small pieces of life. He's talking about the yearning of the soul, that path or source of joy, laughter, fun, devotion, and commitment. And, more often than not, the bliss you wish to follow and fill your life with is one that comes with a price tag, one you have to be willing to pay, which is implicit in the mere fact that 'Follow your bliss' is even a command, at all. If it were natural and without cost, there'd be no need to be encouraged to do it, anymore than one would need encouragement to let the shower water make you wet.

Bliss is that high thing, that 'just a hair out of reach' thing that might be a bit insane to even consider going after; that thing or path that brings a potential for failure or criticism if even pursued. It's that thing that wakes you up in the morning excited to live, or has the power to if you're not doing it yet. It's that path or pursuit that makes life worth living.

What's your bliss? What's the calling of your soul? What's the cost, fear, or thing/person that you allow to keep you from following it? Do you think that might ever stop being such an obstruction in your life? What would it take?

But, all of that said, there's another interesting part to that quote of Campbell's: "follow." Your bliss is not something you find, per se. Rather, it's already beckoning you. The task is not to lead it, but to follow, which requires trusting it, above all else. And it's that trust that is the damn scary part, isn't it? Too often in life we succumb to and sorta follow the fears, instead of the dream. We let our fears, particularly of others' criticism, direct what we do and don't do. Thus, we're not *following* our own dreams or our own self. Instead, we're directing our aspirations, so that they'll not go afoul of our fears of others and fears of failures. Following is hard, because of the trust it demands. But, following your own inner guidance is even harder, because it means relinquishing fears and it means there's no leader to blame when you're feeling down or when the inevitable losses and valleys come. That's just too scary for some folk. So, they choose to live in the fears, instead.

Don't choose fear. It's a lifeless path. It's the path of slow death. Follow *your* bliss, unapologetically.

December 4

No great mind has ever existed without a touch of madness.
-Aristotle, Greek philosopher

When I was a kid and again in my twenties, I had so many people convinced there was something wrong with me. Teachers who couldn't handle me. Lovers who insisted I was bipolar or some other nonsense. And, well, I guess it never really stopped. To this day, there are folks who still want to attach some label, some disease or malady, some choice word for how I am, what I am, or who I am.

Yet, waaaaay back in the beginning, I had parents and, largely, siblings who sorta allowed me and encouraged me to just be different. There was no affliction in their eyes. The only thing that got me a sideways glance or sharp word were bad manners and getting too big for my britches. In such cases, there was always an older brother/sister to bop me on the head or tweak me with words. But different? Nah, different was allowed in our home.

And that set the context for all the denunciations that would come later from others. They stung, but they didn't really land. There was room for my madness, my eccentricities, and my coloring way outside the lines. I think we spend so much time labeling people that we fail to allow for differences and madnesses inside the general definition of normal or acceptable.

What labels have been stuck on you? Or, perhaps, are you seeking a label, because you cannot imagine that different is just fine?

Are you sticking labels on others? To what degree are you uncomfortable with their touches of madness, and thus try to control them, so that you won't feel so uncomfortable? Do you do it to your children? Why? What's the fear driving the behavior?

December 5

*I have often laughed at the weaklings who thought themselves good
because they had no claws.*
-Friedrich Nietzsche, German philosopher

I must be honest, I agree with Nietzsche. Yet, I laugh just as loudly at the base fools who live in the constant cliché of put-on toughness, such as is being sold to searching young men, nowadays. Both are equally clownish, though the former is quiet and the other full of bluster. For, each is a one-sided person, terrified of integrating their innate strong-intense side with their soft-gentle side, as if man, or woman, is not inherently both. Foolishness.

Further, it's not just young men. Too many women, as well, have been enculturated to be either soft or hard, ne'er the twain shall meet. They, too, are being taught silliness, as if a woman isn't, by nature, both fierce and tender.

Is part of the problem in your conception of self that you are trying to choose where no choice reasonably exists? Is it possible you got fed some shallow belief that it's either-or, weak or strong?

I had a young fella reach out to me, this week, and ask what I thought of alpha vs beta in males and the pyramid of value associated with them – alpha = good; beta = weak/bad. I had to tell him precisely what I'm saying here, It's just simplistic crap. The notion that beta is somehow bad is ludicrous. A fully integrated, mature, well-rounded person is at different times different things. It behooves no one to operate always on dominating, high-speed, controlling energy. In fact, to forever live in alpha mode is quite destructive to team-building, intimate relationships (especially if you're in one with another alpha or even a mostly beta). Non-integrated people – people who aren't both – tend to create unnecessary problems, because they lack more than one speed, one mode of thinking and operating, and more than one way of interacting with others and life, itself.

The complete man/person is fully comfortable being both. To be a true badass is to reject conventional norms for thinking and acting, and resolves to just be whomever the hell he/she feels like being in any moment: gentle, kind, sweet, soft, ferocious, dominating, totally recessive, unwavering, and on and on. She does not cave to utterly arbitrary definitions of what a woman is or isn't, or man/person is or isn't. For, each of us is much more complex than simple definitions allow for. True happiness comes from expression and living as one's fullest self in all its forms, to no longer be gripped by ego's fears and perceptions. To walk gracefully and lovingly (to self and others) in this life is to honor one's own complexity, as well as respect and cherish the same complexity in others.

What sides of you are you not expressing, because you're still influenced by the completely contrived societal concepts of who you should be or what is good and bad? Got the courage to step out of those and just be you? Today is the day.

December 6

What I am actually saying is that
we need to be willing to let our intuition guide us,
and then be willing to follow that guidance directly and fearlessly.
-Shakti Gawain, American self-development author

The willingness Gawain writes of is preceded by discontent with living in the unwillingness, or the lack of awareness of intuition's tug. The discontent builds, over decades, particularly in youth, when we're 'guided,' 'encouraged,' pushed or even controlled by external power sources, often mom and dad, to do what they want or recommend, even when contrary to our own inclinations. The internal grating of the inner voice against those voices is faint, at first, and easily squelched by the kid wanting approval, or fearing criticism or a contemptuous look. But, with time, the heap of crappy feels grows, as does the longing for freedom from it and to pursue one's own passions.

Willingness means self-permission, which only comes after having come to terms with and accepting the inevitable backlash and likely ostracism. That's what it means to "follow that guidance directly and fearlessly." "Directly" means there is immediate communication between soul and mind, then action. No calling from the inner voice gets mediated or watered down by anything external to self (or inside of self that comes from an external source, such as the vestigial messages of culture not yet dislodged from self, or the self-beliefs once taught by a long-dead parent). "Fearlessly" means not the absence of fear, in this case, but awareness of the fear-inducing consequences, yet engaging the action or course, anyway.

Are you willing, yet? Why not? Or, why? What scares you most about doing so? What exhilarates you most about doing it despite the fears? Who most wants you to not listen to your own intuition? What's their agenda? Can you live without them or without their incessant pecking and punching your dreams?

December 7

> *Empathy – the ability to identify with someone else's suffering –*
> *is certainly a prerequisite for a genuine apology.*
> -Danielle Ofri, MD/PhD, American writer and professor

Have you ever thought about how apologies work? For instance, if a person inflicts pain multiple times on another person, and then that first person goes and apologizes, simply saying, "I'm sorry for all that I did to you," is that adequate? In other words, is it necessary for an apology to be as significant as the crime or are the simple words "I'm sorry" enough? One of the things I regularly run into over the decades as a soul counselor is people expressing that the person who hurt them did apologize, but the apology didn't feel real, didn't feel significant, or didn't feel like it was enough.

Ever had someone apologize, but it just didn't feel like enough? If so, that raises the question, what does it take for an apology to be significant enough or for the offended person to really feel satisfaction?

I prefer to reverse engineer that question. Rather than asking it from the perspective of the victim, because often that is not a compelling enough argument for the perpetrator to listen or change. What's more effective is to consider it from the perspective of the perp, at least if the perpetrator has the courage to really be honest.

So think about the times when you were the one who hurt another person. When you apologized, if you were to be totally honest right now, how much did you attempt to defend yourself, gloss over it, quickly pivot to 'moving forward,' or not allude to certain things in your apology because those things were more egregious than the others and would make you look, or feel, really bad? In other words, if you were to affix a percentage to it, what percentage of your apology is about protecting you and you looking good, or you not wanting to feel bad, or avoiding backlash? And, what percentage of your apology is for the other person – taking your lumps and taking your medicine because you know it's the right thing to do in alleviating their pain, which you caused?

An authentic apology, an adequate apology, an apology that fits the crime is an apology where you are not protecting yourself. Do you apologize rightly? Are you allowing someone to gloss over their apologies to you?

What ways do you protect yourself in your apologies and thereby act selfishly? What's the fear? What percentage do you truly care more about the other person in your apology? Do you need to up your game to 'Badass' level in your apologies and start *giving* more and self-protecting less?

Oh, and are the apologies followed with changed actions?

December 8

Few red flags are universal – hitting, demeaning, not apologizing.
Most red flags are specific to you. Most red flags become the glaring
problems they forewarn
when you ignore that which feels off or crappy to you.
That's all a red flag is.
This is why the most important relationship
is the one you have with your own intuition and soul.
All important communication starts there.
The soul is where the game of life is won and lost.
-Sven

It's a pretty common experience to be well down the path of problems and struggles in a long-term relationship and then ask yourself the questions, 'Why didn't I see the red flags earlier,' and 'Were there even red flags?' We've all been there. These are excellent questions to be asking, because we're dissecting the relationship, pulling apart the equation to find the variables we missed, so that we can either fix it now or fix the next one.

But, often there are two things operating that we're not aware of, particularly in early adult relationships. The first is, if we've experienced a dearth of love, growing up, to then be in a relationship where there is a seeming glut of love flowing your way, it is profoundly overwhelming in the most sugary of ways. If you grew up in some derivative of a love famine, this new experience feels like heaven on earth, which, in turn, causes you to open up in ways you never have. This, in turn, causes you to bond to this person like you never knew possible, because you're revealing so much more of your real self, believing yourself to be safe.

This, years or decades later, makes the break up even harder, because of your absolute insistence it was real love. Or, almost worse than that, you hold on through sooooooo much hell in the relationship, enduring so much self-abnegating toxicity, giving up soooo much of yourself, because you've so invested with the opening of your real self in a way you never were before.

And it all started simply because you experienced early in the relationship an amount of love well below what might be considered normal by other people's standards. It was at least, sure as hell, more than you had ever experienced previously.

There's a second reason we miss or ignore red flags, hoping they'll just go away. If you've grown up in a home wherein you walked on eggshells, or where your feelings and wants didn't matter, or where you watched your mom shrink, or watched your dad be neutered, or witnessed or experienced abuse, and on and on; if you've grown up with that, then those actions of mistreatment and neglect were normalized. That became your baseline of what love is. Therefore, *there are no red flags!* You were taught that what would be totally heinous and unacceptable for another person were well within the realm of normal for you, because you became an expert at experiencing that, decades ago. Red flags, sirens, and flashing neon lights didn't exist for you. And, if you had two parents – one of them committing the bad stuff and the other tolerating it, then you had it normalized by two people. You were taught by the passive parent that this is how you should act. Or worse, you got your blueprint for acting from the bad parent. Either way, there were no red flags; and this became your definition of love. So, after that, you were attracted to that which was familiar and normal.

No red flags! BOOM!

And, as mentioned, we have to get well down the road of extreme pain, and eventually deconstruct the relationship and our own past, examining forgotten memories, before we realize that ain't love; red flags do and did exist; and that – holy crap! – we actually *did* see it, or feel it deep down, long before the wedding ever happened!

Is it possible your love famine in your family of origin, when mixed with the normalization of awful treatment, caused you to completely miss all the warning signs that the relationship you've now been in for a long time was doomed from the start?

December 9

Change will not occur, until the pain gets bad enough.
-Sven

We become so embedded in our clinging to all that gets us a sense of security that we resist change, even if we know that change is necessary or good. The fear of change and all it might bring – risk, aloneness, financial loss, rebuke from others, to name a few – outweighs the pain, frustration, misery, and discontent of whatever it is you've been enduring. So, you stay in this situation. And you stay.

Then, there is this uniquely transformative effect of compounded time when added to misery. To be miserable is one thing. To be dragged through unrelenting misery, day in day out, year in year out, is a beast of a different stripe. This is why, no matter how tough you think you are in your twenties in enduring all manner of crappy feelings, that same crap carried over another decade or two has a special gift for slowly bleeding every last ounce of strength and courage from a person.

And so, with time, that unceasing suffering, which no clever mind tricks or external distractions or drugs can long assuage, breaks down the very strength and endurance you pride yourself on. With time and a bit of reflection you begin to see that such strength is a curse causing you to tolerate far more than you ever should have. With time, reflection, and a whole lot of daily, yearly pain, you eventually reach the point at which you're simply done; with this path, this purpose, this person, this long-held principle. Whatever it is that tips the balance, you're done.

And that – THAT! – is the day of your birth. That is the day you finally give yourself permission to integrate all of your being, even the part you've been taught to not show or be, the part you've kept down or hidden out of belief that it is bad. But on that day that life finally breaks you, the baby chick is hatched; the proverbial butterfly has finally strengthened its wings enough to kick its way out of the cocoon and fly, never to return to such a constricting prison.

Oddly, yet beautifully, that transformation from prison alters your definition of strength. Now, what you're willing to endure drops significantly. It's no longer strong to endure, but strong to stand up and refuse to allow stuff to get so bad.

But here's the thing: you can't force or hasten that day when the scales are tipped. The day of the pain threshold being reached is different for every person. You may have false starts or attempts, but until you're fully there, you ain't there. Your ability to cling and to endure, coupled with all the fears you have of letting go, are still too great. Simply put, it's not your time yet.

What is the fear that keeps you clinging, refusing to let go? Have you done everything you can to make it work, thus making it easier to walk away, when the time is right? What are you avoiding admitting? What do you really not want to look at or see? What is the great sadness in all of this? When do you face it all and see your life, as it stands, for what it is?

December 10

I pay no attention whatever to anyone's praise or blame.
I simply follow my own feelings.
-Wolfgang Amadeus Mozart, Austrian composer

Isn't it intriguing how Mozart equates the source of his life direction and creativity with his feelings. One is clearly the source of the other for him.

Feelings. The very thing denigrated among so many men...and women, today.

Could it not be argued that the greatest basketball players, business people, doctors, card sharks, teachers, pilots and plumbers so long and so hard learned the fundamentals, the checklists, the workarounds, and the advanced insights that eventually they could really fly by feeeeel? Don't the best at anything have a sixth sense that is intimately correlated to the feel inside, taking the shot in the precise moment, or passing; selling the stock or holding; administering the medicine in the just-right dosage, turning the wrench 'til the fit is where it feels right?

Conversely, isn't doubting the feel the thing that undermines success and trusting your instincts? What often causes you to doubt what you know and are good at: fatigue, hunger, stress, personal problems, past failures, the voices of others? What do you need to do to remove more of the things that are obstructing your trust of the feel? Further, is it possible that all the BS we've been taught by previous generations about feelings was completely wrong?

December 11

> *The only thing standing between you and your goal*
> *is the bullshit story you keep telling yourself as to why you can't achieve it.*
> -Michael Jordan, NBA GOAT

It's kinda hard to argue on the topic of success with the greatest basketball player of all time. Though, it is rather interesting to note that when it came to Jordan's *baseball* career, he was infinitely less successful, never actually making it to the majors. Thus, considering his own quote (above), one is left wondering what his BS story was that he told himself about a baseball career. Now, I say this to throw no shade at Michael Jordan. But, it does highlight a rather distinct dichotomy that we all struggle with, at some point or another, as he had to have struggled with in his baseball career before ever achieving the success he likely dreamed of:

When is quitting "quitting" and
when is quitting the result of realizing this really isn't my dream?

I desired to be a fighter pilot when I was 16-19 years old. I got into and was succeeding at the very top school in the US for becoming a pilot – the US Air Force Academy. To further the passion for that dream, the movie *Top Gun* came out my first year there, for pete's sake! Yet, for as much as I wanted it, in my second year, I knew it wasn't my calling. It lost its luster for me. My marks were fine; military and athletic performances were all well above average. But I quit, even though I didn't know why, except that it didn't feel right, anymore. Maybe that's why MJ chose to quit baseball. Who knows?

In the end, the point is this, you need to be asking yourself and answering with a level of extreme honesty that you push yourself to in only the most extreme situations, Am I quitting because it genuinely doesn't feel deep inside that this is my most authentic path, or am I quitting because I don't believe I can, am afraid of what people will say, am afraid of failing, and am afraid I won't be able to overcome this or that aspect of it?

Are you being truly honest with yourself when it comes to your dreams and passions? I mean really honest. Are your greatest limitations inside of you, not outside you, when it comes to going down the paths that draw you? If they're in you, what precisely are they? Can you dive into who they came from and how much of a chokehold they have on you? Are you okay with all of that history and the severe limitations it all places on your life, today? Most importantly, are you okay with sacrificing your dreams because you're afraid to go into and overcome your limiting fears and belief systems? Do you have the courage to quit in life?

December 12

Talking, always talking.
That's your problem, you always talking.
-Leikeli47, American rapper

You are what you do,
not what you say you'll do.
-Carl G. Jung,
Founding Father of Analytical Psychology

One of the beauties of aging is that the internal BS meter gets much more finely calibrated. We get better at sniffing out crap much sooner. We can tell when someone's a BS-er and when someone is hardcore, a real doer. A pitch without plan, product, or proven history becomes far less enchanting. Pretenders bore us, as we age. Or, perhaps they entertain for a moment, but they're never brought close by the older and wiser. Their words fall flat, unable to sway.

Is it possible that the reason some people have distanced themselves from you is because you're always talking, always selling, but there's little *do* in your past and behind your pitches? Is it possible that the durability and respectability that come with aggressive action aren't yours, because your fears have kept you crippled far too long? Is it possible you're well aware of the fact that your life has been a disappointment to you, because you know your fear of failure, backlash, or disappointing others has been so daunting that you've stayed hidden? And when does the fatigue of being a disappointment to yourself finally catapult you into action to heal your crap inside?

It ain't about whether or not someone has failed; for, generally, the one's who've eagerly failed most have had the brass balls to attempt and *do* the most, which is its own wisdom and power. Similarly difficult to see is the person who's a doer, but also paints a helluva picture; their picture ain't BS; it's been proven.

December 13

> *Quiet the mind,*
> *and the soul will speak.*
> -Buddha, Nepalese teacher

The itch is the body's way of revealing the place that most needs a scratch. An irritant is not a broken bone, screaming with pain. An itch is nagging, small but attention-stealing. The irritant in your life – in your insides – reveals where attention is needed, and often breaks open into major revelations or greater problems.

But, when it comes to the soul, we too often run from the irritants. They scare us. So, we try to make them just go away. But soul work means asking the deeper self why this damn thing is bugging me so much. What is it about it that causes me to obsess over it or not be able to move through it? What's the soul trying to draw my attention to and teach me with this persistent unfinishedness?

List the 5 most persistent irritants in your life. These are not the giant pain sources in your life. These are the incredibly small, yet ever-present drains on your focus, energy, or happiness that seem to always be there.

Now, write out why each of these is such an irritant and how your life would be different (be as specific as possible) if each of these, item by item, were not in your life.

Next, tell me the story in your journal of the single most traumatic event(s) of your life. Or, if there are several, start with the one staring you in the face, at the moment. Allow your fear of this event, this memory, to come, as well. It is the feeling that must be shown the light of day, must be allowed to come up and out, perhaps for the first time ever. It's going to be okay. But you must have the courage! Use as much detail as possible, as well as the most graphic, strong, even offensive language you can, if that is what you authentically feel when writing it. Your writing may be halting, at first, but you know you're down to soul level when it just starts pouring out of you, almost trance-like.

Now, it may seem like the most traumatic events have nothing to do with irritants. But what if they do? In your journaling begin to play with the possibility that irritants find their roots in larger past trauma, or that trauma finds signals and signs in irritants. How are your irritants and traumas interwoven?

December 14

*Because the soul has such deep roots in personal and social life
and its values run so contrary to modern concerns,
caring for the soul may well turn out to be a radical act,
a challenge to accepted norms.*

...

*It is precisely because we resist the darkness in ourselves
that we miss the depths of the loveliness, beauty,
brilliance, creativity, and joy that lie at the core.*
-Thomas Moore, Author of *Soulmates* and *Care of the Soul*

Whether it be the fear of our own individual darkness and the pain it holds, or the fear of orienting our lives to something other than acquisition, fame, money, acceptance/approval, and appearances, there is never a shortage of reasons for running from the calling of the soul, deep inside. And so, we simultaneously miss the sheer beauty of the discovery of authentic self and living in the richness of soulful life. It is, day to day, interacting at a soul level with those we meet, orienting our lives to soul-driven decisions that breathe life into us and speak to truths that move us. Yet, it is the me, too, but in its fullest expression.

It's not a religious thing, at all, or doesn't have to be. It's just a deeply human thing, one that is not solely human, because it's a connection to all of life and spirit and energy that flows between and inside all things animate and inanimate.

To what degree are you, or are you not living the soulful life you know exists within you and beckons to you? What might life look like if you were living a life even just 5% more soulful? 25%? How would you walk differently through life? What decisions, large or small, would you make differently? What is it about the darkness deep inside you most fear facing? Might it be time to no longer be afraid of it? Or, is the fear that you're no longer oriented toward what seemingly everyone around you is oriented toward? Has the longing for a more soulful, connected, deep life become strong enough to warrant a change or three in your life? If not now, when?

December 15

*Don't touch my sh*t!*
-Heard often on the street among homeless folk

Feeling called by my own soul to do so, I gave up all of my life possessions, bit by bit, over time, 'til eventually I made the final move of draining my bank account and giving up everything, except a change of clothes. With that, I went and moved to the street. Taking my gifts where I believed the need to be greatest, I worked with and lived among the homeless of Oakland/Berkeley, California, literally sleeping on concrete every night for 2 ½ years. Every day, I got to know and grow close to the poor, drug-addled, mentally ill, and people who had nothing wrong with them but were just choosing to live this way for their own reasons.

To say I learned a lot would be a silly understatement. Yet, one of the simplest yet most hard-hitting messages I learned was the one above. Folks on the street can be extremely territorial. It makes sense, as often their entire life's possessions are precisely what you see or what they carry on their backs. And so, a fierce reprimand to not go near someone else's belongings, seat, meal, or sleep spot was not an uncommon thing. But the beauty of the statement "Don't touch my sh*t" is that it's a good reminder to each of us in our everyday lives to not go into other people's business uninvited, to not meddle when we're unwanted, to not offer advice or opinions unsolicited. It's a powerful reminder to shut up and honor other people's boundaries.

It's also a great mindset to have when it comes to your own boundaries and life. You are not required to share your life with everyone or even with anyone, if you feel they might mishandle it or if you just don't want to. It's completely okay to not want people touching your sh*t, so to speak. The permission and ability to set and hold boundaries, such as this simple one, is an absolute prerequisite to happiness.

So, what boundaries do you need to reinforce and not back down? How are you not representing yourself well? Or, what unsolicited opinions and meddling are you guilty of and need to really cut back? What's the underlying reason you keep sticking your nose where it's not wanted? What need is being satisfied in you or what fear is being assuaged by you? Is it the need to seem smart and above it all? Is it the fear that if you don't tell them what to do, they will fail or get hurt and then you'd feel bad; thus, you're trying to control them now to save yourself pain later? What is it? What's driving your inclination to take sh*t, do sh*t, say sh*t, and touch sh*t that ain't yours to take, do, say, or touch? When do you finally back off and mind your manners? Or, when do you stop letting others touch your sh*t and start enforcing your own boundaries?

422

December 16

Fear and happiness are inversely correlated.
The more your life is driven by fear, the less happiness there can be.
The more you simply want to be happy and fulfilled in life,
the more you let go of fear controlling it.
-Sven

What percentage of your life is driven by fear? What choices are you making because you are trying to avoid a potential outcome, rather than going boldly toward that which inspires you? Do you live your life trying to do the things that breathe energy into you and be the person you most enjoy being? Or do you live your life fearful of showing the world who you really are, fearful of saying a hearty 'YES' to all you want to do with your life, and saying a decisive 'NO' to all that you are done with and no longer want controlling your life?

If fear drives your decisions, the fears are not yours, per se, as in ownership. Instead, your fears own you. You're their b*tch.

Your fear of looking weak, fear of failure, fear of being alone (or being left) and so many more keep you weak inside, alone inside, and a failure in your own eyes. Ironic, ain't it?

December 17

Worrying is carrying tomorrow's load with today's strength –
carrying two days at once.
It is moving into tomorrow ahead of time.
Worrying doesn't empty tomorrow of its sorrow;
it empties today of its strength.
-Corrie Ten Boom, Dutch (and later American)
watchmaker and writer whose family hid Jews from the Nazis in WWII;
was caught and sent to Ravensbrueck concentration camp

We're all guilty of it, worrying about this or that small or large thing in the future, whether it be tomorrow or next year. We spend so much life energy holding onto tomorrow's problems today, zapping our life energy for today.

It's just so doggone hard to trust that tomorrow there will be new energy, new insights, new solutions, and that we'll find a way through. It's so hard to trust that, no matter what happens, I'll be okay. For, it's that realization that enables us to let go of tomorrow, to loosen our grip on future events and some internal drive that needs to fix them now, or at least stop the mind's desire to churn and churn them over and again.

But, until we reach that realization and can live in that realization, we grow depressed and heavy, losing today, one more day slipping through our fingers.

It is going to be okay. Even if there is loss, hardship, sadness, decay, death, we'll be okay. Some of my fondest memories from my past are from when life was hardest. I was so *ALIVE!* There was a realness, an earthiness; you could feeeel life. So, if that is what's to come for you tomorrow, embrace it. You are alive, feeeling life! And it's going to be okay.

What is the fear in tomorrow or next month, or year, that you need to trust will be okay, or that you'll find a way to sort it out and make the best of it? What is it in tomorrow that is killing your todays? What do you need to let go of?

Hold everything in your hands lightly;
otherwise, it hurts when God (or fate) pries your fingers open.
-Corrie Ten Boom

December 18

A man with outward courage dares to die.
A man with inward courage dares to live.
-Lao Tzu, Chinese philosopher

Boy, if that quote doesn't mess with you a bit!

This is really what it all boils down to. This right here is the difference between *ALIVENESS* and slow death. That feeling of true *ALIVENESS* that we all seek, whether we're aware of it, or not, demands the courage to live as self, which in turn demands the courage to go into solitude then welcome and release all that is killing you, dragging you down from within, and stealing your life force.

Why is that refrain of coming alive so common in epic movies and stories of heroes and those who have accomplished great things? Why is that notion of being 'truly alive' always a revolutionary thought when it hits our ears, always an inspiration to strive outside of our safety zone? Why is that notion even such a powerful point and rallying cry if it isn't by nature rare and courageous?

How miserable, boring, frustrating, numb, or painful does your life have to become before the courage to come alive finally grips your soul and drives you to action? When do you finally feel the courage welling up inside you and no longer fear the critics. When?

December 19

Never mistake an opinion for knowledge,
nor knowledge for wisdom.
An opinion requires a mouth.
Knowledge requires a brain.
Wisdom requires pain and the willingness to relive that pain later
while mining it for the gems of deeper truth
it holds in its terrible claw.
The opinionated will not think,
because it is too hard to open one's mind.
The knowledgeable will not mine,
because it is too scary to feel that pain, again,
and too humiliating to not know things,
too humbling to ask questions,
rather than constantly spout answers.
It is a narrow path to wisdom,
for it demands letting go of comfort and security.
It demands the courage that the opinionated
and the smart do not have.
-Sven

In what areas of your life are you still stuck in the lesser state of opinions? When you give an opinion, do you offer it as such, or do you pretend it to be knowledge or even wisdom?

Are you knowledgeable but still running from or distracting yourself from your past, your pain, and therein your greatest source of possible future wisdom?

Opinions and knowledge are both good things. But neither are final destinations. One is an opening volley; the other an arrived-at good spot. But, ego keeps us stuck in opinion and knowledge, never climbing to the highest summit where we can do the most good – wisdom, depth, plunging insight, and silence.

December 20

> *Most of the successful people I've known*
> *are the ones who do more listening than talking.*
> -Bernard Baruch, American financier

My father used to say that when someone feels truly heard by you they feel as if you've just given them a bouquet of flowers. There were few things my physically powerful father loved more than working in the flower and vegetable gardens with his wife. Flowers made my parents feeeel. Dad's favorites were marigolds. And, Dad was married to the deepest and most connecting listener I've ever known. Anyone who ever knew my mom felt heard, seen....truly cared about.

I had a client, one of many actually, who was a physician with a very successful practice, employing almost exclusively women. After working with me for awhile, she went off on her own and I'd hear back from her every six months or so for a check-up. When she came back, she remarked two things that stuck in me. She said that, since our work together, she's listening far more as an employer/leader, spouting commands and opinions less. On her second check-up, she noted that there is a new sense of connection among her staff and herself.

That other thing she said? "I'm more vulnerable, but feel less vulnerable, now, Sven." She meant both personally and professionally.

To listen requires living in student mode, rather than boss or ego mode. It requires humility. And, the only thing that allows a person to live as such is having gotten out all the antagonistic voices inside, belittling you from within, such that you have to put up a guard on the outside, lest anyone see your weaknesses and frailties inside.

Listening – making someone feel truly heard – is rare, because we so often want the flowers, the attention, for ourselves. People so seldom give those flowers of attention to others. Weak ego and fear inside say, "Don't be vulnerable. Stay in control and look strong and smart."

But someone who has done the work of healing their innards can say, "Screw it. I'm fine. Open up. Be vulnerable. Give 'em love. Just slow down and be present." And that's a damn beautiful thing.

What's the deep message still ringing in you that keeps you from being truly vulnerable, keeps you from slowing down, keeps you from being truly present, and keeps you from being a bearer of flowers in this life?

December 21

Do not set your sail using someone else's star.
-African proverb

Did you know that a ship leaving Los Angeles harbor heading for Hawaii that miscalibrates its navigation by just a few degrees will end up, after traveling thousands of miles across the Pacific, far north, docking in China, or possibly Russia? Lovely countries, but you're going to be very under-dressed.

The slightest of problems at the start, at the root of an endeavor, track to very unexpected, or even unwanted, outcomes. The slightest of changes deep in the soul, as they pass up and through our being into our daily life and behaviors, become massive changes in character. My clients tire of hearing me harp on the fact that just trying to change behaviors on the surface never changes behaviors, long term. Unless you change the core beliefs that are deep down and driving those behaviors – i.e. until you change the navigation down where behaviors and actions begin, deep in the soul – ain't nothin' gonna change; ain't nothin' gonna stick. You will revert back. That's why significant relationship, career, and personality changes require epiphanies and new insights, as well as the inner work that go with them. Claims otherwise seldom bear long term fruit.

What are a few examples from your past where the slightest shift in your core beliefs resulted in a dramatic shift in your actions and, thus, shifts in the results and events in your life? What are the areas of your life where you most need to make a shift of a few degrees in your beliefs? What is the single biggest core belief (to the degree any one person can be aware of their core beliefs without having done the work) harming your life? What would those shifts in belief look like? What's the single biggest thing holding you back from doing so? What's the origin of that original, non-functional belief, to begin with? Who put it in you? When do you finally realize they were wrong?

December 22

Until you love you,
ain't nobody else gonna love you.
Because, if you don't love you,
you're gonna keep being who everyone else wants you to be.
And you'll never let yourself discover who you really are,
let alone show anyone else who you really are.
And how the hell are they gonna love you
when you don't show them who you really are?

-Sven

That's the scary part of life – letting go of being who you think everyone else wants you to be, because that's the only way you've gotten love in the past, when you've gotten it. You've been what they wanted, thinking then they would want you, stay, and give you love, in return. But, it didn't work out that way, did it? And, that's why you're so broken and empty now.

The scary part of life is going inside and purging yourself of all the memories, messages, and pain that caused you to adamantly believe that the real you is not only not good enough but ugly and to be forgotten forever.

The scary part of life is discovering the real you inside, loving on it, and having the courage to more and more become on the outside who you really are on the inside. It is forever casting away the old forms of your existence. It's having the courage to show your authentic self to the world, the naysayers, the detractors, the critics, the family who are convinced they know better and who are quick to judge and criticize you.

The scary part of life is the 'No' to the old you and the becoming of new you. The scary, yet glorious part of life is the becoming; giving yourself permission to become; falling in love with not just new-you, but the process of ushering new-you in.

And, the more we engage the scary, the more miraculous and gorgeous life becomes and we become. And, they'll love you for it, those ones who appreciate true quality and happiness in another person.

Is it time to fall in love with you? Is it time to begin the journey of becoming? New-you awaits!

December 23

*A spiritual leader who wants to be a real leader is the person who is able
to put the full range of his life experiences –
experiences in meditation, in conversation, and in his/her lonely hours –
at the disposal of those who ask him or her to be their spiritual leader.
Spiritual care does not mean
running around nervously trying to redeem people,
to save them at the last moment,
or to put them on the right track by a good idea,
an intelligent remark, or practical advice.
No!
Spiritual care means in the final analysis:
offering your own life experience to your fellow man/woman and,
as Paul Simon sings,
to lay yourself down like a bridge over troubled waters.*
-Henri J.M. Nouwen, Dutch writer, *Creative Ministry*

I really don't expect that quote to resonate with many, even though it stirs my soul. It is the words and belief system of my people, my parents, the many WWII Generation clergy and spiritual leaders in my bloodline. And so, I wrote it for myself. It's my book, f**k off! I need this reminder in my book of who I am and what I know my roots are – roots I re-choose each day.

The scary task in my work is to keep laying myself bare for the benefit and growth of others – my sin, my ugliness, what bits and pieces I've learned, the failures and screw-ups of the paths I've taken, and those gems of wisdom and depth I've been granted.

Spiritual leadership and care is not a job, but a way of life, a nurturing of self for the utter giving of self.

This is badass spiritual leadership.

I think this is really what great parenting is and great leadership of any stripe. Great leadership is always in the business of speaking to people's deepest longings, pain, and insecurities. It's the willingness to not just give of self for others, but to offer up even your failures and vulnerabilities, so that others might feel comforted knowing they are not alone in their own vulnerabilities. It is to be strong enough to show your weaknesses and shortcomings, so that others might grow past their own.

Are you badass enough to do it? What's the real fear keeping you from doing so?

December 24

The sauce to meat is ceremony; Meeting were bare without it.
-William Shakespeare, English playwright

There was not one single day in my entire childhood more special, more sacred, more rapturous than Christmas Eve at the Erlandson house. The presents in the parsonage, though never extravagant or excessive in number, did slowly more populate the skirt in the weeks leading up to this day, as well as on this day as more of my older siblings and mom and dad finished finally wrapping them. The patently original Christmas cookies from Aunt Viv's kitchen, which she often collared nieces and nephews to help her roll or dip, were under literal lock with the key held tightly by one person (mom), lest six sneakthiefs peck and steal in the weeks leading up to the big night. On this day, we played lots of snow football during the day as one or two of us might have to depart at different times to be an acolyte or help with communion or some other duty at Dad's church across the street, or out in the country, when Dad was a rural pastor.

In the late afternoon or early evening, after dad's last daytime service, yet long before his late-night Christmas service, kids would be put to task by mom to set the table with the fine china and silver from Mom and Dad's wedding day, set candles aglow throughout the house and on the table, and turn off all electric lighting, except the lights on the tree. The hand-stitched red Christmas tablecloth adorned a long table now set with the traditional Swedish-American Christmas meal of lutefisk and white sauce, lefse, Varmlandkorv, boiled potatoes, peas, and Swedish limpa rye bread. Even with the lutefisk, it was still my favorite meal of the year. And here it was, my whole family – all of my siblings home, including Kent from the military, Dan, Karla and David home from school, and John and me – around one table. Singing the prayer, lively conversation for hours, and the food!

After dinner, the tradition was that it was the one night of the year mom and dad did the dishes and the six of us went in around the piano, each with the instrument we played (Kent-trumpet, Dan-trombone, Karla-piano/bassoon, David-piano/trumpet, John and me each on violins), playing Christmas songs as well as songs from the Lutheran hymnal. This became a time of kidding, making some music, and jokingly harping on each other for missed notes.

Then we'd sit, in chairs and on the sofa, in a large circle and open gifts one at a time, each getting full attention while opening his or her gift. There was no mad rush, just more conversation and laughter, gratitude, and fun. It's interesting how small amounts of gifts can be so satisfying when you don't have a lot. You each enjoy the moment and each other's gifts, and lots of laughter, and of course a few tears and some bickering, as would happen with any six kids.

Then around 11pm we'd all go over to church. The air never so crisp and clean, the snow never so crunchy, the smell of someone's fireplace burning birch never so dreamily taking you back in time to the memories of the poets and storytellers...as on that night. All of your church friends would be there on this night, looking good, laughing, happy. And, if we weren't performing an old Swedish song as a family for the congregation, we'd each be at service – some sitting with friends, some with mom, one or two acolyting or assisting, and likely at least one sneaking into the church kitchen to steal some sweet treat (because that's what preacher's kids do). Then out into the crisp air to walk back to the parsonage, eat some cookies, play with the new toys, spin the new record, or start the new book.

The sheer power of this ritual with all its smells, tastes, laughter, temperatures, textures, and depth of meaning moves me, even now, 50 years later.

What rituals from your past move you? Much more importantly, what rituals are you creating? Ritual is necessary, grounding, and, with time, quite compelling. It's not always the big High Holy Day rituals that we lean on the most, but the small ones. How you shower and brush your teeth. The ritual of setting the table just so, even when you eat alone. Your bedtime rituals. Where you sit when doing homework. Your workout music is part of your life rituals. How you fold your clothes on laundry day. Your different meals during the week. Your coffee/tea/cigarette ritual. How you arrange your brushes.

Never underestimate the power of rituals, particularly the healing power. Ritual creates a desired feeling – peace, ecstasy, calm, laughter, strength – through repeated actions. When you move to a new place, create small rituals. When you're feeling ungrounded, build a new regular practice, whatever it may be. For, comfort is needed amid the adventures of life. Grace flows through patterns.

December 25

"Come in," she said, "I'll give you shelter from the storm."
-Bob Dylan, GOAT Minnesota rock star

Who brought you in, sheltering you from the storm? Or, perhaps even more significantly, who sheltered and cultivated your talent, your deepest gifts? Who saw your greatness inside you, found that dirty penny and buffed it to a brilliant sheen?

I had never in my life, ever, had someone truly foster my talents and callings. I have been blessed with love from many people – touch, kind words, time together, great listeners, gifts, etc. But the one thing I had never received to any substantive degree was the shepherding of my gifts and aspirations. My entire career, with only the tiniest exceptions, is completely self-made.

Then Karen came along. She had long ago built an $80M company in Midtown Manhattan as a true old-school garmento. She excelled at sourcing and relationships, selling ideas and cultivating talent. But, having grown up in a Bronx Italian family, her primary love language was food, cooking for the ones she loves, and spending laughter-filled time with them. She didn't know what to do with this big guy who ate one meal a day (often low-carb). It made her happy to serve the ones she loved and also those less fortunate. But it frustrated her to no end to feel like she wasn't serving me, even as I strove to serve her, her family, and her interests.

Then it sorta dawned on her, "Wait, you need help with your career? Oh, I can do that. That's simple. *That's* all you need? *That* would make you happy? Oh hell, I can definitely do that!" I had been a near-completely self-made man, up to that point. Then she took my business to the stratosphere – infrastructure, bold new directions, new creative forms. She saw shininess underneath all the accumulated gunk on that penny. She sheltered and shepherded my work through storms.

I had come from a great home, growing up, wherein there was much love. But no one had ever helped me or loved me in this one way – honoring and serving my talents and dreams. And, it was rain in the desert, balm to the soul.

So, whose talent are you sheltering and cultivating? Who cultivated your talent? Who saw the vision you saw? Who brought you back to life with their belief in you? Have you come full circle in your career and life, such that you are now the one finding and shining pennies, breathing life into them. Or perhaps you never had it, and so you make it your mission to be that person for others? That's leadership.

I had an old friend who called people like this "star throwers." Metaphorically speaking, they walk along the oceans' beaches, finding starfishes that have washed up on shore and are drying out, dying. They throw the starfishes back into the ocean, so that they might live again. Starthrowers are badass! Be a starthrower! Be a penny-shiner!

To my penny-shining starthrower, Karen. I cannot even begin to express my deepest gratitude. Thank you and Merry Chritmit!

December 26

**I don't understand a way to work other than
bold-facedly running towards failure.**
-Cate Blanchett, Australian actor

The first hundred times you fail, it can be powerfully debilitating, even soul-crushing. We think, "What are other people thinking of me," after we fail. We fear what they might think, before we even attempt. Fear of failure is more wrapped up in what others might think than perhaps any other of the great fears of life.

But, here's the thing, the more you fail and work through that failure, the less that fear of what others might think grips you, because it loses its sting. Also, you've sorta conditioned those around you to get over it, to leave you alone, to piss off. And, there's a beautiful "Screw it!" mentality that takes over inside. The boldness grows with each new failure. Yes, in the immediate, the failure stings, sure. But it gets smaller and smaller, at times unnoticeable. But a boldness, a devil-may-care sorta craziness can begin to infuse your work. There grows a delight in the attack of the new challenge, and a glorious freefall of f******ck mixed with laughter, that comes with the next failure. There grows a detachment from needing to have the success, and an attachment to the sheer audacity of and love for the work itself. It's a sort of, "What the hell else am I gonna do? This is what I do!"

It's that willingness, that eagerness to fail grand and gloriously, if I must. It's that. That is what drives the work of the most successful, those with real purpose, the truly *ALIVE!*

That willingness to fail and eagerness to fail big are what get converted in the alternator into grit. That passion, that lust to attack, knowing that failure is damn near inevitable, or at least well worth the risk, is what fuels the hard slog, the daily putting in the hours, the extreme focus necessary for extreme achievement.

At what point do you stop giving a crap what people will think if you fail? At what point does the mediocrity of such living bore you and bleed you so much that you dive in and begin your own path of bold failures, grand f-ups, and gorgeous fall-downs? At what point do you unleash your crazy and begin to fail boldly?

December 27

Impractical was not a disqualifier.
Nor was inconvenient, expensive, or extremely labor intensive.
These were merely obstacles to be worked around or run over.
They rendered his quest more difficult,
but in no way altered the reality of what he knew to be within reach.
-Bill Shore, American author & non-profit founder

We're called. Each one of us. By our own soul, more than any universe, god, or other. We are each called to a dream, a vision of reality that only we – only you! – can see. And, the grand question of life is whether you do it, or not.

That's all. You know the stirring of your heart. You know the direction in which you want to run. The only thing that has the power to hold you back from doing so is either your fear of what might happen (or what others might say), or your own lifetime of accrued crud dragging you down inside. By this point in the book you know you have to go in and start identifying and flushing out all that past crap, especially the BS messages you were taught about yourself.

Having done this and faced the fears of rocketing forward in the direction of your dreams, you must take that first step. Then, just keep putting one foot in front of another. Just keep fighting through the impracticalities, expenses, labors, and obstacles. You attack the difficulties and setbacks, and keep fighting forward. At times, you're going to need to rest and lick your wounds. Ain't nothin' wrong with that. Then, when the time is right, get up and get back after it!

You must fight forward! You must have the brazen foolishness and fire to conquer the worlds in which you've been called to run. You must trust the tug of your soul. You must!

It's time!

December 28

All we have to decide is
what to do with the time that is given to us.
-J.R.R. Tolkien, English novelist

Each new day, it is a decision and re-decision. To what do you commit? When you've done the work of cleaning out the soul, jackhammering the cement once poured over the bedrock of your authentic self and inscribed with false messages about yourself, then what? What is worthy of your life energy and the remaining time you have on this spinning rock? What captures and holds your attention? What intrigues you? What feeds the fires of your inner furnace, exciting passion and tightening your focus?

What is it for you? And, for what possible reason would you waste your time and life force on anything else?

When a person can't find a deep sense of meaning,
they distract themselves with pleasure.
-Viktor E. Frankl, Holocaust survivor, psychiatrist,
author of "Man's Search for Meaning"

December 29

Suffering is due entirely to clinging or resisting.
It is a sign of our unwillingness to move on,
to flow with life.
-Nisargardatta Maharaj, Indian Guru

To whom are you still clinging? Who are you still holding onto, hoping they'll come back? Or, perhaps, you know it's done, but you're not done grieving the death of that relationship.

Maybe it's not a relationship, but a business you built, a family you grew up with, a favorite place you lived, a friend group, a beloved person who has died, or a cherished memory that you cannot resurrect. What is it you're clinging to that you just refuse to let go of? Do you see how clinging to something you can no longer have is the root of your pain? The pain comes not from them being gone, but from you still wanting them back – i.e. from the clinging.

One of the grand ugly truths of existence is that life flows on, even when we don't want it to. And so, we resist, often with all our strength. That resistance beats us down.

I grew up one block from the mighty Mississippi River, one of the longest and most powerful in the world. Some friends had constructed a rope swing from a tree that we'd take turns swinging out on then jump off into the running water. And, as you stood up in thigh-deep (or deeper) water, you could feel the strong current trying to push you downstream. Stand there long enough, resisting that current, and your legs will get tired, no matter how fit you are.

Resist the currents of life and you will grow exhausted. Try to force your way back upstream and you'll be fatigued even faster.

Has it occurred to you that your true peace and happiness are downstream, not upstream? But it requires letting go of that which you cannot bear to let go of. Exhausted yet? Depleted yet? Ready yet?

December 30

Sven, everything has a price.
-Rev. LeRoy A. Erlandson, Pastor, Farm boy-at-heart, & Father

Ever wonder why the rich are rich and you're not, whether it be rich in money or rich in happiness, rich in strength or rich in creativity, rich in generosity of spirit or good health, rich in fame or character, rich in independence or title, rich in wisdom or experiences, rich in laughter or compassion? Ever wonder?

It's a bit simplistic, because it disallows factors like luck, but there is massive truth in the fact that the people who've achieved or amassed something you envy have done so, not just because of what they were willing to do, but because of what they were willing to let go of.

In the Latin origin, the word 'decision' is cracked open to reveal a richness of meaning. 'De-' means 'away' or 'off,' and '-cision' comes from *caedere*, which means 'to cut.' Thus, what makes decisions so damn hard, and intimately revealing of who a person really is, is not just what they are choosing, but what they are letting go of or walking away from. Our "no's" say just as much about us, or more, as our "yes-es," because it's so hard to let go of sometimes very good things.

Thus, the fascinating part of being rich is not that someone kept choosing that path and endured, and so forth. The really intriguing, often overlooked part is all they cut away, let go of. Sacrificed.

The ability and willingness, even eagerness, to sacrifice is power; sometimes extraordinary power. It is not just the mark of self-control. It's the mark of focus, extreme focus.

What are you willing to sacrifice? What do those sacrifices reveal about what you really value? What's it like to know yourself better, not by looking at what you want or even what you don't want, but by examining keenly that which you have cut away or want but are willing to cut away?

That person you're trying to understand or figure out; look at their no's. What do their no's tell you about who they are, what they deep-down value, and/or what they fear?

It's fascinating how much of a person is unlocked by peering closely into their sacrifices and no's. The sucky part, of course, is when you're their no…until you later realize that 'no' was a gift that set you free.

December 31

Courage is rightly esteemed the first of human qualities...
because it is the quality which guarantees all others.
-Winston Churchill, 20th Century Badass!

I am a great lover of Winston Churchill, particularly his grit, his laughingly unflinching middle finger, and his razor-sharp wit and oratory, not to mention his Herculean efforts to win WWII.

That notwithstanding, this quote is one of my favorites, not because it's particularly inspiring or witty, as most of his are, but because of the penetrating truth of it, particularly as it relates to my own work in helping others go deep inside themselves. It's not that I have courage, but they do. I know the fears that get stirred up in the soul, as one moves further and further in toward the truth dragons from their past that lay hidden deep in the caves. I know that fear on a personal, visceral level. Additionally, I know the courage required to pass into the fear and slay the dragons. Many have it; many acquire it, step by fearful step; and many run away in fear.

Everything hinges on your courage. It's the fulcrum on which happiness, peace, fulfillment, and the *ALIVENESS* you seek all turn.

The two ultimate questions of life are simply:

Who the hell are you, REALLY?
and
Do you have the courage to be who the hell you really are?

Boom!

Index